Visual Representations and Interpretations

Springer
London
Berlin
Heidelberg
New York
Barcelona
Hong Kong
Milan
Paris
Santa Clara
Singapore
Tokyo

Ray Paton and Irene Neilson (Eds)

Visual Representations and Interpretations

Springer

Dr Ray Paton, B.Ed, PhD, CBiol, MIBiol
Department of Computer Science, Chadwick Building, Liverpool L69 3BX

Dr Irene Neilson, MA, PhD, MSc
Computer Science, Foresight Centre, 3 Brownlow Hill, Liverpool L69 3GL

The cover is based upon a symbolic sculpture entitled 'Intuition' by John Robinson, drawn by Ove Arup. Editions of 'Intuition' can be seen outside Isaac Newton Institute, Cambridge; Field Institute, Toronto and Aspen Institute, Colorado.

ISBN 1-85233-082-1 Springer-Verlag London Berlin Heidelberg

British Library Cataloguing in Publication Data
Visual representations and interpretations
1.Representation (Philosophy) 2.Representation (Philosophy) -Data processing 3.Visualization 4.Visualization - Data processing 5.Communication 6.Communication - Data processing
I.Paton, Ray II.Neilson, Irene
153.3'2
ISBN 1852330821

Library of Congress Cataloging-in-Publication Data
Visual representations and interpretations / Ray Paton and Irene Neilson (eds.).
p. cm.
Includes bibliographical references.
ISBN 1-85233-082-1 (alk. paper)
1. Computer graphics. 2. Visualization. 3. Virtual reality.
I. Paton, Ray. II. Neilson, Irene.
T385.V5765 1999 98-49156
006.6--dc21 CIP

Typesetting: Camera ready by contributors
Printed and bound by the Athenæum Press Ltd., Gateshead, Tyne & Wear
34/3830-543210 Printed on acid-free paper

Preface

The value of multi-disciplinary research and the exchange of ideas and methods across traditional discipline boundaries are well recognised. Indeed, it could be justifiably argued that many of the advances in science and engineering take place because the ideas, methods and the tools of thought from one discipline become re-applied in others. Sadly, it is also the case that many subject areas develop specialised vocabularies and concepts and can consequently approach more general problems in fairly narrow, subject-specific ways. Consequently barriers develop between disciplines that prevent the free flow of ideas and the collaborations that could often bring success. VRI'98, a workshop focused on Visual Representations & Interpretations, was intended to break down such barriers. The workshop was held in the Foresight Conference Centre, which occupies part of the former Liverpool Royal Infirmary, a Grade 2 listed building, which has been recently restored. The building combines a majestic architecture with the latest in new conference facilities and technologies and thus provided a very suitable setting for a workshop aimed at bringing the Arts and the Sciences together.

The main aim of the workshop was to promote inter-disciplinary awareness across a range of disciplines where visual representations and interpretations are exploited. Contributions to the workshop were therefore invited from researchers who are actively investigating visual representations and interpretations: - artists, architects, biologists, chemists, clinicians, cognitive scientists, computer scientists, educationalists, engineers, graphic designers, linguists, mathematicians, philosophers, physicists, psychologists and social scientists. Mailing lists, newsgroups and the WWW provided the means for the organisers of the workshop and the editors of this book to reach a wide range of disciplines outside of their own personal discipline of Computer Science.

The response to this invitation was excellent. All of the above disciplines and others - Film and Media studies, Philosophy of Science, Molecular and Cellular Science, Theatre Studies, Art and Textile design - were represented in the refereed papers presented at the workshop. We were also privileged that Professor Arthur Miller, University College, London and Professor Rom Harré, Linacre College Oxford accepted our invitation to give Keynote Lectures. The former, in his lecture entitled "Visual Imageries of 20th Century Physics: Representing the Invisible", discussed the basic problem in modern science of how to represent nature, both visible and invisible with mathematics, and what these representations mean. The nature of scientific creativity, scientific realism and the role played by metaphors in scientific research were all explored. Professor Rom Harré continued this philosophical theme in his presentation, "Type Hierarchies and Iconic Models". Visual representations and interpretations were related to questions about the nature of knowledge in general. The importance of prototypes in defining conceptual categories was emphasised. Both contributions stimulated intense debate and played an important part in promoting an atmosphere of inquiry at the workshop.

Indeed, the workshop was intensive with much animated discussion over coffee and at lunch, discussion that was frequently continued in the pubs and restaurants of Liverpool in the evening. In the light of such activities, and the constructive criticism and cross-fertilisation of ideas they entailed, the workshop papers have been revised and extended for publication in this book. The selected contributions come from authors in many different disciplines, residing in countries across the globe: New Zealand, Australia, North America, Latin America, as well as many European countries are all represented. Thus this book truly presents a multi-disciplinary, international perspective on visual representations and interpretations.

Acknowledgements

The Workshop was sponsored by Connect, The Department of Computer Science, The University of Liverpool, Unilever Research, and Barclays' Bank. The Tate Gallery, Liverpool, Merseyside Conference Bureau and Merseyside Tourism also made contributions to the success of the Workshop.

We gratefully acknowledge the many staff at the University of Liverpool who helped the Workshop to succeed and especially to Beth James of Connect. We also thank Thelma Williams of Department of Computer Science and Lynne Westbury and Pam Evans of the Foresight Conference Centre. Thanks also to Steve Paton for his efforts to secure some funding.

We also acknowledge all our colleagues in various UK Universities who gave of their time freely to referee workshop contributions.

Table of Contents

Introduction:

Theme 1: Visualisation for Effective Communication

Theme 2: The Visual Dimension of Science

Theme 3: Articulating the Design Process

Theme 4: Psychological and Philosophical Perspectives

Theme 5: Visual Representations and Computational Processes

A Multidisciplinary Perspective on Visual Representations & Interpretations

Irene Neilson,
Connect, The Foresight Centre, The University of Liverpool,
Liverpool, L69 3GL, United Kingdom

Introduction

The chapters in this book present a multi-disciplinary perspective on Visual Representations and Interpretations. Five themes are identified. A variety of different disciplines contribute to each theme. The themes are - Visualisation for Effective Communication, The Visual Dimension of Science, Articulating the Design Process, Psychological and Philosophical Perspectives, and Visual Representations of Computational Processes.

Theme 1: Visualisation for Effective Communication

We might have entitled this section "A picture is worth a thousand words". The effectiveness of a good visual representation in conveying the structure of an argument or theory is well recognised in educational circles. We have, however, a very unclear idea of what constitutes a "good representation". In this section, Harrison attempts to shed light on this question by exploring the nature of models and the relation of model to theory in both the Arts and the Sciences. Lee considers what constitutes a 'good visual representation" through a detailed exposition of the work of Goodman. Lee's strong conclusion is that there is no way of helpfully characterising pictures, if they are considered as symbols, without taking their semantic aspects into account, a position that is also argued by Pineda in Theme 5.

These philosophical perspectives are complemented by a variety of papers reporting empirical work. Brown reports on his attempts to convey the main methods of mathematics to the general public through the Theory of Knots. In this task Brown employed the skills of graphic designers and the sculptor, John Robinson. Robinson created a number of symbolic sculptures, which articulate key mathematical concepts, http://www.bangor.ac.uk/SculMath/. An exhibition of this work was presented at the workshop and can be viewed on-line http://www.bangor.ac.uk/ma/CPM/exhibit/. Kent is also interested in the effective teaching of mathematical principles, particularly those of Dynamics. The understanding of Dynamics, Kent argues, is critically dependent on computational experimentation and visualisation. His paper reports on how Mathematica software might be adapted to effectively communicate key principles in Dynamics. His work also raises interesting questions about the possible integration of the visual and algebraic in a computational object language which is inherently visual http://metric.ma.ic.ac.uk/. The papers by Lund and Paton and de Freitas, respectively, broaden the educational framework by considering the role of visual representations in the teaching of key concepts in other domains. Paton and Lund explore the use of a visual metaphor - that of a hexagonal tube - in the communication of complex concepts in psychotherapy, notably those of Transference and Counter-transference, Projection and Identification, Container-Contained. The mental life of the individual is visualised as being transacted within the lumen of the tube. For further examples of the roles of metaphor in scientific thinking see http://www.csc.liv.ac.uk/~rcp/metaphor.html De Freitas adopts the conceptual framework of plate tectonics to aid in the interpretation of a series of landscape paintings. Her paper highlights the value of applying frameworks from scientific and cultural disciplines to visual paradigms such as the art of contemporary landscape painting.

Discussion of the communicative power of graphics frequently involves contrasting the expressive power of graphical with textual forms of expression. Hill and Wright's paper considers the nature of graphical as opposed to textual representations through an analysis of users' interpretations of various forms of representing causation in accident scenarios. Graphical representations, such as Petri nets and Why-Because Graphs, are compared with equivalent textual reports. One key issue is whether an information mapping scheme can be developed that permits meaningful comparison of the information contained within one form of representation with that contained within another. Finally Antonacopoulos and Delporte remind us of the problems faced by those who cannot readily decipher a visually communicated message. Their paper considers systems for the extraction of the message content from a graphic. Such a system is obviously important for those who have to rely on speech synthesisers for the interpretation of mixed media interfaces such as those commonly found on the WWW.

Theme 2: The Visual Dimension of Science

The first three papers of this section are concerned with philosophical aspects of the impact of visualisations on scientific theory. Harré is concerned with the nature of models, in their construction and in their use in scientific thinking. Specifically he contrasts an "Analogy" account of model making and using with a "Type Hierarchy" account. The latter is favoured but not as an account of how people actually reason but rather as a means through which one can express the 'logic' of typological reasoning of which, he argues, model thinking is a species. The next paper, by Ione, by contrast, is more concerned with the impact the phenomenological image itself has on the development of our understanding of the object and the creative thinking process, both at the level of the individual and that of society. Hendry returns to the question of the relation of theories to models. Drawing on historical examples within science, he explores how models developed to describe one phenomenon in science were utilised in the search for explanation of other phenomena. In so doing, Hendry develops a critique of the semantic approach to the relation of theories to models, which views the former as but a family of models

The remaining selection of papers considers how advances in representational techniques have facilitated understanding of key phenomena in science. Cooper addresses the importance of concepts taken from electronic structure to chemistry. Simple pictorial models of electronic structure are important tools for thought but to carry any real conviction, these models must also retain the high numerical accuracy expected of modern systems. Cooper's paper reports one approach to molecular electronic structure, the spin-coupled valence bond, which provides simple, highly visual representations of the behaviour of correlated electrons in molecules while also producing results of very high accuracy. Visualisation of the output from other complex numerical procedures, such as quantum molecular similarity methodologies, is also discussed. In biochemistry, Parish considers whether there is a language of proteins that would facilitate understanding of the determination of the three-dimensional fold in protein generation. Such a language would need to take account of the 3D interactions between amino acid residues. Goodsell reviews the value of atomistic verses continuous representations in both the physical and biological world. The utility of each form of representation is viewed as a function of the complexity of the system under study, the degree of interactivity between constituent parts from a given perspective. The paper focuses on the synergy of atomistic and continuous representations at the nanometer range of macromolecular structure and function and the representation of cellular mesostructure in molecular detail. Finally Serov, Kirillova and Samsonova consider the role of simulations in the development of student understanding of the mechanisms of cell functioning. A Java applet is used to display a Boolean network implementation of the behaviour of large genetic networks. Students interact with the applet to construct networks and examine their dynamics, http://www.csa.ru:81/Inst/gorb_dep/inbios/Dyn_bool/Dyn.htm.

Theme 3: Articulating the Design Process

The papers in this section are unified by a concern with the processes of interpretation involved in user interaction with on-line graphical systems including virtual reality environments. Transparency in interface design has frequently been emphasised in the human-computer interaction (HCI) literature and indeed in the computer aided design (CAD) literature. All too often, mastering the intricacies of a particular application can stand-in the way of achieving tasks through use of a computer. Various approaches have been proposed to improve interface design. The paper by Malcolm and Goguen explores some applications of algebraic semiotics to the design of user interfaces, particularly that of operating systems. For examples see http://www-cse.ucsd.edu/users/goguen/zoo. Treglown's paper continues the theme of interface design with a focus on the role of metaphor. Many indices in interface design rely on metaphors for their interpretative force. However, as Treglown points out, user interface metaphors can create as many design problems as they solve. England reviews the design of virtual environments for collaborative working. Such environments do not simply map to physical reality but also have to reflect the processes of knowledge creation and sharing.

Human computer interaction also frequently draws on other disciplines for its inspiration. The work reported by Sloane reflects this tradition. Sloane utilises a background in literary and rhetorical studies to consider how on-line representations of fictional characters invite varying interpretations. Of particular interest in her presentation are the elicitation of emotion through visual cues and the potential use of virtual environments in clinical desensitisation therapy.

Frequently the creative use of computers is impeded by the design of the interface or the manner in which information is represented within the system. Earl examines the constraints associated with different representations in his review of the manner in which shapes are considered in design and visualisation. The essential difference between geometric models and subshape descriptions of shape are reviewed and the implications of each form of representation for the interpretation of shape boundaries considered. Carlisle explores how computer based randomisation techniques can be applied to fabric design in order to break the monotony of repeating patterns and give rise to a greater individual and innovative feel to a fabric's design. Fernando, Wimalaratne and Tan, consider the use of Virtual Reality as a tool in the evaluation of ease of assembly and maintenance of proposed product designs in the manufacturing process. Doing this effectively requires the preservation of the geometric surface descriptions and dimensional data of CAD models (most current VR environments are polygon based) and support for run-time specification and management of assembly relationships between engineering parts. Such support is being built into the IPSEAM (Interactive Product Simulation Environment) which the Fernando *et al* paper describes. The CAD systems mentioned by Fernando still do not readily support the early, creative stages of the design process.

Computer support for the early creative stages of the design process is the focus of the papers by Stappers and Hennessey and also Mcfadzean. Stappers and Hennessey discuss the requirements of a system to support conceptual design through an analysis of the designer's ideation activities. Many of the issues they raise – such as expressive renderings, gesture based input - relate to more general research in HCI, Edutainment and Virtual Reality. Mcfadzean considers how the construction of external representations aids problem solving in conceptual design. As part of this research an interesting tool, Computational Sketch Analysis has been developed to capture key features of the sketching process and to aid in protocol analysis of design sessions. The assumption of both these papers - that trying to provide computer support for the early stages of the design process is desirable and/or useful - was challenged by various members of the audience, resulting in a lively debate.

The final paper in this section by Tweed considers our interpretations of the built environment. Visual representations of that environment are argued to focus undue attention on form at the expense of other qualities of that environment, such as its tactile, auditory or olfactory characteristics. Further, Tweed contends, interpretations of form are experientially determined. Architects may share an interpretative framework as a consequence of their training that may well be absent in non-architects. If true, this contention raises many issues such as how can an understanding of the design of a building be shared between architect and client.

Theme 4: Psychological and Philosophical Perspectives

The papers in this group explore the nature of the human perceptual experience. The researchers adopt various strategies of investigation. On the one hand, Welchman and Harris adopt the time-honoured tradition (c.f. Galen (AD130-200), Broca (1824-1880) and Wernicke (1848-1904)) of studying what anomalies in the visual perceptual experience tell us about the normal perceptual process. Their study of the phenomenological experience of artificially induced scotomas leads them to conclude that the brain does not fill in information in order to construct a perfect model of the environment. Such a thesis derives from a mistaken view of the nature of human perceptual processes. The visual system, Welchman and Harris, emphasise has evolved to support action. Holes in perception are not noticed simply because they are not significant to a visual system geared to detecting changes in the environment.

This emphasis on the importance of action in understanding perceptual processes is also to be found in the work of Schubert, Regenbrecht & Friedmann. Their interest is the construction of reality in virtual environments and the strategy adopted for investigation is that of experimental psychology. Of particular interest is the phenomenon of ‘presence’, a participant's sense of ‘being there’ in a virtual environment which Schubert *et al* conceptualise in terms of Glenberg's work on embodied cognition. The latter relates the psychological experience of presence to the cognitive representation of the environment by the perceiver. This emphasis on the involvement of modelling processes in perceptual experience differentiates the perspective of Schubert *et al* from that of Welchman *et al* and led to interesting discussion at the workshop.

Kovordanyi's paper continues this interest in the cognitive processes involved in perceptual experience. Kovordanyi asks “What are the cognitive mechanisms behind the human ability to reinterpret images?” Her desire is to identify the mechanisms, which propel cognitive processing towards the discovery of new visual patterns and concepts in a visual representation and the mechanisms, which obstruct the reinterpretation focus. Knowledge about these mechanisms might suggest alternative means of computer based support for the process of creative design. Her work thus links to that of Fernando, Stappers, Mcfadzean and Tweed in Theme 3. Kordanyani's method of investigation is that of the computer simulation of hypothesised cognitive models.

Marsh & Wright, like Schubert *et al*, are interested in virtual reality but from a different perspective. Marsh *et al's* interest is in the articulation of spatial information in a "natural and intuitive way". They are concerned with finding reliable methods through which subjects can articulate their experience of virtual reality environments and thus offer feedback to designers about the user interface to these environments. The focus of the paper is in on the individual's attempt to make sense of the virtual environment. The methodology is that of experimental psychology as applied in usability engineering. Dormann's paper is also concerned with the design of effective user interfaces to the on-line world. Her paper explores the application of the concepts of rhetorical theory to visual discourse in the context of the design of interactive WWW sites.

Virtual Reality is only one example of how man is constantly developing novel means of representing his environment. Of considerable interest, is the interaction between the medium of expression and the underlying thought process. What is the impact of a new form of expression on understanding? Buckley and Boulter 's paper reflects on this question in respect of the use of visual representations in the teaching of scientific concepts to children. They search for a schema by which the properties of different forms of representation might be related to learning objectives. Their focus is individual understanding. Edwards, by contrast, aims to paint a broader picture. His interest is in the impact of a new form of expression, the photographic negative, developed by Fox Talbot in England in the 1940's on the conventions adopted by societies for the interpretation of images. Controversially he argues that the invention of the photographic negative led to the development of universal codes for the interpretation of images. The study of how such images are interpreted, Edwards argues, has implications for the design of graphical interfaces; especially icons to computer based systems. One wonders, however, about the relative importance of this particular form of imagery. Indeed, in the paper which follows Edwards, Manley argues for the importance of attending to the conventions governing the interpretation of theatrical performance when considering the design of 3D virtual environments.

The remaining papers in this section, those by Clapin and Biggs, analyse the nature of visual representations from the perspective of philosophical enquiry. The work of Goodman, also referenced by Lee in Theme 1 and Hendry in Theme 2, receives considerable attention. Biggs adopts a content-model for the interpretation of some of Wittgenstein's graphics while Clapin considers representational schemes within the framework of the work of Haugeland. The taxonomy he presents offers an interesting contrast with that proposed earlier by Dormann.

Theme 5: Visual Representations of Computational Processes

As was emphasised in Theme 1 visualisation is arguably one of the most potent means of communicating information. Within Computer Science, considerable attention has been paid to the development of software visualisation techniques aimed at improving the comprehension of large software systems. Several papers in this section explore this issue. The problems in comprehending complex and sequential parallel programs are addressed by Beaumont, Jackson and Usher. Their particular interest is the representation of program control flow and concurrency in visual programming languages, two notoriously difficult problem areas. Petri nets are suggested as the basis for a concurrent, high-level visual language. Young and Munro are particularly interested in the use of 3D Graphics and Virtual Reality to model the overall structure of a piece of software. The traditional method of displaying structure is through the use of call graphs visualised as a directed graph but this itself often presents problems of interpretation as the scale and complexity of the information to be presented increases. Neary and Woodward's work returns to the issue of representing complex mathematical ideas. This time the focus is algebraic specifications. These have proven useful tools in the software development process offering precision, consistency, completeness and reduced ambiguity. But they are a form of representation that people find difficult to understand. Neary and Woodward consider how such specifications, in particular term re-writing in OBJ, may be visualised in order to improve comprehension. Yap and Holcombe's paper also addresses the issue of visual expressions of formal specifications. Their interest is in the development of an iconic interface through which novice formal methods users can readily create expressions in the Z specification language. The design of one tool, VisualiZer, is described in detail. Novice formal methods users were observed to make fewer errors in constructing Z specifications when using this tool as compared with their performance when constructing such expressions on paper.

The choice of a representation for a particular problem always involves a trade-off. The paper by Brown, Coenen and Knight discusses this issue in the context of the appropriateness of various spatial representation techniques for reasoning about a possible noise pollution problem. Specifically, the paper details the advantages of linear quad-tesseral addressing systems over cartesian systems when using AI reasoning techniques.

Multimodal scenarios present particular problems in choice of underlying representations and inference mechanisms. Pineda and Garza consider this problem in detail and offer a multimodel system of representation and inference based on the assumption that graphical expressions may be considered a language with a well-defined syntax and semantics. The relation of graphical to natural language expression is consequently viewed as one of translation.

The other papers in this group attend to the problem of the design of effective mechanisms for document retrieval from the large complex archives of resources offered by modern computer systems and the WWW. The difficulty that users' experience in correctly specifying search queries in Boolean logic terms is well known. Burdeck, Eibl and Krause explore how query visualisation might facilitate the adoption of effective search strategies by the user. Alternative systems for representing a search query are explored – from systems based on the simple Venn diagram, through those used in InfoCrystal, VIBE, LyberSphere and Vineta to the authors' own (based on set theory). Reid and Gittings are also concerned with information retrieval but from a different perspective. Their interest is in facilitating users' awareness of pages of interest on large WWW sites thus facilitating their navigation of these sites. Their aim is to design an unobtrusive mechanism whereby suggestions can be made to users of sites of interest based on knowledge about what other users with a similar profile have found interesting. Most of the current work on this topic requires users to explicitly define their interests by filling in a profile form. Reid and Gittings adopt an alternative approach. A user's profile is defined from their behaviour, from the sequence of pages they initially visit. This sequence serves as the user's signature. Genetic algorithm techniques are then used to create an environment in which signatures can interact and mutate over time.

Conclusion

This book, reflecting the work of 44 authors from 11 countries and approximately 18 disciplines, presents a kaleidoscope of perspectives on Visual Representations and Interpretations. As such, it demonstrates the value of multi-disciplinary research and the exchange of ideas and methods across traditional discipline boundaries.

THEME 1

Visualisation for Effective Communication

A. Harrison

J.R. Lee

R. Brown

P.Kent

C.A. Lund and R.C. Paton

N. de Freitas

J. Hill and P. Wright

A. Antonacopoulos and F. Delporte

Realism and Representation: Pictures, Models and Theories

Andrew Harrison

Department of Philosophy, University of Bristol

1 Introduction

A primary function of certain sorts of models, I shall argue, is that of *legitimising qualities*. Depiction in art - drawing, painting, sculpture - is I believe also a species of modelling[1]. What follows here is a preliminary to a discussion of a problem in aesthetics, namely the legitimisation of what we may loosely call 'aesthetic qualities'. To show that a description of the world is legitimate, that it has a fair chance of not being dismissed as fanciful, or subjectively private but may be respectably true, false or fictional, can be focused on how we may conduct more or less successful forms of representation. The starting point is adjacent to the philosophy of science.

The present consensus is that scientific theories and explanations inevitably involve, or are even equivalent to, 'modelling'. It is still unsettled whether model construction is to be distinguished from theory making or whether the distinction between theories and models in science is at best imprecise or merely one of nomenclature and style. However the common use of the word 'model' is still remarkably wide, and still seems to show a degree of ambiguity from context to context that suggests a radical conceptual divergence not yet quite captured by linguistic use. For who would suppose that there is now much in common between the ideas of a 'current model' in a contentious scientific area of enquiry and that of a model ship, train or Action Man, or indeed a supermodel on a catwalk, or 'the very model of a modern major general'? Yet these uses of 'model' are really far more traditional than the idea of a model in science. It would seem an absurd mistake of categories to suppose that any of them are theories.

What links all these different senses of model is essentially that two conditions go together which seem to oppose one another. One is the idea of a projective representation which may depend on a structural analogy that has little or nothing to do with mere resemblance, the other that models may *present*, exemplify or exhibit qualities or properties which they at the same time represent. While I do not wish to run our understanding of art and science together, whether models are used in art or in science, realism and its obverse seem to stand to one another as two sides of the same coin.

2 Is modelling a good thing to do?

The idea of modelling as a core activity in the rational pursuit of scientific understanding is comparatively recent. The 'old' OED, recently replaced by the current edition, gives 'to model' as a verb in scientific enquiry as 'obsolete and derogative', quoting in evidence Milton's jibe in *Paradise Lost* Bk. VIII at those who would 'model the heavens'. Since that OED entry dates from the '30s it provides a timely reminder of just how much theoretical and terminological water has flowed under the bridge since then. But it is not all that easy to guess what it may have been that Milton had in mind at the time of writing *Paradise Lost*. Clearly the general polemic in this passage is against a form of scientific realism, but the subtleties underlying that issue were no more straightforward for Milton's immediate predecessors than they are for present-day philosophy of science. We might, for example, imagine two different cases of 'modelling the heavens' in the pre-Newtonian period of the scientific revolution. One, apparently baroque, having more apparent affinities to art than to plain science, might be Kepler's imaginary models of the harmony and proportion of the heavens, perhaps his earliest jewel-like conception of the planetary orbits as the set of regular solids enclosing and enfolding planetary orbits and nested in sequence. A naturally sceptical 'anti-realist' response to this would be to insist that there is no good reason at all to identify the mathematical 'devices' of calculation as having any more 'reality' than is required for the pragmatic purposes of 'saving the appearances'. A quite different kind of model-making might, however, have been Gilbert's experimental models of the earth (as it may be presumed to be located in the heavens)[2]. Gilbert's small pieces of lodestone turned and carved to different shapes, were, we may suppose, thought of by him as scaled-down versions of the magnetic earth - small enough to be experimented with on a work bench as a device for finding out new things about the properties of the full size earth.

This is a form of modelling-realism of a quite different order. In the Keplerian case, as also in the case of Galileo's imagined 'thought-experiments', 'models' construct a 'conceptual picture' out of fully prepared empirical and conceptual ingredients: Gilbert's, by contrast, make the assumption that we may make direct empirical investigations of the miniature earths and then extrapolate that data from the model to claim parallel discoveries concerning its topic. Sceptical worries about either kind of imaginative device will be different. Gilbert's conception of a model, in contrast both to the most natural interpretations either of Kepler's constructions or Galileo's thought experiments, is of far the greater interest if we have worries about realism. It corresponds closely to how models are used in empirical engineering. It also corresponds equally closely to our everyday concepts of modelling, whether we are concerned with the simplest children's toys or the most sophisticated works of art. Models, used or conceived of in this way, *exemplify properties*. Models that do this might be called 'Gilbertian' with acknowledgement to both William, and with 'the very model of a modern major general' in mind, W S, Gilbert. The difference between the two is that William Gilbert's models are different kinds of things from what they model (small pieces of turned lodestone, rather than the earth itself) whereas the very model of a modern major general is still a major general, even if an absurdly perfect one - an actual, rather than imaginary paradigm case. (It may be an open question to which category a supermodel on a catwalk belongs). My main interest here is with Gilbertian models of the first kind. So long as we trust them they can serve the purpose of making properties transportable and demonstrable across 'analogy gaps'. It matters that it is *properties* we are dealing with in such cases not predicates: real properties are open to empirical experiment, predicates are open only to conceptual thought-experiment. Both sorts of experiment are, of course vital to enquiry. The question of how to trust experimental models addresses therefore a particularly strong sort of realism, for their success requires that the very same properties that we suppose to reside in the model's referent (what, real or imagined, it is a model of) can be more conveniently presented to us in the model itself. This is so even when from all other points of view the model may be *radically unlike* what it models.

To understand this we need to recognise that models of this sort represent what they do in two quite different ways. Success in the first stage of representation is a condition of success at the second. The first stage requires that we recognise a model as a *projective analogue* of its topic. That is to say to be able to recognise that *m* is a model of *t* we need to understand, or imagine, construe, both *m* and *t* as having a common structure (that is to say a commonly recognisable pattern of internal relationships - nothing deeper need be suggested) such that we can regard recognisable units in *m* as corresponding systematically with appropriate units in *t*. Within these constraints (which may be quite tight ones) we have a tremendous amount of freedom. This freedom permits quite radical simplifications of how we may, *via* the model, construe its topic. What we make salient depends on what properties we wish to exhibit. For example, a model of a bridge may succeed simply by isolating within the structural analogue just the fact that there are two supporting uprights joined by a cross member. (Two books and a stick of blackboard chalk might do). Similarly, a child may be perfectly satisfied with a model car that isolates just the fact that it is a rectangular object that may be moved from one place to another: a wooden brick may serve perfectly well. Being capable of such general patterns of location and movement in space may be quite enough to provide a modelling analogy,. Here the analogy is provided by the recognised common pattern between one activity and another that may constitute a child's game. How elaborate the child's game is determines how 'naturalistic' the toy needs to be. This is the nub of E. H. Gombrich's early, simple and profound, essay *Reflections on a hobby horse.*[3] As Gombrich makes clear, the underlying thought here is not really to do with the imaginative phenomenology of the child's play but with the 'logical structure' of simple model-representation, namely that which provides the simplest projective analogue for whatever the purposes of the model may be.

3 Pictures and perception

Rather naturally, most discussion of pictorial representation since the publication of *Art and Illusion,*[4] Gombrich's most seminal work, has concentrated on the negotiations our recognition of pictures involve between recognition of visually perceived objects and the phenomenology of our recognition of pictures of them. *Art and Illusion* tracks deep connections between psychological theories of visual recognition and our capacity to recognise pictures. The common question has been how far the psychological facts of 'normal' visual perception ground our recognition of visual representations of objects we see, or might see. There is a virtual consensus (from which only Goodman apparently defected[5]) that, as Wollheim has put it, any theory of the pictorial that is not 'rooted in the visual is doomed from the start'[6]. Regarded in one way this is manifestly right: visual art *is* irreducibly about the visual. But, equally obviously, recognition is at its simplest far more elusive than that would suggest. As the case of the hobby horse shows this need not be confined to the visual. There is no rivalry between such an account of representation and the specific claims for pictures (especially those studied by Gombrich within the history of art) that do locate them within the arena of the visual. For the key concept here is not visual *experience* as such but visual experience embedded within other modes of *recognition*. All philosophical positions, whether Kant's or Quine's that deny that there is a bare input of un-construed un-interpreted experience agree in paying homage to that rather trivial truth. What, however, many such philosophical theories fail to recognise is that this fact contrasts *recognition* strategies, certainly as they may be incorporated within the functions of pictures and most everyday models, with explicit *theories*, patterns of belief, argument and explanation. Theories are not models, nor are models theories, however intimate their association may be. Recognition may be 'theory laden', but by that same token 'pure' explicit, non-mysterious theories will always be compromised by their liaison with models in their everyday function in recognition.

But as far as pictures are concerned this leaves a question un-addressed. This is how recognition-strategies or depictive, more generally modelling, strategies interact. For it would be naive to suppose that it is obviously a one way traffic. While many pictures such as movies or video, may be thought of as extensions (prosthetic enhancements) of our normal visual abilities, other pictures, typically drawings, could not be regarded in this way. Drawing is always interpretative. Seen objects, for example will certainly present horizons, since they occlude one another when seen from a point of view. They also have surfaces that have directions relative to one another. What they do not have 'in reality' is outlines or indications of planar direction. But drawings cannot represent except in terms of such things. As any painter knows, pictorial devices as much point towards ways of recognition as they derive from them. A painter as much sees the picture in a landscape (sees the landscape in terms of the medium of depiction, in oil paint, water colour or pencil, say) as any 'properly informed' beholder (in Wollheim's words) sees the landscape in the picture. But this fact, important as it may be for understanding art, applies equally to any form of modelling representation.

It is essentially this inter-connection between modelling and the variability of imagination-charged recognition that underlies the traditional suspicion of modelling. But such suspicion, though well grounded from the point of view of a demand for unsullied theory, would if taken to any extreme, vitiate most of our normal practical strategies of recognition and representation. We cannot have unsullied theory, and we will not make theory purer by granting modelling a theoretical purity it cannot have.

4.'Anti-naturalism' and 'uncompromising realism'

Two consequences follow from this. The first is that since all modelling involves a simplification of how we, *via* the model, conceive of or imagine its topic - and most modelling involves very *radical* simplification - the idea of a model straightforwardly resembling what it is a model 'of' has no clear sense. All sorts of simplification may be equally right All sorts of simplifications can establish ways in which the picture or model invites us to conceive of, or imagine, its topic. We are inclined to overlook this especially in the case of marvellous replicas; but even they may be a different size (larger or smaller) and will thus have different internal patterns of physical strength and weakness, even very different textures or colour. What makes a model intelligible is itself what provides our conceptions of relevant similarities between the model and its topic. Rightness and relevance of resemblance is a *consequence* of successful modelling not the other way about. To this extent Nelson Goodman's notorious denial that visual resemblance could explain successful pictorial representation is (almost, though not quite) trivially true. Resemblance (without qualification) is neither a necessary nor a sufficient condition for representation: the required qualification is that what a model represents, or a picture depicts, is the 'intentional content' of *how* we are to regard, see, make imaginative sense of, its subject. This applies equally to structural resemblance, *tout court.* This is the 'anti-naturalistic' (anti-realist) consequence.

However, the second consequence of these considerations brings back resemblance with a vengeance, as a form of uncompromising realism. For if we think of a paradigm case of modelling being an engineer's model, such as Gilbert's tellurian spheres, or a ship designer's model hull for water tank testing, the function of such models will be to test *transferred properties.* (Goodman's term for this is 'representation by exemplification'[7]. His account applies this apparently to W.S. Gilbert's type of model, but it must apply to Gilbertian models generally). It depends on two conditions. The first is whether the projective analogy implicit in the model is successful enough for us to be sure what (real or imagined) the model is a model of, thus which bit of which corresponds to what, or in the case of paradigm samples, a matter of appropriate selection. The second condition is whether, granted the first, the variation between the model and its topic is such that the model will in fact (often, though not always as a matter of physics) exhibit the required properties. Will the model bridge that preserves the (scaled down) appearance and aesthetic features of the projected or actual bridge also enable us to test the properties of (say) tensile strength or compression? Will the scaled-down model ship have the right properties to test the flow of water, and so on? The art of experimental modelling largely consists in getting this right.

This may seem to provide an obvious objection to the idea that experimental modelling could in principle advance the understanding and truth of those scientific theories such modelling seems at the same time to presuppose. The immediate appearance can be of a badly circular argument (in effect the objection to William Gilbert). I do not think this is so for two reasons. The first is that one stage of understanding and knowledge will always be capable of bootstrapping another. The second is that while such models are not theories, but may 'illustrate' or test possible consequences of theories (precisely as pictures may illustrate stories, but not tell them) so the formal circularity is avoided, modelling may progressively modify the theory behind it by articulating the very idea of structural simplification (of what is salient in perceived or understood structure) on which the model depends. It is as if the interaction between experimental model and background theory constantly forced questions of definition: what, from the relevant point of view *is* a bridge, a hull form, a large building...? The constructed context provides such questions with their sense.

5 Experimenting with aesthetic qualities

That model-projection (including picturing) requires a structural analogue implies that *simple* properties (in terms of the modelling strategy) *cannot* be modelled or pictured, for they cannot present sufficient structure to get the analogue off the ground. One cannot model tensile strength, so long as this is thought of as a non-structured property. Yet a simplified model bridge may *itself* exhibit that property in various ways. So similarly, while a picture cannot *depict* the aesthetic quality of gracefulness or relaxation, it may still *exhibit* that quality. A picture of (say) a nude or a tree succeeds in representing such qualities by *itself* possessing them: the relaxed or energetic quality of the picture's subject is represented by exemplification in the picture (or sculpture) itself. The work demands that we regard the object that is depicted by it in the light of how we regard its own depiction. Representation by projection sets the conditions for such representation by exemplification.

But if model-exemplification is a way of legitimising even aesthetic properties this suggests a quite dramatic philosophical heresy. Traditional common sense orthodoxy suggests that it is simply *obvious* that aesthetic features of the world are paradigmatically 'subjective'. Beauty is proverbially in the eye of the beholder, with the mostly tacit proviso that each beholder's eye may be as different as may be from the eye of the next. I can see no reason for assuming any such thing. The commonest practices of the representational arts would be unintelligible if this orthodoxy were correct. The point is not that aesthetic features of the world are 'there in reality' as material properties may be but that, rather, aesthetic properties may be as much the subject of experimental transferability as the properties explored by other 'Gilbertian' models.

Outside the arts we do not normally attend to the aesthetic qualities of the representation *itself* as part of the idea of it *as a representation.*[8] In art (whether 'pure' or 'applied') we do. The relevant qualities may be 'objectified', made manifest to inspection and investigation *via* the representational powers of what we make. An architect's model of a bridge may explore by exemplification both the qualities of interest to a structural engineer and the qualities of interest to a designer. Both respectable philosophical or common sense orthodoxy would see these questions as wildly diverse. Model-making treats them very much the same. It also presents us with exactly parallel risks. How are we to be sure that the exemplified properties may really be a fair sample? How may we be sure that the properties of tellurian spheres are those of the magnetic field of the real earth? The analogy might be forced, unreliable, badly sampled. Similarly in art. No exemplification is self-validating. Rather, the point is how to make the *risks* inherent in the procedure *manifest.*

An apparent ontological difference between aesthetic properties, like gracefulness or ungainliness, and material properties, such as tensile strength or weakness, is that in the latter case we do not seem have to arrest the modelling process at a privileged point in the scale reduction. The fine scale of a piece of brittle material may be explained by a further model of a structure that has all the apparent properties of not being properly tied together. Often this may be hazardous. Seventeenth Century further-modelling suggestions, following on from Gilbert, offered a mechanical picture of hooks and eyes to account for magnetic attraction and repulsion[9]. What was appealing about such models was that they seemed to illustrate what mechanical, corpuscularian theory would suppose must happen across the distances of magnetic attraction. Such models derived entirely from causal theory (essentially a metaphysical theory that denied action at a distance). In this sense they were truly imaginary models, but ones with at least some hope of becoming less imaginary. Aesthetic qualities, such as gracefulness, do not seem to offer even a hope of such - even imaginary - finer scaling. Elegance at one scale may disappear at another. There is, it seems, no finer structure to draw on, nothing 'down there' in an underlying reality. This makes it seem obvious that such qualities are not part of the fabric of the world. Unlike magnetism or brittleness there is nothing further to be wrong about. Rock bottom is at the surface - a most unsatisfactory place for it to be.

This, however, confuses reductionism with legitimisation. Experimental models cannot be reductionist unless we are prepared only to permit such models at the level of a final explanation, and such a restriction would rob them of all use. Successful depiction incorporates differences between recognising woods and seeing trees The idea that property-ascription is legitimate only if there are endless vistas of plausibly imaginary fine scale modelling assumes that all such modelling can remain within the same representational methods, as if a fine scale drawing of what we have a large scale charcoal study for should itself be in charcoal, only finer. Neither drawing nor modelling works like that. If what is made salient in a fully realised broad wash is to be examined further this is unlikely to be achieved by focusing on finer details.

Gilbert's triumph was first of all to legitimise what mariners reported (in particular the phenomenon of compass 'dip' as a ship approached the poles). Supposing that there are exhibited properties open to empirical examination in new domains is necessarily risky. But it was this which opened the door for further speculations concerning deeper explanations. But without that such speculations would have been pointless. Much the same applies to aesthetic exemplification. One reason why it can be so hard to focus explanations of aesthetic judgements is that we pay far too little attention to this stage in the process - the exhibition of aesthetic properties whose (non-conceptual and in this modest sense empirical) examination is one of the primary functions of art.

The demands of exemplification are demands for a place for theories of error. If aesthetic qualities were as subjective as they are frequently supposed to be there would be no room for such a theory. For the legitimisation of the ascription of properties requires that we may have a public 'discourse' for this in which we may be capable of being able in principle to grasp distinctions between fact, fiction and fantasy. This applies dramatically to the ascription of aesthetic properties.

An inadequately discussed fact about pictorial - including sculptural - representation is that such depiction involves a specific danger in its potential for corrupting imagination and belief that is not shared by linguistic description and assertion - not shared by theory. Pictures, images, even children's toys, invite fear of fantasy and (in religious contexts) idolatry. Both errors of imagination derive from a temptation to confuse the properties of a representation with those of its referent. The reason why this temptation can be so strong is that it is, just sometimes, perfectly proper not to resist it. In fact serious art *normally* invites our response to exemplified qualities: if we are merely satisfied with the attractions of a picture that reside in the qualities of the depicted object alone, we have missed the point of representational art.. As Gilbertian models make material properties present, subtler forms of depiction make subtler qualities equally present to us. Iconoclasm (which is an extreme response to the fear of this) has produced so many crimes against civilisation that it is philosophical embarrassing to ask what reasonable caution may underlie such unreasonable reactions. If we attend, however to the Seventeenth Century reaction to rash modelling in science, we may find the parallel drawn quite explicitly. For Milton modelling was a form of idolatry - a maximum risk.

A child's toy, is a kind of model, which has given far too little attention by the philosophy of art. Neither an explanatory model nor a work of art, its function may illuminate both categories.. Consider the role of a cuddly toy to a child. By representing a certain sort of friendly animal the beloved toy can present not merely softness (which is a simple quality of the cloth) but cuddliness. It is easy to think of this quality of cuddliness as a highly subjective product of a form of private projective imagination on the part of the child, but given the representational capacity of the 'model' bear and given the materials of its construction the cuddliness is thereby *presented* in a quite non-fanciful manner It is equally a fact about the Teddy bear that it has be worn out by much hugging. But children not only cuddle their stuffed toys, they love them. Yet most children are equally content with the knowledge that these friends of theirs are made of cloth and sawdust. Do they then think that such mindless matter may nonetheless have thoughts and feelings? In fact they happily entertain a fiction. A fiction of which we may be sure, sure because it is rooted in fact, is not *thereby* something which we (or children) *need* to mistake for fact.

The fact in which such fiction is rooted is the fact of *presence.*[10] At its simplest presence is merely a form of (here fictional) exemplification. We rightly fear its dangers. The dangers are (in the case of children who have missed the point of their toys) those of fantasy, in religious contexts the corresponding danger is that of idolatry, the belief that an object, that *represents* a god and *presents* some of the qualities of an imagined god in the power and energy of its sculptural representation of the god, is itself divine. and is at the same time constituted of quite un-divine material. A more contemporary danger would be that of being imaginatively tempted by the overwhelming sense of presence inherent in varieties of virtual reality to suppose that the 'reality' is more than 'virtual'. In each case the risks derive from the fact that the presented qualities go far beyond mere conceptual 'experiment' with a possible extension of common predicates. In each case we are presented with properties.

Examples within art may bring out the relationships between theory and depictive modelling more dramatically than any others. Consider haloes. We might start with imagining a halo as a circle round the head of a depiction of a holy person as tantamount to the linguistic statement (the proposition) 'here be a saint'. The picture might be misconstrued as a depiction of a person with a soup-plate on his head or wearing a large straw hat at a strange angle. But the circle is not a depiction at all but a graphically encoded assertion. This circle may, further, be painted with lapis lazuli or gold, not to depict the blue or gold (gold itself is a bad material for depicting gold in paint) but in order to present to the beholder the glory of rarity and value transferred from the depicting surface to the depicted object. We have, then, a sample of a quality, but this only works if we, the beholders, can know what it is that is depicted in the first place. What quality is being appropriately re-presented to us as a transferred property presupposes that we know what it is that is being represented to us The aesthetic/theological theory of the School of Chartres was that the glory of jewels and gold and of rare and precious beauty would present to the beholder a small - scale sample of the glory of Heaven. The (contemporary) theological response was in effect that this was to mis-identify the appropriate qualities - to St Bernard a form or radical mis-sampling[11]. At a later stage Leonardo, for example, painted nimbuses, using whitish paint to depict, 'naturalistically', the imagined light about the head of the holy person. What is involved here is the exemplification of aesthetic qualities. It is the painting's qualities of strange beauty that we are to imagine as a how we are to grasp its (imaginary) referent. *That* (as the picture is) is the quality that is exemplified.

The objection to modelling that underlies Milton's satire in *Paradise Lost* is that bad science may ascribe to reality qualities (not merely Gilbert's experimental qualities , but qualities of intelligibility and order, of harmony and beauty) that belong merely to representations not to referents. In effect this warns against naive modelling without proper supporting theory. Manifestly, we need to learn how not to ascribe qualities to what pictures depict that properly belong to the pictures themselves. A picture in monochrome is not thereby a picture of a monochrome object, and an ugly picture no more a picture of an ugly object than a beautiful picture is thereby of a beautiful object. Children learn these distinctions early, but they do have to be learned. More subtly, pictorial features, especially those that derive from whatever system of depiction the medium or style of drawing may dictate need to be distinguished from directly perceptual features of the visual world. It is easy to be seduced by these facts into overlooking their converse. What Gilbertian modelling shows is why this matters. Modelling of this sort can provide us with the ability to make available to experiment and to public ostension qualities that can, just sometimes, be legitimately transferred from referent to representation. The challenge of such representation in both science and art is how this may be warranted. Here theory has to come to the aid of modelling. That is another story, but the point to emphasise here is that however sceptical such theory may need to be its anti-naturalistic emphasis should not override the peculiar sort of realism inherent in modelling and depiction.

---

[1] See Andrew Harrison, ' A minimal syntax for the pictorial' in *The Language of Art History*, ed. Salim Kemal and Ivan Gaskell (Cambridge University Press 1991) and *Philosophy and the Arts, seeing and believing* (Bristol: Thoemmes Press 1997)

[2] William Gilbert *de Magnete* trans. P Fleury Mottely (New York: Dover 1958)

[3] E.H. Gombrich *Meditations on a Hobby Horse and other essays* (Oxford: Phaidon 1985)

[4] E.H. Gombrich, *Art and Illusion* (London: Pantheon Books 1960)

[5] Nelson Goodman *Languages of Art* (Indianapolis: Hackett, 1976)

[6] Richard Wollheim, *Painting as an Art* (London: Thames and Hudson, 1987)

[7] Nelson Goodman *Ways of World-making* (Indianapolis: Hackett, 1978)

[8] see Andrew Harrison 'Style' in David Cooper (ed.) *A Companion to Aesthetics* (Oxford: Blackwell, 1992)

[9] see Copenhaven's discussion of Gassendi in *The Cambridge History of Seventeenth Century Philosophy* .472 ff. (Cambridge: C.U.P. 1998)

[10] For a fuller discussion of this see Andrew Harrison 'The Terror of Aesthetic Presence' in *Reconciling Art and Objectivity in Art Education* (Ed. Neil Brown) (Sydney: The University of New South Wales 1993)

[11] see Umberto Eco *Art and Beauty in the Middle Ages* (trans.) Hugh Bredin (New Haven: Yale U.P. 1986)

Words and Pictures — Goodman Revisited

John R. Lee
Human Communication Research Centre
and EdCAAD, Dept. of Architecture
University of Edinburgh
Edinburgh, Scotland

Abstract

The distinction between words and pictures is approached via Nelson Goodman's theories about symbol systems and notations, denotation and exemplification. It is argued that his attempt to draw a purely syntactic distinction fails. An attempt is made to reconcile Goodman with a notion of pictures as based on interest-relative structure-mappings. Comparisons are drawn between e.g. Goodman's concept of "repleteness" and the "systematicity" of structural mappings.

1 Goodman's Theory of Notation

This discussion addresses the distinction between linguistic and pictorial representations. It pursues the general idea that the pictorial is to be identified through the notion of an interest-relative structure-mapping [1]. This prompts a reassessment of some of Goodman's well-known views on symbolic representation.

The *locus classicus* of comparative study between graphical and linguistic systems is Nelson Goodman's *Languages of Art* [2]. Goodman is concerned with a general issue about how representation works—how marks on paper are related to various kinds of things in the world[1]—in a range of cases such as pictures, music and other kinds of notation. His cornerstone is to establish what distinguishes a "notational symbol system" from other kinds of symbol system. His approach forms the prototype for most later formal theories in this area, in as much as he considers even pictures to be symbol systems which represent not in virtue of any notion such as resemblance, but due to their being subject to certain systematic rules of use.

According to Goodman, there are five basic conditions required for a symbol system to be notational. The first two of these are syntactic, the others semantic.

1. It must consist of symbols (utterances, inscriptions, marks) which form equivalence classes (*characters*) on the basis that they can be exchanged without syntactical effect. Alphabets are a prototypical example—any "a" is as good as any other; they are "character-indifferent", and the characters have to be disjoint, so that

---

[1] In fact, Goodman does not consider this to be representation, a term he reserves for pictorial systems that are semantically dense and replete in the senses discussed below. In his terms, we are speaking here of denotation, but we will continue to use "representation" in the way that is now conventional.

no mark qualifies as an instance of more than one character. In general, Goodman takes compound inscriptions (e.g. sentences) to be characters as well.

2. Characters have to be "finitely differentiable" (or "articulate") in the sense that their disjointness is feasibly testable, which rules out, in particular, "dense" systems where any two (ordered) characters have another between them.

3. Notational systems must be *unambiguous*, so that the extension (which Goodman calls the "compliance-class") of an inscription is invariant with respect to time, context, etc.

4. The compliance-classes of all characters must be disjoint. (Also, the system will ideally be non-redundant.)

5. Compliance-classes must also be finitely differentiable. Thus, for example, any system which is "semantically dense", in that its compliants form an ordering such that any two have another between them, is excluded.

Goodman elaborates these points in relation to clocks and pressure gauges, which measure quantities that are infinitely variable. Here, the semantic domain can always be seen as dense, and if there are no marks on the dial, then there is no syntactic differentiation of characters, so the representation system is clearly non-notational. It can become syntactically notational if, say, dots are distributed around the dial and each is taken to be the centre of a disjoint region such that the pointer appearing anywhere within that region counts as an inscription of a certain character. If the ranges of pressure correlated with these regions are also disjoint (and articulate), then the system meets the semantic requirements as well, and hence is simply a notation. On a clock face, the hour hand is typically used notationally in this way, whereas the minute hand may be seen as marking the absolute elapsed time since the passing of a particular mark, and hence is non-notational.

Diagrams, one might think, are typically non-notational. Goodman observes that many topological diagrams are in fact entirely notational. This also applies e.g. to many drawings used in architecture and design, where although there may be a non-notational impression of form, measurements etc. are always given and the use of the drawing becomes largely notational. Road maps are a common example of mixed diagrams, with both notational and non-notational aspects. Non-notational diagrams are equivalent to two-dimensional *models*, taking the latter term (which in general can mean "almost anything from a naked blonde to a quadratic equation") to exclude descriptions and samples. Models, like diagrams, of molecules are usually entirely notational; others range all the way to being entirely non-notational.

Goodman approaches the difference between diagrams and *pictures* by introducing a further notion of "repleteness". A symbol is relatively replete if a relatively large number of its properties are involved in its identity as a symbol; something is more a picture, and less a mere diagram, if there is less about it that can be changed without making it into a different picture. This concept receives more detailed discussion below.

Goodman's general view is summarised as follows:

> Descriptions are distinguished from depictions not through being more arbitrary but through belonging to articulate rather than to dense schemes; and words are more conventional than pictures only if convention is construed in terms of differentiation rather than of artificiality. (230-231)

According to his own account, however, Goodman is not here trying to define the pictorial. Writing much later, in "Representation re-presented" ([3], ch. VIII), he says:

> Nowhere in my writing to date have I proposed a definition of depiction, but have only suggested that the everyday classification of symbols into pictures and nonpictures is related in an important way to the line between symbols in a dense or 'analog' system and those in a finitely differentiated or 'digital' system. [3] (123)

This characterisation is then sharpened up somewhat by noting that the distinction between analog and digital does not depend on the semantics of the system. Considering only the syntactic aspect (called a *scheme*, where clearly a scheme, being susceptible of having different denotations assigned to it, can belong to more than one system), Goodman notes that digital and analog schemes can be categorised on the basis of differentiation among the symbols in the scheme. Goodman is thus led to claim that the pictorial can be distinguished from the verbal on a purely syntactic basis, despite the apparently paradoxical facts that "all symbols belong to many digital and analog schemes", and "some schemes consisting entirely of pictures ... are digital" [3] (130). The key to resolving this paradox is said to lie in considering the *comprehensive* or *full* scheme for a whole language (e.g. English) or pictorial system (e.g. our pretheoretical idea of pictures).

2 Symbol Systems in Use

There is a tension between this account from ch. VIII of [3] and ch. VII of the same book. In ch. VII, the point is hammered home that our competence to understand novel representations using some system cannot in practice be accounted for on the basis of syntax and semantics alone, scorning "a pair of related misconceptions: ... the conviction that understanding a symbol is an all-or-nothing affair [and] that a symbol has a single, uniquely correct interpretation" (119). Invariably, contextual and often background knowledge is brought into play. "Literal" meaning is ill-defined; metaphor is rife. Language use does not depend simply on the application of rules, and picture use does not depend on our capacity for visual recognition of resemblances[2].

This vehemently expounded argument begins to call into question the very existence, or at least definiteness, of the system of rules; the syntax and semantics. The identification—and hence identity—of a word, or its location in a grammatical category, becomes open to question. If we look back at Goodman's approach to defining a syntax, we note that it depends on discriminable marks that fall into equivalence classes and are interpreted unambiguously. In fact, few symbol systems in practical use will meet these criteria, and the observations in the previous paragraph serve to emphasise that even when they may appear to this is likely to be an illusion. How, in fact, are the relevant equivalence classes identified?—By the patterns of *use* that the symbols are subject to, e.g. what can be exchanged "without syntactical effect". But such effects can only be identified on the basis of a certain amount of theorising, which in generating the distinction

[2] This account of why pictorial understanding does not depend on resemblance appears strikingly different from Goodman's claim in *Languages of Art* that pictures are in fact highly conventional and depend on the application of rules.

between syntax and semantics (and that which is neither) departs from the reality of practice where context and relation to experience are everything. Any distinction so generated is surely to be regarded as bounded and perhaps temporary, certainly subject to revision in the face of different kinds of usage.

In these circumstances, can we really speak of a *comprehensive* symbol scheme? Difficult as this must be for the symbols of a language, it seems still more so for those constituting a pictorial system. As Goodman himself emphasises, one and the same picture may appear in one situation as a digital character, in another as an analog picture. It seems manifestly implausible that we can tell which is which on purely syntactic grounds, because this requires us to establish when the picture can be substituted by another; and even if this can be found out from an agnostic scrutiny of patterns of usage, it surely still depends on what the picture is taken to represent. On the one hand, it is deeply problematic to identify the system that is at hand when any symbol is being considered; on the other hand, as far as pictures are concerned it appears that when used analogically each is a unique exemplar of a symbol and hence, as Elkins observes [4], that "there is very little sense in calling non-notational images 'systems'" (361).

A defence of the syntactic approach is mounted by Scholz [5] (101-2) on the basis that pictures are common enough which do not denote at all—e.g. pictures of fictional objects. We can accept this without finding it very helpful. In all symbol systems there's a sense in which what something means is distinct from the question of whether anything corresponds to this. Elgin [6] (135), responding to Scholz, makes a related point in observing that *reference*, as understood by herself and Goodman, encompasses more than *denotation*, including e.g. exemplification, expression and allusion. For these or other reasons, we surely have to insist that symbols which fail to denote "real world" objects are not thereby shown to lack interesting semantic properties; but also it is hard to see that syntactic properties alone can suffice to distinguish pictures from other symbols.

Goodman worries that

> The pictorial is distinguished not by the likeness of pictures to something else but by some lack of effective differentiation among them. Can it be that—ironically, iconically—a ghost of likeness, as nondifferentiation, sneaks back to haunt our distinction between pictures and predicates? [3] (131)

The ghost has some substance. Nondifferentiated pictures are not necessarily "like" each other in the sense that they visually *resemble* each other, but rather in that they have similar *uses*; and though this use may not be identified through their likeness to something else, it seems difficult to disentangle from their *reference* to something else.

3 Structure Mappings

If we accept this, we are thrown back once again into the difficult area of determining what is distinctive about the way pictures, as compared with words, secure reference to their objects. We accept that likeness is not, in any simple sense, the answer here, and nor is recognitional capacity (as proposed by Schier [7]; cf. discussion in [1]). The notion of structural mapping, which goes so naturally with the notion of analog (and analogical) representation, seems the most promising direction in which to seek progress.

It can be said that any formal semantics is based on a structure-mapping. Wittgenstein's so-called "picture theory of meaning" is a prototypical way of presenting the semantics of natural language as a relation between the structure of the linguistic expressions and the (logical) structure of the world. More modern versions of the story use mappings between set-theoretic models or algebraic signatures to achieve a similar result. What is emphasised by Wittgenstein's later work, however, is that there's no definitive, given way of doing the mapping. Various kinds of symbol systems come into being and acquire such mappings only in virtue of being used by communities of people for various, typically communicative ends. Conventions evolve that "standardise" to some extent the ways in which this is done, so that people can usefully generalise their understanding from one case to another, but there is always a good deal of latitude. The organisation of symbols into systems emerges from the development of these conventions, but then it also emerges that symbols and systems have many different kinds of properties at different levels of structural abstraction. Not only that, but there are different ways of structuring the "world" onto which symbol structures are mapped: it can be subjected to different schemes of conceptualisation, some of which may be more conventional than others. Following Gurr [8] [9] we call these abstract scheme- and world-representations "α-worlds".

The upshot is that we have a mapping between two structures (α-worlds) that are susceptible of the same general kind of formal description. The mapping constitutes *denotation*, going from the abstraction of the representing scheme (e.g. some formalisation of a type of graphics) to an abstraction of the represented domain. The formalisation allows us to examine particular properties of the mapping. One property that seems to be important has been called *systematicity* (cf. [9]). A mapping between two structures is systematic, crudely speaking, when the mapping involves and preserves properties and higher-order properties (i.e. properties of properties, such as *transitivity* etc.) that hold among the entities mapped. Thus a family tree can be based on a systematic mapping in that connections by lines (intransitive) represent parenthood relations (intransitive), whereas *being above* represents *being an ancestor of*, which are transitive relations. If lines to represent parenthood were drawn in random directions[3], the diagram would still in principle be usable, but a number of useful topological features of trees would no longer be shared by the diagram, and e.g. ancestorhood would have to be inferred by following multiple parenthood links, rather than being represented directly. Relative to an α-world in which the ancestorhood relation is explicit, this diagram would be less systematic than the tree. Systematicity of this kind is important when using diagrams for reasoning; but it is also relevant to depiction.

Note here that systematicity is a property of the *relation* between α-worlds, and not of the abstractions themselves. If both α-worlds are very "flat" and contain only first-order relations, then a mapping that only maps these relations may still be maximally systematic (i.e. isomorphic at all levels). We may feel that a set of parenthood relations just inevitably induces the ancestorhood relation. However, this remains a feature of the domain that we might not have included explicitly in our abstraction; in which case its omission is no fault of a diagram intended to

[3] Arrows or a similar device would have to be added to capture directedness, since this is normally also shown implicitly by the vertical dimension.

communicate that abstraction. Arguably in such a case the tree, with its tendency to be read as illustrating a transitive relation, would be implying *too much*.

4 Structure and Repleteness

Systematicity can be compared, and to some degree contrasted, with Goodman's notion of *relative repleteness*. The latter is defined [2] (229f) in terms of a distinction between features of symbols that are *constitutive* or *contingent* in a given scheme, i.e. the features that are relevant to distinguishing between symbols. For a given diagram, it might be that most of its geometrical features are irrelevant, hence contingent, and can be varied without affecting its identity, provided that the topology is maintained. In that case, the diagram is less replete than a picture where (Goodman suggests) changing almost any detail will turn it into a *different picture*. It might thus be argued that the family tree is more replete than the diagram where arrows point in all directions, since the directions of the arrows are constitutive in the one, and can be inconsequentially changed (or changed more) in the other. Since repleteness is a very "flat" notion, in that it relates only to the surface features of a symbol (its first-order properties), it seems somewhat less useful in explanatory terms than the systematicity of a proposed mapping. However, in another sense it might be thought a fuller notion in that it is not at first sight relativised to the construction of some particular pair of α-worlds. Being supposedly syntactic, it can be evaluated by simply looking at whether a particular diagram, seen as a symbol, just has more constitutive properties. A picture like the *Mona Lisa* seems to have far more constitutive properties than a tree diagram. But here we are returned to our earlier difficulty of determining what *seen as a symbol* might mean. How can one make sense of this, especially for analog symbols, in purely syntactic terms? In fact, characterisation of a range of items, e.g. marks on paper, as a symbol scheme amounts to defining the α-world on one side of a semantic mapping and, as Goodman observes, different such schemes will treat the same marks very differently. In general, and especially for analog schemes, this procedure is only coherent in relation to some other α-world onto which a mapping will be defined. What systematicity requires is that wherever a scheme is relatively more *or less* replete, so will have to be the α-world description of the domain it represents. The smile of the *Mona Lisa* is merely contingent if her image is treated as a symbol for *any girl*—the symbol has fewer constitutive properties. Although it may be true, in principle, that a scheme with this syntax can be described purely in terms of those properties, it is clearly neither feasible nor useful to do so without adverting to the intended *use* as a representation of arbitrary girls.

We said: "especially for analog schemes". Repleteness, as Goodman uses it, seems to apply only to analog schemes, but it can also be considered in relation to notations, such as text. Features like spatial layout seem clearly able to have a function. Petre and Green [10] discuss the concept of *secondary notation*. Where there exists a well-defined diagrammatic system, diagrams may often be constructed which go beyond the defined system—prototypically, items in an electronic chip design may be grouped by experienced designers in ways that indicate useful facts about their relationships even though these groupings are formally undefined. By the standards of the simplest parenthood abstraction, use of the vertical direction to induce ancestorhood in the family trees discussed in the last section could be seen as a case of secondary notational use of the arrow-based representation. However, it would always be possible to define a new α-world with respect to which the secondary notation is well-defined and hence now "primary". This would also be a system entailing a scheme in which more properties were relevant to symbolic identity, and hence more replete. Though Petre and Green speak of diagrams, the idea of secondary notation appears to cover aspects of text, as in the issue of spatial layout. Since natural language is not a well-defined system, let's consider as an example computer programming languages. These are very commonly defined without regard to the nature of the "white-space" characters between the various lexical items, but whether a character is a space, a tab or a newline has a dramatic effect on the visual appearance of the program code (text), as normally presented. The resulting layout is crucial to the usability of the text for a human reader, precisely because there is a relationship, though it may be intuitive, vague and hard to define, between the layout structure and the abstract structure of the program. This may be in some sense implicit in (derivable from) the unformatted code itself, but in that form it's *unavailable* to the human user. Layout here implies a secondary representation system with a more replete scheme and a systematic mapping to a more explicit abstraction of the domain structure.

For Goodman, secondary notation may often not be notation. Though a programming language is probably as close to a true notation, in his terms, as anything in practical use will get, the various uses of layout are likely to fail the five criteria[4]. But this is perhaps true of all real notations, including Goodman's favourite example, musical notation. Elkins [4] discusses a Bach autograph score, suggesting in effect (without of course using this terminology) that many of its features—the ways notes are grouped, etc.—may be seen as a more replete secondary notation. Aspects of natural language text, such as layout, the use of various fonts, italics, etc.—and likewise prosody in speech—seem plausibly to fall under a similar account. Perhaps also, though this is less clear, the approach will extend to those aspects of language known as "iconicity" among linguists (see e.g. [11]; briefly discussed in [12]), where for example the sequencing of items in sentences may relate to temporal ordering, etc. The sharp dichotomy that Goodman sets up between the continuous and the discrete is valuable in theory but often as blurred in practice as even the sharp formal edges of well-defined symbol systems.

5 The Role of the Interpretant

Our discussion has emphasised that the relationship between a symbol and what it represents is dependent on a particular way of abstracting a view of the latter. Goodman is indeed keen also to make this point, and it has been seized on by others as a way of responding to his critique of the role of resemblance in representation. Files [13], for example, draws an instructive analogy with Peirce's tripartite distinction between representation (symbol), representational object and interpretant (interpretation in an interpreting agent). The interpretant corresponds to what has been here repeatedly termed the *use* of a representation[5]. In non-artificial

---

[4] Though, as we observed earlier, many diagrams are notational.

[5] Files speaks of the "behavioural dispositions" of the interpreting agent; I suppose all relevant such dispositions (if nothing else) to fall under the term *use*.

symbol systems (including e.g. painting and natural language), considerations of use give us our only basis for describing the abstractions that are in play. In artificial systems, as we have seen, secondary uses are likely to usurp the supposedly clean and well-defined abstract semantics which is supposed to account fully for issues of interpretation. Files urges that whereas this framework may explain how something can be a symbol at all, more is required to explain, or *ground*, what in particular it represents—its content. He suggests that resemblance plays a role in grounding iconic representations. Our alternative is to ascribe something like this role to structure-mapping in general: it grounds by modulating the use of representations in relation to objects. Mappings will only affect use if they can be somehow apprehended by the user; to this extent, mappings that coextend with what are usually thought of as (visual or other) resemblances may well be important, but they are accorded no special status. It is not clear that mappings where the resemblance is obscured, e.g. anamorphic pictures which require curved mirrors before their resemblance to their object can be recognised, have any less right to be called "pictures" (cf. [1]), or to be considered any less effectively grounded as representations.

Another view of the tripartite nature of representation is offered by Bull [14], who combines Goodman's approach with that of Gombrich to produce an interesting emphasis on the notion of a *schema*, described (in terms that for present purposes are undesirably mentalistic) as "our prior concept of an object's appearance" (214). So we have images, objects and schemata, where the latter form a differentiated symbol scheme which can be used to link images and objects by denoting both. Though taking a very different route, Bull seems to arrive somewhere quite close to Files' position. The schema has very much the role of an interpretant: "We recognise an image correctly if and only if we see it as the schema with which it complies, but the act of recognition does not itself depend on the compliance relationship" (214)[6]. We wish to stress here that equally the compliance relationship does not depend on the act of recognition. Rather it depends on a structural mapping—an *abstract* schema—that provides for a certain kind of use of the image as a representation. Resemblance and the assistance of visual recognition is just one kind of way in which a mapping can facilitate such use. And this is not to disagree with Elgin [15], who notes that

> ... the scheme/content distinction has come into disrepute, and rightly so. The orders we find are neither entirely of our own making nor entirely forced upon us. There is no saying what aspects of our symbols are matters of conventional stipulation and what are matters of hard fact. For there are few purely conventional stipulations, and no hard facts. [15] (18)

The parallel construction of α-worlds reflects just this kind of mutual interdetermination of our conceptions and our ways of representing them.

6 Exemplification

Goodman, as was noted in passing above, deepens his account of reference in a way that is illuminating here, by observing that the notion is not exhausted by denotation. There are other ways of referring, and one of the most important he

---

[6] Recall that, for Goodman, to comply with a symbol is to be denoted by it.

calls *exemplification*. A sample, e.g. a swatch of cloth, is used to refer to other items, and in this way it obtains a symbolic role. Goodman [2] (52ff) analyses this as the *converse* of denotation. A symbol that denotes is called a *label*: when a label denotes something, then what it denotes becomes (i.e. can now be *used as*) a symbol that exemplifies the label. This is clearest in relation to predicates, e.g. *red*. A predicate is analysed as denoting all its compliants, in this case all red things; and any red thing exemplifies *red*.

Exemplification is in no way limited to linguistic labels. A diagram has some given denotation; it is then exemplified by its referent(s). The family-tree diagram is exemplified by the set of relationships in the depicted family. This is again dependent on the particular abstractions that are invoked on either side of the mapping: the relationship of being *father of* will exemplify the spatial relationship of being *above* only where the latter has been established as denoting the former in some symbolic system. Systematicity is therefore as relevant to exemplification as to denotation. In a fully systematic mapping between two sets of abstractions—an isomorphism—exemplification is the exact converse of denotation. Lapses in systematicity raise dangers of misunderstanding in both directions.

Goodman notes that the taylor's swatch exemplifies only certain properties of the bolt from which it comes, such as the colour and weave, and not e.g. being made on a Tuesday. This seems not unlike the doctrine of constitutive and contingent properties: here, the day of manufacture is contingent with respect to exemplification, which is as much as to say that no such label as "made on a Tuesday" is part of the abstract description (of both the swatch and the bolt of cloth) which is in use for present purposes. We assume that there is an abstract label—describing, say, the weave—which refers to some property of both the swatch and the bolt, and this label is then exemplified by both of its referents. We now see that the role of the label here is similar to that of the schema discussed in the last section, denoting both the referring symbol and the thing referred to. The swatch may loosely be said to *exemplify the bolt* at best by some sort of analogy, but it is the possibility of some such connection that supports our normal talk of swatches as samples of bolts.

A suggestion one might make then, along the lines of Bull's use of schemata, is that pictures and their objects be treated as related via common referenthood with respect to some abstract set of labels. We would then say that a picture depicts what it does because we can describe both the same way: a picture and its object would both exemplify the same description. In a sense, Goodman does say this, but avoids the extra layer of abstraction by maintaining that a picture can be a non-linguistic label that denotes, and hence exemplifies, *itself* as well as its object ([2], 59ff; see also Elgin [16], 77-8). This situation is uncommon with words: "sesquipedalian", being a word that means[7] "a long and ponderous word", denotes and exemplifies itself, as does "polysyllabic", but relatively few words behave thus. Perhaps all pictures do? Elgin seems to imply as much: "In exemplifying, a symbol in [a pictorial] system functions as a label that denotes itself and the other things that match it", and again "[t]wo symbols exemplify the same label if they match each other and refer to the same shared feature" [16] (78). She also applies this idea to rhythms, musical phrases etc. It may now appear that the essential arbitrariness of denotation has been usurped, though something of this seems

[7] Ignoring the complication that this is clearly metaphorical.

natural in cases of self-reference[8], and also that the notion of "matching" is suspiciously like *resemblance*, which with Bull we agreed should be independent of compliance (and hence exemplification). But again an alternative is structure-mapping at some appropriate level of abstraction. If pictures and other such structures are somehow necessarily self-referential, this marks them out from words in a rather interesting way, and certainly in a way consistent with the idea that their reference is based on structure-mapping, since of course anything structured shares its own structure. We have almost the appearance of Goodman (and Elgin) offering, without explicit mention of structure, a nonetheless structure-based account; and one, moreover, in which the structures that matter are just those that serve the interests of the users of the symbolic system that they and their uses determine.

7 Repleteness and Relativity

We return briefly to secondary notations, and note that their emergence has to be explained at an extra-systematic level, relative to the original symbol system. There must be a process whereby a new α-world abstraction is (in effect) devised and found to be a proper extension of the original. Alternative such abstractions inevitably exist, and cannot, of course, be evaluated against the original system; instead their evaluation (and indeed the motivation for creating them in the first place) must come from some consideration of the *purpose* for which they are being used. This may be to do with reasoning, in which case a fairly minimal scheme is likely to be attractive, reducing the danger of unwanted implicatures[9] and other worries. Or it may be to do with aesthetic appreciation.

I look up and see on the wall a painting by Cezanne which appears to depict a group of women bathers. It is important to my understanding and appreciation of the work that I see it as a picture of such a group, but it does not matter whether there ever actually existed such a group[10], or whether if so they were very much as depicted. With respect to groups of women, the nature of this painting can be compared to that of a somewhat abstract diagram, and perhaps one way to think of this is that it exemplifies a group of women. It exemplifies the label "group of women", which due to the self-referentiality of pictures also gives it the denotational role of that label. The seeming sophism here can perhaps be dissolved by considerations of structure. Properly to exemplify the label "group of women", one might think, something should actually *be* a group of women, so what the picture really exemplifies is the label "group-of-women-label"; but now if we accept that (at least for pictures) to exemplify is to share structure at a suitable level, it becomes possible to collapse this threatening regress.

---

8 Even with autological words, as in the examples above, there is usually some aspect of the structure, sound or orthography of the word that is exploited. Exceptions may be e.g. "recondite" or "meaningful", which perhaps serve as samples of their own function rather than structure.

9 Unwanted implicatures arise, for example, when users of a representation may read more into it than is intended. Cf. [17].

10 Though if we assume there did, we can avoid many of Goodman's nominalistic contortions associated with fictive labels.

Here, systematicity and repleteness seem again to come apart. This picture has very many properties—line, colour, composition, etc.—that are critical to its appreciation but are of no significant representational interest. In as much as these properties are constitutive of the identity of the painting as an artwork, but largely contingent in relation to what it might depict or exemplify, we see how thoroughly repleteness is a relative notion: the painting is replete or not only as considered for the time being as a particular kind of symbol in a particular scheme. For a fuller account of its aesthetic qualities we will have to look beyond its symbolic aspects. Here, however, we restate: notwithstanding that the precise semantics is in many respects unimportant, the representational nature of the work *in so far as it is considered to be a symbol* is central. The relevant scheme (syntax) cannot be coherently identified except as part of some particular system (including semantics), and once again the system will ideally exhibit thoroughgoing systematicity.

Acknowledgements

The author is grateful for the support of HCRC, an Interdisciplinary Research Centre established by the UK Economic and Social Research Council (ESRC).

References

1. Lee, J. (1997) Similarity and Depiction. In Proceedings of the Interdisciplinary Workshop on Similarity and Categorisation (SimCat '97), M. Ramscar and U. Hahn (eds.) Dept. of Artificial Intelligence, University of Edinburgh.
2. Goodman, N. (1969) Languages of Art. Oxford University Press.
3. Goodman, N. & Elgin, C.Z. (1988) Reconceptions in Philosophy and Other Arts and Sciences. Routledge.
4. Elkins, J. (1993) What really happens in pictures: misreading with Goodman. Word and Image 9:4, 349-362.
5. Scholz, O. (1993) When is a picture? Synthese 95:1, 95-106.
6. Elgin, C.Z. (1993) Outstanding problems. Synthese 95:1, 129-140.
7. Schier, F. (1986) Deeper into Pictures. Cambridge University Press.
8. Gurr, C. (1998) On the Isomorphism, or Lack of it, of Representations. In Theories of Visual Languages, K. Marriot and B. Meyer eds. 288-301, Springer-Verlag.
9. Gurr, C., Lee, J. and Stenning, K. (1998, in press) Theories of diagrammatic reasoning: distinguishing component problems. Minds and Machines.
10. Petre, M. and Green, T.R.G. (1992) Requirements of graphical notations for professional users: electronics CAD systems as a case study. Le Travail Humain 55, 47-70.
11. Haiman, J. (1985) Iconicity in Syntax (ed.). John Benjamin.
12. Lee, J. and Stenning, K. (1998) Anaphora in Multimodal Discourse. In Multimodal Human-Computer Communication, Harry Bunt, Robbert-Jan Beun, Tijn Borghuis eds. 250-263 Springer-Verlag.
13. Files, C. (1996) Goodman's rejection of resemblance. British Journal of Aesthetics 36:4, 398-412.
14. Bull, M. (1994) Scheming schemata. British Journal of Aesthetics 34:3, 207-217.
15. Elgin, C.Z. (1991) Sign, symbol and system. Journal of Aesthetic Education 25:1, 11-21.
16. Elgin, C.Z. (1983) With reference to reference. Hackett Publishing Co.
17. Oberlander, J. (1996) Grice for graphics: pragmatic implicature in network diagrams. Information Design Journal 8:2, 163-179.

Mathematics and Knots

Ronald Brown
School of Mathematics, University of Wales, Bangor
Bangor, Gwynedd

Abstract

The exhibition `*Mathematics and Knots*' is intended to present some methods of mathematics to the general public. We explain these methods and the design underlying the presentation.

1. Introduction

The Popularisation of Mathematics is a considerable challenge. The fascination of the subject is shown by the popularity of recent biographies of Wiles, of Erdos, and of Nash, as well as by the Royal Institution Christmas Lectures and books by Ian Stewart. Nonetheless, it is not clear if the biographies provide good rôle models or encourage students to take up the subject, and in all of these the nature of mathematics remains to some extent a mystery. It is not easy to find brief statements on: the objects of study of the subject; its methods; and its main achievements. Even a popular writer such as Deutsch [5] makes statements such as: `Mathematics is the study of absolutely necessary truths.', which to most people conveys nothing, and as a view of mathematics was discounted by the discovery of Non Euclidean Geometry in the early 19th century [7].

Instead of this fruitless philosophising, trying to make external justification for mathematics, it is worthwhile to show the practice of mathematics, and to relate it to the usual means by which we investigate and attempt to understand the world.

Through teaching the Theory of Knots to mathematics undergraduates at Bangor since about 1975 we have found its value for explaining some basic methods of the subject, and began to use some of the ideas in public presentations. For example, I gave a BAAS lecture at Sussex in 1983, a London Mathematical Popular Lecture in 1984, and a Mermaid Molecule Lecture in 1985. For these we accumulated a lot of visual material and in 1985 set about making this into a travelling exhibition.

The start was to discuss with a graphic designer, who gave us the basic format of mounted A2 boards with aluminium surround, and a travelling case. Over the four years of the exhibition's gestation, we consulted with three greatly helpful graphics designers, and this input was essential for the successful production for the Pop Maths Roadshow which opened at Leeds University in 1989 and then toured the UK. Support from a number of organisations, including one of the first COPUS Grants, was essential for the costs of all this work. We were fortunate in

1988 to get an ESF Grant for training of young people in IT, which supported two students to implement the exhibition in the first version of Pagemaker

The Exhibition was put on the web in 1997, with further support [1].

We started out very naive and had not realised that the exhibition format is one of the hardest. The reasons are:

1. The impact has to be predominantly visual.
2. Each board has to tell its own story.
3. Each board has to be properly related in content to the other boards.
4. Each board has to be properly related visually to the other boards.

In particular, a grid design has to be used so that there is a certain visual rhythm. A basic fault is also to try to put much on one board. The initial content of one board on Knots and Numbers was finally spread over three boards. The final graphic design, including the hand drawing of all the knots, was done by John Round.

In determining the content of each board according to these gradually realised principles, we also found that our views on the structure of the presentation and the nature of mathematics were changing. The emphasis developed in terms of the methodology of mathematics, rather than its nature. Indeed a full treatment of mathematics would have to involve understanding on matters of psychology, language and neurology way beyond current possibilities. What we can do is show how the mathematicians go about their business and how they use standard methods of investigation to advance their subject. In this way we demythologise the subject, and also we hope make it more exciting.

The theory of knots has many advantages for our purposes. The major one is that the objects of study are familiar to all. So also are its basic problems, as anyone who has tried to untangle string will know. The long history of knots is also an advantage: the oldest known pierced object is a wolf's tooth, presumably part of a necklace, and dates at 300,000 BP [8]. Perhaps the Stone Age should be called the Age of String!

The mathematics of knots begins in 1867 with the now forgotten Vortex Theory of the Atom. A theory of the atom had to explain:

- The stability of atoms.
- The variety of atoms, as shown by the periodic table of elements.
- The vibrational properties of atoms, as shown by their spectral lines.

Lord Kelvin had seen smoke rings of his physicist friend P.G. Tait, and was impressed by their stability, and vibrational properties. He had a vision of atoms as vortices in the aether, an imaginary substance which was supposed to fill all space. How to explain the variety of atoms? In 1867, Kelvin presented a paper to the Royal Society of Edinburgh, part of which read:

> Models of knotted and linked vortex atoms were presented to the Society, the infinite variety of which is more than sufficient to explain the allotropies and affinities of all known matter.

The first job was to compare a list of knots with the periodic table of the elements, and so Tait set about preparing a list of knots. The vortex theory of the atom soon disappeared, but Tait's 10 years of work on his list of knots of up to 10 crossings and the conjectures he made (some of which have been proved only recently) have been an inspiration ever since. Further, to determine what is meant by `a list of knots' required solving difficult conceptual problems.

The solution to these problems is basic to our presentation, and gave the underlying structure of our exhibition.

2. Analysis of the methodology

The objects with which mathematics deals may be said to be `structures'. We do not define this precisely, but this term conveys two impressions:

1) The objects have parts, which are related.

2) Mathematics deals with *abstract structures*, which means we have a notion of an instance of a general idea; for example a knot in this piece of string is an instance of the general notion of a knot. This abstractness is a basic aspect of language.

The first problem with examining a species of structure is that of:

2.1 Representation

We have to find some way of showing, describing, presenting, or whatever, for the structure under consideration. In the case of knots, we can in a lecture bring a piece of string with us, but on paper we resort to diagrams of knots.

We start with a piece of string as on the left below and tie a knot in it as on the right:

Assuming you are holding both ends, the right hand string cannot be changed to the left by any kind of manipulation of the string, but only by cutting and retying, or letting go of one end.

This shows the basic mathematical problem: how do you *prove* that the string cannot be untied? This may sound a silly question because some minutes' experiment shows it cannot be done. However a mathematician is asking for more certainty, and is asking for methods that can be applied not just to this problem but to more complex knots where the situation would not be so intuitively clear.

As a start, we find it bothersome holding both ends of the string, so we join them. In this way we get the unknot, and our simplest knots, the trefoil and its mirror image:

Thus our representation of knots is by these *knot diagrams*, in which at each crossover only two parts of the string cross.

2.2 Classification

A basic urge to make sense of the world is to classify. For example, we do not list all the insects in a piece of jungle but we do try to list all the insect species.

So we need to know when two knot diagrams represent the same knot. A knotted loop of string has essentially the same `knottiness', however it is pulled, twisted or crumpled. This kind of change has to be shown in terms of knot diagrams. We will say more on this later. However the idea is illustrated by the following diagram, which shows how the figure eight knot is the same knot as its mirror image.

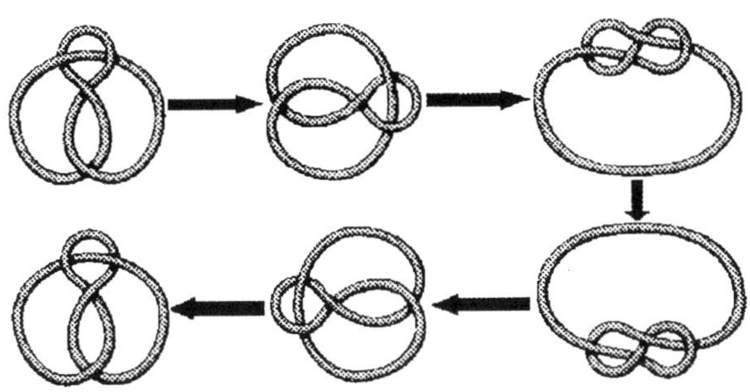

2.3 Invariants

To prove two knots are the same, that is, to prove two knot diagrams represent the same knot, you only have to move one diagram into the other. This is not easy as it looks: Tait's table of knots contained two 10 crossing knots that were proved the same only in 1974 by Perko.

A considerably harder problem is to prove two knots are not the same, because you have to prove that no possible movement can move one into the other, and there is no way of examining all the infinite number of possible movements. For example, the trefoil knot is not the same as its mirror image. This is a central problem in knot theory, and there is still no complete solution. The method for partial solutions is to find *knot invariants* which can be defined in terms of the diagram, which give the same result for equivalent knot diagrams, and for which there is some method of calculation. The exhibition gives details of: *crossing number, unknotting number, bridge number, three colouring.* For example, the trefoil knot can be coloured in three colours in a precise sense, but this would not be possible if the trefoil knot were an unknot. This gives a reasonably easy proof that the trefoil, and a number of other knots, are in fact knotted.

The *crossing number* of a knot is defined as the smallest number of crossings which can occur in a diagram of the knot. This illustrates a standard mathematical procedure, namely choose the least of a set of whole numbers, but is any case standard practice, since in drawing knot diagrams you tend to try to give the one which seems the simplest. The crossing number is easy to define but hard to determine for a complicated knot, since the definition is in terms of the infinite number of possible diagrams.

2.4 Decomposition into simple elements: Reidemeister moves

The process to be decomposed into simple basic elements is that of changing one knot diagram into another without changing the knot.

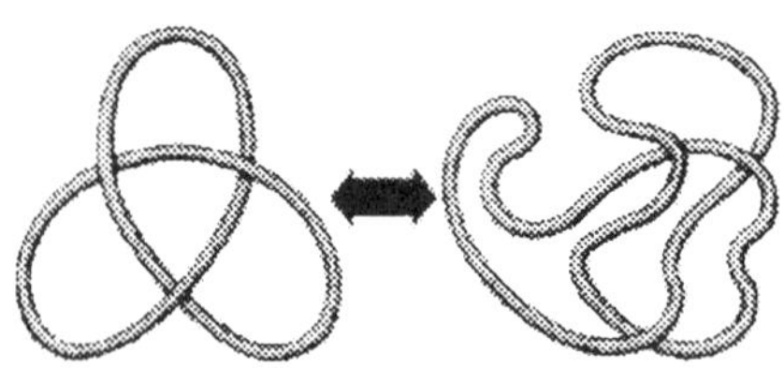

Reidemeister showed in the 1920s that two knot diagrams define the same knot if and only if one can be changed to the other by a sequence of five basic moves: the first is to distort the diagram without changing the crossings, as in the diagram on the left. The other four moves are to change crossings in one of the following ways:

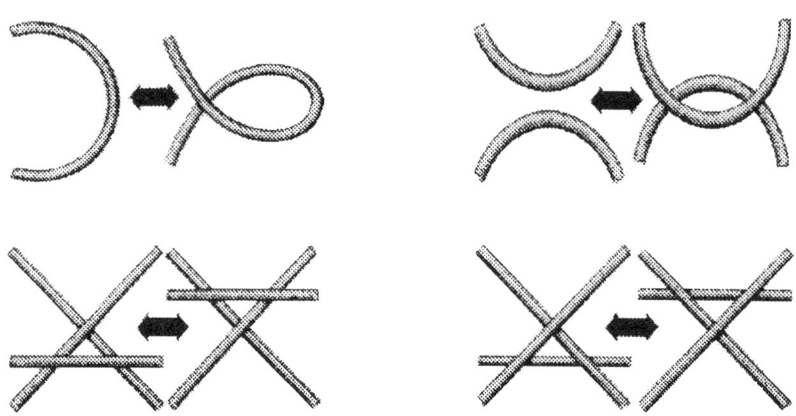

These moves are an important tool. For example, to prove a proposed knot invariant is invariant, all you have to do is show it is unchanged by the Reidemeister moves. Invariance under distortion is often easily verified, and we have only four other moves to check. This reduction to four cases is a considerable advance on studying an infinite number of cases, and is the method used to show 3-colourability is an invariant. Try it!

2.5 Analogy

Although the word is rarely used in this context, analogy is in fact central to mathematical practice. The abstract nature of mathematics is precisely because it deals with `structures', and we want to see how a particular structure occurs in many situations. This gives us the excitement of `that reminds me of", and allows for the transfer of knowledge from one situation to another. Such a transfer often leads to the solution of problems, and is indeed sought for this purpose, in the style of: `If I could apply these techniques to that problem then ....!' The more surprising the analogy the better, and the finding of such a new analogy may be called an *insight.*

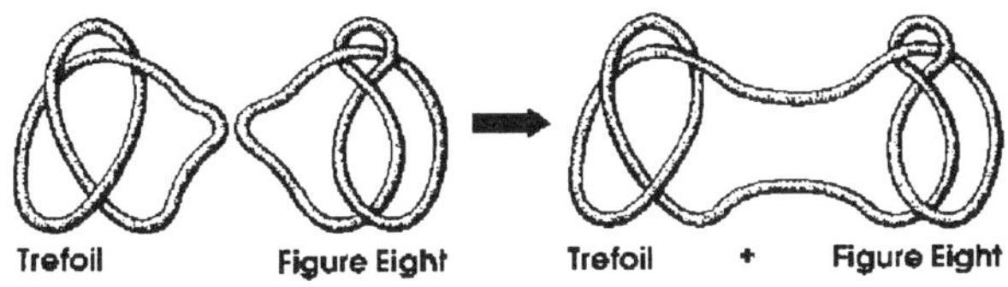

The analogy we can show here relates knots and numbers, and relies on a method of combining knots which we here call *addition*. This is illustrated above: pull a piece out of both knots and join them as shown. It is important that that this process is independent of where on each knot one starts to join them. This is proved by the type of diagram on the left, which also shows that addition of knots is *commutative*: $K+L=L+K$

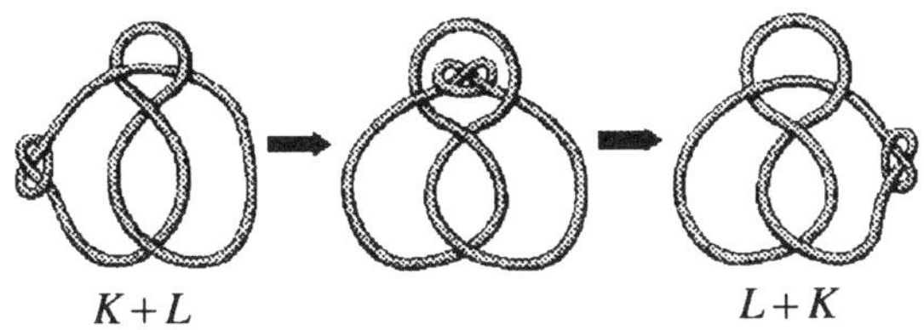

We can prove additional laws. If we write the unknot as 0 then it is easy to see that for any knot L we have $L+0=0+L=L$. Another useful rule is *associativity:* $K+(L+M)=(K+L)+M$.

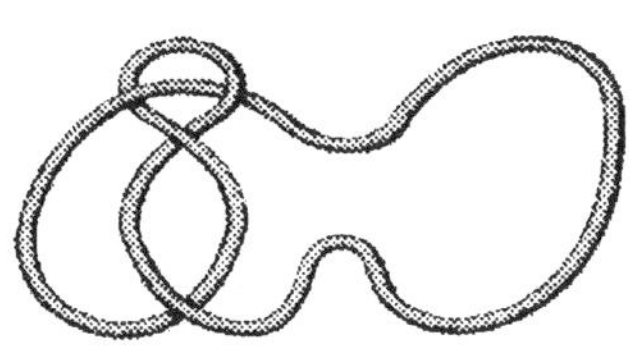

$L+0=L$

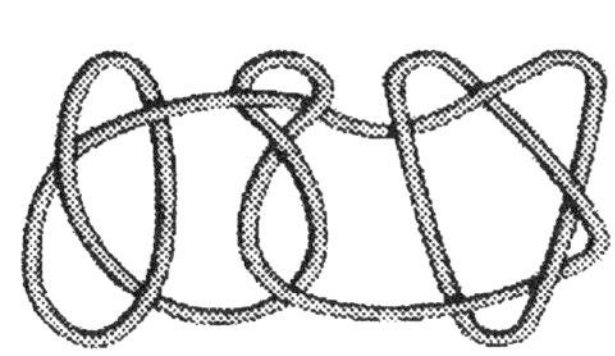

$K+L+M$

These rules, or laws, are shown by the above diagrams.

In formulating these laws we are using two analogies.

One of them is between the behaviour of knots and the behaviour of numbers. In fact we make the analogy between the *addition* of knots and the *product* of numbers. So the associativity rule for the product of numbers has the instance $3 \times (4 \times 5) = (3 \times 4) \times 5$, that is $3 \times 20 = 12 \times 5$. The important feature is that a relation between numbers has analogies with a relation between knots: there are common structural features when you consider all knots and all numbers. There are also differences: there is no negative of a knot and no subtraction for knots. It is true that if $K+L=K+M$ then $L=M$, but this needs some ideas for its proof that we cannot give here.

The other analogy is between laws in different situations. By drawing attention to the commutative laws for addition and multiplication of numbers

$$m+n=n+m, \quad m\times n=n\times m$$

we are making an analogy between addition and multiplication. Mathematics is indeed *abstract*, and this abstractness has a clear purpose, to allow for analogies.

There are two reasons why we have called this `composition' of knots addition rather than multiplication, as is common in the literature on knots. One is that the notation 0 for the unknot is more intuitive than the notation 1. The other is to emphasise that we can have analogies between structures with different names.

2.6 Decomposition into simple elements: Prime knots

Now we have another example of decomposition into simple elements. We say that a knot K is *prime* if it is not the sum of simpler knots, that is if whenever we try to express K as a sum of knots $K=L+M$ then $L=0$ or $M=0$. The trefoil and the figure eight knot are prime knots, and so are all the knots in the family illustrated on the right. These are the *torus knots* because they can all be wrapped around an inner tube, a shape mathematicians call a torus.

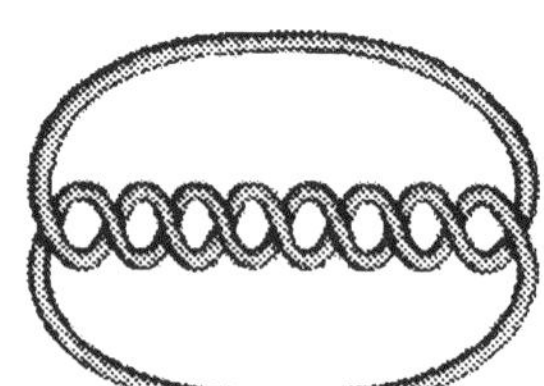

On the left is an example of a torus knot with the torus shown. This idea is not developed in the exhibition, but is on the web site related to sculptures of John Robinson, since four of them can be described as torus knots.

In any case, the prime knots are the simple elements in the whole family of knots. The example of torus knots shows that there are infinitely many prime knots, though the proof that torus knots are prime is hard.

A remarkable similarity between the addition of knots and the product of numbers is that there is essentially only one way of writing a knot as a sum of prime knots. Again, this result needs for its proof ideas not given here. There is no algorithm for finding the decomposition of a knot into the sum of prime knots. So the analogy between knots and numbers is not complete. On the other hand, the factorisation of large numbers, with say 200 digits, is beyond the reach of current computers in reasonable time, a fact that is the basis of a form of cryptography, and so in a way the analogy resumes for large numbers.

From all this we see that one of the uses of analogy is to formulate questions. We wish to know in what ways two systems are analogous, and what ways not.

2.7 Laws

The laws obeyed by the addition of knots have already been discussed, but the theme needs some elaboration. These laws can be taken as the *axioms* of an algebraic system. A lot of mathematics is concerned with developing the consequences of some chosen axioms. This has led to the view that `Mathematics is the subject where we don't know what we are talking about and where we don't know whether what we are talking about is true.' Related views are that:

`The method of "postulating" what we want has many advantages; they are the same as the advantages of theft over honest toil.' [6,p.71]

`Mathematics is non creative because it is concerned only with the consequences of given rules.' [Heard in a lecture for young people by an established scientist.]

These views miss the point. Axioms (postulates) are tools for defining the structures we wish to study. The finding and choosing of these axioms for their relevance to the structures we wish to study is a key part of the creative process. Conjecturing and proving interesting consequences of axioms, that is, formulating and proving theorems, is a basic part of the creation of new mathematics, and often requires new concepts to state the theorems.

The Nobel Prize winning physicist Wigner [8] had a clear view of mathematics:

`Mathematics is the science of skilful operations with concepts and rules invented just for this purpose. [this purpose being the skilful operation ....] '

`The principal emphasis is on the invention of concepts.'

`The depth of thought which goes into the formation of mathematical concepts is later justified by the skill with which these concepts are used. '

2.8 Generalisation

Now we reach into areas not touched on in the exhibition. It was pointed out in the 19th century by Klein that a knot can be untied in 4 dimensions. To see why this is so we again use analogy. A beetle on a table may be blocked in its passage by a vertical wall. If it is allowed the third dimension, for example by flying, then it can easily move over the barrier.

It is the crossings in a knot diagram which give the barrier to untying the knot. If we are allowed a 4th dimension, then it is easy to see we can then move one portion of string `over' another, and so change any crossing. In this why, it is easy to untie any knot in 4 dimensions.

The generalisation is to ask what we can tie in 4 dimensions? The answer is the surface of a balloon, which mathematicians call a 2-sphere. As expected, such a 2-knot can be untied in 5 dimensions.

More generally, an n-sphere can be tied in $(n+2)$-dimensions and untied in $(n+3)$-dimensions. The proof of this is rather hard, and was carried out by E.C. Zeeman. The general situation cannot be properly visualised. The formulation and representation of the abstract properties which describe the situation, and the logical argument with these, is where we have to rely, rather than on visualisation and interpretation, which is simply a starting point for our intuition. The problem is indeed that of building up our intuition of what is going on, and what might happen, in these dimly grasped complicated structures.

2.9 Applications

The picture on the left shows some knotted flow lines arising in chaotic flows resulting from some differential equations related to weather.

One of the points we wished to show in the exhibition is that many applications rely on all the above aspects to be effective. Even the original, and abandoned, idea of Vortex Atoms required the formulation of the subtle concepts of classification of knots, and their arithmetic, to decide that it was not going to work.

The two modern applications we mention are to chaotic flows, as above, and to DNA.

The second results from developments started as recently as 1985 and which have had remarkable effects on the theory of knots and its applications. This is a new theory of knot polynomials. It started at a seminar by Vaughan Jones in Geneva on a branch of mathematics called operator algebra theory. He obtained some laws for certain elements of this algebra, and a member of the audience remarked that these rules also arose in another

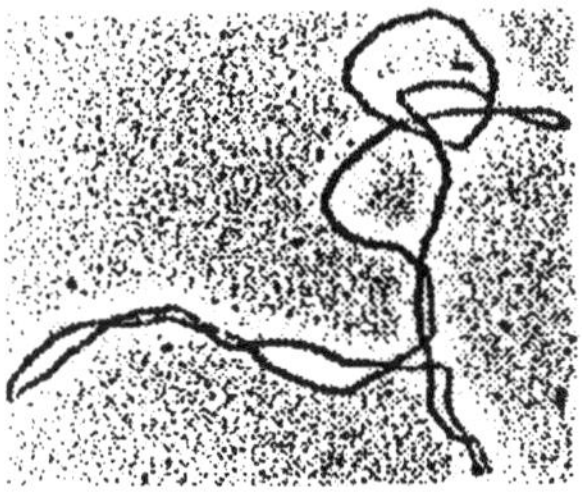

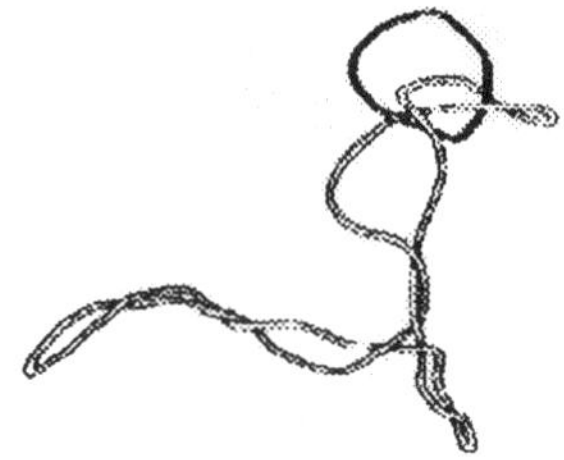

branch of mathematics, closely related to knot theory, called braid theory. In pursuing this idea with experts, a new theory of knot polynomials was born. These have been applied in studying the way DNA untangles itself when it divides. On the previous page is a micrograph and sketch of knotted and linked DNA (due to N. Cozarelli).

3. The link with art

One original aim of the exhibition was to show knots in history, art and technology. This was gradually seen to be too ambitious, but the opportunity came to ask John Robinson to exhibit his sculptures at the Pop Maths Roadshow in 1989. This exhibition and its catalogue [2] became the start of an extensive collaboration in opening the academic world to knowledge of his work.

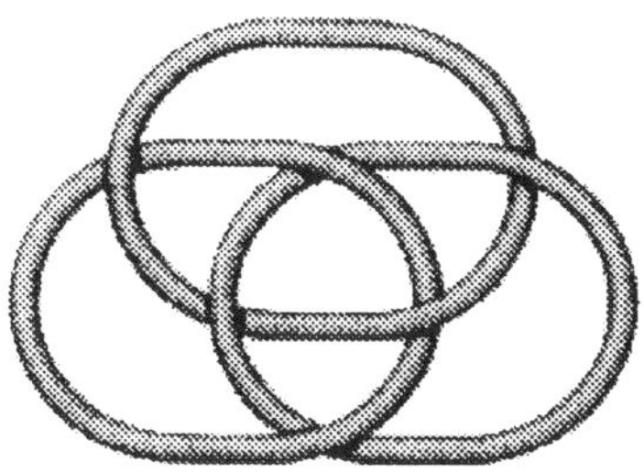

The Borromean Rings, as on the left, is called a `link', rather than a knot, since it has three loops, whereas a knot has, by definition, only one loop. In this link, no two of the circles are linked, but the whole cannot be pulled apart. Such links, of which this is one of the simplest, show ways in which the whole is more than the sum of its pieces, that is the parts are placed together to form a *structure*. It is part of the job of mathematics to invent language to describe and determine the properties of structures, and to find interesting and extraordinary ones. Some of these structures model aspects of the world, and often have been developed for this reason. The peculiar properties of mathematical language is its rigour and exactness, and the way the

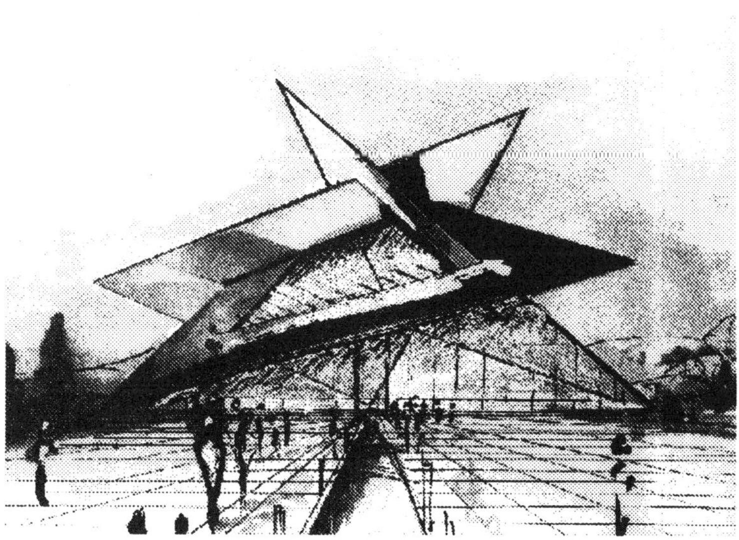

consistency of the structures developed has been tested by thousands of matehmaticians and scientists particularly over the last 200 years.

Robinson has made various sculptures based on the Borromean Rings. In view of the architects present at this meeting, I would like to end with an example of Robinson's sculpture *Intuition,* which he saw could be a central structure to a building proposed as a Pantheon of Mathematics, and sketched here by Ove Arup.

Acknowledgements: Support from: COPUS; London Mathematical Society; University of Wales, Bangor; British Ropes Ltd/Bridon; Anglesey Aluminium plc; Midland Bank plc; Ferranti plc; British Gas; Pilkington plc; The Philip Trust; Edition Limitée; Centre for the Popularisation of Mathematics.

Designers: Robert Williams; Jill Evans; John Round.

WWW production: Cara Quinton.

References

1. Brown, R., Gilbert, N.D. and Porter, T., Mathematics and Knots, Public Exhibition, (1989), Brochure (1989), Mathematics and Knots, Bangor, 1997. Web site: http://www.bangor.ac.uk/ma/CPM/exhibit/ .
2. Robinson, J., Symbolic Sculpture: catalogue for the exhibition at the Pop Maths Roadshow, Mathematics and Knots, 1989.
3. Brown, R., Quinton, C., Robinson, J., Symbolic Sculpture and Mathematics, Web site: http://www.bangor.ac.uk/SculMath/
4. Brown, R. and Porter, T., Making a mathematical exhibition, in The popularization of mathematics, edited A.G.Howson and J.-P. Kahane, ICMI Study Series, Cambridge University Press, 1990; 51-64.
5. Deutsch, D., The fabric of reality, Penguin 1997.
6. Russell, B, Introduction to mathematical philosophy, George, Allen and Unwin, 1919.
7. Trudeau, R.J., The Non-Euclidean Revolution, Birkhäuser, Boston, 1987.
8. Turner, J.C. and Van de Griend, P., History and science of knots, World Scientific, Singapore, 1995.
9. Wigner, E.P., The unreasonable effectiveness of mathematics in the natural sciences, Comm. in Pure Appl. Math. (1960), reprinted in Symmetries and reflections: scientific essays of Eugene P. Wigner, Bloomington Indiana University Press (1967).

A Visual, Computational Object Language for Mathematics

Phillip Kent
Mathematics Department, Imperial College,
London SW7 2BZ, United Kingdom

Abstract

I describe work in progress on using the computer mathematics system, *Mathematica*, to construct a special "object language" to be used by undergraduate mathematics learners. In this language, graphical objects have a peculiar kind of in-between existence as "visual" data structures that can be manipulated through programs. I attempt to elucidate the nature of this existence, and its possible usefulness for mathematical thinking, and learning, using the example of visualising a four-dimensional "hypercube".

1. Introduction

This paper describes work in progress on the development of a "visualisation toolkit" intended for an advanced undergraduate mathematics course on dynamics (i.e. classical mechanics, and nonlinear dynamics—popularly known as "chaos"). However, since this is not a mathematics-oriented proceedings, and since I would like to point up the cross-disciplinary aspects of this work (with respect to computer science, in particular), I will restrict the mathematical topics to the more accessible domain of geometry.

The toolkit is based on the "computer mathematics system", *Mathematica* [1]. Like similar systems (e.g. Derive, Maple, and even the more powerful recent models of graphical calculators), *Mathematica* combines functions for symbolic manipulation, functions for graphical output, and a programming language. What particularly distinguishes *Mathematica*, as I will try to demonstrate, is the tight integration of these three aspects.

In computer science, the idea of graphics being the output of computational procedures is familiar enough, as is the contrasting paradigm of directly manipulable "virtual reality" graphical environments for drawing and design (e.g. anything from Microsoft's "Paint" accessory to professional CAD packages). What I have been studying is, I would say, an idea somewhere in-between: *a system where graphical objects exist as data structures, manipulated through programs*, and just one of the possible manipulations is to produce graphical output. The basic functionality for this is built into the *Mathematica* software; what I have been working on is exploiting it for the purposes of mathematical visualisation, and learning.

1. Mathematica Graphics: What *is* the Output?

Here is a simple *Mathematica* plot:

```
plot1 = Plot[Sin[x], {x,0,2π}]
```

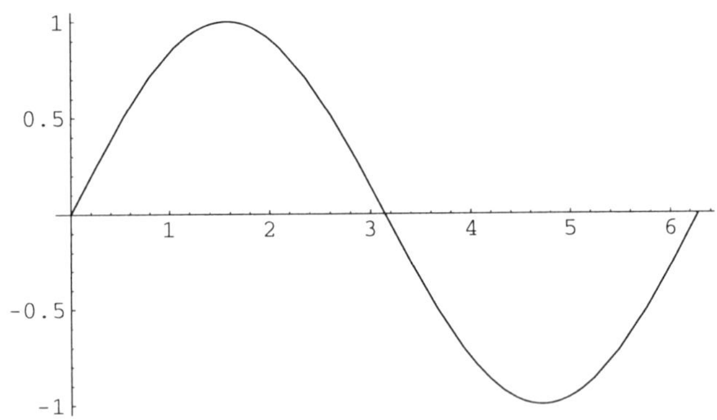

-Graphics-

(I'll use `Courier` for inputs to *Mathematica* and *`Italic Courier`* for outputs). Actually, there are two outputs here, the picture itself and the funny object "*-Graphics-*". Let's look inside that:

```
Part[plot1, 1]
```

{{Line[{{0.0, 0.0}, {0.25489, 0.25214}, {0.53287, 0.50801}, {0.79394, 0.71312}, {1.04501, 0.86492}, ..., {6.01652, -0.26351}, {6.26682,-0.01636}, {6.28318, 0.0}}]}}

So the sine "curve" is actually created as a sequence of 82 short straight lines (from (0, 0) to (0.255, 0.252), and so on). And, *Mathematica*'s graphical output contains a complete "geometrical" description of the objects in the plot. Moreover, graphical objects such as "Line" are not just outputs from plots but can also be used as *inputs* to plots.

2. A System Where Graphical Objects Exist as Data Structures, Manipulated Through Programs

Here is another standard graphical "data structure"[1]:

```
Circle[{1,3}, 1.5]
```

This defines a circle by its centre, (1, 3), and radius, 1.5 (and in fact, this is precisely one of the *mathematical* definitions for a circle). One type of operation is graphical output:

```
Draw[Circle[{1,3}, 1.5], Axes->True]
```

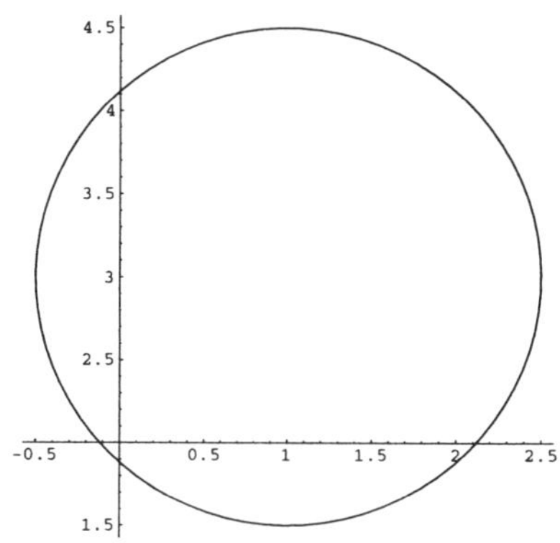

-Graphics-

(*Note*: I have abbreviated and modified the *Mathematica* inputs in this paper a little for presentation purposes. "Draw" is a special definition. You can find full working versions of the *Mathematica* code on the web at the address given at the end. Also, I'll omit the "*-Graphics-*" outputs from now on.)

But since this is a piece of data like any other in *Mathematica*, I can perform all kinds of operations on it, including *mathematical* ones, such as those developed by Wickham-Jones for coordinate geometry [2]. Let's define a triangle:

```
P = {0,0}; Q = {12,0}; R = {12,5};
triangle1 = Polygon[{P,Q,R}];
```

Now I'll use the "InCircle" function defined by Wickham-Jones to compute the inscribed circle of triangle1:

```
InCircle[triangle1]
```

Circle[{10,2), 2]

---

[1] Actually, *Mathematica*'s language has no distinction between data and program: "everything is an expression" [ref. 1, section 2.1.1].

```
Draw[{Boundary[triangle1], InCircle[triangle1]}]
```

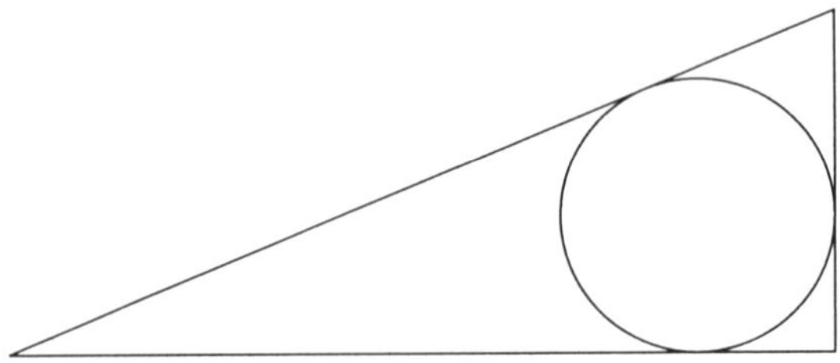

One might also want to demonstrate the geometrical construction of the inscribed circle, as the intersection point of the angular bisectors of the triangle:

```
Bisector[Line[{P,Q}],Line[{P,R}]]
```

Line[{{0, 0}, {625/52, 125/52}}]

```
Draw[{Line[{P,Q}],Line[{P,R}], Dashing[{0.01,0.01}],
  Bisector[Line[{P,Q}],Line[{P,R}]]}]
```

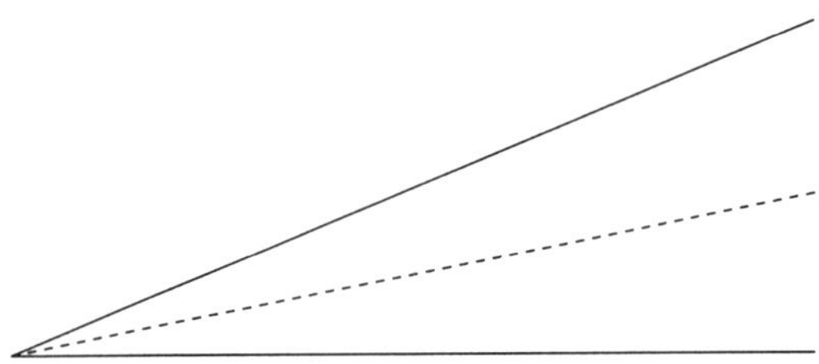

```
ipoint=IntersectionPoint[
  Bisector[Line[{P,Q}],Line[{P,R}]],
  Bisector[Line[{Q,P}],Line[{Q,R}]]]
```

{10,2}

```
Draw[{InCircle[triangle1],
  Line[{P,Q}],Line[{P,R}],Line[{Q,R}],
  Dashing[{0.01,0.01}],
  Bisector[Line[{P,Q}],Line[{P,R}]],
  Bisector[Line[{Q,P}],Line[{Q,R}]],
  PointSize[0.015], Point[ipoint],
}]
```

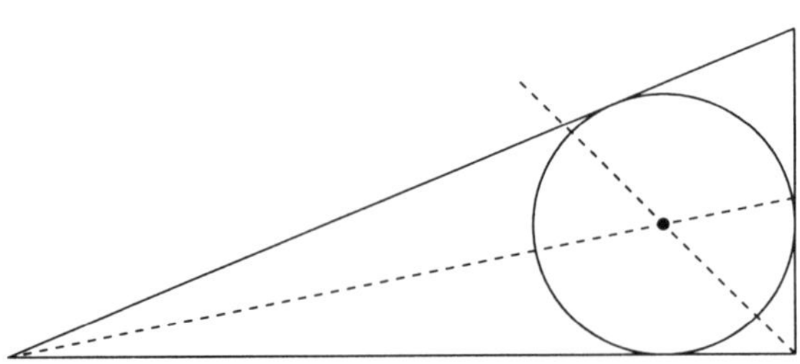

3. Objects and Operations

Graphical objects of the type just described interest me because they have both a mathematical structure and a visual "resonance": I cannot read or write terms like "Circle", "Line", "Bisector", "IntersectionPoint" without a host of visual images coming to mind.

And the act of *naming* objects gains even more conceptual power when it is combined with having sets of operations to create and transform objects: the objects and operations form an *object language* for talking about and doing mathematics. I'm using the term language informally at the moment; I do want to sharpen up my thinking in terms of computer science and, perhaps, linguistics.

I would like to offer some speculative proposals on the usefulness of such a visual object language for mathematics in the context of thinking about mathematical "hyperspace".

4. Visualising Hyperspace

Dealing with objects defined in hyperspace—a space of more than three dimensions—is a well-studied part of mathematics (see, for example, [3]). But hyperspace exists only as a mathematical construct, and whilst it is true that algebra and formal geometry can supply answers, there is a deep-seated need, especially for learners, to "see" what is going on. Of course, seeing and understanding have a strong conceptual relationship (as in, "I see what you mean"), and in mathematics, this is bound up with making use of formal manipulations (algebraic, geometric, etc). I'm not suggesting that formality can be replaced by something "visual"; on the contrary, I'm interested in what ways object languages could offer learners access to formal ways of thinking.

One approach to hyperspace makes use of analogy: as in Abbott's classic book *Flatland* [4], one tries to imagine hyperspace by comparing how three-dimensional space would seem like to a two-dimensional being, who can perceive only slices and projections (shadows) of the three-dimensional world. To demonstrate this approach, I've used my object language in *Mathematica* to construct some movie sequences for: (1) the 2-D projection of a cube rotating in three dimensions, (2) the 3-D projection of a "hypercube" rotating in four dimensions.

Figure 1 shows the construction method for the cube projection: from a fixed "view point" straight lines are drawn through each vertex (corner) of the cube; where these lines intersect a "view plane", the "shadow" of the cube can be constructed.

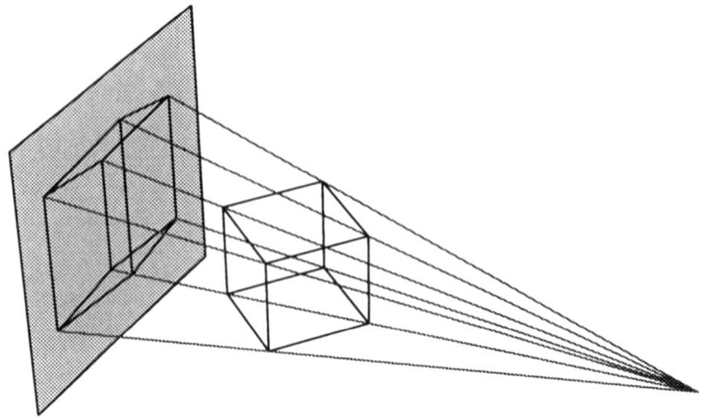

Figure 1: Constructing the (point) projection of a cube.

Figure 2 shows some frames from the movie of the projection as the cube rotates around a vertical axis.

Figure 3 shows some frames for the 3-D projection of a rotating hypercube. At first sight, this is a strange kind of object, a "shadow" from the unseen world of the fourth dimension. However, as Dudeney says [5]:

> Every time the hypercube in the program is rotated the vertices swing into new positions and a new, oddly confusing view of the object results. With continued experimentation, however, the views begin to make a strange kind of sense, and one feels on the threshold of something awesomely spacious and inviting.

Analogy is a powerful aid here. Compare Figures 2 and 3: when the rotation is 0, 90 and 180 degrees, the projection of the cube contains a square within a square; of the hypercube, a cube within a cube. At 45 and 135 degrees, one sees the shapes "edge on". There are more analogies in the way that edges (or rather the shadows of the edges) transform into one another as the rotation progresses; but these are difficult to pick up from static images.

So far, so good. However, there's nothing special about these movies that I've constructed—they could be made using any programmable graphics system. So, what *is* special about an object language?

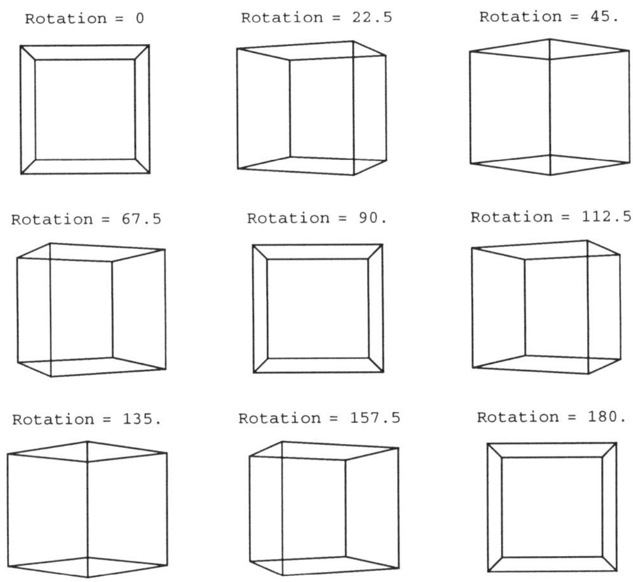

Figure 2: 2-D projection of a rotating cube.

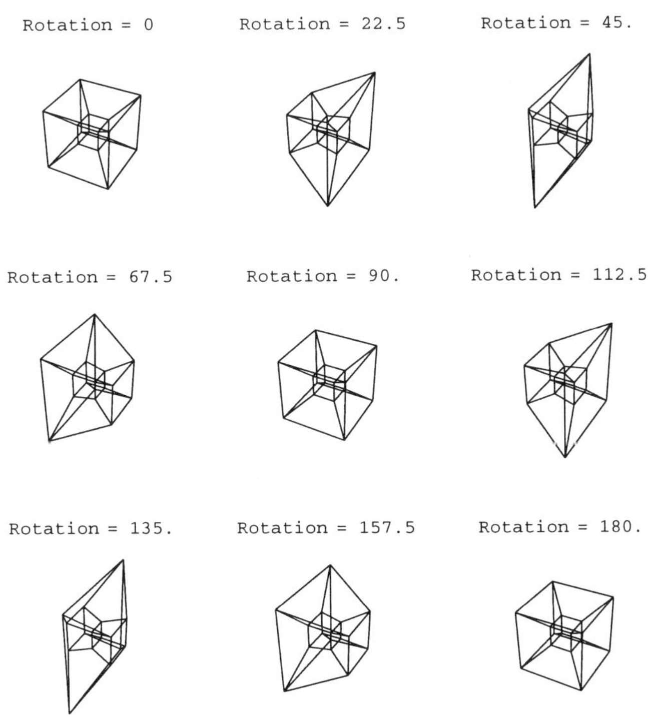

Figure 3: 3-D projection of a rotating hypercube.

5. Analogous Objects and Operations for Cubes and Hypercubes

In my object language, 4-D objects are represented by the same (analogous) structures as 2 or 3-D objects. So, the cube was defined by a set of 12 edges, that is 3-D Line objects:

```
cube={Line[{{1,1,1},{-1,1,1}}],Line[{{1,1,1},{1,-1,1}}],
Line[{{1,1,1},{1,1,-1}}],Line[{{-1,1,1},{-1,-1,1}}],
Line[{{-1,1,1},{-1,1,-1}}],Line[{{1,-1,1},{-1,-1,1}}],
Line[{{1,-1,1},{1,-1,-1}}],Line[{{1,1,-1},{-1,1,-1}}],
Line[{{1,1,-1},{1,-1,-1}}],Line[{{-1,-1,1},{-1,-1,-1}}],
Line[{{-1,1,-1},{-1,-1,-1}}],Line[{{1,-1,-1},{-1,-1,-1}}]}
```

And the hypercube was defined by a set of 32 edges, i.e. 4-D Line objects:

```
hypercube={Line[{{1,1,1,1},{-1,1,1,1}}],
Line[{{1,1,1,1},{1,-1,1,1}}],Line[{{1,1,1,1},{1,1,-1,1}}],
Line[{{1,1,1,1},{1,1,1,-1}}],Line[{{-1,1,1,1},{-1,-1,1,1}}],
Line[{{-1,1,1,1},{-1,1,-1,1}}],Line[{{-1,1,1,1},{-1,1,1,-1}}],
Line[{{1,-1,1,1},{-1,-1,1,1}}],Line[{{1,-1,1,1},{1,-1,-1,1}}],
Line[{{1,-1,1,1},{1,-1,1,-1}}],Line[{{1,1,-1,1},{-1,1,-1,1}}],
Line[{{1,1,-1,1},{1,-1,-1,1}}],Line[{{1,1,-1,1},{1,1,-1,-1}}],
Line[{{1,1,1,-1},{-1,1,1,-1}}],Line[{{1,1,1,-1},{1,-1,1,-1}}],
Line[{{1,1,1,-1},{1,1,-1,-1}}],Line[{{-1,-1,1,1},{-1,-1,-1,1}}],
Line[{{-1,-1,1,1},{-1,-1,1,-1}}],Line[{{-1,1,-1,1},{-1,-1,-1,1}}],
Line[{{-1,1,-1,1},{-1,1,-1,-1}}],Line[{{-1,1,1,-1},{-1,-1,1,-1}}],
Line[{{-1,1,1,-1},{-1,1,-1,-1}}],Line[{{1,-1,-1,1},{-1,-1,-1,1}}],
Line[{{1,-1,-1,1},{1,-1,-1,-1}}],Line[{{1,-1,1,-1},{-1,-1,1,-1}}],
Line[{{1,-1,1,-1},{1,-1,-1,-1}}],Line[{{1,1,-1,-1},{-1,1,-1,-1}}],
Line[{{1,1,-1,-1},{1,-1,-1,-1}}],Line[{{-1,-1,-1,1},{-1,-1,-1,-1}}],
Line[{{-1,-1,1,-1},{-1,-1,-1,-1}}],
Line[{{-1,1,-1,-1},{-1,-1,-1,-1}}],
Line[{{1,-1,-1,-1},{-1,-1,-1,-1}}]}
```

Moreover, the operations that I needed to perform on these objects to make the projections—i.e. constructing the straight lines from a fixed view point through all the vertices of the objects, and finding where those lines strike the view plane—use the same *Mathematica* program, IntersectionPoint, based on the same mathematical construction. Here is the basic operation for the cube projection:

```
IntersectionPoint[
  Line[{{8,0,0}, {X,Y,Z}}],
  Plane[{-4,0,0}, {1,0,0}]
]
```

where {X, Y, Z} is substituted by the coordinates of each vertex. And here is the basic operation for the hypercube projection:

```
IntersectionPoint[
  Line[{{2,0,0,0}, {X,Y,Z,W}}],
  Plane[{-2,0,0,0}, {1,0,0,0}]
]
```

where {X, Y, Z, W} is substituted by the coordinates of each vertex.

6. Conclusion: Uniting the Visual and the Algebraic?

I think the upshot of the object language approach for mathematics learning is that working with such a language requires the manipulations of objects to be expressed as formal (computational) operations, which are "representations" of formal mathematics. And an important geometrical aspect is that these operations may often have the same structure in different numbers of spatial dimensions.

In a curious way, therefore, the visual and the algebraic seem to be united in a computational object language which is inherently "visual" (i.e. graphical objects *are* data structures). Although I cannot physically draw a four-dimensional hypercube, I *can* represent it in a "visual" language, and I can "see" it by manipulating it computationally.

In this paper, I have spoken about learners entirely in the abstract. A substantial report is in preparation, which will include detailed evaluation of my *Mathematica* object language with undergraduate students. This report will be available from the web address given below.

Note

Further information about the work described here, including *Mathematica* programs and movies corresponding to Figures 1-3, is available at http://metric.ma.ic.ac.uk/articles/vri98.

References

1. Wolfram S. The Mathematica book, third edition. Cambridge University Press, New York, 1996
2. Wickham-Jones T. Mathematica graphics. Springer-Verlag, New York, 1994
3. Banchoff T. Beyond the third dimension: geometry, computer graphics and higher dimensions. Freeman/Scientific American Library, New York, 1990
4. Abbott E A. Flatland: a romance of many dimensions. Dover Publications, New York
5. Dewdney, A K. The armchair universe: an exploration of computer worlds. Freeman, New York, 1988

A Visual Metaphor for Psychoanalytic Training and Supervision

C. A. Lund[1] and R. C. Paton[2]

[1] Claremont House, Royal Victoria Infirmary
Newcastle NE2 4AA, U.K.

[2] Department of Computer Science, University of Liverpool
Liverpool L69 3BX, U.K.

Abstract

This paper reports collaborative work between a psychiatrist and a computer scientist on the application of visual metaphor for clarifying a number of key concepts in psychotherapy. A number of conceptual difficulties are reviewed and a visual metaphor is proposed which seeks to clarify potential misconceptions. The metaphor is elaborated and applied to the domain of study.

1 Background

The material reported in this paper has grown out of an ongoing dialogue between a psychiatrist and a computer scientist. The former is concerned with the development of meaningful communication between an expert practitioner in psychotherapy and trainees especially within the context of supervision, and the latter with the characterisation of complex domains of knowledge in relation to the possible development of computer-based support systems [1]. In order to facilitate dialogue, and building on previous research ([2], [3], [4]) we have focussed on metaphors and theoretical frameworks appropriate to dealing with some abstract ideas.

The general approach we discuss here may be described as "constructive hermeneutics". Its focus is for an expert and a hermeneut (interpreter) to come to share a common view on a domain of knowledge through dialogue involving words and diagrams albeit to different levels of detail (see Figure 1). One major method of achieving this is by establishing a common visual dialogue and also identifying and exploring pervasive metaphors.

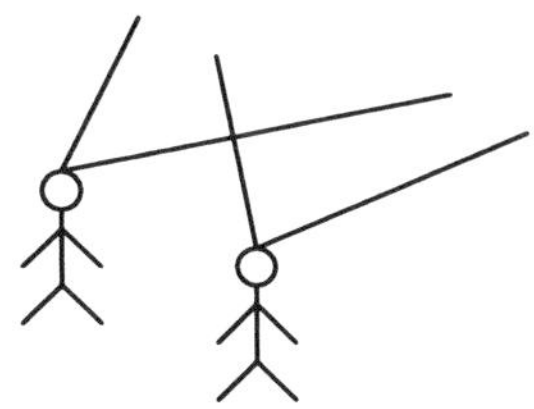

Figure 1 - Constructive Hermeneutics as Sharing a Similar Perspective between Expert and Hermeneut

The domain under consideration is conceptually rich and involves a number of highly abstract and non picturable ideas. This paper reports on how one problem within the domain of psychoanalytic training and supervision has been explored and enhanced using this ideographic method.

2 The Context and Nature of the Problem

The phenomena involved are closely related and therefore can all too readily and frequently be confused as the following quotation from a standard text illustrates:

> "*Hand in hand with transference is, of course, counter-transference. The term here is used in its more contemporary sense as referring to the understanding that some of the feelings aroused in the psychotherapist are unconsciously projected into him by the patient. The unconscious hope is that the container/therapist can manage and process projected feelings which can be introjected by the patient, along with the possibility that he (the patient) may be able to do likewise.*"
>
> from [5] page 212

This example demonstrates how at present a number of terms are often used in confusingly overlapping ways in psychotherapy supervisions, discussions and texts. The effects of such `confusion are an imprecision of thinking by practitioners, a restriction in the choice of responses to patients' communications by the therapist and unnecessary difficulty for students who are trying to make sense of complex phenomena. The purpose of this paper is to explore some aspects of this misunderstanding and introduce a visual metaphor that seeks to provide an integrative framework for discussing these difficult ideas.

The terms to be discussed are not esoteric side issues but concepts that are central to the understanding of what is happening in relational terms between human beings in general and available for study in the patient-therapist relationship in particular. These terms can be thought of as pairs of linked concepts:

a) Transference - Counter-transference
b) Projection - Identification
c) Container - Contained

In some relation to these concepts are other ideas which often enter into conversations or texts in the domain under consideration. Examples of such concepts would be: holding, parallel process and reflection.

2.1 Transference - Counter-transference

Probably the best starting point for this discussion is a direct quote from Freud [6]

> *"What are transferences? They are new editions or facsimiles of the impulses and phantasies which are aroused during the process of analysis, but they have this peculiarity, which is characteristic of their species, that they replace some earlier person by the person of the physician. To put it another way a whole series of psychological experiences are revived, not as belonging to the past but as applying to the person of the physician at the present moment".*
>
> from [7] page 38

It is to be noted that Freud was writing of phenomena that involved phantasies and impulses and that he is clear that the experience of some other person in the past is being contemporaneously experienced in the present. At other points he clearly is aware that different past family members can be reproduced in the transference relationship.

Counter-transference as a concept has had a checkered career, beginning as an observation that therapists too had their transferential hang-ups! This use of the term emphasises that the therapist may have "blind-spots" or inappropriate responses to the patient's communications. This clearly can and does occur. However, an alternative complementary insight was developed by Heimann [8] in which she drew attention to the inner capacity of the therapist to read off within him or herself the emotional reactions being aroused by the patient,

> *"... sustain the feelings which are stirred up in him as opposed to discharging them (as does the patient), in order to subordinate them to the analytic task in which he functions as the patient's mirror reflection"*

... "that the analyst's unconscious understands that of his patient. The rapport on the deep level comes to the surface in the form of feelings which the analyst notices in response to his patient, in his 'counter-transference' ".

from [7] page 65

While these quotes are designed primarily to illustrate the changing use of the concept of counter-transference from a hindrance to a help in the work of the psycho-analyst, it also gives an intimation of the next pair of concepts to be discussed. However, the changing emphasis in respect of counter-transference toward the study of the emotional exchanges between patient and analyst inadvertently drew attention away from Freud's original ideas about transference where different people in the patient's past elicited different responses.

It is one of the aims of developing the visual metaphor for psycho-analysis that it will encourage analysts and psychotherapists to take stock of the change in the day-to-day use of transference as a concept. This has come about as a consequence of the term counter-transference becoming confused with or overlapping with the terms projection and identification.

2.2 Projection - Identification

The notions of projection and identification began their lives in the psycho-analytic literature as separate terms. Each described an aspect of mental defence whereby a person maintained his or her psychic equilibrium under the pressure of emotional states ranging from everyday relating to grief or internal events such as powerful emotions, phantasies and impulses. Thus a person harbours feelings or attributes that do not accord with their view of themselves, these feelings are projected into others and are familiar in racism, religious intolerance and homophobia. Identification is the contrary phenomenon in that the person psychically allies him or herself with another. It is seen in identification with football teams, with elements of the dead during bereavement and also in pathological states such as identification with the aggressor when some concentration camp victims identified with the guards and mistreated fellow prisoners or the sexually abused who become the abusers.

The degree to which these two complementary features were so recognised led to the use of the notion of projective identification. An authoritative summary of the term has been produced by Ogden [9]:

"Projective identification is a psychological process that is at once a type of defence, a model of communication, a primitive form of object relation and a pathway for psychological change. As a defence, projective identification serves to create a psychological distance from the unwanted, often frightening aspects of the self. As a mode of communication projective identification is the process by which feelings congruent with ones's own are induced in another person, thereby creating a sense of being understood, or "at one with" the other person.

As a type of object relations, projective identification constitutes a way of being with and relating to a partially separate object. Finally, as a pathway for psychological change, projective identification is a process by which feelings like those that one is struggling with are psychologically processed by another person and made available for reinternalisation in an altered form".

from [5] page 213

While for the most part the definitions of projective identification which have to do with it as a form of defence, a model of communication and recapitulation of the earliest forms of baby-mother relating are generally accepted as sitting easily inside the concept, the idea of it also being a pathway for psychological change is less so. To understand the conceptual difficulties here we need to consider the final pair of concepts, Container-Contained.

2.3 Container - Contained

While closely related to the concept of projective identification, Meltzer [10] argued that the main originator of the concept of container-contained, namely Bion [11] was making a "tactical not a theoretical error" in using the term projective identification for the particular form of communication he was describing. Bion was describing an unconscious phantasy "implementing the non-lexical aspects of language and behaviour aimed at communication rather than action" [10] page 96.

In more homely terms what we are considering in this concept of container-contained can be thought of in terms of the example of a six year old child returning frightened from school having been subjected to bullying. The most helpful thing would be for the parent to listen to the child, take in what is being said, offering an appropriate amount of comfort, and after considering the situation over a period of time either suggest to the child how best to handle the situation next day and/or to intervene with the school. Less helpfully the parent may go into a rage or fill the child with memories of their own bullied childhood thereby reinforcing the terror of the situation.

Linking this example to Bion, while the facts of the bullying need attending to, the deeper issue is how the bullying episode has mobilised, given flesh to, deeper, more unconscious persecutory phantasies. And that while the parent's conscious mind is appropriately working out how best to practically help the child, the parent's unconscious mind is working with the child's unconscious mind to detoxify the six year old's phantasies. Indeed this unconscious work is seen in the use of the concept of container-contained, as the underlying basis of any conscious practical action. That is to say, if the parents own persecutory anxieties have not been adequately contained in their development, then the parent will be emotionally unable to contain the persecuted upset presented by the child either at an emotional or practical level. Where the parent is able to contain the child's anxiety this will not only deal with the current situation but will also provide a learning experience by which the child, when it in turn is a parent, will have available an increased capacity to contain his or her own child's anxiety.

This has necessarily been a very brief statement about complex observations and interpretations in a practical setting. What will now be presented is a visual metaphor that spatially places the concepts of transference - counter-transference, projective indentification and container-contained in relation to each other. Our hope is that in this way the teaching of these concepts will be made easier and that therapists will have a framework by which they can remind themselves to be clear about which transferential relationship is subject to projective identification and perhaps containment at any given point in an on-going therapy.

3 The Hexagonal Tube Metaphor

Having outlined some general features of the problem we now look at the development of the visual metaphor which seeks to offset the possible confusions by providing a single integrated explanatory model of the situation. Broadly, the mental life of the individual can be visualised as being transacted within the lumen of a tube. The length of the tube represents time and is the co-terminous with the duration of life of the individual. It should here be stressed that it is not being suggested that such a hexagon exists in this form in the mind of the individual. It is a metaphoric device whereby complex relationships can be thought about with greater clarity.

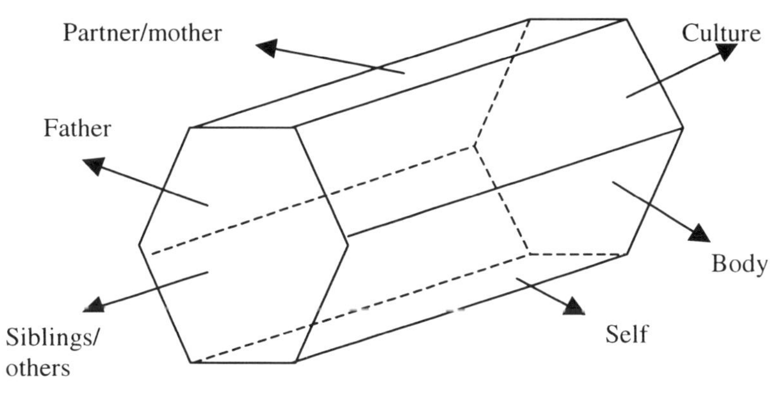

Figure 2 - Hexagonal Tube Metaphor

We begin with the bottom plate in Figure 2 which represents the ongoing mental life of the individual from conception to death. The spatial arrangement of the other plates will be described in relation to this plate.

The vertically opposite (top) plate represents the primary other which in early life is the mother and in later life, the partner. Clearly these are not the only possibilities encountered in practice but this aspect of the metaphor does serve to emphasise the degree to which, for both sexes, patterns relating to the primary other are carried over into partner relationships.

The right hand side can be thought of as comprising two plates. The lower plate, adjacent to the self is the representation of the body of the individual. The plate between that and the primary other represents the cultural heritage and the setting of the individuals in their social context.

The left hand lower plate initially represents siblings and friends but later others, including children while the left upper plate represents father and subsequent authority structures.

It should **not** be taken that this in any way implies an ideal or model state of mental or family life. From the point of view of couples it should already be apparent that not only may the partner at times be better conceived of a s occupying other plates than the primary other e.g., father plate, but that the interaction between self and partner can be profoundly affected by the communication passing between other plates that boundary their relationship.

The two aspects of interpersonal and intrapsychic communication that are central to this visual metaphor are affects and phantasies. Briefly, the activity of the affects in terms of tension states and discharge states is conceived of much as is summarised by Jacobson [12] and Lund [13]. In the revised metaphor developed from these authors and presented here more attention is paid to the site of impact and the interpersonal transformation of discharged emotions than in earlier formulations. The disposition of feelings and phantasies, in some ways resembles Kleinian Object Relations concepts but is conceived of less in corpuscular terms and more in inter-personal wave-form terms. That is, the metaphor that carries the concepts is less the homeomorphic internalisation of an image of mother, rather the image carrying the concept is more of a to and fro discharge between contact points on the plates that, like a neon light gives steadiness of light that belies its evanescent pulsatile nature. Likewise, it is posited that there is transmission of phantasies between plates that can be, at different times conscious and unconscious.

There is clearly a lot of new terminology and historical comment in this domain and the ideas are abstract. From the point-of-view of facilitating greater clarity we can immediately begin to envisage spatially related events in a mathematical structure. Several issues arise such as: why choose a tube, what is the nature of the lumen, are these plates rigid like metal or more plastic, why are the plates juxtaposed in the way described ?

4 The Form and Function of the Plates

Each plate can be thought of as a very long strip of metal beginning at or near the commencement of a person's mental life. The surface of the plate is scored longitudinally by grooves (see Figure 3).

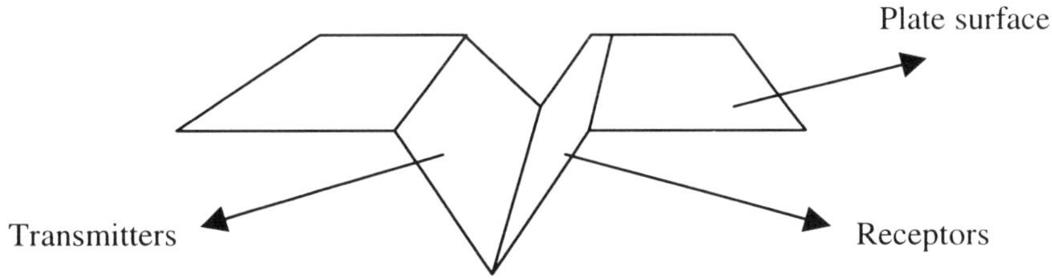

Figure 3 - Cross-section of Plate Groove

A key to the value of the visual metaphor is that some of the grooves receive and transmit affects and some receive and transmit phantasies. Any groove can be either in the mode of receiving only, transmitting only, simultaneously receiving and transmitting or performing neither of these functions. It is posited that there is a field of interaction on the plate whereby the activity of affect and phantasy grooves influence each other in terms of the switching on or off of receptor or transmitter activity. In this model, if the transmit groove side is active the plate is projecting, if the receptor groove side is active it is introjecting, if both sides are active containment is taking place and if neither is active that plate is currently inactive.

It is further suggested that there is a capacity in the system to remember patterns of relating and particularly to remember the differential patterns of relating as between the different plates.

We are now in a position to return to the earlier critique of the confusion of terms. It should now be apparent that the issues normally conveyed by the terms transference and counter-transference refer to the "dialogue" between plates. That aspect of transference which refers to misapperception of current figures in terms of earlier figures can be represented by an emotional "flashback" along the length of the tube from the self plate in the present to the memory of another plate at some distant point in the tube.

If transference can be delineated in this way, then issues of projection, introjection and containment can be conceptualised in relation to "grooves" in the manner just described. That this relates to Ogden's description of the fundamental communication relationship building function of projective identification can be illustrated with relation to falling in love.

It is suggested that phantasies are the more immediate signal transmitted and received. The transmission of phantasies produces images in the plates which have as their form the scenarios of dream fragments. Such phantasies influence the receptivity of other grooves on the plate. Including affect grooves. Insofar as the phantasy is shared by two people/plates the initial basis for relating exists. Such states are most vividly seen in the early phases of falling in love. Subsequently the phantasy is in-filled with love, any hate being transformed into idealisation [14].

In states of unrequited love the phantasy is not shared. It is held in one plate and either undergoes decay or becomes the basis for hallucinatory or delusional phantasies. Even where the relationship becomes more substantial, in terms not only of duration, but also the ever-more complex interweaving of other affects and phantasies, even then the situation is not static. It is proposed that there is repeated, relatively rapid makes/breaks of affect and phantasy connectedness which makes for adaptability and openness of relating between two people. Where there is fixity of phantasy or feeling states there is usually a pathology. For example, the role of abiding guilt between a couple leading to variable admixture of depression and sado-masochistic functioning.

5 The Location of the Model and the Therapist

If the proposed metaphor has found any acceptance with the reader, two questions follow. Where is the model located and where is the therapist located? We are now starting to move to the 'common ground' of visualising the key issue of the domain and clarifying the possible application and limitations of the model.

It is first suggested that the model be available in the mind of the teacher/therapist as an aide-memoire, as a prompt to be as clear as possible in describing the relationship between transference issues and projective identification issues. Second, it may be a guide to the therapist's reasoning processes in clarifying which transference is active and what inter-active potentials exist. It may also serve as an uncomfortable reminder that the "blank screen" therapist does not exist and that the therapist is actively projecting/introjecting from at least one of the plates depending on the predominant transferential mode. That is to say, by mobilising his or her negative capability wittingly or unwittingly the therapist will at different times be occupying each of the sides of the hexagon. Failure to appreciate this often leads to therapists interpreting from a restricted position of, say, maternal transference, when another transferential plate may be more alive, relevant and appropriate.

Finally, the metaphor emphasises that in exercising a containing function, the therapist should consider at each phase of therapy, which transferential plate he/she is occupying as a container. Because much of the theory of containment was initially described by Winnicott and Bion in relation to maternal containment there has been relatively scant regard paid to containment offered by fathers, siblings and the Culture generally in many aspects of the psycho-analytic literature. The metaphor introduced here could help form a link with other therapy modalities that do stress wider containment occurring in group therapy.

References

1. Paton, R.C., Lynch, S., Jones, D., Nwana, H.S., Bench-Capon, T.J.M. & Shave, M.J.R. Domain Characterisation for Knowledge Based Systems. In Proceedings of A.I. 94 - Fourteenth International Avignon Conference, 1994, Volume 1, 41-54.
2. Meyer, M.A. & Paton, R.C. Towards an Analysis and Classification of Approaches to Knowledge Acquisition from Examination of Textual Metaphor. Knowledge Acquisition 1992; 4: 347-369.
3. Paton, R.C. Towards a Metaphorical Biology. Biology and Philosophy 1992, 7, 279-294.
4. Lund, C.A. & Paton, R.C. Metaphor, Science and Psychotherapy: a Shared Muse? Submitted to Brit. J. Psychotherapy.
5. Ruszczynski, S. Thinking about and Working with Couples. In Ruszezynski, S. (ed) Psychotherapy with Couples 1993. London: Karnac Books.
6. Freud, S. (1905) Fragment of an Analysis of a Case of Hysteria. Standard Edition, 7. London: Hogarth Press.
7. Sandler, J., Dare, C. & Holder, A. The Patient and the Analyst: The Basis of the Psychoanalytic Process 1979, London: Karnac Books.
8. Heiman, P. On Counter-transference. Brit. J. Medical Psychology 1950; 33: 9-15.
9. Ogden, T. Projective Identification and Psychotherapeutic Technique 1982. New York: Jason Aronson.
10. Meltzer, D. *et al.* The Conceptual Difference between Projective Identification (Klein) and Container-contained (Bion). Appears in Studies in Extended Metapsychology: Clinical Applications of Bion's Ideas. Cited from Ruszczynski, S. & Fisher, J. (eds) Intrusiveness and Intimacy in the Couple 1995. London: Karnac Books.
11. Bion,W.R. Learning from Experience 1962. London, Heineman.
12. Jacobson, E. Depression, Comparative Studies of Normal, Neurotic and Psychotic Conditions 1971. N.Y.: International Universities Press.
13. Lund, C.A. Psychotic Depression: Psychoanalytic Psychopathology in Relation to Treatment and Management, Brit. J. Psychiatry 1991, 158, 523-528.
14. Kernberg, O.F. Love Relations: Normality and Pathology 1995. London: Yale University Press.

Geomentality: Reframing the Landscape

Nancy de Freitas
School of Art and Design, Auckland Institute of Technology
New Zealand

Introduction

This work is part of a wider investigation into a notion of landscape that includes the sense of belonging to, remembering and viewing land and space. It has come about as a result of the need for a language of interpretation that is effective in relation to the work of artists dealing with land and space who may not be primarily concerned with its appearance. The paper is set out in the form of four conceptual maps of the land. It is structured according to these four sites in order to present different sides of a model of thinking about landscape painting that encompasses historical perspectives, cultural positions and individual artistic orientation, all of which are present to varying degrees in a particular work. For the fourth mapping of this concept, the author's own work will be used as an example. The paper does not set out to deal with the history of landscape painting, nor with the philosophy or theory of landscape painting. It is an attempt to synthesise a few ideas from different disciplines into a discourse that could serve as a model for thinking and speaking about the intentions and concerns of contemporary artists dealing with notions of land. It attempts to locate this contemporary practice in relation to the tradition of landscape painting on one hand, and on the other, in the context of a decentred and global spatial network.

Background

The painter Rene Magritte provides a starting point. He gave a lecture in 1938 in which he explained his painting *La Condition Humaine*. It shows a landscape and a painted representation of it merging indistinguishably. "This is how we see the world. We see it as being outside ourselves even though it is only a mental representation of what we experience on the inside."[1] Magritte acknowledges the way in which Nature is invariably seen through the frame of culture.

Magritte's understanding of how landscape is felt and remembered as much as it is seen is an eloquent explanation of the way in which culture and convention provide the blueprints for our experiences. His description reveals an artist's geomentality. It offers an insight into his own personal frame of mind in relation to the land and also reveals something about the social geomentality of his time.

---

1 Cited in Whitfield [1].

Geomentality is defined by Yoon [2] as "an established and lasting frame (state) of mind regarding the environment. It is necessarily translated into a particular behavioural pattern in dealing with the environment, and is reflected in the pattern of the cultural landscape." Yoon coined this term to identify the different mental frameworks that are at the core of traditional East Asian and modern European systems of classifying landforms. The root "geo" derives from the Greek for earth and "mentality" refers to frame of mind including mode of thought.

This concept of geomentality is proposed here as a useful platform on which to build a contemporary discourse in relation to landscape painting or painting that deals with the land. There are private and public facets to the concept, inseparable components that comprise mental space and social reality. Yoon's neologism adds another conceptual dimension to a pair of terms coined by Wright [3] that later came into general use in Human Geography namely, "geosophy" and "geopiety". These will be discussed in context at a later stage.

The following four sections present the ideas that make up this model for the reframing of landscape interpretation as four conceptual maps. The first two maps deal with a relatively broad view, the third concentrates on a narrower cultural view and the fourth deals with an individual example, the author's own work for a look at the more specific issues that can be encompassed in the notion of geomentality.

First Map - Colonial Geomentality

It was a European geomentality that accompanied the colonists and deported citizens who arrived in Australia, New Zealand, North America and elsewhere. Examples of this frame of mind can be found in all of these countries, in the landscape painting of the period. These colonial artists were said by some to have misrepresented their new territory through the tinted glasses of their European landscape taste and their visual prejudices (Illus. 1). This criticism of the work of early landscape painters in New Zealand was an incomplete reading of the work that did not take into account the geomentality of those recent immigrants and temporary residents. The same type of criticism was levelled at other colonial artists in other parts of the world.

Painters in the colonies remembered the landscapes of their cultural and physical past. Without the actual landscape of the homeland, as long as there was the memory of it, they could still make visual 'maps' in the guise of the new country. In her 1997 novel *Fugitive Pieces,* with its extraordinary evocations of landscape memory, Anne Michaels frames it this way: "What is dearest to us is often clearer to us than the truth [4]."

It took several generations of artists to evolve into the nationalist and then post-nationalist movements that began to display the strong new geomentality of individuals grounded in the time and space of their now not so new homelands. For

Illus. 1 A European geomentality, the picturesque.

colonial painters, the changing and maturing of geomentality came about through familiarity with the life of the new land, its antipodean seasons, indigenous culture, its particular colour, flora and fauna and its temperament (Illus.2). Eventually colonial painters everywhere did shake off the interpretive sensibilities and cultural formulas of the mother country, to assimilate from the physical world around them and the cultural production of the community, a distinctive geomentality. This newer geomentality was characterised by a degree of geopiety, a concept that refers to thoughtful respect for and devotion to the natural world and geographical space. Moreover, it may account for feelings of territoriality and strong nationalist sentiments. A full definition is given in The Dictionary of Human Geography [5].

Both life and art contributed to the shaping of mental space and social reality and the characteristic geomentalities that evolved in the colonies were at least in part the result of artists' familiarity with other artists' responses to the land in painting and poetry. Inevitably, the landscape that they observed through sight was interpreted in painted representations of space which in their turn, influenced later viewing and interpretation.

For New Zealand painters, the landscape became, "...a landscape much ravished and loved: that which has long been prepared, posed and anointed by painters and writers, powdered with pigments and words, mascara'd with ink and lubricated with oils, made into a painted surface [6]".

Illus. 2 Familiarity with the life of the new land.

Illus. 3 A topographical approach.

Writers commenting on 19th and early 20th century New Zealand landscape painting have identified and argued two opposing painterly inclinations. Some artists chose a topographical form that relied on an immediate response to the landscape (Illus. 3), and some imposed on the New Zealand scene the atmosphere, light and characteristic form of the homelands in Europe. It was the work of these latter artists that prompted the emergence of a generally accepted myth concerning the quality of light in New Zealand that was considered a unique and defining characteristic of the place. The writer and critic Francis Pound [7] challenged this assumption, causing an unexpected furore at the time.

> *This fallacy, baldly stated, is that there is a 'real' New Zealand landscape, with its 'real' qualities of light and atmosphere, to which some artists are true and others untrue, the true artists being the 'good' and the untrue 'bad'. And a corollary fallacy: that the real New Zealand causes style in paintings – a kind of geographical determinism.*

Second Map – From Wilderness to Deep Ecology

What European colonisers everywhere did not take with them was any notion of nature as a vulnerable system. There was no philosophical equivalent to the eastern concept of geomancy (*feng-shui* in Chinese) which acknowledges the vulnerability of nature. On the contrary, European colonisers braved the New World with the righteous intention of carving up and taming the wilderness. This western geomentality, according to Yoon [8], was framed in a profound way by the biblical idea of "human dominion over nature."

> *Be fruitful and multiply, and fill the earth and subdue it; and have dominion over the fish of the sea and over the birds of the air and over every living thing that moves upon the earth.*
> (Genesis, chapter 1, v. 27-28).

Examples of such a frame of mind can be found extensively in the literature, the visual arts, architecture and landscape design. One particularly persuasive example of big vision, this masculine taste for potency and control is the monumental project at Mount Rushmore by the sculptor Gutzon Borglum who announced at the first of the unveiling ceremonies that the monument would outlast the civilisation it represented.[2]

This western geomentality that had its roots in the Scriptures, recognised that the wilderness was a desolate place forsaken by God and inhabited by demons. It was, for the most part, the place to which the damned would be banished. The New England Puritans who established their communities in North America in the late

---

[2] An interesting account of the proposal to include Susan B. Anthony in the monument is to be found in Schama, Ch 7, i The Woman on Mount Rushmore [9].

16th and 17th centuries saw it as their task to create a fertile garden out of the untamed expanses [10].

The wilderness was seen as an obstacle and a threat to the livelihood of the settlers, something to be contested and to be won. By the 19th century, the perceptions of North Americans were divided. Contrasting qualities were recognised. Some pioneers continued to relate to the wild environment with a geomentality that perceived negative characteristics, the difficulties and the obstacles, the positive aspect being the associated toughness and virility that was required to deal with it. However, growing communities of urban dwellers, including artists and poets had a different geomentality, one that identified the elegant solitude of the wilderness, the sublime qualities, the potential for contemplation and for spiritual renewal. Artists at this time, like Caspar David Friedrich, portrayed the natural landscape as a site of spiritual redemption while writers like James Audubon, Thomas Cole, Henry David Thoreau and others, saw a serious decline taking place. Commenting on the state of the wilderness, they expressed concern at the removal of natural forests, the penetration of inaccessible areas and the impact of urbanisation. These concerns reflected a growing understanding of place and space, a knowledge of the land that geographers call geosophy.

In the antipodes, colonists named the wilderness "the bush". The Australian and New Zealand versions of evolving colonial geomentality took place over a much shorter period of time. More importantly, the European geomentality that arrived in Australia and New Zealand in the late 18th and early 19th centuries respectively, was very different to that which arrived in North America two hundred years earlier. In the antipodes, the Arcadian idyll, bolstered by the artists of the time, became the facade that masked the true effects of land confiscation and cultural domination.

The romanticising of nature became a movement in literary and artistic circles and subsequently created a divergence in environmental perception. By the late 20th century, wilderness had come to be widely and symbolically perceived as the ultimate salvation of a polluted and depleted global environment, representing the robust and proper processes of nature. The course of this transformation in the way that the land and environment is conceived can be tracked throughout the period in the literary and visual arts, reflecting a shift in geomentality.

Third Map - The Naming of Land: Genealogy as Landscape

The word "landscape" in connection with colonial painting in New Zealand is a word that has, more often than not, included notions of boundaries and ownership. This is of particular significance in connection with the renaming of the land and subsequent obliteration of original names. Possession was a forceful aspect of colonial western geomentality and landscape painting contributed to the sense of ownership of that which could be viewed.

Maori are the indigenous Polynesians of New Zealand. Their language has no word that means a view of land as in "landscape". The closest equivalent word, "whenua", means place. To describe place as landscape, requires the use of a phrase such as 'te aahua whenua', meaning the appearance of the land, or nowadays, a photo of the land. The word "papatuanuku" commonly used as "papa", means land or earth mother in relation to sky father and comes with all its legendary associations from the Maori creation myth. The geomentality that is evident in these words for land and place is one that acknowledges origin, as in the creation myth, or embodies history and local significance (Illus. 4).

Illus. 4 Genealogy as Landscape.

Maori iwi, or tribal affiliations, are based on common ancestry, but the most important social groups are the hapu, the sub-tribes who are the corporate landholding groups. Traditional Maori geomentality did not recognise private ownership of land. This fundamental difference in geomentality was, at least in part, responsible for the different views and expectations of the signatories to the Treaty of Waitangi, signed in 1840. This was the historic pact between Great Britain and a number of New Zealand Maori tribes of the North Island that was supposed to protect Maori rights and was the immediate basis of the British annexation of New Zealand.

The clash of indigenous Maori and non-Maori (Pakeha) geomentalities has had profound effects on all aspects of society and culture in New Zealand. In the art world, it has resulted in a contemporary landscape tradition that is both vigorous and distinctive. Maori artists who have trained in the art schools are using both traditional sources and materials as well as European media. The cultural interface in New Zealand has been a fertile location for artists in the second half of this century. This is often politicised as a bi-cultural interface. But, given the waves of immigration that have brought Pacific Islanders and other cultures to the country, the social/cultural reality is more complex.

Fourth Map – An Immigrant Geomentality: Landscape with Memory

We live in post-colonial times and recent immigrant geomentalities have replaced the colonial ones. As with the colonial geomentality, the immigrant frame of mind, knows every moment as two moments, history and memory, the actual and the perceived. Every image of place and land, in the broadest interpretation of this concept, retains the stain of the other view.

Referring to "spatial practice" in the way that Lefebvre [11] has theorised space, that is, perceived space, there is visible evidence in urban and rural environments of the structural marks of early conquerors and settlers. Just as visible, but even more complex, however, has been the effect of the diaspora in contemporary microcosms. Within cities, suburban subdivisions and isolated rural communities in many places, there are areas that bear evidence of this, through the distinguishable, idiosyncratic responses to land and space of their immigrant communities. The immigrant geomentality is identifiable in terms of spatial practice, in the visible adaptations and modifications that are made to the environment and in terms of their cultural production such as painting.

Referring specifically to capitalist spatialisation, Burgin [12] asserts that "There is a Boston in Los Angeles, a Lower Manhattan and a South Bronx, a Sao Paulo and a Singapore." This is a description of transplanted urban identities, but the reality for many immigrants, displaced people and inhabitants of rapidly transforming communities is that there is a palpable loss of identity. It is this loss of identity and associated difficulty in making connection with the land that underpins the immigrant geomentality. If we examine a series of works that reflect this geomentality, it may be possible to tease out the significant characteristics.

As an immigrant painter, my imaging of space in paintings (or *representations of space* as Lefebvre would have put it), is framed by my particular geomentality. For me, there is no connection with the visible landscape, only with its pulse. The contemporary New Zealand born painter Don Binney, can relate to the familiar land view (Illus. 5), but I am drawn to its underside.

Illus. 5 Contemporary view from the window.

Drawings from the Plate Tectonic series in long vertical format, seemingly at odds with the concept of landscape, are in fact much closer to my concern for an interpretation of land that recognises its human correlation. The long format is like a fragmentary glimpse, incomplete and relative (Illus. 6). It is like a geological core sample, pulled into the cultural domain, offering fragments of information from which we try to construct a picture, an interpretation of what this place is and who we are. The vertical format of the drawings is an attempt to evoke a sense of time that is not effectively delivered in the wide horizontal view. The horizontal view, which is the conventional landscape format, describes a moment of viewing. The hands here refer

Illus. 6 Landscape felt rather than seen.

to connection with land, to correlation. They are comparable to those impressions that humans have described on cave walls, on cliff faces and in transient sand, noting their connection to and curiosity about the Earth.

Artists often find it difficult dealing with precise definitions. They are to be avoided. I prefer a description or a concept that is meaningful in as much as it escapes precision and finality. It is the evocation that is important. This is a geomentality that has been shaped by childhood experiences in another colonial environment, the West Indies, where the childhood attachment to land and place was undermined by the social construct of home being elsewhere. Home, the real place, was where we had come from. But that place could not be home, it was an abstract place, a world constructed from books, pictures and family albums and stories. It was not the everyday lived reality, and the everyday reality was not home either.

Our significant memories accompany us from childhood into adulthood, from one place to another. For the immigrant, and for the refugee, images of the land and place from which one has emigrated are the memory component of the experienced new land. Our entire relationship with nature, that is, the physical land or the represented landscape of painting and photography, is a complex mix of observation and intellectual and emotional perceptions.

The woven or unravelling structures in the *Plate Tectonic Series* represent a metaphorical view of land, of the Earth, of the idea of place (Illus.7). This is not the recognisable, visual terrain that we expect to see in a traditional landscape, but the notion of land as force, or as a dynamic correlation. This is not the Hauraki Plains of New Zealand or the Sahara Desert of Africa or the Canadian Shield. It is all of these, present and past. The strands of interwoven structures present both a constructive and a decomposing possibility open to our interpretation. The hand gestures offer clues to the human, conscious and spiritual component, interrelated and interdependent. They refer to the whole realm of human manufacture that is on its way to becoming a geological layer: the terraced fields, the cities, the railways the formal gardens, the parking lots. Several works in the series contain a personal genealogy in the metaphorical vegetation. They contain the painted hands of members of my family, representing three generations. Their identities are embedded in the land, the trees and the water. The hand is the vegetation itself. All the represented fragments of human anatomy in these works offer small gestures as clues to the human, conscious and spiritual part of the cultural relationship, the most significant clue being the closed hand with fingers touching. This is a gesture representative of all of the finest motor actions possible by human beings. It is seen in the use of a scalpel, the holding of minute fragments, the feeling for texture and the use of a writing instrument. The intention in the work is to go beyond geology and vegetation into myth and memory.

Illus. 7 The soul embedded in land, the hand as vegetation itself.

Immigrants necessarily take with them the flavours and colours of past experience. They retain the learned and felt disposition of the land/place from which they have emigrated. Oscillations or phases are a characteristic of the personal immigrant geomentality as it moves between the well-known space of memory and the new place of hope. Old knowledge is planted in the new country in ways that significantly and permanently alter it. But it takes time to make the adjustment, and in the interim, the perception of the new place is problematic. The author V.S.Naipaul described the dilemma well, referring to his arrival in England [13]:

> *I saw what I saw very clearly. But I didn't know what I was looking at. I had nothing to fit it into. I was still in a kind of limbo.*

To understand a place one has to take some knowledge to it and the knowledge that serves best is provided by that very place. This is the "sagesse de la terre", the wiseness of the land that comes from living with it.

Turning From the Window

Artists choose to depict only certain facets of reality and the language of critique attempts to deal with those facets. Foucault [14] argued that after all uncertainties in relation to the senses have been removed, only the narrow area of sight remains, for definition of the observable world, its lines, surfaces, forms and reliefs. Hearsay, taste and smell were considered to lack certainty, and feelings would not have counted for much. The use of a vocabulary based on sight provided adequate explanation and critique of representational landscape painting in the past. That was when artists were painting an arrangement of natural and man-made features in rough perspective to represent a setting for human activity. But it is clearly inadequate today in relation to the work of contemporary artists who deal with issues of land, space and place.

These artists are likely to be engaged with an exploration of cultural boundaries, intellectual projections, tectonics, memory, latitudes, histories, antipodes, itineraries, legends, genealogies, "rootedness [15]" or authenticity. This is no longer the view from the window and the language of analysis and critique needs to change. The concept of geomentality offers another perspective that encompasses more than sight, is more relevant in the contemporary context, and can still be used in comparisons with earlier work, as I have shown.

I would like to conclude with a suggestion for a neologism that embodies concepts appropriate to contemporary work. I propose the term *geolegend* to denote work that is intentionally concerned with land, place and space, but not primarily with the appearance. It is a term that can accommodate a number of concepts. 1) It suggests a moving away from the certainty of vision to make representations and interpretations that incorporate other forms of knowledge, including the colloquial, the mythical, the true and the false. 2) It suggests place and space intersecting with human desire, motivation or prejudice. 3) Legends are often the written versions of oral histories of non-writing cultures. This association adds a useful nuance in relation to the representation of something that has long been known or felt. 4) Legends are often used as a cue for the interpretation of experiences or the translation of signs, as in cartography. All of these nuances of meaning in the term geolegend work well in reference to those images created by artists working today whose concerns go beyond the view from the window.

Illustrations

Illus. 1 Eugene Von Guerard. *Lake Wakitipu with Mount Earnslaw, Middle Island, New Zealand* 1877-1879. Oil on canvas. Mackelvie Trust Collection, Auckland City Art Gallery Toi o Tamaki.

Illus. 2 George O'Brien. *Otago Heads from Signal Hill* 1872. Watercolour. Auckland City Art Gallery Toi o Tamaki.

Illus. 3 Christopher Perkins. *Taranaki* 1931. Oil on canvas. Auckland City Art Gallery Toi o Tamaki.

Illus. 4 Verandah panels from *Rongopai* c1860. Rongopai Marae.

Illus. 5 Don Binney. *Sun shall not burn Thee by day nor moon by night* 1966. Oil and acrylic on canvas. Auckland City Art Gallery Toi o Tamaki.

Illus. 6 Nancy de Freitas. *Study for a Rift Landscape* 1995. Charcoal on Arches Aquarelle. Private Collection.

Illus. 7 Nancy de Freitas. *Landscape with Vegetation* 1994. Acrylic on cotton duck. Collection of the artist.

References

1. Whitfield S. Magritte. London, 1992, p 62

2. Yoon H. K. Maori Mind , Maori Land: Essays on the Cultural Geography of the Maori People from an Outsider's Perspective. Peter Lang, Berne, 1986, pp 39-46

3. Wright J. K. Human Nature in Geography: Fourteen Papers, 1925-1965. Harvard University Press, 1966

4. Michaels A. Fugitive Pieces. Bloomsbury, 1997, p 166

5. Johnstone R. J. et al, (eds.). The Dictionary of Human Geography. Third Edition. Blackwell, 1994

6. Pound F. Signatures of Place. Paintings and Place Names. Govett-Brewster Art Gallery exhibition catalogue, 1991, p 23

7. Pound F. Frames on the Land. Early Landscape Painting in New Zealand. Collins, 1983, p 11

8. Yoon H. K. Two Different Geomentalities, Two Different Gardens: The French and the Japanese Cases. GeoJournal, 33.4, 1994, p 473

9. Schama S. Landscape and Memory. Fontana Press, Harper Collins, 1995

10. Tuan Y. F. Topophilia: a Study of Environmental Perception, Attitudes and Values. Prentice-Hall Inc., Englewood Cliffs, NJ, 1974

11. Lefebvre H. The Production of Space. Oxford and Cambridge (Massachusetts), Basil Blackwell, 1991

12. Burgin V. In/Different Spaces. Place and memory in visual culture. University of California Press, 1996, p 24

13. Naipaul V. S. The Enigma of Arrival. Viking, London, 1987, p 12

14. Foucault M. The Order of things. An Archaeology of the Human Sciences. Random House, 1970

15. Relph E. Place and Placelessness. Pion, London, 1976, p 37

Graphically Representing Causal Sequences in Accident Scenarios: Just Some of the Issues

Julia Hill & Peter Wright
Human Computer Interaction Group,
Department of Computer Science, University of York
Email: <julia>,<pcw>@cs.york.ac.uk

Abstract

This paper aims to explore the analytical issues surrounding the graphical representation of causation in accident scenarios. Two types of graphical renderings, Petri Nets and Why-Because Graphs, are introduced and the different ways in which they denote accident causation are explored. The second part reports an experiment undertaken to explore whether graphical renderings of causality have any benefits over text, and if one of the two graphs is superior to the other. In so doing, this paper aims to draw out our visual understanding of graphical renderings and how these map from the original representation, the accident scenario, to the secondary representation.

1. Introduction

Safety and the improvement of safety is an emotive issue in today's society. This is especially the case with respect to failures in safety critical systems such as aircraft, oil rigs, nuclear power plants and ambulance services. Failure in this type of system can have catastrophic consequences (eg. multiple deaths and environmental damage). Learning from such failures is a key component of accident prevention. When accidents happen detailed investigations take place and the findings are published in incident or accident reports[1]. For example, aircraft accident reports are published by the Air Accident Investigation Branch (AAIB). These reports serve a number of purposes and are used by many different communities including members of the general public, legal experts and technical experts such as aircraft designers and airworthiness authorities. They contain factual and analytical information, findings, conclusions and the recommendations of the accident investigators. The complexity of accident report reflects the complexity of incident/accident[2] themselves and it has been argued that the textual format common in these reports could be made more accessible to

---

[1] In this paper, I use the phrase *accident report* to refer to incident and accident reports.

[2] In this paper, I use the term *accident* to refer to both incident and accident.

wide range of audiences by the use of graphical notations. Johnson et al. [1], for example, argue that one particular form of graphical representation, Petri Nets (PNs), can help "visualise the relationships between the various events", especially causal and temporal relationships. PNs were chosen because they were already well known within the design community and because of their relatively simple syntax. Others [2] have developed their own graphical notations, Why-Because Graphs (WB-Graphs), specifically for representing causality in accidents.

These attempts to make accident reports more accessible are premised upon the assumption that supplementary graphical notations aid comprehension in some way. Larkin and Simon [3] have argued that in some situations, problem solving can be enhanced by the use of diagrams. Glenberg and Langston [4] have shown that sequential instructions can be made more comprehensible by the use of flow-chart diagrams. But there is no research in the literature that tests these assumptions with respect to causal analysis in accident reports. The primary aim of the experiment reported in this paper is to determine whether or not PNs and WB-Graphs enhance readers' understanding of accident causality over and above text only narratives. Before reporting the experiment we describe some of the problems with text only descriptions and some of the features and differences between PNs and WB-Graphs.

2 Describing Causality

2.1 Causal Relations in Accident Texts

There is no single way in which causal relations are described in accident texts. Syntactic and semantic clues both serve to aid the reader in constructing a causal understanding of the accident. Information needed to piece together causal relations may dispersed through the text. Sometimes there are explicit semantic references in the text but often causal relations are implicit. In this situation syntactical clues can be used to extract implicit references. The following extract from the Cowly incident [5] has examples of explicit and implicit references to causal relations. The extract explicitly says why the commander was not allowed a lower cruise level by using the conjunction "because" as a semantic indicator. However, it is implicitly implied by the sentences being in sequence that the commander requested a lower cruise level was because of sleet and rain.

> " During the period that the aircraft was in cloud the crew observed sleet and rain. At FL154 the commander requested Air Traffic Control for a reduction in his cleared cruised level to FL140 but the controller was unable to approve the lower level immediately because it had already been allocated to another aircraft..." .

2.2 Causal Relations in the Graphs

Despite PNs and WB-Graphs belonging to the same genre of directed graphs, there are fundamental differences in the way they are used to represent accident scenarios. Firstly, PNs were adopted to remove ambiguities in accident texts, thus giving a precise and explicit account of the accident in conjunction with the text itself [1]. In so doing, the PN tends to highlight a mixture sequential and concurrent temporal sequences in combination with causal relations. WB-Graphs were specifically designed to represent only causal sequence in accident scenarios in order to question the causal findings in the accident report [2].

Both the graphs, however, make relationships explicit through a series of interconnecting arcs (arrows) and nodes (states and events). States represent the state of the flight in the accident sequence, whereas an event represents an instantaneous action which brings about a change in the state of the flight. PNs (Appendix A) use a graphical notation of circles and rectangles to denote states and events, respectively, in a state-event-state syntax. The linear form of the net represents logical time in sequence where concurrent events (occurring approximately at the same time) are highlighted graphically on the x-axis.

WB-Graphs (Appendix B[3]), in addition to states (hexagons) and events (rectangles), have processes (octagons) which are events that occur over a period of time. However, they do not have the same rigid syntax as PNs since the nodes can be placed in any order. Also their placement on 2D space does not indicate any additional information, including logical time. Finally the graph itself can be read from right to left asking, "Why did X happen? Because of A, B, C".

2.3 Effectiveness and Efficiency of Graphical Representations

In the literature on accident reports it has so far been taken for granted that PNs and WB-Graphs enhance comprehension. But in more general fields, researchers have attempted to analyse what makes for an effective and efficient representation.

For example, Zhang [7] identifies a general class of displays including alphanumeric, graphical and tabular displays which he calls Relational Information Displays (RIDs), and argues that the physical properties of the graphical display must clearly and unambiguously map the properties of the information being represented. Failure to achieve a clear mapping may lead users of the graphical representation to make incorrect inferences about the information being represented. He then goes on to consider how different information structures support general information processing tasks. Using, for example, a graphical user interface he identifies three general tasks: information retrieval (e.g., what is the size of the word file called *work*?); comparison (is the word file *final* bigger than the word file *work*?); and integration (for example, integrating information about breadth and depth to determine area). Zhang argues that although there is no task-independent way of determining the best graphical representation, there is a general principle that can be derived from the RID framework, namely that "the information perceivable from a RID should exactly

---

[3] This example of a WB-Graph is a highly simplified one created for the experiment. Therefore, causal relations are not shown in depth. For a more detailed example see [2].

match the information required for a task, no less and no more". If the display does not obey this so-called "mapping principle" then the task cannot be achieved unless the user has other information internally represented.

From the point of view of graphical representations to support accident texts, Zhang's analysis provides two clear messages. The first is that the nature of the task for which the report is being used may be an important feature in determining the value of graphical enhancements. Secondly, one graphical notation may have advantages over another by virtue of the simplicity of the mapping of causal relations onto graphical features of the notation. In order to start exploring the value of graphical notations in this area, an experiment was carried out. The following section gives an account of this experiment.

3. Experiment

3.1 Aim

The experiment had the aim of finding out whether graphical representations used alongside accident scenario texts improved the understanding of accident scenarios, and whether PNs or WB-Graphs were more successful. Two possible uses of graphs were identified: (i) to give an overview of the accident scenario; and (ii) to retrieve information about particular causes of accident sequences.

The experiment was divided into three phases. Phase 1, **Memory Recall**, explored whether using a graphical representation alongside accident text assisted or hindered a subject's ability to gain an overview of the accident scenario. Phase 2, **Information Retrieval**, explored whether using a graphical representation alongside the accident text aided or hindered the detailed analysis of the events in the accident scenario text. Phase 3, **Informal Interview,** explored how subjects felt about using graphical representations.

3.2. Method

Two texts with two conditions each were examined. Each text was presented to the subject as a text only condition or a text plus graph condition. Due to subject number and time constraints (16 subjects, 1 hour each), the texts in the text plus graph condition were examined with either the PN or the WB-Graph but not both. Subjects were divided into two groups with each group being given one text in the text only condition and the other text in the text plus graph condition. Table 1 summaries this.

Phase 1 - Memory Recall. Subjects, at the beginning of Part 1 and 2, were given a text (or text and graph, depending on condition) to read for 5 minutes. They were told to read the text and/or graph with respect to understanding the main events in the scenario text and to expect to answer questions later. In the text plus graph condition, the amount of time that subjects spent on using either the text or graph was observed and recorded. This was achieved by watching them closely and marking down at what time they swapped between the representations.

	Part 1 -Text only Condition		Part 2 - Text plus Graph Condition		Part 3 - Informal Interview
	phase 1-memory recall	phase 2-information retrieval	phase 1-memory recall	phase 2 - information retrieval	phase 3 - informal interview
Grp A	text 1 (Cowly)		text 2 plus WB		
Grp B	text 2 (Ronaldsway)		text 1 plus PN		

Table 1: Summary of testing conditions

After 5 minutes, the text (and graph) were removed and subjects were asked to write down a summary of the accident scenario including what they understood to be the main events. Five minutes was given to do this.

The subjects' summaries were marked in two ways. They were first of all marked against a list of 10 main events in the scenario that had been previously selected. The subjects in the text plus graph condition were also marked in accordance with how they used the materials during the reading period.

Phase 2 - Information Retrieval. After phase 1, subjects, in part 1 and 2, were asked to answer seven questions on the accident scenario. This time they had the text (and graph) to use in answering the questions. They were asked to speak their thoughts out loud as they did this and had 10 minutes in which to complete the task. Subjects actions were observed and noted while doing this in the text plus graph condition with respect to how the materials were used. This phase was audio-taped.

The subjects' answers were marked in two main ways. Their answers were first of all marked against a list of answers previously constructed. Four out of the seven questions in text 1 were further marked with respect to whether subjects noticed ambiguities in the text. Three out of the seven questions in text 2 were also marked in this way[4]. Secondly, based on observations made during the experiment, the scripts were marked with respect to the frequency in which subjects had used the text and graph to answer the questions.

Phase 3 - Informal Interview. Subjects in the remainder of the experiment session (10-15 mins) were given an informal interview which involved the

[4] Both sets of questions before the experiment had 3 questions each marked for ambiguity. However, during the course of the experiment it was realised that a fourth question in the text 1 set had a fourth ambiguous answer. Consequently, text 1 results are out of 4, while text 2 results are out of 3.

experimenter asking the subjects a number of questions concerning their background, accident text familiarity, and their opinions on how they found using the graphical representation that they were given. This final phase was also audio-taped.

3.3 Results and Analysis

Phase 1 - Memory Recall. The results (figure 1) show that subjects in text 1 only and text 2 plus PN conditions performed about the same, while subjects in the text 2 plus WB condition performed much better than subjects in the text 2 only condition. This is confirmed by a t-test showing a significant difference between the two conditions of text 2 (t=-3.52, tcrit = 2.145, df=(14), $p<0.05$) and no significant difference between the two conditions of text 1 (t=0.18, tcrit = 2.145, df=(14), $p>0.05$). There is also a significant difference between the two text only results of text 1 and 2 (t=-6.24, tcrit = 2.145, df=(14), $p<0.05$).

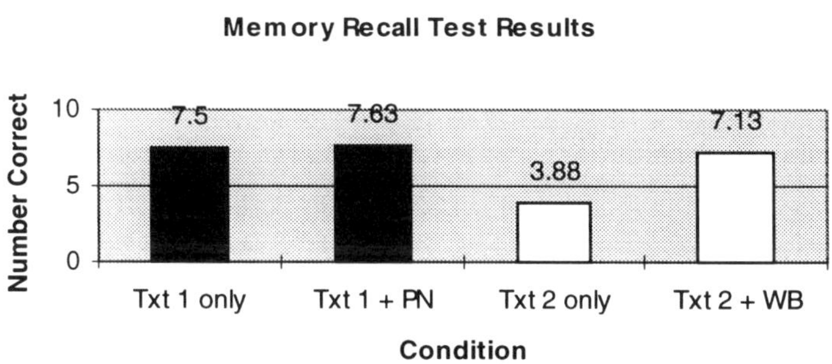

Figure 1: Average number correct in phase 1

Overall it appears that WB representations of causal relations help in recall and understanding over and above text only. We can see this looking at the difference between the text 2 only condition and text 2 plus WB condition. Interestingly enough this is not replicated for the PNs. Why could this be?

One possible explanation for the difference between the two sets of results is that text 1 was easier than text 2 to understand. Text 1 is a shorter text than text 2 (2 pages compared to 3) and, therefore, subjects have less to read and understand in the 5 minutes compared to those given text 2. The relative simplicity of text 1 is corroborated by the fact that subjects performed so well in the text 1 only condition. It would have been hard for those in the text plus PN condition to perform much better.

Since text 2 is a longer text, subjects in the text only condition struggled to read and understand the accident scenario in the time given. The subjects in the text 2 plus WB condition performed nearly as well as those in both the text 1 conditions. Consequently subjects in the text 2 plus WB condition benefited a lot from the extra representation.

We have seen that the WB condition assisted subjects in the Memory Recall task. Of interest is how much time subjects with access to graphs spent using them. Fifteen out of the 16 subjects read the text first before looking at the graph, and 11 of those 15 subjects read the text for at least 3.5 minutes out of a possible 5 minutes. In figure 2 the bar chart shows the average time in seconds that each subject spent on reading the graphical representation given to them.

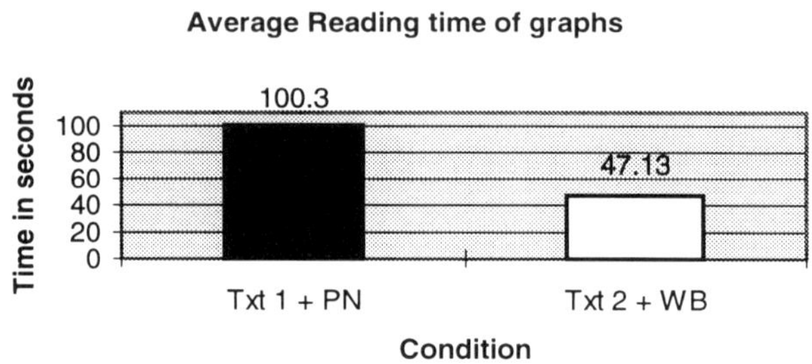

Figure 2: Average reading time of graphs with maximum time of 300 seconds

We can see that the those in the text 1 plus PN condition spent more time reading the graph than those in the text 2 plus WB condition. This might be surprising because we have seen that subjects in the text 2 plus WB condition performed much better than subjects in the text 2 only condition. We could have expected then that subjects in the text 2 plus WB condition spent more time using the graph than those in the text 1 plus PN condition. A possible explanation for this is that since text 1 is shorter than text 2, subjects had more time to spend reading the PN than subjects in the text 2 plus WB condition.

Another interpretation of this data could be that subjects in the text 2 plus WB condition used their limited time with the graph more effectively than those in the text 1 plus PN condition. We could also interpret that WB-Graphs themselves are more effective than PNs. More data is required to substantiate this interpretation.

Phase 2 - Information Retrieval. Figure 3 shows the average scores for phase 2 part of the experiment. The subjects were marked out of seven. Because their answers were audio-taped, marks were also given for answers given verbally even if not written down on the answer sheet. Furthermore, marks are included for subjects noticing ambiguities in the text when answering ambiguously marked questions. We can see on the bar chart that subjects in the text only condition for both texts performed better than subjects in each of the text plus graph conditions. A t-test was carried out on each condition for each text. Differences were significant between the text 1 conditions ($t=-2.70$, $t_{crit} = 2.145$, $df=(14)$, $p<0.05$), but not between the text 2 conditions ($t=2.11$, $t_{crit} = 2.145$, $df=(14)$, $p>0.05$). In further analysis, the number of questions answered using text only and graph only (PN and WB) for both texts were collated. The analysis of the results showed that 78% of questions were answered correctly using text only while the same was true for 66% of questions answered using graphical representations only.

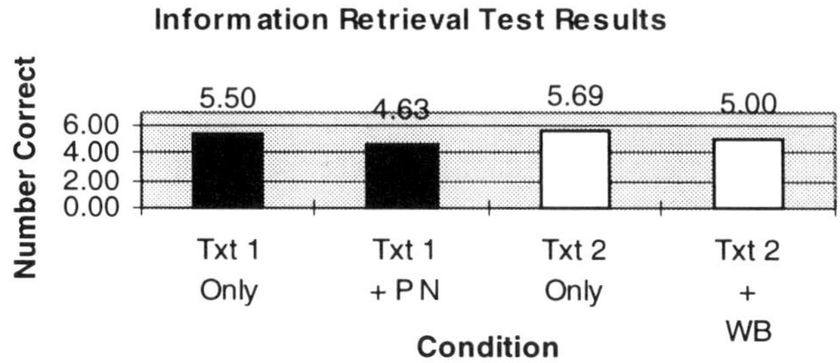

Figure 3: Average correct in phase 2

The results suggest that both graph conditions hinder detailed analysis of information in the text rather than aiding it. While this seems surprising at first, an interpretation of this data is as follows (see [8]). Graphical representations of causal sequence in accident texts provide an unambiguous reading of the information in the text. In contrast, being able to analyse the text without a complementary graphical representation allows readers to pick up on ambiguities and allows them to interpret the information more freely. If this interpretation is correct, analysis of the data should indicate that subjects did notice more ambiguities in the text only condition.

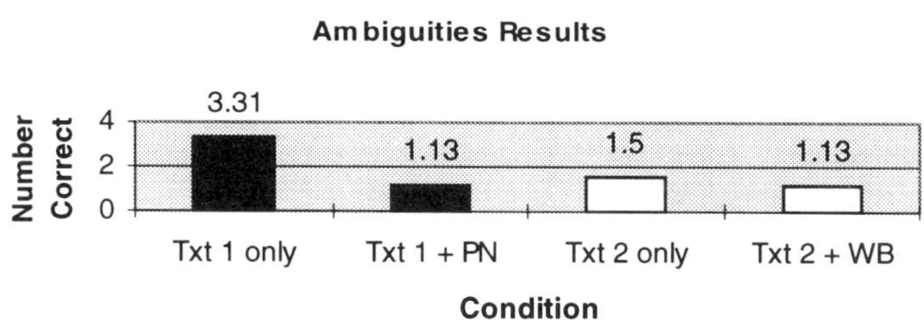

Figure 4: Ambiguity results[3]

Figure 4 shows that subjects with respect to text 1 noticed the ambiguities far better when they were in the text only condition compared to those in the text plus PN condition. However, for text 2 there is little difference between the results. A t-test confirmed significance between the text 1 conditions 2 ($t=5.09$, $t_{crit} = 2.145$, $df=(14)$, $p<0.05$) and the no significance between the text 2 conditions (2 ($t=0.94$, $t_{crit} = 2.145$, $df=(14)$, $p>0.05$).

The difference between the results in the text 1 conditions confirms the hypothesis that graphical representations hinder the detailed analysis of the information in the text. There are number of reasons why the results between the text 2 conditions are not the same. Firstly, having only 3 ambiguities to mark does not allow for much freedom of movement between groups of marks[3]. Secondly, text 2 could be less ambiguous than text 1 for some reason, or WB-Graphs allow for some freedom of interpretation compared to the PN.

Phase 3 - Informal Interview. The informal interview highlighted a number of things. Firstly, subjects said that the graphical representations were useful as an overview in that it helped them to understand or confirm the information in the text. Secondly, subjects said that they found the graphical representations useful for indexing information during the information retrieval task. For example, subjects used the graphs to find a certain chunk of information and then related this back to their reading of the text.

After looking at both the graphs, subjects commented that they thought there was more information in the WB-Graph than the PN. It was also remarked upon that having the text inside the nodes themselves strengthened the relationship between the physical dimensions of the graphs and the text.

4. Discussion and Conclusions

Do graphical notations aid the accident analyst in their understanding of accident scenarios? The experiment has certainly moved us a step closer in answering this question although more research needs to be done. It has shown us that the WB-Graph in the Memory Recall task was successful in aiding subjects to remember the accident scenario, and that both notations in the Information Retrieval task, prevented subjects from noticing ambiguities in the accident scenario text. However, further work is required with respect to the benefit of PNs.

What does this all mean? Firstly the success of WB-Graphs points us in the direction of Larkin & Simon [3] who argue that it tends to be the case that a successful representation is one that offers the information required by a user at reasonable computational cost. The results do suggest that the WB-Graph offers enough information with respect to the memory recall type tasks and, therefore, are suitable to this type of task. This point follows from the arguments of Zhang [7] demonstrated in section 2.3. On the other hand, with respect to information retrieval type tasks, freedom to analyse information freely is removed using such representations. At the same time, however, we have seen that subjects found the graphs useful for indexing events.

This paper has only looked at the user of accident texts and corresponding graphical notations. A further issue of great interest and importance is that of the author. Authoring such notations would allow accident investigators, for example, to focus on what happened and why by making them pull together all the bits of information in a systematic way. Maybe it is this area in which the power of using graphical representations lie. If this is the case then a possible next step in this research is to look in depth at authoring with respect to the single and multiple author. Exploring the authoring issues surrounding the multiple author may open group work in design industries and, therefore, as groups explore and understand the accident scenario in greater depth.

This research was undertaken as part of a case studentship funded by the EPSRC and British Aerospace plc.

References

1. Johnson, C. W., McCarthy, J. C., & Wright, P. C. (1995), *Using a formal language to support natural language in accident reports*, Ergonomics, 36(6).
2. Gerdsmeier, T., Ladkin, P. & Loer, K. (1997), *Analysing the Cali accident with a WB-Graph*, Technical Report RVS-RR-97-06, Faculty of Technology, Bielefeld University.
3. Larkin, J. H. & Simon H. A. (1987), *Why a diagram is (sometimes) worth ten thousand Words,* Cognitive Science, 11.
4. Glenberg, A. M. & Langston , W. E. (1992), *Comprehension of illustrated text: pictures help to build mental models,* Journal of Memory and Language, 31.
5. AAIB (1992), *Report on the incident to British Aerospace ATP, G-BYMK 10 Miles north of Cowly, near Oxford, on 11 August 1991,* Air Accident Report 4/92, Air Accidents Investigation branch, Department of Transport, HMSO, UK.
6. AAIB (1991), *Report on the accident to British Aerospace ATP, G-OATP at Ronaldsway Airport, Isle of Man on 23 December 1990,* Air Accident Report 1/91, Air Accidents Investigation Branch, Department of Transport, HMSO, UK.
7. Zhang, J. (1996), *A representational analysis of relational information displays,* International Journal of Human-Computer Studies, 45.
8. Hill, J. C. & Wright, P. C. (1997), *From text to petri nets: the difficulties of describing accident scenarios formally,* in Harrison, M. D. & Torres, J. C. (eds.), Design, Specification and Verification of Interactive Systems'97, Springer-Verlag, New York.

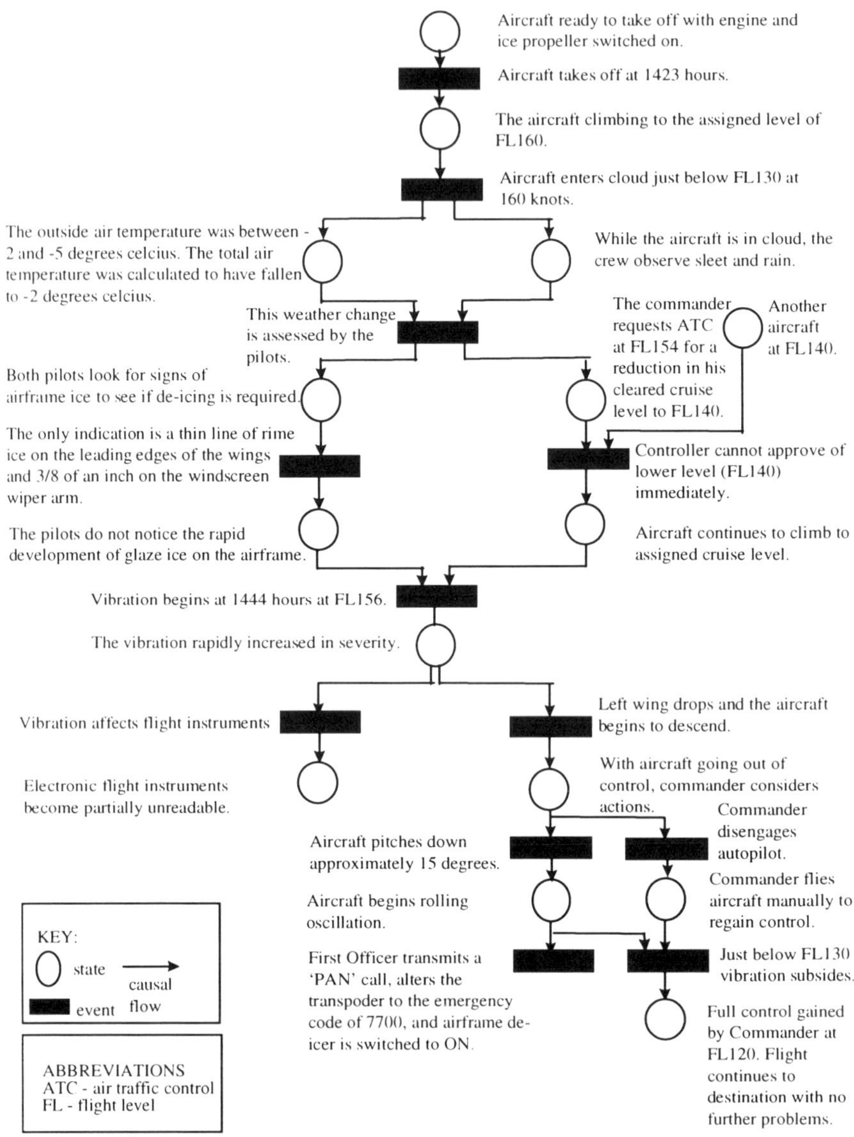

Appendix A: Petri Net of the Cowly Incident [5]

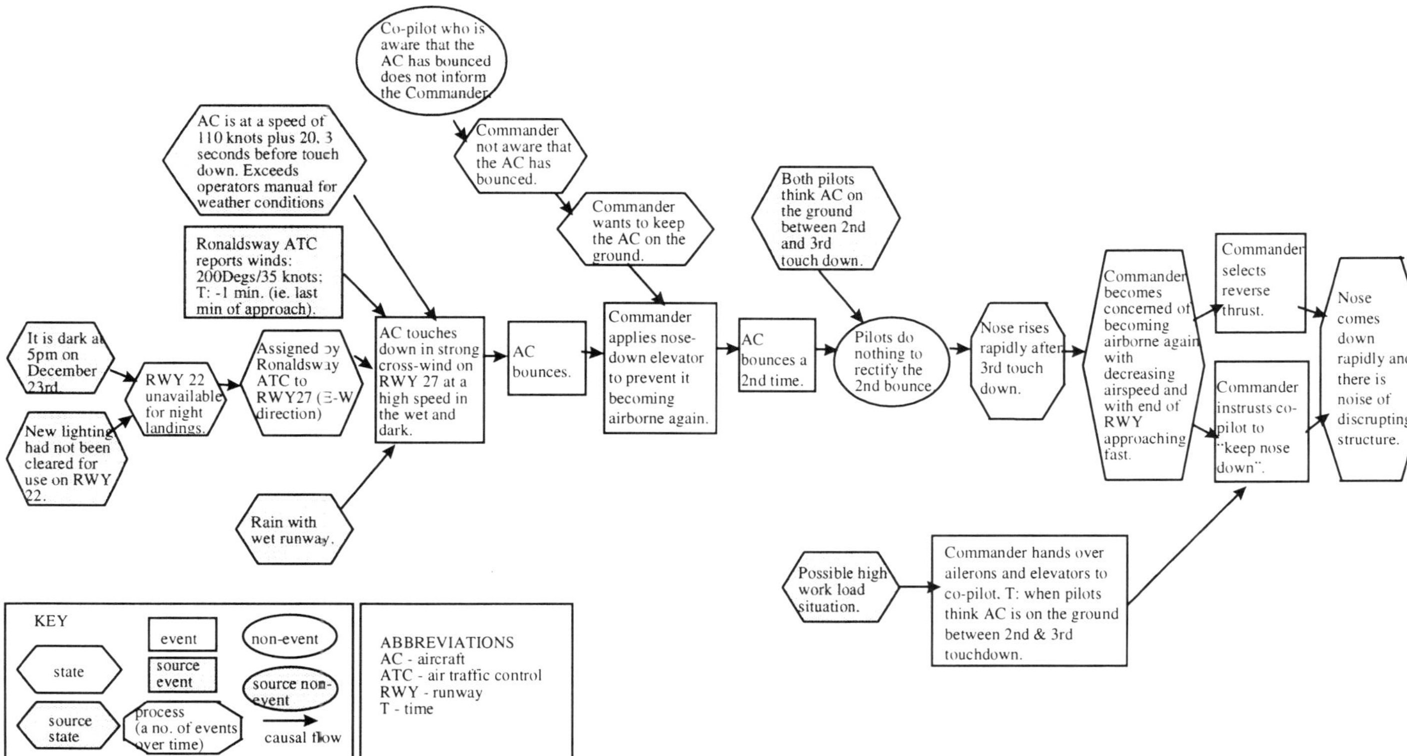

Appendix B: Why-Because Graph of the Ronaldsway Accident [6]

Automated Interpretation of Visual Representations: Extracting Textual Information from WWW Images*

A. Antonacopoulos[1] and F. Delporte[2]
[1]Dept. of Computer Science, University of Liverpool, Liverpool, UK
[2]Dépt. de Mathématiques Appliquées, Ecole Polytechnique, Paris, France

Abstract

There is a widening gap between the *creation* of visual content and its analysis and interpretation by machine, an increasingly essential requirement for correct indexing and filtering. In the case of the WWW, for instance, although there are efficient methods to process the encoded (e.g. ASCII) text, there are no such methods for the (significant) visual content. This paper focuses on the methods developed by the authors to address the problem of extracting the characters from WWW images containing text.

1 Introduction

The role of visual representation is significant in conveying information. Advances in technology in the last few years have made possible the widespread creation and dissemination of visual content. However, there is a very wide gap between the *creation* of visual content and its analysis and interpretation by machine. This automated analysis and understanding is an increasingly essential requirement for coping with the plethora of visual information on offer.

A familiar example is the WWW. The relatively recent success of the WWW has resulted in visual information being commonplace, embedded in electronic documents and disseminated on a large scale. Furthermore, the phenomenal growth of the WWW has seen a very rapid increase in the volume of electronic documents. Still images, video and graphics are frequently part of these electronic documents. As the volume of information on the WWW is increasingly becoming impossible for humans to navigate through and identify useful information, more sophisticated automated search and filtering techniques are required.

Information retrieval techniques have matured and are able to intelligently distil the essence of encoded (e.g., ASCII) text. However, methods to extract useful information from the visual data with similar efficiency are not available. This is a significant problem for two main reasons. First, important information contained in the images, which could characterise the content of a WWW page far better than the ASCII text alone, is currently being ignored by search engines. Secondly, as HTML lacks certain more advanced formatting and layout capabilities (e.g. the

* The project is generously supported by Hewlett-Packard (equipment grant).

ability to draw certain fonts, diagrams, special symbols, equations, etc.), an increasingly large number of images have to be embedded in a WWW page to achieve the desired effects.

Artistically presented text on the WWW, usually in image form, is a case in point. Although the human reader is able to extract this information, no automated analysis can be performed on such text at present. It should be noted that an easily verifiable fact is that the provision of alternative text (i.e., using the ALT tag) for textual WWW images is in most cases wrong, incomplete or non-existent.

In a recent survey [1] it was reported that between 2% and 45% of text in WWW pages is in graphic form. Furthermore, on average 18% of text in graphic form does not appear elsewhere in the document. Having these facts in mind, the current inability of machines to "read" the text presented in image form poses the following problems. First, search engines are not able to analyse the whole content of WWW pages and therefore may not be able to index them accurately. The fact that titles and headings (most important fields for indexing) are regularly created in graphic form intensifies the problem.

Secondly, users who do not see images (visually impaired people and users who have opted to ignore images in order to improve transfer speed) miss potentially vital information. In many cases it is not possible to read and understand the full message, due to important text being encoded only in graphic form.

The trend of representing textual information in graphic form is rapidly increasing. More WWW sites are being developed professionally by graphic designers who place the main emphasis on visual effect. There is therefore a pressing need to develop new methods to analyse and interpret such textual information.

As an example of the confusing reality of the lack of suitable textual description the reader is referred to the WWW page of Figure 1. One can see that the text present in the page is far from representative of the true information content of the site. On the other hand, the same page with the images displayed (Figure 2) contains the full information. Clearly, the text in the images is very important.

This paper outlines the research carried out by the authors to extract characters from a variety of types of WWW images. The emphasis is on providing the text for indexing (for search engines or for personal use) and for validation (check whether the alternative text is valid). A brief study of the characteristics of the problem is presented in Section 2. The techniques developed so far are outlined in Section 3, each in a separate subsection. The paper concludes with the presentation of experimental results and a discussion of the issues arising from the research.

2 Problem Characteristics

The task of identifying the characters in WWW images can, at first, appear to have similarities with traditional optical character recognition (OCR) techniques. However, the nature of the WWW images is quite different, making in most cases the application of OCR impossible.

First, an advantageous difference is that images of characters on the WWW are created directly by software. This means that there are no digitisation artefacts (e.g., skew and noise), a common problem in scanned printed documents.

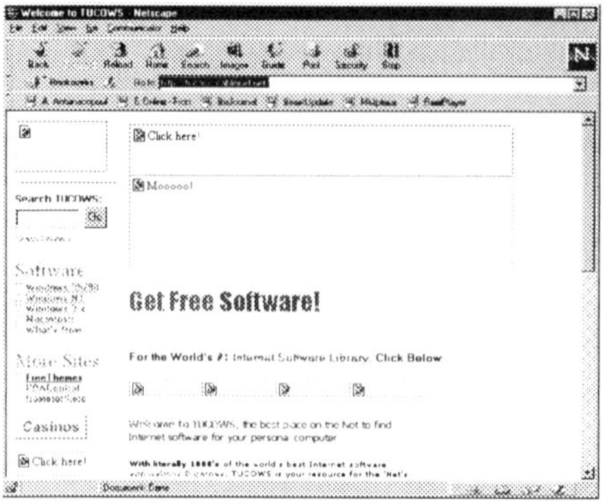

Figure 1. A WWW page without the images.

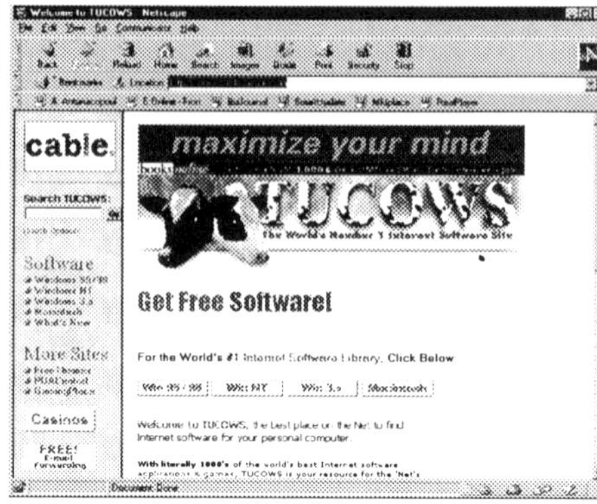

Figure 2. The WWW page of Figure 1 with the images.

Secondly, however, major difficulties arise due to the fact that in WWW images:

a) text can be present in different colours/textures and placed on complex backgrounds (in contrast, in the vast majority of cases, OCR works on a binary image),
b) the resolution is about 75 dpi which is of very low quality compared to the minimum of 300 dpi required by OCR methods,
c) most characters are of very small size (5 – 7 pt) compared with the characters present in traditional documents (usually at least 9 – 10 pt),
d) there could be artefacts resulting from the colour quantization process used in the authoring software, and
e) there are serious artefacts resulting from the lossy compression (e.g., JPEG) of the WWW images.

The above characteristics indicate the large degree of difficulty in the character extraction task. Previous methods [1–2] concentrate on the identification of single-coloured text, ignore very small text, and perform a global analysis of the colour information. Furthermore, the typical methods for the analysis of texture [3] can be computationally too expensive for practical application.

3 Method

The proposed method aims to improve on past approaches by avoiding the use of traditional texture analysis methods and by extending the capability to handle more difficult cases, such as gradient background and non-uniform text colour.

The main steps are described in the following subsections.

3.1 Bit Dropping

The images found on the WWW are mostly encoded in GIF (256 colours, 8 bits per pixel) or more increasingly in JPEG (millions of colours, 24 bits per pixel) format. To enable the efficient analysis of the image, the first step in the processing is to reduce the amount of colours that a pixel can have (JPEG images only). The reduction in the number of colours is achieved by dropping the five least-significant bits for each of the three 8-bit channels (red, green and blue) associated with every pixel. The remaining 9 bits allow the description of 512 colours. Experimental observation has shown that this number of colours is adequate for the purpose of colour distinction while also preserving a reasonable degree of quality.

3.2 Colour Clustering

In order to identify the differently coloured parts of the image, the colours present in the image have to be grouped in clusters according to their similarity. This is the most critical step as there can be a variety of similarly looking but different colours and various effects, such as gradient fill, may be present. The clustering of colours is achieved using one of two methods.

In the first method, after bit dropping, the histogram of the available colours is computed. The colours are then ordered according to their prominence in the image. The most dominant colour is taken as the centre of the first cluster. The distance between each of the remaining colours and this centre is computed and, if it shorter than a fixed threshold, the colour is assigned to the cluster. The most important of the remaining (unassigned) colours is then taken as the centre of a new cluster and process continues until all colours have been assigned to a cluster.

The choice of the threshold is important. However, although using the threshold does not guarantee that each cluster will fit within it, in cases of simpler graphics (limited number of distinct colours) this method is fast and the results are adequate.

The second method is applied to more complex situations such as that of Figure 3. This refined clustering algorithm is based on the Euclidean minimum-spanning-tree technique, for which more information can be found in [4]. A graph is considered in which nodes represent colours in the reduced-colour image and the value of each of the edges represents the distance between two colours. A threshold is computed based on the values of the graph edges. Experimental observations have indicated that the average distance produces reasonably good results. Given the threshold, the next step involves the removal of all graph edges with value below it. The result is a number of disconnected graphs, each of which represents colours that are close to each other. The complexity of this algorithm is $O(N^2)$, where N is the number of colours resulting after bit dropping.

3.3 Connected Components Analysis

Having identified the main colours (belonging to each of the clusters), regions whose pixel colours belong in the same cluster are extracted. A fast one-pass labelling technique (similar in principle to [5]) is used to identify connected components (regions of connected pixels with colours in the same cluster).

It should be noted that, for characters and/or background printed in gradient colour a different component extraction method is required. In such cases, it is important to identify and use the contour of components. The contours of image regions that form closed shapes are identified and by examining the topological relationships between regions (e.g., inclusion of a region in another) potential character components are extracted.

Character candidates are identified next, by analysing the extracted connected components. The following features are used to determine whether a given connected component could be a character or not.

a) The total area covered by a connected component. This feature is used to filter out noise (components having area less than a threshold).
b) Spatial extent of component (i.e., width, height).
c) Aspect ratio (i.e., width/height).
d) Number of strokes crossed by each image scanline. For instance, each letter should have up to 4 strokes on a scanline (case of letter 'M').

The above rules perform an initial selection of possible characters among all connected components. The possible character components are further examined to form words. To do so, the similarity and proximity between adjacent characters is considered. The similarity and proximity characteristics are expressed using the following features:

a) The colour of components must belong in the same cluster.
b) The components must share the same baseline (allowing for descenders).
c) The aspect ratio of components should be similar.
d) Components must be close to each other.

Special rules apply to ensure that the composite components corresponding to the 'i' and 'j' characters are correctly identified (the dot is not discarded).

The connected components believed to represent characters can then be passed to a commercial OCR package in a suitable form (i.e., black text on white background) to obtain the corresponding character encoding.

4 Results and Discussion

Initial results indicate the effectiveness of the methods proposed in this paper. The method can successfully extract coloured characters from backgrounds of distinctly different colour. Both the character and the background colours may be non-uniform (e.g., gradient, or different colours with similar hue). Figures 3 to 6 illustrate the results of the method. Figure 3 shows the original image containing an outer background (off-white), a more complex inner background (various shades of orange), and text in the foreground (varying shades of dark blue). The identified outer background is shown in Figure 4 (darker region). Figure 5 (darker region) shows the inner background as identified by the method. Finally, the identified text is shown (in white) in Figure 6.

An important issue that affects the performance of the method is the accurate selection of a threshold for the clustering of colours. This is a difficult task to perform optimally in the first attempt for a large number of different situations. The method currently uses experimentally determined values. Given the wide variety of graphics and colour combinations present, it would be useful to process the image using a number of independent processes in parallel with different thresholds. The results can be evaluated at the end and possibly fused to achieve higher accuracy in difficult situations. A similar approach can be taken in the

Figure 3: Original image.

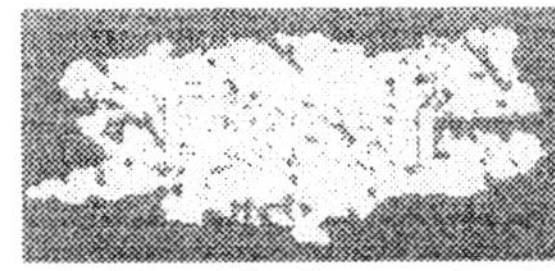

Figure 4: Identified outer background.

Figure 5: Identified inner background.

Figure 6: Identified text (in white).

absence of knowledge about the texture of characters. If only simple distinct colours are present, less complex and faster algorithms can be used. However, if textured characters and backgrounds are used, more complex algorithms are required. Therefore, a number of independent processes can be launched and the best results selected.

Further work, in addition to the combination of differently parameterised processes, will concentrate on the analysis and description of texture to identify characters and backgrounds in complex situations. Simpler textures (i.e., parametrically representable) as well as more complex ones will be targeted.

Finally, the recognition of the extracted characters is currently deferred to a commercial OCR package by presenting the extracted characters in binary (black and white) form. It will be advantageous in some cases (as also pointed out in [6]) to be able to use the existing colour information to recognise characters, especially in the presence of the artefacts mentioned in Section 2. Further work will be carried out in this direction to devise efficient methods to achieve this task.

References

[1] Zhou J, Lopresti D. Extracting Text from WWW Images. In: Proc 4th Int Conf on Document Analysis and Recognition, Ulm, Germany, August, 1997

[2] Köpen M, Lohmann L, Nickolay B. An Image Consulting Framework for Document Image Analysis of Internet Graphics. In: Proc 4th Int Conf on Document Analysis and Recognition, Ulm, Germany, August, 1997

[3] Sonka M, Hlavac V, Boyle R. Image Processing, Analysis and Machine Vision. International Thomson Computer Press, 1993.

[4] Zahn CT. Graph Theoretical methods for Detecting and Describing Gestalt Clusters. IEEE Trans on Computers 1971; 20

[5] Antonacopoulos A. Page Segmentation Using the Description of the Background. Computer Vision and Image Understanding 1998; 70: 350–369

[6] Zhou J, Lopresti D. OCR for World Wide Web Images. In: Proc. IS&T/SPIE Int Symposium on Electronic Imaging, San Jose, CA, USA, 1997

THEME 2

The Visual Dimension of Science

R. Harré

A. Ione

R.F. Hendry

D.L. Cooper

J.H. Parish

D.S. Goodsell

V.N. Serov, O.V. Kilillova and M.G. Samsonova

Models and Type-hierarchies: Cognitive Foundations of Iconic Thinking

Rom Harré
Linacre College
Oxford

1 Introduction

1.1 Models and cognition

In the sciences there are two main devices that are used for iconic thinking, graphical representations and models. Though models can appear in different modes of expression, from pictures to bench-top gadgets, they are abstractions from, idealisations of and/or analogues of those `matters' which they represent, which we shall call their `subjects'. In thinking about some subject matter with the help of models we thinking about something other than the model, what it represents, stands for or in place of. Model-thinking is thus a species of Polanyi's proximal/distal principle, thinking of something through something else [1].

Traditionally the cognitive processes by which model thinking is carried on have been assumed to be those involved in reasoning by analogy, that is `thinking through' the model by balancing the import of similarities, differences and undetermined attributes of one thing as a model of another. Thus in thinking of the state in terms of the human body, one supposedly balances up the similarities and differences between the king and the head, the farmers and the stomach and so on, exploring the analogy by further investigating those aspects of the human body that are not registered in the original act of model making.

However, recently, drawing on work in Artificial Intelligence, a rather different mode of cognition has been suggested as the `grammar' of reasoning through models [2]. Rather than making analogy the basic relation between models and their subjects, the idea is to make models and their subjects subtypes of the same supertype. Type-hierarchies become the cognitive tools of thinking through models.

1.2 Models in Formal Contexts

Before looking in more detail into type-hierarchical thinking it will be useful to contrast the way models are used in science with the way models are defined in the formal sciences, such as mathematics and logic. M, some assemblage of elements and relations, is a model for a system of uninterpreted signs, S, if the sentences which result from interpreting S by means of M are all true of M. This makes modelling an internal relation between an assemblage of elements and relations and a discourse consisting of the interpreted sentences of S, each being nicely adjusted to the other. I do not wish to suggest that this procedure, which presumes that the formal calculus exists prior to the act of model building, is never resorted to in science. But it is rare. Choice of models, as we shall see, is constrained by ontological considerations. There is no place for these, except as *ad hoc* `add ons' in the formal procedure of model creation. If at least some models are to be a guide to reality, then ontological plausibility, being representations of possible states of affairs in the world, must be a consideration.

An iconic model stands for or in place of something else, that which is the subject of the model. Thus a scaled-downed prototype of an airliner can stand in place of the full scale object for testing in a wind tunnel. The Bohr planetary model of the atom was thought, at least for a while, to stand for or represent the structure of real atoms in real materials.

1.3 Kinds of `standing for'

What sort of `standings for' does cognitive psychology recognise? We seem to depend, in our uses of symbols, on three main kinds of representing.

1. ARBITRARY: the relation between a sign, it might be a word in the sense of a vocable, and an object or object-type. Thus `cow' in English is an arbitrary sign for an animal which is called `vaca' somewhere else, and `vache' in another place. Or `>' is used in some contexts to mean `greater than' and in others to mean `later than', and so on.

2. FORMAL: we find this kind of representing relation exemplified in Wittgenstein's famous `picture theory of meaning' in his *Tractatus Logico-Philosophicus* [3]. According to the well known but long since rejected account of how a sentence means something there is an isomorphism of structure between a sentence and the state of affairs it is used to describe. To understand a sentence is, in part, to recognise that structure. According to Wittgenstein, the elements of these structures are simple names. Each name is an object serving as a sign for an elementary object in the state of affairs described by (represented by) the sentence. Names are arbitrarily related to the elementary objects of which a material state of affairs is composed.

3. SUBSTANTIVE: there is a real resemblance between that which represents and that which is represented. Models are in just such a relation to that of which they are models. A map, an architectural drawing, a toy car and so on share certain properties with that which they represent, but differ in certain ways. The differences are partly a reflection of the practical role of the model. Maps, for example, must be smaller than the terrain they represent, and so on. To prescribe a journey one could mark a map, highlighting a certain track, using the map as a model of the terrain. This is an iconic presentation of `how to get there'. One

could describe each twist and turn, presenting journey discursively rather than iconically.

1.4 Modes of Iconicity

The current tendency is to highlight, in our discussions of the role and nature of models, those iconic representations that are visualisable [4]. This is part of the modern tendency to privilege the sense of sight over other sensory modalities, but also reflects the major technologies of experiment, such as microscopes and telescopes, giving visual access to previously unknown states of the world. But at other times, particularly the Renaissance, the other senses were fruitful sources of iconic models. For example, Kepler [5] used auditory models, drawn from the music of his time as representations of the structure of the solar system. The `sound' of each planet had a definite pitch, and these were related according to the principles of harmony. These principles were derived from the pentatonic scale, which was itself derived from the natural harmonics of plucked strings. Planetary motets are out of favour today, not because they gave hopeless results so much as because we have abandoned the neo-Platonic metaphysics and ontology that made them appropriate as representations of the structure of the world.

2 The Two most Important Roles that Models Play in the Sciences

To follow some of the patterns of iconic thinking in science I propose to outline two of the ways models are used in scientific practice. Both have pragmatic virtues, but, it will be suggested they have epistemic or knowledge engendering powers as well.

2.1 The Analytic Role

Models are often used to achieve abstractions and simplifications of complex set-ups, structures and processes, by highlighting structures analogous to those they exhibit. The model is applied to the material situation. In such a use a model serves to highlight a figure against a ground.

An example of an analytic model was the spring which animated Boyle's method of studying some aspects of the behaviour of gases [6]. Gas, in its natural state, is a highly inchoate and complex material stuff. But Hooke had been studying springs, both in compression and in tension, during which he discovered Hooke's Law. By creating a gas spring, in the famous U-tube experiment, Boyle was able to investigate `the spring of the air', the law for which bears his name. Here the idea of a comparison procedure seems the natural way to treat the cognitive processes involved. There are springs and there are gases and the apparatus is designed to enable a comparison between them. However to think of this as the fundamental cognitive process involved in Boyle's reasoning leaves much unexplained. In particular, there is an interesting question in linguistics as to whether we should call the use of the word `spring' in Boyle's own title of his research, a metaphor for some trapped air, or should we interpret it as a new use, in short read Boyle as putting forward a view of the model and the phenomena which amounts to assuming that there are two kinds of springs, metal springs and air springs?

At this point the value of thinking of Boyle's pattern of reasoning in terms of type-hierarchies begins to show. We might try to resolve the issue about the semantic status of the word `spring' by imagining a type-hierarchy in which <elastic stuffs> is the supertype, and the two main subtypes are <solid> and <gaseous>. <solid> has <metallic> and <non-metallic> as subtypes and the latter has <compression> and <tension> as yet more specific subtypes. The question of whether the Boyle's usage is literal or metaphorical seems to have been by-passed, since we can now see fairly clearly what the semantic structure could be.

What do we get by using models in this way? The complex and inchoate material world can be made to yield reasonably manageable *phenomena* from which, with a little sleight of hand, we can abstract the kind of data from which a formal law, such as `PV = K', can be induced.

There are also plenty of examples of this kind of model use in the social sciences. A famous analytical model frequently resorted to is the dramaturgical approach to small scale social interactions. Adopting this model as a tool of analysis of complex, and superficially baffling social episodes, such as departmental meetings in Universities, we envisage the goings on as if a play were being performed, with staging, scenery, roles, costumes, a director, an audience and so on [7].

2.2 The Explanatory Use

The other main way that models are used in the sciences is as representations or stand ins for that which cannot be observed even by sense-extending instruments. Of course the boundary that is implied in that account is historically contingent. X-rays made previously unobservable bones structures visible, in conditions under which it would have been impossible to observe them before. And so on. By using an analytical model phenomena have been made available to the people using them, phenomena which cry out for explanation. Usually the issue is causal: what brought about these phenomena? Models of the unknown that is unobservable, structures, entities, processes and properties that constitute the `hidden mechanisms' that cause the phenomena, in the relevant circumstances, are created.

But such models are not free creations. They are created under a constraint of internal consistency and plausibility. In practice these constraints are provided by the source from which the relevant model is constructed. A simple but exemplary case is Darwin's route to his theory of organic evolution [8]. On his travels with Captain Fitzroy in the Beagle he observed variations in species generation by generation. And he observed that species changed, that there were novel species, if we start to think in geological time. What closed the theoretical gap between natural variation and natural novelty? To construct a model of the unknown, that is unobservable mechanisms involved, he explicitly drew on the procedures that farmers and gardeners use to create new varieties, that is the differential selection of breeding stock. So we have another pattern, <domestic variation - domestic selection - domestic novelty (new varieties)>. Using this pattern as a guide or model source Darwin gives us the pattern <natural variation - natural selection - natural novelty (new species)>. This is laid out in the early chapters of the *Origin of Species*, while the working out of the differences between domestic and natural selection, particularly answering the question what is the selection agent or agents in the wild, occupies the rest of the book. In the introduction Darwin had argued against a rigid demarcation between species and varieties, leaving the key relation for his forthcoming selectionist model as that between the mechanisms by which selective breeding is brought about.

According to the traditional view the cognitive processes involved are analogical, and that in turn devolves into assessments and explorations of similarities, differences and indeterminacies, between the model, its source and its subject, in this case the unobservable processes by which natural selection is brought about. But let us look at the underlying cognitive processes of Darwin and his co-evolutionists in terms of type-hierarchies. The basis of the theory is the acceptance of what some have called `processes of negative causality' as the supertype. As a subtype we have domestic selection, in which the characteristics of the succeeding generation are achieved by eliminating the undesirable. The farmer does not create the new characters, but lets them survive. Darwin's innovation could be thought of as locating his theory as an additional subtype of negative causality. Now the similarities and differences that constitute the analogy between domestic and natural selection are consequences of the structure of the type-hierarchy and the location of the two relevant subtypes. And there might be many other subtypes and subsubtypes to be found or inserted into that same type-hierarchy, for example the history of steam engines, and so on.

3 Which Cognitive Scheme?

We now have two uses of models, and we have noted two main accounts of the modelling relation. There is that in which the cognitive process is assessing similarities and differences according to the structure of an analogy, and that in which the model and its subject and its source are thought of as subtypes of the same supertype. The principles of type-hierarchies are taxonomic, judging how instances fall under types. We can now step back and assess the viability of each of the main contenders for the cognitive psychology of model making and using.

3.1 The Analogy Account

M (a gas `spring') is a model of (for) its subject Su (a gas), if M and Su are analogous. Similarly an analogy relation is held to obtain between the model M and its source, So (a metal spring). According to the analogy account a model is related to its source and its subject by similarities (the positive analogy), differences (the negative analogy) and properties of model, subject and source which have not yet been firmly assigned to either similarities or differences (the neutral analogy), among the properties characteristic of entities of the types of M, Su and So. The strength of the analogies and the plausibility of the model will depend on the balance between the three sets of property relations in each of the analogies, to subject and to source, and the salience of the components of each to the explanatory job in hand. That can be looked on as the realising of certain natural kind constraints on what might be a plausible model, deriving from the natural kind of the model's source. The cognitive grounding of model thinking as analogical reasoning then is a matter of making comparisons. In many cases these are iconic, and of these many are based on real or imagined visualisations. The presentation of the intuitions captured by the modelling relations as a theory is produced by recording these relations discursively.

3.2 The Type-hierarchy Account

M is a model of (for) Su, its subject if the types of M and Su are subtypes of the same supertype. The type of the source, So, must also be a subtype of the same supertype. All three, M (natural selection), Su (the causes of the production of new species) and So (domestic selection), have properties in common because they share a supertype, (selective reproduction). Their differences are irrelevant and indeterminate. The salience of the groups of similar properties in M and Su is determined by the prior choice of supertype, which could be put down, in many cases, to choice of model source. The cognitive grounding of model thinking is classification, taxonomic reasoning, a matter of relations between species and genera, families, orders and so on. If there are analogies between model, subject and source they are secondary and inessential to the modelling relation. However, as we shall see, it is not obvious what sort of cognitions are involved in taxonomic reasoning. To that issue I will return.

3.3 Problems with the Analogy Account

Why are we inclined to choose the type-hierarchy account of thinking through models over the analogy account? There are serious difficulties in carrying through the analogy account in detail. The problems that beset the analogical, positive, negative and neutral comparison view are fairly obvious. Searle [9] and others have complained that analogical reasoning, depending as it does on balancing up similarities and differences, requires *ad hoc* decisions as to the salience of the properties chosen as those on which the role of the analogy in either of its scientific uses depends. Since anything is similar to and different from anything else in some way or another, without a way of determining the relative importance of this or that similarity or difference in properties, the whole notion of modelling becomes too weak to sustain such a central role as many have given to it in scientific thinking. Any analytical model could fit any situation to some extent, and any explanatory model could be similar in some way to the source from which it is drawn. Unless we can give an account of why one type of property should be more important in assessing similarities than another the process of modelling is arbitrary.

The second problem is rather more recondite, and appears only in specific scientific contexts. If an explanatory model is supposed to represent an unknown or unobservable something as its subject, that for which it stands, the second term in the explanatory analogy relation is not available for comparison, since *a fortiori* it is not able to be examined. That was why the model was created in the first place. And so the plausibility of the model as a representation of the unknown explanatory level, is determined only by its relation to its source, So, and not by any comparison between the characteristics of the model M and that of its subject, Su. Since Darwin could not compare his model, Natural Selection, with what was going on in the genesis of new species, the only check on its plausibility must come from whence it came, the source, Domestic Selection. But we already know that there is an analogy relation between M and So, since we drew M from So by analogy, according to the analogy theory of models.

One solution to this difficulty has been to distinguish between substantive similarities between model and subject, unknown when an explanatory model is first developed, and behavioural similarities and differences between phenomena the model is imagined to produce, and phenomena observed to have been produced by the activity of the model's unknown subject. This is all very well, and indeed provides good pragmatic reasons for choosing one model rather than another, but leaves the issue of the plausibility of the model as a representation undetermined. It is perfectly compatible with the neo-positivist views advocated by such `empiricists' as van Fraasen [10].

3.4 Resolutions of these Problems by the Adoption of the Type-hierarchy Account

Both the problems with the analogy account disappear if we adopt the type-hierarchy approach. The salience of any particular property in the model is predetermined by choice of supertype. Since the model is related to its subject taxonomically, the question of plausibility of a model as a representative of an unknown and unobserved source of activity is settled by their common relation to the same supertype. Even if nothing else is known about the subject, the unknown for which the model provides a *pro tempore* representation, it must be thought of in terms of a common ontology, that of the sciences of the day, realised in the supertype or types of the type-hierarchies in common use. For example, exchange particles in quantum field theory are all subtypes of a general photonic supertype, which settles the ontological question, `What sort of beings are these?' in advance of any further working out of the detail of exchange models of particle interactions. I conclude that it is better to think of reasoning with models as a form of taxonomic thinking rather than as the making of comparisons between the terms of an analogy. This needs spelling out in more detail, since we have still to settle the question of how taxonomic thinking takes place and by what means.

4 Type-hierarchies and Cognitive Science

Laying out the structure of reasoning with models in the form of a type-hierarchy of the kind used in the examples discussed so far, might leave one with the impression that it is these structures that are involved in real life scientific reasoning. But we shall see that this assumption must be mistaken. It could be defended for certain purposes as an abstraction, made for philosophical and expository purposes, just as grammar is an abstraction for various practical purposes of the norms of language use. Before modulating into the cognitive science mode however it will be desirable to explain typological reasoning in the abstract form invoked in the examples. Whatever else the more psychological account must preserve it must preserve concrete realisations of some of the abstract relations that structure any classificatory hierarchy.

4.1 `Inheritance' as the Basic Structure

The relation between subtypes and supertypes is created by a relation between the properties included in each. All subtypes under a common supertype inherit the properties of the supertype, and all subsubtypes under a common subtype inherit the properties of that subtype and therefore the properties of the relevant supertype. Thus if we classify cats as felines and tigers as felines, the cat-type and tiger-type will share all the properties that belong in the feline-type. And since felines are animals, the cat-type and tiger-type will include all the properties that are in the animal-type.

Formal presentations of this kind of relational structure, for instance in the binary structure of the Porphyry tree [11] can be achieved by analysing each type at each level into sets of necessary and sufficient conditions for membership and then comparing these sets. The necessary and sufficient conditions for being a cat must include those necessary and sufficient to be feline and those necessary and sufficient to be an animal. It is easy to see that this sort of cognitive work is well suited to a computational engine based on the Turing machine. Registers can be compared mechanically in just the way that would represent deciding whether the necessary and sufficient conditions for being a cat included those for being an animal. However we will have reason to query whether this kind of formal treatment of taxonomic thinking is much use as a guide to how people, including scientists, actually manage typologies and type-hierarchies. On the type-hierarchy view, thinking with models is thinking in terms of types and subtypes. How is this thinking carried on by real people in real life?

4.2 The Empirical Psychology of Typological Reasoning

The seminal studies in how people reason typologically are to be credited to E. Roche (for a discussion of prototypes, their strengths and limitations in typological thinking, see [12]). Since her work many other studies of everyday patterns of taxonomic reasoning have been made. However, while subsequent work has brought out all sorts of variants and refinements in our conception of how people do this cognitive work, the basic Roche thesis has been substantiated over and over again. I will describe the cognitive processes that seem to be involved using the original Roche terminology of `prototypes'. Other terms have been proposed and defended for describing the foundations of classificatory activities, but the essential idea of typological thinking as involving reflection on concrete images has been found to be substantiated very widely.

When people are asked such a question as `Is a donkey a mammal?' they do not generally report making an abstract comparison between two sets of necessary and sufficient conditions, the one for falling under the type `mammal' and the other for membership of the type `donkey', to determine whether one set is a proper subset of the other, and so to answer the question. Instead they report thinking of a prototype mammal, and for most people in the West this is probably a cow, and asking themselves how like a cow is a donkey. I have done experiments myself along these lines, for example asking `subjects' questions like `Is fettucini pasta?'. In answering such questions the majority of people in my samples refer to a prototype pasta, which is usually spaghetti, and compare, usually in quite a visual way, the one prototype with the other. One person has told me that when asked to think of pasta he thought, not of a prototype like spaghetti, but of stuff made of durum wheat flour and extruded through a mould. This too was a prototype, and not surprisingly he turned out to be an enthusiastic cook!

The cognitive process involved is highly iconic: does the candidate entity, structure, property, stuff, process and so on `appear' (and that often means `look') like the prototype that carries the typological force of the generic concept. In short people do not carry around abstract type-hierarchies, consisting of formal sets and subsets of necessary and sufficient conditions, expressed propositionally perhaps. They carry round complex and ever changing clusters of prototypes, with which they accomplish taxonomic tasks. There is a strong historical echo to be heard here, coming from the account of generalised reasoning proposed by Berkeley [13]. Criticising Locke's thesis that there were abstract ideas as actual mental contents used in typological thinking he claimed that reasoning about types was carried on by the use of particular images (ideas) which were used and understood in a certain way, that is to stand for types (universals). And this is more or less the same view that has re-emerged in the empirical studies of real typological reasoning in this century.

If model thinking is a species of thinking typologically, then the type-hierarchies with which one can express the `logic' of this mode of reasoning are abstract representations drawn up for expository purposes, say by philosophers of science, or botanical taxonomists in the Linnaean tradition. They are not representations of how people actually reason.

It is easy to be seduced into a serious mistake at this point. It might seem as if `behind' the play of prototypes there *must be* abstract type-hierarchies. Since such structures are very well suited to being expressed in GOFAI[1] machines, we can be led into thinking that because some much thinking is typological therefore the brain which is being used by someone to do such thinking must itself be a GOFAI machine. Of course the fact that it is convenient for a logician to display subtype-supertype relations in terms of sets of necessary and sufficient membership conditions does nothing to show that that is how people, including scientists using their models, actually reason.

4.3 Models as subtypes in type-hierarchies

We can now use these insights to give a general account of model building and model use, filling out the examples cited above. A model, its source and its subject are all subtypes of a common supertype. Thus, each inherits the properties of that supertype, and all types superior to it in the type-hierarchy. Only those supertypes which all three have in common are scientifically relevant properties.

The ontological constraints on model building, constraints that ensure a measure of plausibility to the model as a representation of some unknown because unobservable state of affairs, derive directly from the choice of supertype. Since there are indefinitely many possible type-hierarchies within which an entity can find a place the choice of type-hierarchy is provisional, and subject to success `in the market place'. Furthermore type-hierarchies have histories, and their internal structures are not fixed for all time. New subtypes are being added and others deleted, while supertypes are also, under the same kinds of pressures, continually undergoing minor and major revisions, particularly through abandonment of some and adoption of other prototypes.

It is also important to notice that the inheritance relation creates similarities between models, sources and subjects. It has nothing to tell us about differences. The fact that everything differs from everything else in some way or another is irrelevant to typological thinking. We can set aside the Searle-type objection to making analogical thinking basic as not relevant to typological thinking.

[1] `GOFAI', that is `good old-fashioned artificial intelligence', is the standpoint according to which thinking is computational and probably implemented, behind the scenes, by something like the formalism of Frege-Russell logic.

However the so-called ` neutral analogy', the range of attributes that a model prototype and a source or subject prototype might or might not share provides a further aspect of the dynamics of model thinking, in that empirical work on such indeterminacies can lead to a transformation of a type-hierarchy or a masking out of part of it as irrelevant to the standing of a model. The fact that a type-hierarchy of substances with `matter' as the common supertype includes solids, liquids and gases as subtypes, and only solids and gases are elastic, does not make the Boyle-Hooke exploitation of a type-hierarchy of elastic materials defective. That part of the `matter' type-hierarchy is masked in this pattern of reasoning. Once again we see the superiority of the prototype or Berkeleyian account of typological reasoning over the necessary and sufficient conditions or Linnaean form. It is hard to see how there could be a way of masking some necessary conditions and not others, that was other than arbitrary. But choice of prototypes is task related, and so readily defended in any particular research programme.

It should now be clear why, in general, the idea that model thinking is a form of cognition that is based on assessing similarities and differences, the alleged basis of analogical thinking became popular. But on this view analogies are secondary cognitive formations that appear once the primary formation, the type-hierarchy has been set up. And that has to be understood in terms of clusters of prototypes, concrete iconic mental and material phenomena, through which types are manifested. The final step in this discussion is taken when we see that the fact that it is prototypes and not the logician's abstractions from them that are the tools for model building, that shows how perfectly natural it is to make models on the laboratory bench, to display them on the screens of computers or to draw them as diagrams. Only if we think in prototype terms can the iconic character of model thinking fit in to a general cognitive theory of scientific reasoning and theory construction.

5 Experiments Understood as Models

The thrust of the argument so far can be expressed in another way. Hitherto philosophers have tried to understand the nature of scientific knowledge gathering and indeed of scientific knowledge in general as the product of that gathering in terms of a logico-linguistic account of theories. The presentation of a theory in discursive form is taken to be fundamental and, as in the logical notion of modelling, the attachment of iconic content, a secondary and perhaps not strictly necessary add on extra. Duhem [14] famously professed this point of view and many have followed. The view I am presenting, drawn from Aronson, Harré and Way [15] proposes a different order of priorities. If models and modelling are taken as the heart of the processes of scientific thinking, and projective or substantive symbols are basic, then the discursive presentation of a theory is the add on and optional extra, adopted for pragmatic purposes, such as presenting results of research in a journal article. Among the many reasons for adopting the iconic point of view is the fundamental role played by thought experiments in the development of physics. What are these but icons, sensorily expressed intuitions as to the character of some natural phenomenon? For example the first steps towards relativity were taken by Galileo in a famous thought experiment, in which he imagines a ship as a sort of model of the world. The portholes are closed, and in the cabin a scientist does all sorts of experiments involving force and motion. Galileo tells us that whatever may be the uniform motion of the ship with respect to the stationary ocean, the experiments will all come out the same. The laws of nature are covariant under the Galilean transformation, substituting V + U for V. This is the discursive presentation of the physical intuition that is carried by the image of the thought experiment using a ship as a model of the world.

But there is another context where the suggestion that models are prior to discourses helps to resolve all sort of problems, that is in our understanding of the nature of experiments and of experimental apparatus. This topic has hardly been broached in mainstream philosophy of science. It is mostly taken for granted that experiments are ways of arriving at propositions, in the Aristotelian I and O forms (`Some A is B' and `Some A is not B') which can be used to assess the value of general hypotheses in the Aristotelian A and E forms (`All A are B' and `No A are B'). Which of the I and O forms is the most important has attracted different answers. For inductivists it is the I and for fallabilists like Popper and Francis Bacon it is the O.

Yet experiments, when scrutinised without assuming the priority of the discursive mode of presentation of scientific thought, can come to seem very different. What if an experimental apparatus is a kind of model of processes that occur in Nature, but in forms and locations and epochs that make their direct study difficult if not impossible. In the Nineteenth century there was a good deal of family scientific entertainment. After dinner experiments would be set up to amuse the guests and enlighten the children. Electrical experiments were popular, and none more so than the discharge of electricity though an attenuated gas. One's own *aurora borealis* in the drawing room. Faraday, invited to dinner with one of his friends, watched such an evening demonstration, and of course, being the greatest experimentalist of all time, noticed the dark space near one of the electrodes, the banding of the glow and so on, and began his own laboratory studies of the phenomenon shortly of after. He recreated a model with the *aurora* as source, but more importantly a manageable model of electrical discharge in attenuated gases in general as subject.

Looked at in the light of our type-hierarchy view of models we can say that experimental apparatus is often what it is by virtue of exemplifying a subtype of a supertype, another of the subtypes of which is some natural phenomenon; just as cows are the domestic subtypes of the common supertype, bovine, of which aurocs (extinct European wild cattle) are among the feral subtypes. We can learn a good deal about aurocs by studying cows. Taking this stance to them, it seems that experiments are not primarily to test hypotheses but to produce phenomena to order [16]. Roughly if I can build the apparatus, reproduce the phenomena at will, then to that extent I understand them.

6 Measuring the Truth of Theories

Truth seems to be a concept that philosophers, at least in the Anglo-saxon tradition, have taken for granted to be appropriate to propositions, particularly as they are constitutive of fact-stating discourses, and particularly the genre of scientific discourses. Yet for all sorts of reasons the conditions for the proper application of the term, with its correlative, `false' have proved to be elusive. The correspondence theory of truth runs foul of the problem of making sense of how any such incommensurable types of beings, propositions and states of affairs should correspond to one another. Even more difficult to make philosophical sense of is the ordinary notion of degrees of truth. And this notion is inescapable in science.

We could cut this Gordian knot by shifting away from discourse to models that scientific discourses describe. Now we can say something like this: to the extent that an iconic model and its subject, some natural phenomenon, are subtypes of the same supertype the theoretical discourse about the model is true of the subject of that model. This move does not beg the question since the relationship between the theory and its model is not one of description, but prescription. We can best look on the laws exemplified by the model as the very rules or instructions we use to create it. Thus the molecular law `$pv = 1/3nmc^2$' specifies rather than describes the molecular model of gases.

The hardest problem to solve is that of the relative truth of theories about unobservable realms of the material world. But using the idea of the type-hierarchy we can follow Aronson [17] in developing a metric for measuring the degree of truth of a model as a representation of something in the world. (Of course the model is, in a sense, also in the world). When we compare models and their subjects we are comparing things with things, not propositions with states of affairs. If the things match then the prescription for the model is a good approximation to a true description of the subject o that model. Since both the subject and any models that purport to represent it are subtypes of the same supertype, it is easy to develop a formal measure of verisimilitude. It is simply the relative number of nodes or branching points in the type-hierarchy currently being employed to manage this part of our knowledge. It does not follow that we have to hand a method of assessing the measure, but, as Aronson has stressed, we have shown that we can give a satisfactory definition of the concept.

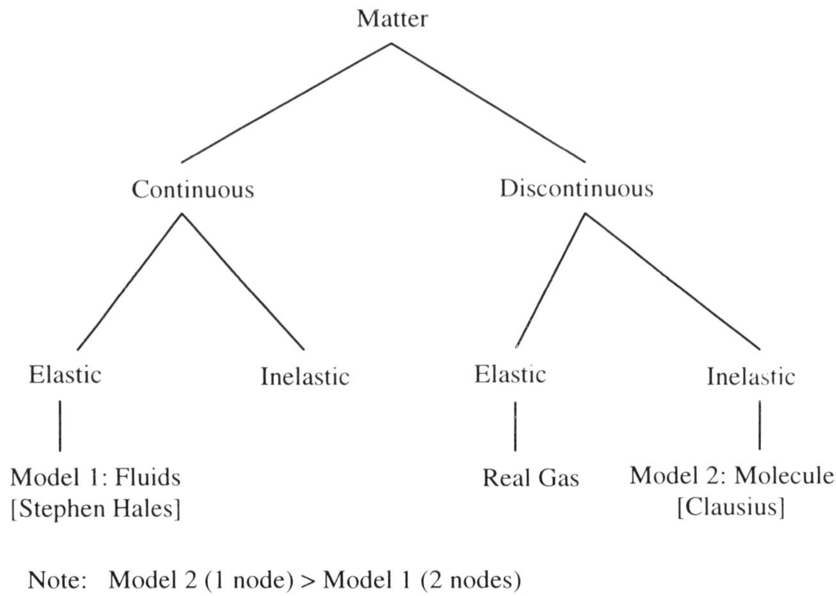

Figure 1 - A Metric for Model Verisimilitude: the Nature of Gases

7 Summary

In the use of models we find a scientific practice that is fruitful in two dimensions. Models, `laid alongside' complex and obscure phenomena, processes, entities and so on can be used to highlight and abstract aspects of their subjects difficult to observe without their aid. But models can also stand in for or represent unknown processes etc. which can be observed only in their effects. What sort of thinking is thinking through models?

Traditionally models have been taken to be based on analogy relations to both their subjects and their sources. It turns out that deeper examination of this account shows it to be seriously defective at just those points at which it should be at its best, namely in reducing the indeterminacy of abstract theorising. Model thinking is iconic thinking [4].

However, there is another way of accounting for the power of models as devices for scientific thinking, namely as subtypes of type-hierarchies within which their sources and subjects also have places as subtypes. Though there are great advantages in this approach it is still somewhat abstract and unrealistic. People, be they scientists or lay folk, do not think by assessing the formal relations between two sets of necessary and sufficient conditions for class membership. Research has shown that concrete prototypes serve the necessary cognitive role. They too are models, in a sense.

References

1 Polanyi, M. Personal Knowledge 1962. London: Routledge and Kegan Paul

2 Way, E. C. Knowledge Representation and Metaphor 1991. Dordrecht: Kluwer.

3 Wittgenstein, L. Tractatus Logico-Philosophicus 1922. London: Routledge and Kegan Paul.

4 Miller, A. Imagery in Scientific Thought 1984. Boston: Birkhauser.

5 Kepler, J. Harmonices Mundi 1619. Leinz: Gottfreid Tampach.

6 Boyle, R. New Experiments, Physico-mechanicall, touching the Spring of the Air 1660. London: Davis.

7 Goffman, E. The Presentation of Self in Everyday Life 1969. London: Allen Lane.

8 Darwin, C. The Origin of Species 1859. London: Murray.

9 Searle, J. `On determinables and resemblances' Aristotelian Society, Supplementary Volume 1959, **33** 141 - 158.

10 van Fraasen, B. The Scientific Image 1980.Oxford: Oxford University Press.

11 Sowa, J. F. `Semantic networks'. In E. Shapiro (ed) Encyclopedia of Artificial Intelligence 1987. New York: John Wiley.

12 Medin, D. L. Concepts and conceptual structure. American Psychologist 1988. 44 1469 - 81.

13 Berkeley, G.A. Treatise Concerning the Principles of Human Knowledge 1710. London.

14 Duhem, P. The Aim and Structure of Physical Theory 1914 and 1954. Princeton, N.J.: Princeton University Press.

15 Aronson, J. L., Harré, R. and Way, E. C. Realism Rescued 1994. London: Duckworth.

16 Gooding, D. Experiments and the Making of Meaning 1990. Dordrecht: Kluwer.

17 Aronson, J. L. Testing for convergent realism. In A. Fine and J. Leplin (eds) Proceedings of the 1988 Biennial Meeting of the Philosophy of Science Association 1988. I, 188 - 193.

Defining Visual Representation as a Creative and Interactive Modality

Amy Ione
Berkeley, California

Abstract

This paper explores visual representations as a creative and interactive modality. Non-optical technologies and artistic representations are analyzed in the context of scientific communication, artistic creativity, and cognitive science research.

1 Introduction

Images are everywhere today and when we look at them closely it quickly becomes clear that the technological innovations of the twentieth century have allowed us to see formerly unavailable information. One compelling aspect of this, and my primary area of concern in this paper, is that while artists have pierced through surfaces and created dynamic pictures of the brain working, scientific imaging technologies have generated images that have revolutionized our understanding of our minds. This paper discusses these new ways of 'seeing' the world and ourselves, defining visual representation as a creative and interactive modality.

2 Ways of Seeing Images

People often define images in terms of iconography, meaning the images offer symbolic or descriptive illustrations of a subject. This kind of definition mitigates the element of communication that is a part of image-making and a part of the relationship we establish with an image when we look at it. The film maker Sergei Eisenstein clearly described this interactive form of creativity when he wrote:

> In fact, every spectator, in correspondence with his individuality, in his own way and out of his own experience . . . creates an image in accordance with the representational guidance suggested by the author leading him to understanding and experience of the author's theme. This is the same image that was planned and created by the author, but this image is at the same time created by the spectator himself. [1, p. 33; 2, p. 261]

Let me propose that even adding this interactive element to our perception of an image still fails to adequately address how images have enlarged our body of knowledge, our sense of who we are, and have also expanded our visual range. Non-optical images, as is shown below, illustrate how this expansion is possible. Thus these images offer excellent examples of creativity as an interactive modality, as well as good examples of how images have helped create our consciousness and our cultural environment.

More specifically, and turning to scientific discovery first, in 1873 Sir John Eric Ericksen, a British surgeon appointed Surgeon-Extraordinary to Queen Victoria, said "The abdomen, the chest, and the brain will forever be shut from the intrusion of the wise and humane surgeon." These words clearly did not leave room for the discovery of non-optical imaging in 1895, two years later. This discovery made it possible to see inside our bodies without cutting and before physical disintegration of the flesh.

The non-optical revolution per se could be said to have begun when Wilhelm Conrad Roentgen discovered that radiation can penetrate solid, opaque substances like human skin and that it has the same effect on a photographic plate as light. Roentgen called this discovery the X-ray, having no idea what it was. Today, the event is generally characterized by the skeletal image of a ringed X-ray hand.

This image was not trivial. The exceptional element relevant to my thesis that images offer an interactive modality that can expand human understanding beyond known parameters becomes evident when we look at the electromagnetic spectrum. The electromagnetic spectrum has a visible portion that includes wavelengths ranging from red light (at about 700 nanometers) down to violet light (at about 400 nanometers). This is the section where we find all of the colors of the rainbow. The self-propagating waves that comprise the entire spectrum include a variety of electric and magnetic fields that like visible rays travel at the speed of light. These invisible waves, however, have different frequencies from visible light and it is frequency that determines whether we characterize waves as radio, microwave, infrared, visible light, ultraviolet, X-rays, or gamma rays.

The evidence that there are both visible and invisible waves explains why we cannot pierce through opaque surfaces like skin with our eyes or even with photography per se, but can do so with invisible radiation. We can also use invisible radiation to create maps, and since Roentgen's time, many non-optical inventions have been developed to help us map and explore areas formerly unknown to the human mind. The key points here are, first, the discovery of the X-ray is what made the investigation into domains invisible to the eye possible. Second, although others had noticed the anomaly, it was because Roentgen investigated it that he became the first person to realize how the use of invisible radiation can produce and record a visible image of an invisible object property [3]. In sum, his inquiry offers an example of how mind and phenomena can come together to define a scientific problem that formerly did not exist.

3 Images and Creative Interaction

The investigation of the image, however, ultimately highlights areas that stretch far beyond the initial X-ray image. Thus these areas are critical in considering visual representation and interpretation, especially from a cognitive perspective. For example, one intriguing element we find here is that Roentgen's discovery was a non-algorithmic insight. This means that the insight that opened a new domain scientifically, medically, culturally, and philosophically cannot be classified as something that followed a logical or strictly empirical pattern. On the one hand, this was because the image revealed something that was not directly perceived — since both the radiation and the human bones are invisible to the unaided human eye. On the other hand, the image was not directly received. In sum, the event was not an insight alone or a revelation Roentgen intuited indirectly since the interaction between the mind and the physical world led to the insight. This means it is essentially incomplete to characterize the event as something that was analytically, intuitively, or psychically conceptualized. Moreover, it cannot be emphasized enough that there was no mathematical correlate initially. All people, including Roentgen, first grasped what they saw with their eyes and then conceptualized that other possibilities existed. This led some to then develop the dependable and mathematically-driven technologies that are now capable of making the skin as well as other physical and opaque surfaces transparent.

These technologies have now become so familiar that people overlook the that the initial discovery was needed to suggest this direction as an option. The extent to which these technologies altered the way people experience the world has also been overlooked. For example, while scientists like Roentgen were enthusiastic about creating extensions that would allow them to open additional doors to formerly unavailable information, some lay-people like Frau Roentgen had little enthusiasm for the new information being revealed. After confronting her skeletal hand in her husband's laboratory Frau Roentgen was convinced it was an omen of death and never returned. As events like the nuclear disaster at Chernobyl show, Frau Roentgen sensed there was a negative side to radiation and this side has slowly revealed its face to human society.

There were also people, like the Russian painter Pavel Tchelitchew, who saw the X-rays as a door to another dimension. He creativity recorded his perception and because he documented it we can now see it in his painting Hide-and-Seek (see Figure 1), a work produced in 1942. Tchelitchew's painting quickly authenticates itself as a twentieth century artifact, for in looking at the image closely one sees it displays a chorus of X-ray images of children's see-through heads arranged in puzzle-like patterns as parts of a growing tree. The veins and bones of the children merge with the roots and bark of the tree in a now-you-see-it, now-you-don't puzzle pattern of arteries and landscape [4]. The piece also conveys the interior of the bodies and includes an accurate physiological rendering of skeletal structure as well as the kinds of internal elements that became transparent only with the imaging technologies that developed as a result of the X-ray image and knowledge of radiation waves [4].

It should be noted that what is not included in the image also identifies Hide-and-Seek as a piece of the twentieth century. For example, history shows the idea of rays piercing the body was not in and of itself totally novel to the twentieth century. To the contrary, ideas of rays had been around for centuries. Even as far back as the thirteenth century the philosopher Roger Bacon had noted that no substrate is so dense that it can prevent rays from passing through and Bacon pointed out that the walls of a vessel of gold or brass show this when they heat up [4]. There was also the belief that spiritual rays emanated from the body to the outside world, and these were often portrayed in paintings by halos around the heads of saints and religious figures.

Figure 1

TCHELITCHEW, Pavel. *Hide-and Seek {Cache-cache]*. 1940-42

Oil on canvas, 6' 6 ½" x 7' ¾" (199.3 x 215.3 com)

The Museum of Modern Art, New York. Mrs Simon Guggenheim Fund.

Yet, and this is a key point, these earlier ideas were not actually the ideas validated by imaging science. Visual representations of earlier artists and philosophers did not suggest that any rays, whether passing from the inside or emerging from the soul out through the skin, could reveal everything beneath the skin to a human eye — the way a non-optical image does. There was also no suggestion that the images could leave an impression on something else, like a shadow on a wall or a permanent imprint on glass or film. Yet radiation rays were soon tamed to do so.

This is not to say that art and artistic representations did not continue to inform the human dialogue. For example, Gerald D. Fischbach, a Professor of Neurobiology, described Hide-and-Seek as a painting that

> [C]aptures the interplay between the mind and environment that influences the brain's development as well as its architecture. Hidden forms are embedded figures, a delicate test of mental function. Roots, branches and vines suggest neuronal arborization and the ability of such structures to change. [5, p. 49]

On reviewing Fishbach's description in relation to the discovery of non-optical imaging one is inclined to ask why cognitive scientists have mainly devoted their efforts to the study of laboratory problems. Short laboratory exercises cannot address or replicate the complexity of a work of art or the kind of creative activity that Roentgen's discovery reveals.* In Roentgen's case, as explained earlier, problem-solving could not even begin until he actually recognized that there was a problem that needed to be solved. Until the image was visually present to Roentgen, there was no 'problem' to solve. It was simply understood that we cannot see through our

---

* Gestalt images are often used to represent brain-mapping. Like the brain-mapping itself, however, a gestalt image fails to represent the kind of discovery that raises the two-sided whole to another level. Emergence is the term generally used to explain this kind of conceptual development and how this cognitive development is a part of parallel processing. While the concept emergence seems to infer development, actually explaining what it is has proved to be difficult. Of more concern is that the growing acceptance of the idea of emergence has led people to use the term as if it stands for something 'real,' despite the fact that it is only a theoretical idea that resolves something we know happens that essentially continues to be a mystery. The critical point here is that, on the one hand, the idea does fill the definitional vacuum. On the other hand, the growing acceptance of the idea brings to mind that when Newton introduced the idea of gravity he specifically stated that *he did not know* what gravity is. He was using the word to explain something evident in his mathematical equations. As history shows, eventually people became so accustomed to the idea that gravity was a 'real' force that no one looked further, at least not until Einstein's relativity challenged some basic assumptions within the Newtonian system. Two books that attempt to make sense of the problems evident in the idea of emergence are Alywin Scott's *Stairway to the mind: the controversial new science of consciousness* and John Holland's *Emergence: From Chaos to Order* [6; 7].

skin. This kind of unknown problem is the kind of creative experience that can not be tested for in a lab.

The larger point is that this kind of creative and interactive modality is hard to derive experimentally and often becomes mentally transparent to us once a new discovery is actively being incorporated into scientific work and our cultural experience.* For example, to continue to build on the case study the X-ray provides, once discovery of non-optical image formation made it possible to see beyond the visible as it had been previously defined, the technology was quickly combined with computers. This combination generated an avalanche of data-driven inventions, all instrumental in expanding how we know the physical, the invisible, who we are, and how our bodies function. Now when reviewing the assortment of simulations, photographs, and digital renderings that are used to describe our world, our bodies, and our ideas, it is difficult to categorize what is virtual, what is actually seen, and what is better described as a representation of something outside of our visual reach.

Perhaps it is this knowing that there is always information beyond our reach that has led some, like Semir Zeki, a Professor of Neurobiology and Co-head of the Wellcome Department of Cognitive Neurology at University College London, to ask if art offers an uncharted area. In a recent article called "Art and the Brain," Zeki correctly notes that while a great deal has been written about the visual brain, little has been written in relation to one of its major products, art.[8, p. 71]. Zeki then writes:

> I hold the somewhat unusual view that artists are neurologists, studying the brain with techniques that are unique to them and reaching interesting but unspecified conclusions about the organization of the brain. Or, rather, that they are exploiting the characteristics of the parallel processing-perceptual systems of the brain to create their works . . . [8, p. 77].

This intriguing statement is worth exploring in light of how cognitive neuroscience uses brain imaging methodology and how the imaging technology is providing a biological link to complex tasks such as visual attentional control, memory storage, language interpretation, and brain functions. The resulting maps illustrate human coritical processing with millimeter and millisecond resolution and

---

*Even if we use the Gestalt idea that the whole is more than (different from) the sum of the parts the Gestalt interpretations can only account for the horizontal mental exchange. Saying the patterning and relatedness between the parts and a whole is more than (different from) the sum of its parts is not represented. It is a conceptual idea. Thus the image does not explicitly convey how an emergent leap beyond all that is presently known among us comes to be a part of our knowledge base as a whole. In other words, we know the image and its parts differently *after* the cognitive leap that allowed us to see the ambiguous reading is possible. Moreover, each time this kind of cognitive leap occurs we are reminded that there is a clear and distinct difference between an 'old' way and a 'new' way of 'seeing.' The 'new' way of seeing was simply not possible within the 'old' framework. It must be emphasized that the history of creativity and discovery shows that *each* time we see anew, we are *once again* reminded that all conclusions are drafts subject to change.'

follow chemical processes in normals. Recent technological advances have also made it feasible to create pictures of our brains as we think, learn, read, and visualize. Images of these kinds of processes are generally formed over time by an orderly set of operations that include, for example, placing the parts of the images in their proper relationship and scanning the content for specific features [9]. As a result, and for the first time, scientists are able to render certain aspects of thought visible by recording the physical effects of brain activity. Overall, the images generate descriptions of mental processes, show active and dormant areas of the brain, and show that component operations can be precisely and visually specified. The excitement surrounding this new information attests to the undeniable ways in which visual representations have extended our understanding of brain functionality. The images do not, however, provide the kind of methodological reach that necessarily acknowledges images as a creative and interactive modality.

4 Areas for Future Investigation

The failure to see how the development of non-optical images added a new perspective is an area that has not yet been effectively been addressed in cognitive neuroscience research. Given this, I would like to propose that the relationship among the following four elements is of primary importance to a comprehensive understanding of cognitive involvement with visual representations. I would also like to propose that these four areas should be given more attention as a whole — especially if we are to forge a more comprehensive understanding of what images are and how new discoveries inform both science and culture.

First, as outlined earlier, the discovery of x-rays made it possible for researchers to see a domain not accounted for in earlier philosophical, religious, artistic, and scientific investigations. Thus it raises the question of whether it is possible to design an experiment that is in fact capable of mapping, cataloging, and characterizing visual and logical possibilities not yet imagined in any fashion. Given the scope of this question, I will only state here that research by myself [10-13] and others [14-16] shows the answer is no. In another context, the Nobel Prize winner Leon Lederman recently explained the problem many are pushing aside when he said: "There's always a place at the edge of our knowledge, when what's beyond is unimaginable, and that edge, of course, moves. . ." [17].

Second, and on the counter-side, the x-rays led to the discovery of the various data-driven non-optical technologies researchers now depend on to map and study the brain. This use of new technologies to map and monitor our minds indicates that once we have developed new means to access data and engage in intelligent problem-solving we can creatively extend how we know and use available information. This is not research into a new and unknown domain, but a form of discovery that consolidates information using comparative and correlative forms. It is creative to some degree but, again, not a way of addressing 'unexpected' discoveries so much as a way that extends ideas easily characterized as within the range of problems researchers are already actively pursuing.

Third, cognitive science literature and the literature on consciousness has tended to either ignore creativity or to assume that problem-solving and personal insight are the only viable options we can apply to creative developments. The limitations within this perception are readily apparent when we look at how creative work develops, be it in art, science, or elsewhere. This is an especially important point given that many in psychology, philosophy, the history of science, and art history — who do not adopt the cognitive science approach — have shown that the stress on universals favored by cognitive scientists cannot address the complexity of individuals, the nature of creative products, and the dynamics of a living and evolving creative process. [14; 16]. Moreover, as has been documented, even cognitive scientists who are known for their interest in creativity, like Newell and Simon [18-20], do not even have entries for creativity or even creative thinking in their indexes. Thus, despite the fact that they propose their scientific work in problem-solving is relevant to creative thinking, whatever their understanding of creativity is remains implicit to them, rather than expressed.

Finally, it is not just our experiments that must be looked at closely. We must also look at the way in which human minds and cultural ideas work in tandem, a point David Teplica, a Chicago based photographer and plastic surgeon, alludes to by incorporating radiographs into his 1989 "Birth of Man with Homage to Michelangelo."

> Teplica gives the impression that he has simply X-rayed Michelangelo's original image, a kind of stylistic allusion that acknowledges art of the past while taking it out of context to be used in a new way. [4, p. 283]

Michelangelo would never have been able to conceptualize why Teplica is using X-rays in his replication of God touching Adam, or even explain what the radiographs are. An even larger, by still related point, and one I have expanded on in previous work [10; 11; 21], is that implicit prejudice often engages our minds and these biases cannot be logically refuted since they are mentally invisible and impossible to physically model and study in a lab.

5 Conclusion

In summary, visual representations offer a means to consider how problem-finding, problem-solving, iconography, and image development differ and interpenetrate. As I have demonstrated, scientists are using some measure of artistry to evolve digital image formation, interpretation, and clarity. Artists, on the other hand, have used digital advancements as well as traditional artmaking techniques to personalize the domain scientific technologies has revealed. The sum total of this is that we have become a more visual culture, a culture that has shown visual representations are a creative and interactive modality.

References

1. Eisenstein, S. Film sense. Harcourt, Brace & World New York, 1947
2. Gruber, H. E., & Davis, S. N. In: R. J. Sternberg (ed.) Inching our way up Mount Olympus: the evolving-systems approach to creative thinking. The nature of creativity: contemporary psychological perspectives, Cambridge University Press Cambridge,1988, 243-270
3. Beck, R. N. In: T. Umiker-Sebeok (ed.) The Future of Imaging Science. Advances in Visual Semiotics -- The Semiotic Web Walter de Gruyter, Mouton Publications, Berline, 1994, 609-642
4. Kevles, B. H. Naked to the bone: medical imaging in the twentieth century. Rutgers University Press New Brunswick, New Jersey, 1997
5. Fischbach, G. D. Mind and brain. Scientific American, September, 1992; 2673: 48-57
6. Holland, J. H. Emergence: from chaos to order. Addison-Wesley: A Helix Book Reading, Mass, 1998
7. Scott, A. Stairway to the mind: the controversial new science of consciousness. Springer-Verlag New York, 1995
8. Zeki, S. Art and the brain, Daedalus, 1998; 1272: 71-104
9. Posner, M. I., & Raichle, M. E. Images of mind. Scientific American Library New York, 1997.
10. Ione, A. Information: Description, Cognition, Invention, Informatica, 1997; 213: 421-434
11. Ione, A. An investigation into emergence consciousness, Performance Practice, 1998; 3:16-18
12. Ione, A. "Science: method, myth, metaphor?" Alexandria, 5:1999, in press
13. Ione, A. Multiple Discovery, Encyclopedia of Creativity Academic Press San Diego, 1999, in press.
14. Gardner, H. Extraordinary minds. Basic Books New York, 1997
15. Csikszentmihalyi, M. Creativity: flow and the psychology of discovery and invention. HarperCollins New York, 1996
16. Sternberg, R. J. (ed.). The nature of creativity: contemporary psychological perspectives. Cambridge University Press, Cambridge, 1988
17. Dreifus, C. Science is serious business to the 'Mel Brooks of physics'. New York Times, July 14, 1998
18. Simon, H. A. Models of my life. Basic Books New York, 1991
19. Newell, A., Simon, H. A. In: J. Haurgeland (ed.) Mind Design. Computer science as empirical inquiry: symbols and search. A Bradford Book, Cambridge and London, 1981, 35-66
20. Newell, A., Simon, H. A. Human problem solving. Prentice-Hall Englewood Cliffs, NJ, 1972.
21. Ione, A. Implicit cognition in scientific speculation and development. Paper presented at the first conference of the Association for the Scientific Study of Consciousness, Claremont Colleges and Claremont Graduate School, Claremont, California, June 14-16, 1997

Theories and Models: the Interactive View

Robin Findlay Hendry
Department of Philosophy, University of Durham,
Durham UK

Abstract

The semantic view of theories presents theories as families of models. I argue that while the semantic view has helped to make important insights into physical theorising, it tends to obscure the complex nature of theories, which may combine elements from different representational media. I explore this claim in the context of three short case studies.

1 Philosophical Views of Theories and Models

In the philosophy of science, model building has been the subject of much discussion, enjoying the status of 'primary phenomenon' of applied physical theorising. There is broad agreement that models are extralinguistic items that represent the real systems that constitute the subject matter of scientific theorising. However, there are competing philosophical accounts of how theories and models are related, and of how models represent systems and relationships in nature. Any such view must be able to provide a plausible account of how theories and models are used, primarily in explanation and prediction. In this first section I will critically examine one influential account of the structure of theories, the semantic view, according to which theories are analysed as families of models. My arguments in this section are indebted to a joint paper [1]. In Section 2, I will present some brief examples of historical and contemporary model construction from physics and chemistry, that, I hope, help to throw some light on the relationship between theories and models, and the nature of theoretical representation.

On the semantic conception of theories, to present a theory is to present a family of models. Given that, in the mathematical sciences at least, the primary presentation of a theory is via some set of equations, satisfaction of the relevant equations must be the criterion of family membership. Note that a 'model' is an extra-linguistic entity. Defenders of the semantic view have always stressed that the notions of model in science and in mathematical logic are close, but there are differences, even under the semantic view. In textbooks of mathematical logic, a model of a set of sentences of a (formal) language is an interpretation of the sentences under which they come out true. As van Fraassen ([2], p 366, note 4), notes, a 'model' in this sense is a partially linguistic entity, since it involves a structure, and a function onto that structure from elements of a particular formal language. So to free a theory from its particular formulations, the notion of a model that is at work in the semantic view must be that of the non-linguistic *structure* in which the sentences constituting a particular formulation of the theory at hand find an interpretation under which they are true. Now consider the set of structures that can be picked out as models of some particular formulation of a theory: it is that, according to the semantic view, on which an analysis of the theory must concentrate. The more fundamental relationship, on the semantic view, is that of class membership: the membership of a model in a particular class of models that, in the analysis of a particular theory, is picked out by examination of some formulation of the theory. A theory may well be associated with a particular linguistic formulation (that may take the form of a set of equations), but this should not be mistaken for the theory itself.

It is helpful at this point to distinguish strong and weak construals of the semantic view. On the weak construal, the claim is only that models should be 'occupying center stage' in the analysis of theories, as Giere ([3], p 79) has put it. On the strong construal, a theory is to be *identified* with its family of models. Two kinds of argument have been offered in support of the semantic view. The first is that the semantic view is closer to scientific practice than the received view, partly because it is relatively simple matter to identify a class of models from the presentation of a theory in a scientific paper or textbook, and partly because the semantic view allows for more perspicuous accounts of both the internal structure of theories, and the uses to which theories are put, such as prediction and explanation. This kind of argument, I would claim, tells primarily in favour of the weak semantic view, but does not establish that theories are to be identified with classes of models. The second major kind of argument, which I will call the 'multiple formulations' argument, has been offered explicitly by Suppe, but endorsement of it is hinted at by others. This argument, if successful, would support the strong semantic view. I will briefly review these two kinds of argument.

It must be admitted that the semantic view has indeed allowed for plausible and natural analyses of the internal structure of particular theories, of relations between theories and phenomena, and of approximation and idealisation in theories. Thus Giere has provided an elegant analysis of classical mechanics in terms of hierarchically arranged clusters of models at different levels of generality, picked out and ordered by Newton's laws of motion plus the various force-functions ([3], Chapter 3). Lloyd has done a similar service for evolutionary theory [4]. As for relations between theory and phenomena, Suppes neatly captured the relationship between theories and phenomena, and the revisability of 'empirical' laws, with the insight that the relationship is primarily one that holds between models: models of data on the one hand, and theoretical models on the other [5]. This insight has been developed by van Fraassen, who construes the claim that a particular theory is empirically adequate (that is, adequate to the phenomena) as the claim that a data model can be embedded in one of the theory's models, which is to say that the data model is isomorphic to what he calls the empirical substructure of one of the theory's models [6]. Another variant, due to Giere, is that a claim of adequacy for a theory is a claim that some class of real systems is similar in specified degrees and respects to some model of the theory ([3], pp 80-1). Now van Fraassen used this account of relations between theory and phenomena as the basis of an elegant analysis of the problematic distinction between what can and what cannot be observed in science, but it is clear that some considerable idealisation is involved in the account.

I have argued elsewhere [7] that two different notions of 'model' seem to be at work in van Fraassen's account of the relationship between theory and data. On the one hand there is the kind of model that is central to the semantic view: a structure that satisfies some set of equations. On the other hand, there is the kind of model that represents some particular real item, much as a model of the Eiffel Tower does. Both van Fraassen's and Giere's accounts of theoretical representation trade on the identification of the two different kinds of model: we apply a theory by selecting one of its models to represent some real system. This does not do justice to practice, however, for the scientist's model of a real system will often fail to satisfy the equations of the theories of which it is an application. Nomologically disuniform models, models that fall under no *one* set of theoretical laws, are common in quantum chemistry at least. And this is not atypical: Nancy Cartwright has long argued that physical theories (like quantum mechanics) typically supply models that represent *parts* of real systems, and that these may be embedded in representative models that belong to no particular theory [8]. A theoretical model may represent, but only in the context of a wider model, much as a line in a particular drawing may represent something—like a guitar string—only in the context of the drawing of the guitar as a whole (for an example see [7], and section 2.3, below). Furthermore, van Fraassen's neat picture neglects the role of idealisation and approximation in physical theorising, although French and Ladyman have addressed some of these issues within the 'partial structures' version of the semantic view [9].

The undoubted advantages of the semantic view tell primarily in favour of its weak version. But Suppe ([10], pp 204-5; [11], p 82) has claimed that theories are to be *identified with* (collections of) abstract, non-linguistic entities, arguing from the possibility of different linguistic formulations of a single theory. Suppose, says Suppe, that a theory formulated first in English is translated into French. If we would deny that a new theory had been offered in the French, we must identify the theory with something extralinguistic that has been presented in two languages. As more telling examples, he cites the equivalent formulations of the quantum theory offered by matrix and wave mechanics ([10], p 205) and of classical particle mechanics by its Lagrangian and Hamiltonian formulations ([11], p 82). In all cases, the argument goes, we must distinguish between a theory and its formulations: a theory should be *identified* with something extralinguistic, that is, with something which can formulated in different languages.

While van Fraassen ([2], p 188) and Giere ([3], p 84) have hinted at similar claims, on similar grounds, they each add important qualifications. For Giere, the central equations of a theory serve only to define its class of models: the equations themselves can do no representational work on their own. The relationship between theory and reality is given only by something linguistic, a 'theoretical hypothesis', that asserts a relationship of similarity between one of the theory's models and some class of real systems. But if the (linguistic) theoretical hypotheses are not part of the theory itself, there must be a distinction between the theory itself, and what it has to say about real systems. But what a theory is a theory of (its subject matter) is surely part of the theory itself: it was surely essential to Bohr's atomic theory of 1913 that it was a theory about the structure of atoms. It may well be possible (and even important) to distinguish between a theory's (mathematical) *structure* and what that theory has to say about real systems, but this is a different distinction, and one that can be captured only by recognising that mathematical structures can represent real systems only when 'framed' (as it were) by natural language. So it would seem unnatural, on Giere's view, to identify the theory with its class of models. Now van Fraassen ([2], p.222), also expresses some reservation about 'reifying' theories (that is, identifying them with anything at all), but these reservations are beside the present point, since van Fraassen goes on to say that although 'effective communication proceeds by language', 'in the discussion of the structure of theories it [i.e. language] can largely be ignored'. It will be part of my argument that to ignore language and its relationships to other representational media is to misunderstand the nature of theoretical representation.

In the joint paper with Stathis Psillos, I have argued that Suppe presents the relation between model and equation as far too close to that which, in philosophical logic, holds between a sentence and the proposition it expresses ([1], Section 3). Two objections arise from understanding the theory-model relationship in that way: firstly, models are no more required to play the role of primary bearers of linguistic meaning than were propositions before them; secondly, in putting models in this position, the semantic view obscures the fact that models *themselves* are representational devices.

Turning to the first point, suppose that sets of sentences in two or more different languages are formulations of one and the same theory: the theory could then be identified with all the equivalent linguistic formulations. We need not invoke an *abstract* extralinguistic entity to account for semantic relations between 'snow is white', 'la neige est blanche' and 'der schnee ist weiss', but can merely say that there is something that can be said equivalently in the languages of the different formulations. Identity of truth-conditions can be invoked if something extra-linguistic is required. Now matrix and wave mechanics are a case in point: here we have historically independent but 'equivalent' formulations of the same theory, according to Suppe. But are they formulations of the same theory? This is a complex historical question. An intimate mathematical relationship between the two theories was proved: that a model of one could be turned into a model of the other. But mathematics aside, it is hard to imagine two theories that were further apart in what they had to say about the nature of the physical world, in their "fleshly clothing" ([12], p 59) as Schrödinger once put it. If historical hindsight has deemed the two theories to be one, this was more a product of their joint mathematical subsumption under a later (Hilbert-space) formalism than a sign of equivalence in any sense wider than the mathematical (but see section 2.2. for further comments).

So to the second point. The meaning of a physical theory is what it has to say about real-worldly physical systems. We use equations to say these things, but equations are linguistic items that are written down, solved, interpreted and re-interpreted. They can be used to represent parts of the world (like hydrogen atoms) as being certain ways, or having certain kinds of structure. Proponents of the semantic view are right to stress that models are central to an understanding of how equations can do representational work: the equations define the model, and the model represents the real system, in the sense that it is the model that is isomorphic to, or similar to, some class of real systems. But surely models cannot both be the meanings of the sentences that constitute a particular theory-formulation *and* be apt to represent real systems. Even if one can accept reifying them, the meanings of sentences are not the kinds of things that bear relationships like isomorphism or similarity to the real systems that are the subject matter of those sentences. The semantic view is right to stress models as the means by which equations convey their message. But the mathematical structure of the theory—that which that bears a definitional relationship to the equations—is not itself the content of the theory.

2 The Interactive View of Theories and Models

Scientists make claims using equations, diagrams, models, analogies and of course natural language. I have argued elsewhere that within both the received and the semantic views, scientific theories are 'reconstructed' [1]. That is, the representational tools that are associated with any particular theory are analysed so that the basic claims of the theory can be distilled out and presented in some canonical way. In the joint paper, we were keen to distinguish these artefacts of analysis from the real historical theories for which they often play proxy in philosophical arguments about science. What concerns me here, however, is how interactions *between* the different representational media associated with a particular theory determine what the theory can be used to explain and predict.

2.1 Bohr's First Atomic Model

In a well-known paper of 1913, Niels Bohr presented the first successful quantum-theoretic model of the atom (see [13], pp 161-85). This was a mathematical treatment of the nuclear model that had been developed by Ernest Rutherford in 1911 to account for the statistics of alpha-particle scattering from thin gold foils. The crucial feature of the published model—that won it acceptance by an initially sceptical scientific audience—was that it offered a detailed account of the origin of atomic spectra, and, crucially, allowed accurate calculation of both known and novel series in the hydrogen spectrum. So much is well documented [14], [15]: what I will do here is use the details of the heuristic background to Bohr's model to make two connected points about the use of mathematics in physical theories.

Bohr first outlined the model in a memorandum to Rutherford ([13], pp 135-43): he began by assuming that electrons could inhabit stable circular orbits around a stationary nucleus (so that electrostatic and centrifugal forces balance). Bohr then noted that if a continuum of possible orbits were allowed, there would be no obvious way to account for the characteristic atomic volumes displayed by every element. Introducing what he called a 'special assumption', he then restricted the number of possible orbits, allowing only a countable number: hence the stable states could be characterised by integer terms. That much mathematical structure would have been sufficient (bar certain constants) to fix the energy terms that he would later draw on to explain the atomic spectrum of hydrogen, but it is noteworthy that at this point, Bohr explicitly ruled out any such explanation. A clue to what was going on is given by a letter he subsequently wrote to Rutherford, on 31 January 1913, in which Bohr compared his own model to that of a contemporary, J. W. Nicholson ([13], pp 579-80). According to Bohr, Nicholson's model described the 'less stable' (i.e. excited) states of atoms, such as are produced in stellar nebulae and discharge tubes, environments in which atoms are 'constantly broken up and formed again' ([13], p 579). In contrast, his own model centred on the 'permanent' states of atoms, and hence would be able to account for the characteristic atomic volumes observed in lower-energy environments. So at that time, it would seem that Bohr thought that atomic spectra were produced by a mechanism intimately involving the reformation of atoms from ions (see also [14]). Thus it was natural for Bohr to conclude 'I do not at all deal with the question of calculation of the frequencies corresponding to the lines in the visible spectrum' ([13], pp 580).

Within just a few weeks, Bohr had submitted the final version of the paper, in which there *did* appear calculations of frequencies corresponding to the visible lines of the spectrum of hydrogen, along with a mechanism for their production. As before, an electron in a hydrogen atom could occupy a number of different stationary states, characterised by integer terms. Frequencies in the atomic spectrum corresponded (via a re-interpreted Planck equation) to differences between the energies of these states. But it is interesting to note that the published paper contains two different derivations of the spectral frequencies. In the first derivation, Bohr contends that the spectral frequency associated with a particular stationary state corresponds to half the mechanical frequency of the electron's orbit in that state. The justification for this claim is that the mechanical frequency of the 'initial' state in the process by which the spectral line is produced is zero. This suggests two things: firstly, that he had not yet broken (as he was very shortly to do) the close link that there had been in classical mechanics between optical and mechanical frequencies. Secondly, if the initial states in the radiation process are characterised by a mechanical frequency of zero, the electron must be at infinity: the 'initial' states of radiating systems must be ions. Curiously, then, this first derivation seems intimately to involve the 'old' mechanism for radiation that Bohr hinted at in his earlier letter to Rutherford. In the second derivation, Bohr derives his energy terms, and identifies them (presumably by inspection) with difference terms that appear in empirical formulae for spectral lines, strongly suggesting that spectral lines are produced by transitions between stationary states. He then goes on to use what he would later call the correspondence principle to fix a constant. It is this derivation that appears in his later papers.

There are two interesting features of Bohr's route to his model that I would like to discuss here: firstly that he imported a developed and tractable set of mathematical tools from classical mechanics; and secondly that he re-interpreted his equations in the course of developing his model. Bohr's initial choice of idealising assumptions for his model (stationary nucleus, circular orbits), and his later developments and refinements (reduced mass replacing electronic mass, elliptical rather than circular orbits, precessing orbits) suggest a close analogical connection between Bohr's model and the detailed accounts of planetary motions that had been developed around central-forces models within classical mechanics. In carrying over these mathematical tools from their original applications, Bohr was representing the hydrogen atom as a miniature solar system, albeit an anomalous one. Although it would be too strong to say that the analogy was psychologically important for Bohr, it would certainly seem that the analogy provided what Lakatos called a 'positive heuristic', that is, an open list of 'natural' sophistications that can be introduced into an idealised model in the face of empirical or theoretical objections [16]. For Lakatos, a positive heuristic is what distinguishes well-motivated improvements from *ad hoc* fudge factors. If Lakatos is right, heuristic factors are central to a theory's explanatory and predictive power. But the heuristic associated with Bohr's model depends on the historically contingent prior development of central forces models to account for planetary motions. So the link between equations and their representative content—what they can be used to predict or explain—is a historically contingent one too.

The contingency of that link also shows up in another aspect of Bohr's progress: that he was unable to offer an account of spectral lines until he was in possession of a plausible mechanism for their production, even although he had the mathematical resources to derive the frequencies of spectral lines from an early stage. If 'Bohr's model' was something that could be used to explain—something that involved a mechanism for radiation—then mathematical structure is not all there is to Bohr's model. In conclusion, then, the mathematical structure of Bohr's model was a representational medium, but not the model itself. Firstly, the mathematics was portable: part of the mathematical structure had been carried over from a previous application, in which it had been used to represent something else (the solar system), and this previous use informed its application to the hydrogen atom. Secondly, the mathematics did not itself fix the way that Bohr's model represented the hydrogen atom. Bohr interpreted and re-interpreted his equations: to track the evolving interpretations, we must look to the claims, made in natural language, that 'frame' his uses of the mathematical resources of his theory, determining their representational content, and justifying his derivations.

2.2 Wave Mechanics and Matrix Mechanics

In 1925-26, famously, two different quantum theories were proposed: one (the matrix mechanics of Born, Heisenberg and Jordan) was an avowedly agnostic attempt to save the complexity of line spectra, while the other (Schrödinger's wave mechanics) was a speculative mix of gas statistics and wave equation. In 1926, Schrödinger, Eckart and Pauli produced proofs of an intimate theoretical relationship between the two theories [17], [18]. The proofs showed how to turn a matrix-mechanical model into a wave-mechanical model, and vice versa. The relationship between the two theories has sometimes been read as one of equivalence: here were two theories that in some sense 'said the same thing'. But that reading is plausible only on an impoverished view of theories. If the proof was correct (and Müller [18] has voiced important reservations on this point), what was established was that an arbitrary wave-mechanical model would have a matrix-mechanical counterpart. But this would show only that the equations that resulted from an application of wave mechanics would have a counterpart in matrix mechanics, not that that counterpart would be a well-motivated description of the same system. It is an open question whether the two theories would have yielded equivalent descriptions when applied to real systems, had the required descriptions been developed independently within the two theories.

Schrödinger's interpretation in particular suffused his presentation and development of wave mechanics. In wave mechanics he had consciously imported a second-order differential equation that in classical mechanics had been used to describe wave processes. Not only were the backgrounds to the two theories very different, but their authors envisaged different futures for them. Schrödinger hoped to substitute his wavefunctions into classical electromagnetic field equations, while the authors of matrix mechanics set about quantising the electromagnetic field at an early stage in their research programme. Interestingly, Schrödinger indicated that the first wave-mechanical treatments of the hydrogen atom were necessarily but first approximations, because they were based on Coulombic Hamiltonians ([12], pp 57-60). Interactions in the old quantum theory, from which matrix mechanics grew, had been Coulombic ever since Bohr explicitly suspended classical electromagnetic theory in the first few pages of his 1913 paper. So Schrödinger thought that wave mechanics and matrix mechanics might become mathematically *non-equivalent*, if developed, independently, along the lines that their authors originally intended. Hence the contingent historical associations of the equations with which Schrödinger formulated wave mechanics are required to distinguish it from its rival, matrix mechanics, although the mathematical tools developed by the different authors were intimately related.

2.3 Quantum Chemistry

The relationship between a theory and a representational model in which it is applied need not be a *hierarchical* one. As Nancy Cartwright has long argued [8], the central equations of such general theories as classical or quantum mechanics themselves yield no direct information about real systems. Further information is required: a force-function in classical mechanics, a Hamiltonian in quantum mechanics. Suppose that there were general methods that, in each of those theories, could be applied to the description of particular systems, yielding a force function or Hamiltonian as appropriate. This would support the view, suggested by accounts of representation within the semantic conception of theories, that theories like quantum and classical mechanics predict and explain by providing theoretical models (structures that satisfy the central equations of the theory) that represent real systems. But in fact there are no such methods for either theory. Textbooks of quantum chemistry are sometimes written as if there is a general method for writing down Hamiltonians for molecules, that begins by enumerating the charges and masses of electrons and nuclei present. But these Hamiltonians are laid aside when the real task of explaining and predicting molecular behaviour begins. It should not be thought that the problem is one merely one of tractability, for an arbitrary solution to a Schrödinger equation that results from applying this method would not have the right symmetry properties to be a suitable basis for chemical explanations. So if one wants quantum-mechanical molecular models to be explanatorily useful, one needs to put the required structure in by hand, and although this procedure is sometimes misleadingly called the Born-Oppenheimer 'approximation', it can be interpreted as suspending quantum mechanics for the molecular skeleton [19], [20].

So representative models of molecules are not simply models of quantum mechanics, because they are *nomologically disuniform*. The treatment of carbon dioxide by one textbook of spectroscopy, for instance, begins with the structure of the carbon dioxide molecule, which 'is linear and contains three atoms; therefore it has four fundamental vibrations'. Detailed analysis of its motions allows symmetry considerations to be applied: 'The symmetrical stretching vibration is inactive in the infrared since it produces no change in the dipole moment of the molecule. The bending vibrations ... are equivalent, and are the resolved components of bending motion oriented at any angle to the internuclear axis; they have the same frequency and are said to be doubly degenerate' ([21], p 96). The next step is to apply quantum mechanics. There are models in quantum mechanics for simple rotating bodies, and for simple oscillators: they are usually to be found in the chapter of the textbook on quantum mechanics *after* the chapter in which the Schrödinger equation was introduced. With some adjustments, the quantum-mechanical rigid rotator and harmonic oscillator allow us to quantise the rotational and vibrational motions that background chemical theory tells us the carbon dioxide molecule must exhibit. This provides the energy levels: differences between these energy levels correspond to spectral lines (in the infrared region in the case of the vibrational modes of the carbon dioxide molecule). These explanations—and the models that ground them—do not seem to fit the accounts of application that are offered within the semantic view: motley collections of theory-fragments from different areas (classical molecular structure, idealised quantum-mechanical systems, statistical mechanics) pull together in the explanatory process. If satisfaction of a Schrödinger equation be the criterion for a representative model being an application of quantum mechanics (as it would seem to be on the semantic conception), then the above model of carbon dioxide does *not* constitute an application of quantum mechanics.

References

1. Hendry RF, Psillos S. Theories as Complexes of Representational Media. To be presented at the 16th Biennial Meeting of the Philosophy of Science Association, Kansas City, October 1998
2. van Fraassen, B. Laws and symmetry. Clarendon Press, Oxford, 1989
3. Giere R. Explaining science: a cognitive approach. University of Chicago Press, Chicago, 1988
4. Lloyd E. The structure and confirmation of evolutionary theory. Princeton University Press, Princeton, 1994
5. Suppes P. Models of data. In: Studies in methodology and foundations of science. Reidel, Dordrecht, 1969, pp 24-35
6. van Fraassen, B. The scientific image. Clarendon Press, Oxford, 1980

7. Hendry RF. Empirical adequacy and the semantic conception of theories. In: Childers T, Kolár P, Svoboda V (eds) Logica '96: proceedings of the 10th international symposium. Filosofia, Prague, 1997, pp 136-50
8. Cartwright N. How the laws of physics lie. Clarendon, Oxford, 1983
9. French S, Ladyman J. Semantic perspective on idealization in quantum mechanics. In: Shanks N (ed) Poznan studies in the philosophy of the sciences and the humanities, vol 63, Idealization in contemporary physics. Rodopi, Amsterdam, Atlanta, 1998, pp 51-73
10. Suppe F. The search for philosophic understanding of scientific theories. In: Suppe F (ed) The structure of scientific theories, second edition. University of Illinois Press, Urbana, 1977, pp 3-241
11. Suppe F. The semantic conception of theories and scientific realism. University of Illinois Press, Urbana, 1989
12. Schrödinger E. On the relation between the quantum mechanics of Heisenberg, Born, and Jordan, and that of Schrödinger. In: Collected papers on wave mechanics. Blackie, London, 1928, pp 45-61
13. Bohr N. Collected works, vol 2, Work on atomic physics 1912-1917. North-Holland, Amsterdam, 1981
14. Heilbron J, and Kuhn T. The genesis of the Bohr atom. Historical Studies in the Physical Sciences 1969; 1:211-290
15. Darrigol O. From c-numbers to q-numbers. University of California Press, Berkeley, 1992
16. Lakatos I. Falsification and the methodology of scientific research programmes. In: Lakatos I, Musgrave A (eds) Criticism and the growth of knowledge. Cambridge University Press, Cambridge, 1970, pp 91-196
17. van der Waerden BL. From matrix mechanics and wave mechanics to unified quantum mechanics. In: Mehra J (ed) The physicist's conception of nature. Reidel, Dordrecht, 1973, pp 276-93
18. Müller F. The equivalence myth of quantum mechanics, Parts I and II. Studies in history and philosophy of modern physics 1997; 28B:35-61; 28B:219-47
19. Woolley RG, Quantum theory and molecular structure. Advances in Physics 1976; 25:27-52
20. Hendry RF. Models and approximations in quantum chemistry. In: Shanks N (ed) Poznan studies in the philosophy of the sciences and the humanities, vol 63, Idealization in contemporary physics. Rodopi, Amsterdam, Atlanta, 1998, pp 123-42
21. Silverstein R, Bassler G, Morrill T. Spectrometric identification of organic compounds, fourth edition. Wiley, New York, 1981

Visual Representations and Interpretations of Molecular Electronic Structure: The Survival and Re-emergence of Valence Bond Theory

David L. Cooper
Department of Chemistry, University of Liverpool,
P.O. Box 147, Liverpool, UK L69 7ZD
e mail: dlc@liv.ac.uk

Abstract

We present a non-specialist overview of the survival in chemistry of valence bond theory and of its re-emergence, in 'modern' form, as a powerful technique for visualizing and interpreting molecular electronic structure.

1 Introduction

Molecules are composed of atoms, bonded together by sharing electrons, and it has long been the experience of much of chemistry that it proves useful to identify certain bonds, such as C–H, and certain groupings of atoms, such as the methyl group (CH_3), whose characteristic properties, while certainly not constant, vary relatively little from one molecule to another. In order to be considered successful, a theory of electronic structure and bonding needs to be able to explain features such as these, as well as the numbers of bonds formed by particular atoms and also any strong preferences for particular geometrical arrangements.

Because nuclei are orders of magnitude more massive than electrons, we may usually consider the description of the behaviour of the electrons as a separate problem from that of the motions of the nuclei. For a fixed geometrical arrangement of the nuclei, the most important contributions to the total energy of a molecule consist of the kinetic energies of all of the electrons and a potential energy term arising from the electrostatic interactions between the electrons and/or nuclei.

One of the first successful attempts to account for chemical bonding can be traced back to Gilbert Lewis in 1916, several years before the advent of quantum mechanics. The basic idea behind Lewis structures is that the various atoms in a molecule share some or all of their outer or 'valence' electrons, forming electron pairs so as to attain the same number of valence electrons as the nearest noble gas element, as in Figure 1.

Each of the shared pairs of electrons may be termed a covalent bond. Pairs of electrons which are not involved in the bonding (*i.e.* which are not shared) are termed nonbonding or lone pairs. The valence shell electron pair repulsion or

VSEPR model, which relies on notions of the repulsions between shared pairs and/or lone pairs, subsequently provided chemists with qualitative tools for predicting geometrical arrangements.

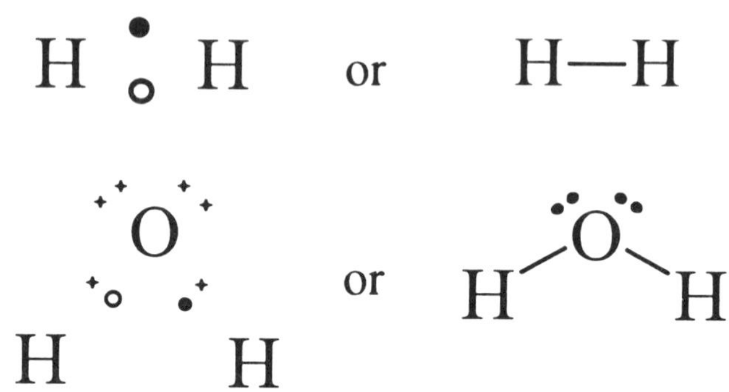

Figure 1. Lewis structures for H_2 and H_2O.

Soon after the advent of the Schrödinger equation, chemistry was advanced significantly by the introduction of valence bond or VB theory, which recognises from the outset that molecules are built from atoms or larger fragments which often have very similar properties from one system to another. This model, which involves accommodating the electrons in highly-localized, atom-centred one-electron wavefunctions (or 'orbitals') which overlap with one another, provides highly visual representations of molecular electronic structure and a direct link with Lewis structures and with VSEPR ideas. The language of VB theory (*e.g.* 'covalent', 'ionic', 'lone pair', 'double bond', 'sp^3 hybridization') plays a pivotal role in the way chemists visualize molecular electronic structure and it provides successful predictions of trends in geometries, properties and reactivity.

Early computational implementations of VB theory were beset by obstacles linked to the nonorthogonality of the orbitals and the approach was soon eclipsed by molecular orbital or MO theory, which accommodates the electrons in orthogonal orbitals that are more delocalized. Not only was MO theory more tractable, but it turned out that in order to achieve comparable accuracy, the simple VB description had to be augmented with a plethora of additional ('ionic') configurations, such that the original conceptual simplicity was all but completely lost.

Continuing progress in the development of new tools of computational chemistry, in parallel with impressive advances in computing technology, have certainly reached the stage where reliable calculations may be carried out for 'real', chemically-interesting systems. Most of the modern, 'state-of-the-art' approaches to electronic structure rely on using large-scale computations, firmly based in quantum mechanics, to calculate total energies and electron distributions (and other properties) of all the species in which we might be interested. Such pragmatic approaches can provide accurate numbers which are of great importance to modern chemistry and which are crucial in the interpretation of a wide variety of experiments. On the other hand, the increasing accuracy and sophistication of quantum chemical methods is usually linked to further complexity in the corresponding wavefunctions, so that their interpretation becomes more and more difficult. It can be especially difficult to find direct links between the results of modern calculations and the more classical models, in terms of which most chemists visualize and interpret molecular electronic structure. Of course, the creation of simple models of molecular electronic structure is not, in itself, a difficult task. However, if these models are to carry any real conviction, then they must also retain much of the high numerical accuracy that we have come to expect.

Chemistry suffered many decades of this schism between variants of MO theory, for producing numbers, and simple VB ideas, for visualizing electronic structure, and the debate became fairly acrimonious and even became entangled with political ideology.

2 An example: benzene

Benzene, C_6H_6, is an important organic molecule in its own right and the description of the bonding in this system is central to much of our understanding of the chemistry of 'aromatic' compounds. This planar molecule features a regular hexagonal framework and is most usually represented by Kekulé structures, as in Figure 2. The double-headed arrow signifies in this case the averaging of these

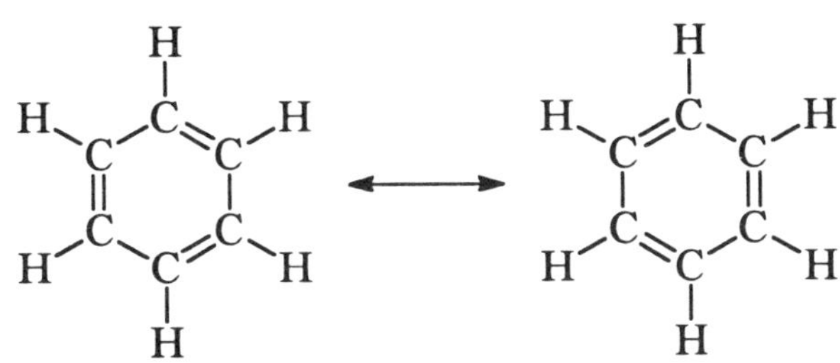

Figure 2. Kekulé structures for benzene.

two VB structures ('resonance'). An alternative graphical representation of benzene is the hexagon-and-circle device:

which indicates more clearly the high symmetry of the molecule. Although the Kekulé-like description does not arise in MO theory, it is that type of visual representation that is most widely used by organic chemists, especially in explanations of reaction mechanisms. Similarly, practicing chemists continue to represent supposed movements of electron pairs in chemical reactions by means of 'curly arrows', as in the nucleophilic substitution reaction:

An attitude fostered by many organic chemistry textbooks is that MO theory is in some sense 'more fundamental' or 'better' than the VB model: they justify continuing to use instead the VB description because it is so easy to visualize. Furthermore, the authors of some of these books claim to 'know' that the visual representations of reaction mechanisms provided by curly arrows bear no resemblance at all to what is really going on, but that this simple device is far too useful to be abandoned. On the other hand, some organic chemists admit to a feeling of unease when using VB-based arguments in the presence of quantum chemists.

3 Coulson and Fischer

In the original valence bond approach of Heitler and London [1], we recognize that the H_2 molecule consists of two hydrogen atoms (A and B), each with one electron (1 and 2) in a 1s orbital. The Heitler-London wavefunction takes the form

$$\Psi_{covalent}=[1s_A(1)\ 1s_B(2) + 1s_A(2)\ 1s_B(1)]\ \Theta^2_{00}$$

in which Θ^2_{00} is the total spin function that corresponds to pairing of the two electron spins. This wavefunction provides a fairly realistic description of the binding in the ground state of H_2, with the strength of the covalent bond linked to the degree of overlap between the two 1s orbitals. A better description requires the admixture of a small component of 'ionic' character (H^-H^+ and H^+H^-) via

$$\Psi_{ionic}=[1s_A(1)\ 1s_A(2) + 1s_B(1)\ 1s_B(2)]\ \Theta^2_{00}$$

A physical interpretation of the role of Ψ_{ionic} is that it accounts for distortion of the electron clouds around individual atoms when the two fragments are brought together. Indeed, some shifting of electron density towards neighbouring nuclei is likely to improve the overlap between different orbitals. Coulson and Fischer [2] abandoned strictly-localized orbitals and rewrote the covalent VB wavefunction in the form

$$\Psi_{CF}=[\phi_A(1)\ \phi_B(2) + \phi_A(2)\ \phi_B(1)]\ \Theta^2_{00}$$

in which $\phi_A=(1s_A+\lambda\ 1s_B)$ and $\phi_B=(1s_B+\lambda\ 1s_A)$. Notice that setting $\lambda=0$ gives the covalent-only Heitler-London model. On the other hand, $\lambda=1$ corresponds exactly to the basic MO description. Instead, Coulson and Fischer reoptimized λ for each geometry. Their optimal λ values correspond to relatively small distortions of the atomic orbitals. In this way, Ψ_{CF} combines the conceptual simplicity of the Heitler-London model with enhanced accuracy. Modern valence bond theory builds directly on this simple Coulson-Fischer idea, such that any of the one-electron orbitals for a polyatomic system can distort towards any atomic centre.

4 Spin-coupled valence bond theory

Developments of efficient computational algorithms, often relying on group theory and on graphical indexing techniques, led to tractable schemes and, alongside the enormous advances in computing power, have resulted in the re-emergence of (modern) valence bond theory as a serious tool for computational chemistry. Much of our own research involves the *spin-coupled valence bond* approach to molecular electronic structure [3]. This method provides compact, highly visual representations of the correlated behaviour of electrons in molecules, whilst also producing results of very high accuracy. Applications span all of the main branches of chemistry.

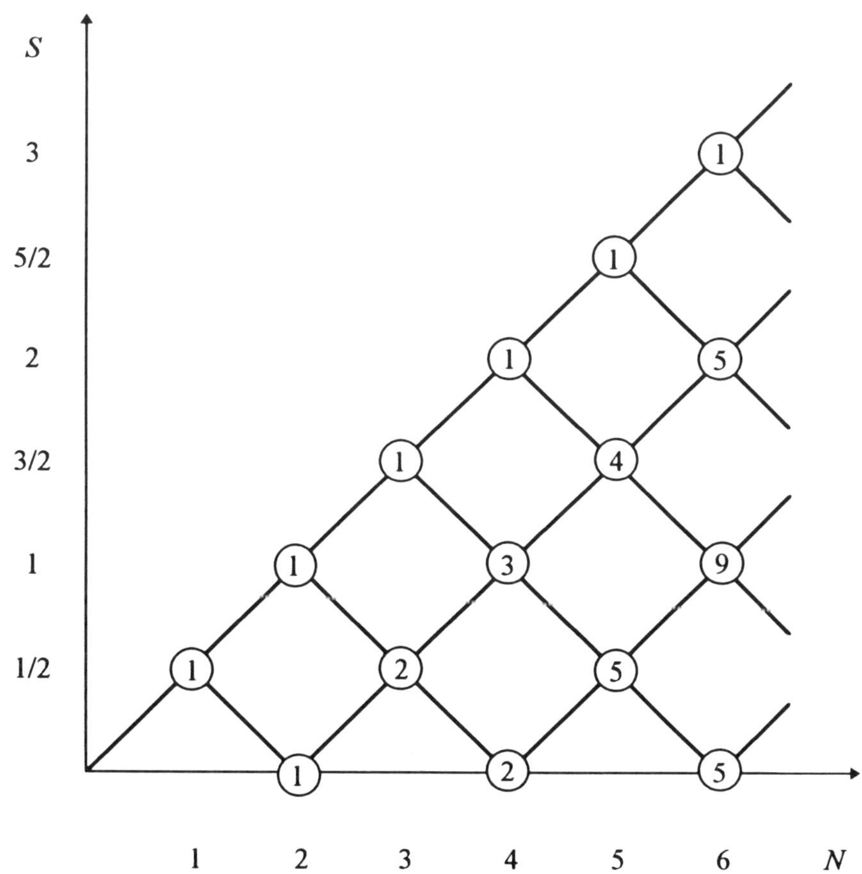

Figure 3. Branching diagram.

In the case of the benzene molecule, for example, it is natural to concentrate attention on the six 'π electrons' (where π signifies here a change of phase on reflection in the molecular plane). The total electronic spin is zero and we must recognize that there are multiple linearly-independent ways of coupling together the spins functions (α and β) of the individual electrons so as to achieve this. This feature of many-electron systems is most easily visualized in terms of a branching diagram (see Figure 3), in which we plot total spin S against the number of electrons N. Each rightwards path corresponds to a different linearly independent mode; the integers in the circles are the numbers of such paths. For N=6 and S=0, there are five linearly independent modes of spin coupling.

We may exploit infinite lattitude in our choice of spin functions to span the full space, and there are efficient schemes to transform from one basis to another. In the case of benzene, it proves convenient to adopt the so-called Rumer basis. An elegant scheme for constructing the Rumer spin functions is to mark N=6 points on a circle, and to join pairs of them in all possible ways such that no two lines cross and all arrows go towards higher numbers (see Figure 4). There are graphical rules for 'uncrossing' lines and reversing arrows. An arrow $i \rightarrow j$ corresponds to pairing of the spins associated with the electrons labelled i and j, and it signifies a factor in the total spin function of $2^{-1/2}[\alpha(i)\beta(j) - \alpha(j)\beta(i)]$. The similarity of R_1 and R_4 to Kekulé structures for benzene should be obvious. The other functions may be associated with the three para-bonded or Dewar structures.

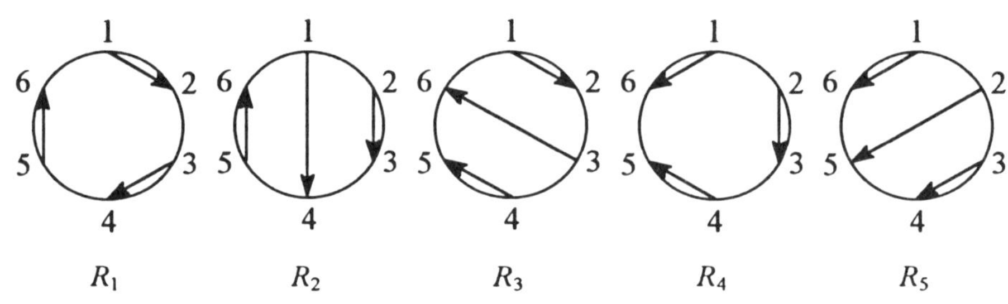

Figure 4. Rumer diagrams for N=6 and S=0.

Unbiased optimization for benzene of the (modern) VB orbitals and of the mode of spin coupling results in weights for the various R_i that are remarkably similar to those given many years ago by Pauling [4] in his original, and much simplified, classical VB calculation, and discussed by Coulson [5] in his textbook, and used by organic chemists. We find six symmetry-equivalent $2p_\pi$ orbitals, each associated with a given carbon atom (as postulated in classical VB theory), but exhibiting some deformation towards the neighbouring C atoms on each side, as is shown in Figure 5. Except for these small, but crucial distortions, it is striking that a description which provides accurate numbers closely resembles the appealing visual representation provided by classical VB, and still so extensively used in much of chemistry.

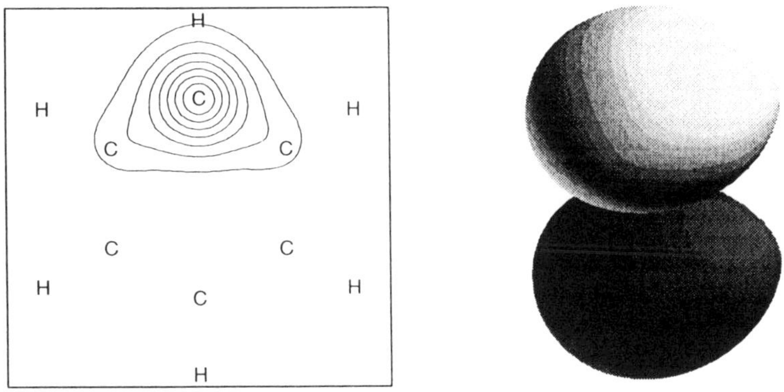

Figure 5. Spin-coupled orbital for benzene. Left: contours in a plane 1 bohr above the molecular plane. Right: a representative isosurface (three-dimensional contour).

Other applications of spin-coupled valence bond theory have shown that visual representations of organic reactions in terms of the synchronized movements of electrons (*e.g.* 'curly arrows') may not be so unrealistic after all. However, it is important to stress that there are many classes of systems for which the modern valence bond representation, although not more complicated, is somewhat different from its classical VB counterpart, and provides new insights.

As is well known, certain types of multiconfigurational MO wavefunctions are invariant to linear transformations of the defining orbitals. We may exploit this invariance to carry out nonunitary transformations of complete active space self-consistent field wavefunctions to representations based on nonorthogonal orbitals. With appropriate criteria for choosing such transformations, we find that an extraordinarily high proportion of such an MO-theory wavefunction can be expressed in terms of a component of modern valence bond form [6]. It seems now that the MO/VB divide was rather artificial.

5 Conclusions

Concepts taken from electronic structure theory have been of immense importance in the historical development of chemistry, and they continue to play a key role in the modern understanding of molecular electronic structure and reactivity. Such ideas not only allow us to interpret and to rationalize experimental observations, but they also enable reliable predictions to be made for whole new classes of systems. Many of the most useful of these concepts are realized in the form of pictorial representations.

Spin-coupled valence bond theory combines the high accuracy that we seek from modern calculations, with relatively simple, highly visual representations that allow us to interpret molecular electronic structure [3]. In addition to the fully-variational optimization of fairly general types of (multiconfigurational) modern-VB wavefunction, our codes may be used to generate modern-VB representations of MO-based wavefunctions [6]. Chemists who continue to use traditional visual representations and interpretations of molecular electronic structure may now do so (albeit with some modifications) with the confidence that such descriptions arise from high quality, 'respectable' calculations.

References

1. Heitler W, London F. Z Phys 1927; 44:455
2. Coulson CA, Fischer I. Phil Mag 1949; 40:386
3. For recent reviews see:
   (a) Cooper DL, Gerratt J, Raimondi M. Chem Rev 1991; 91:929
   (b) Gerratt J, Cooper DL, Karadakov PB, Raimondi M. Chem Soc Rev 1997; 26:87
   (c) Cooper DL, Gerratt J, Raimondi M. In: Maksic ZB, Orville-Thomas WJ (ed) Pauling's Legacy – Modern Modelling of the Chemical Bond. Elsevier, Amsterdam, 1998
4. Pauling L. J Chem Phys 1933; 1:280
5. Coulson CA. Valence, 2nd edn. Clarendon, Oxford, 1961, chapter 9
6. Thorsteinsson T, Cooper DL, Gerratt J, Raimondi M. Theor Chim Acta 1997; 95:131

The Language of Proteins

J H Parish
School of Biochemistry and Molecular Biology, The University of Leeds
Leeds LS2 9JT, U.K.

Abstract

The expression of genes involves processes for which the decoding of a language represents a metaphor. The final part of the process involves the acquisition of a three dimensional fold and to extend the metaphor the protein sequence is like a prose description of a three dimensional object. The rules for interpreting this language might not be the same for all protein families and, in this sense, the protein sequences might be regarded as automata.

1 Background

In biochemistry and molecular biology proteins represent a class of large molecules, representatives of which are found in all living organisms. Proteins fulfil several functions in living cells: haemoglobin, the oxygen-carrying component of the blood of most vertebrates[1] is a protein; collagens and keratins (structural components of many tissues) are proteins and most enzymes are proteins. Enzymes are "nature's catalysts". A biochemist would say, "I recognise an enzyme catalysed reaction when I see one". What (s)he probably means is that an enzyme catalysed reaction shows more-or-less specificity for the reactants (biochemists refer to these as 'substrates') and has a characteristic kinetic mechanism based on the idea that the rate is 'saturable'. We say "most" because some of these enzymes are RNA molecules, not proteins. One of the commonest functions of proteins is the transport of other substances (substrates for growth, toxins etc.) into or out of cells or their components. These proteins are integral components of biological membranes: the kinetics of these processes are saturable so "we biochemists" regard them as enzymes. Haemoglobin represent a more contentious case: it has saturable kinetics but does not actually convert the substrate, oxygen, to anything else.

Genes are sequences in DNA: the expression of genes consists of the use of DNA as a template for the biogenesis of a related molecule, RNA and certain RNA molecules ("the messengers") are used as templates for the synthesis of proteins.

[1] For those fascinated by biological exotica, arctic fishes adapted to live in sub-zero temperatures represent an interesting exception.

The overall process is referred to as 'gene expression'. In many (not all) cases the regulation of this process involves the interaction of regulatory protein molecules with selective 'regulatory' sequences in the DNA. The implied caveat is that in a few natural examples (and many genetically engineered examples in crop plant biotechnology) the regulatory molecules are not proteins but RNAs.

Thus many molecules that regulate gene expression and (as many enzymes are proteins) and metabolism are proteins. In contrast, DNA (the chemical basis of heredity in all organisms and some viruses[2]) and many of the intermediates in gene expression are not proteins: nor are starch, the bacterial cell wall and the carapaces of invertebrates.

Proteins are examples of 'informational macromolecules'. Biologists are preoccupied with ideas of a 'biological template' to distinguish from a 'chemical template'. We can use an example to differentiate 'biological' and 'chemical'' templates. Leaving aside certain ontological problems for the present[3] and resorting to crude anthropomorphism, there is a sense in which chemical templates are more simplistic than biological templates. Place a crystal of salt in a saturated salt solution and allow this to evaporate slowly. The crystal will grow, not in a random fashion, rather the new parts of the growing crystal will not be different in morphology from the original: they will contain ions of sodium and chloride in the same relative spatial orientations as those in the original (seed) crystal. The salt crystal is therefore a template of sorts. In contrast biological templates can be described in terms of a language metaphor (Fig. 1).

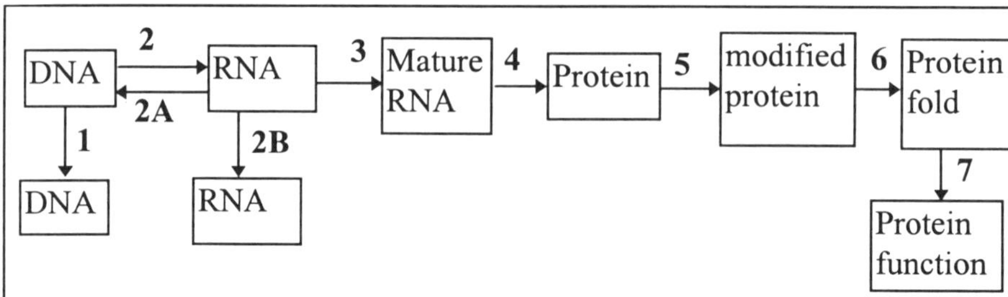

Fig. 1. The 'central axiom': information processing in living cells.

The processes of Fig. 1 involve template-product relationships (Table 1). Biochemists use a confusing mixture of genetic and linguistic terminology and metaphor for describing these processes but, in terms of information processing, the principles underlying most of the processes are fairly straightforward.

The sequences (i.e. the sequences of residues) in RNA and DNA can be regarded as strings of characters in a language with only four letters in the alphabet (T, C, A and G for DNA and U, C, A and G for RNA). Such sequences are templates for new synthesis and the rules are very simple: each letter determines the

[2] Some viruses (e.g. HIV, polio, influenza, rabies, EBOLA, leukaemia viruses) have RNA as their genetic material; others (e.g., herpes, smallpox, hepatitis B and some cancer viruses) are DNA viruses.

[3] "for the present", i.e. the whole of this article.

Process number	Role	Template-product rules	Biochemists' name	Biochemical components
1	Inheritance	A:T, C:G T:A, G:C	DNA replication	DNA polymerase etc.
2	Intermediate Temple	A:U, C:G T:A, G:C	Transcription	RNA polymerase
2A	Inheritance certain viruses[4]	A:T, C:G U:A, G:C	Reverse transcription	Reverse transcriptase
2B	Inheritance certain viruses[5]	A:U, C:G U:A, G:C	RNA replication	RNA replicase
3	Synthesis of m-,t- and r-RNA	specific sites	post-transcriptional modification	enzymes
4	Protein synthesis	Genetic code	Translation	ribosomes, tRNA, factors etc.
5	Covalent modification[6]	several	Many names	Many enzymes
6	Protein folding	this paper	Folding	Nothing and/or chaperones[7]
7	Definition of function	?	Biochemistry	Probably nothing

Table 1. Template-product relationships implied by Fig. 1.

incorporation in the new molecule of a complementary letter and the rules of complementarity are A:T(or U) and G:C. Following the synthesis of RNA (process 2) the nascent molecules are modified and lead to the functional classes of RNA, one of which, mRNA (messenger RNA) is the informational template for the biogenesis of proteins. The mRNA is written in a language with a four letter

[4] e.g. HIV.

[5] e.g. RNA viruses of plants such as tomato mosaic virus.

[6] Some proteins contain chemical bonds not introduced at the point of biogenesis. Examples include the cutting of precursors into mature proteins including several hormones, 'S-S cross links", phosphoproteins, glycosylation and non-S-S cross-links (collagens).

[7] Chaperones are proteins that assist the acquisition of the "correct" fold.

alphabet and the proteins are written in a language with 20 letters (see however next paragraph). There is therefore not a one-for-one rule such as the complementarity that applies to DNA replication and transcription and the relationship between mRNA sequences and protein sequences, the Genetic Code, uses 3-letter 'words', codons, that specify an amino acid. Three of the codons are the equivalent of full stops and, in general, the code involves several codons specifying more than one amino acid.

It is a fairly straightforward code although the start position is specified by the context in which a 'start codon' finds itself and there is a context-sensitive meaning to a codon that might be either a full stop or the '21st amino acid', selenocysteine. Variations in the Genetic Code in certain organisms and organelles are minor and equivalent to dialects in human languages. The idea that there is a simple code or decryption mechanism that relates mRNA to proteins is an anthropomorphic metaphor: the process of protein biogenesis involves mRNA, tRNA, ribosomes and other factors and the 'decoding process' involves physicochemical interactions. However the idea of a code or language led to a fundamentally heuristic method for deducing the code: from a knowledge of the sequence of synthetic mRNA molecules or tiny fragments ('synthetic codons') and the amino acids they might incorporate, the Genetic Code was 'cracked' by the laboratories of Nirenberg and Khorana in the 1960s. The work involved a large number of very difficult and time-consuming experiments but, in essence, the Code could be unravelled today by comparing the sequences of mRNA molecules and their corresponding proteins[8]. This correlation was possible at a time when the mechanism of protein synthesis was poorly understood.

The fundamental question remaining in the scheme of Table 1 is whether there is a language or code that relates protein sequence to structure and function in process 6 (Fig. 1 and Table 1). We should be in a stronger position than that the crackers of the Genetic Code found themselves in because there is a wealth of structural and biochemical data: we know the sequences of hundreds of thousands of proteins and the structures of thousands of these. There are classification schemes for the structures including a hierarchic tree-like structure [1]. The rules have nevertheless eluded biochemists but one thing is clear: the information required is embedded in the sequence and is probably relatively sparse.

2 A search for a language of proteins

We have chosen as an example hevamine A, an enzyme (chitinase II/lysozyme) from the latex of the rubber tree. Its sequence (written in the 20-letter protein alaphabet) is in Fig. 2(a).

In Fig. 3 we show the structure of hevamine A drawn according to two conventions. In Fig. 3(a) we see the atoms represented as balls and in Fig,. 3(b) a schematic

[8] At the time of the cracking of the Code, mRNA could not be isolated and sequenced.

Fig. 2. (a) the sequence of hevamine A. (b) The secondary structure elements E (extended), H (helical) and X (others) followed their lengths. (c) Key residues (explained in the text).

(a)

```
GGIAIYWGQNGNEGTLTQTCSTRKYSYVNIAFLNKFGNGQTPQINLAGHC
NPAAGGCTIVSNGIRSCQIQGIKVMLSLGGGIGSYTLASQADAKNVADYL
WNNFLGGKSSSRPLGDAVLDGIDFDIEHGSTLYWDDLARYLSAYSKQGKK
VYLTAAPQCPFPDRYLGTALNTGLFDYVWVQFYNNPPCQYSSGNINNIIN
SWNRWTTSINAGKIFLGLPAAPEAAGSGYVPPDVLISRILPEIKKSPKYG
GVMLWSKFYDDKNGYSSSILDSV
```

(b)

```
X1 E6 X3 H3 X2 H7 X4 E4 X16 H3 X2 H13 X2 E7 X10 H14
X16 E5 X8 H4 X4 E4 X11 E5 X4 H3 X7 H13 X4 E7 X2 H3
X7 H6 X2 H6 X3 E7 X1 H7 X1 H5
```

(c)

[5,14](f) Y(e) 19-23(f) I(e) 2(f) F(e) 2(f) [I,V,L](e) 2(e) [C,L](e) [7,9](e) [M,V,E,I,L](e) 2[e] [L,I,V](e) 23(f) L(e) [10,17,19,20](f) G(e) 1(e) [D,H,I](e) 0(e) [F,I](f) [12,23](f) L(e) 3(e) [L,T,I](e) 12(f) [L,V](e) [24,48](f) [Y,W](e) 2(e) [10,29,30](f) [F,V](e) [27,23,37,44,9](e) [I,L,V](e) [10,20,30](f) [Y,F](e) 1(e) [S,T](e)

Fig. 2. From Sequence to Residue Patterns

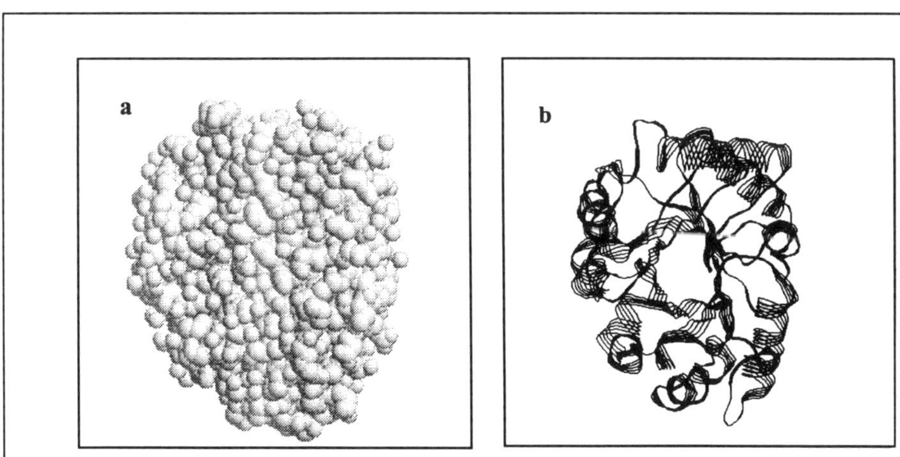

Fig. 3. Two representations of the structure of hevamine A (see text for discussion). The two models are drawn from the same view point.

diagram of the backbones. Fig. 3(a) tells us that hevamine A is a more-or-less globular but we cannot see the conformation of the protein chains because the image is dominated by the atoms in the amino acid residues at the surface of the structure. Proteins can be regarded as having a number of secondary structure 'elements": Fig. 2(b) summarises these for hevamine A and we can see the elements in a schematic cartoon in Fig. 3(b): the H elements look like bed springs and the E elements are aligned (e.g. there are four of them at about "1 to 3 o'clock"). The cartoon of the element geometries (Fig. 3(b)) shows an open structure, known to biochemists in this case as a "TIM barrel' but when we draw in the atoms, we realise the structure is very compact with a lot of atom-atom contacts so we cannot see into the barrel in Fig. 3(a). The ordering of elements in Fig. 2(b) is different from anything that is apparent from Fig. 3(b) because we cannot (in the resolution of Fig. 3(b)) see the topology: i.e. the route taken by the strings of Fig. 2 as they thread through the 3D structure. Nevertheless there is likely to be information to be gathered [3] perhaps by concentrating on the contacts made between elements. If we study the detailed structure of hevamine A and catalogue amino acid residues in multiple contacts between elements we can obtain a signature which we to refine by comparing it with other proteins of known structure and the same fold (there are 4 others in this case) and we obtain a signature (Fig. 2(c)). The signature consists of the lengths of gaps followed by an amino acid. Alternatives are given in square brackets and following each values is an abbreviation (e) for exact or (f) fuzzy. In the implementation of this method [2] the "fuzzy" concept is quantified and there is a scoring system. This particular signature (M Spencelayh and the authors of Ison et al., unpublished) detects unambiguously proteins of the chitinase II family and adds a fifth example of the success of signatures of this type.

2.1 Vocabulary, signatures, syntax and grammar.

What we have achieved so far is a method for deriving signatures for five protein folds. There are approximately 800 such folds in the classification of Hubbard et al. [1] so there is some way to go because we cannot judge whether 5/5 represents 100% but we might work this out sooner rather than later as two of us (S C Daniel and the author) are seeking to automate the refinement stage by using dynamic programming methods Needleman and Wunsch [4] and other techniques.

Nevertheless we are going to end up with a very large dictionary that will be difficult to use. However, help is probably available: if we can predict the position in the classification [1] of a protein in terms of a summary such as Fig. 2(b) we should have a more coarse grained predictor (G J Warner and the author are investigating this) we might have a predictor based on the nature of the element types: within, hopefully months rather than years, we should know whether the granularities of these approaches will overlap or lead to the conclusion that there are additional criteria that need to be considered before we can claim to have deciphered the language of proteins. The question as to how the protein interprets its signature is outside the scope of this article but we close on a cautionary note. We started by observing that we have a metaphor: the sequence of a protein is like a sentence with a three dimensional meaning or containing a three dimensional description. We have seen that the details of the 'signature' are very sparse. What do the other letters 'mean'? There is no reason *a priori* to suppose that the protein-folding language needs to be universal in the sense that the Genetic Code is universal. Possibly the grammar and syntax are embedded in the sequence also; in other words the sequences are automata with their data sets (the signatures) but also their own programs (other parts of the sequence).

Acknowledgements

Matthew Blades, Steve Daniel, Jon Ison, Michael Spencelayh and Guy Warner did the work that justifies the ideas in this paper.

References

1. Hubbard, T.J.P., Murzin, A.G., Brenner, S.E., & Chothia, C. SCOP: A structural classification of proteins database. 1997; Nucl. Acids Res. 25, 236-239.
2. Ison J.C., Parish J.H., Blades M.J., Daniel S.C., Bleasby A.J., Findlay J.B.C.F. A Key Residues Approach to Protein Fold Detection - Development of a Novel Method for generating Signatures for Protein Families based on Analysis of Contacts between Elements of Secondary Structure 1998; submitted
3. Jones D.T. Progress in protein structure prediction. 1997 Curr. Biol. 7: 377-387
4. Needleman S.B., Wunsch C.D. A general method applicable to the search for similarities in the amino acid sequence of two proteins. 1970; J. Mol. Biol. 48: 443-453

Atomistic vs. Continuous Representations in Molecular Biology

David S. Goodsell
Department of Molecular Biology, The Scripps Research Institute
La Jolla, CA 92037 U.S.A.

Abstract

Representations used in science may be separated into two classes: atomistic representations, which model discrete entities interacting through pair-wise forces, and continuous representations, which model derived properties that vary continuously through space. The choice of an atomistic or a continuous model is governed primarily by the complexity of the system: atomistic models are useful in systems with several thousand interacting entities, whereas continuous models are necessary in larger systems. In molecular biology, atomistic models are used at two levels: at the atomic level, where the atomic structure of molecules is studied, and at the molecular level, where the molecular structure of cells is studied. Continuous models are also useful at both levels, for simplifying the atomic details of large, complex molecules, and for simplifying the molecular details of entire cells.

Introduction

Science often represents our physical world in two different, but complementary, ways: *atomistically*, represented as discrete entities interacting through pair-wise interactions, and *continuously*, represented by derived properties that vary continuously through space. Imagine the way a scientist might look at a glass of water. One will see it as a continuous cylindrical volume of liquid of a given temperature that responds to foreign objects with a given viscosity. Another scientist will see the glass of water as an atomistic ensemble of molecules, interacting through directional bonds and moving with a characteristic distribution of velocities. Both representations are valid and each captures different physical characteristics of the system. A hydroelectric engineer will use a continuous model when looking at turbulence; a computational chemist will use an atomistic model when looking at molecular solvation.

These dichotomous representations, in order to be useful, must be consistent with one another. The interactions of molecules in the atomistic representation must converge, when averaged over large ensembles, to give the viscosity; the molecular velocities must average to give the temperature. Microscopic statistical mechanics must provide the foundation for macroscopic thermodynamics.

The utility of each type of representation is typically a function of the complexity of the system under study. Systems that are composed of several thousand interacting entities are often treated with atomistic models. Systems with far more interacting species, in which individuals lose their character and the properties of the ensemble dominate, are perforce treated continuously. Numerous examples may be found: atomistic models of individual sand grains yield to continuous models of sand dune formation or beach erosion, atomistic models of individual nerve action yield to continuous models of brain function, atomistic models of particular prey/predator interactions yield to continuous models of biological evolution, atomistic models of planetary and stellar gravitation yield to continuous models of galactic evolution.

The study of biological molecules shows a similar dichotomy of representations. The range from atoms to organisms separates naturally into four scale domains, as shown in Figure 1. Within each scale domain, the preferred representation shifts from atomistic at the lower end of the range to continuous at higher end. In the first domain, the atomistic entities are subatomic particles, and as the scale increases to representation of atoms, a continuous, quantum mechanical model is most useful.

The second domain ranges from atoms as the atomistic entities to large biological molecules at the upper limit. Atomistic models are commonly used for the study of molecular structure and function, at a scale level of 1-10 nanometers. Common molecular models show the location of each atom and represent explicitly their covalent and non-bonded interactions. As we move to the study of macromolecules and assemblies of macromolecules, at a scale level of 10-100 nanometers, atomistic models become cumbersome because of the numbers of atoms involved, so continuous models that smooth out atomic detail will often yield more insight. These models include protein ribbon models, solvent accessible surfaces, electrostatic and affinity potentials, and other abstracted molecular representations.

At a factor of ten larger, we reach the third domain: the cellular mesoscale. At this level, an atomistic representation is again useful for analyzing micron-sized portions of cells, using entire molecules as the discrete interacting units. Continuous models, however, are essential for the study of cell physiology, at the level of 10-100 microns, describing the diffusion of molecules through cells, concentration gradients, action potentials, and other derived properties of the underlying molecules.

The final domain treats cells as the atomistic individuals. At the lower end of the range, individual cellular interactions are treated, and processes such as phagocytosis, coordination of muscle contraction, and the early steps of embryogenesis may be effectively studied. At the high end, cells are not treated individually, and grosser physiological properties are studied, such as the mechanics of muscular and skeletal systems, the hydraulics of the circulatory system, and the wiring of the nervous system.

In each of these scale domains, the atomistic representation builds upon the lower level of continuous representation. For instance, the representation of atoms as individual entities that interact through pair-wise forces is an approximation of the more detailed continuous quantum mechanical representation of electrons that is used at the lower scale domain. The non-bonded van der Waals interaction, which leads us to think of atoms as being hard, non-interpenetrating spheres, is a simplification of the dispersion and repulsion effects of the cloud of electrons surrounding each atom. In the atomistic model, the complex interaction of these electron clouds is approximated by a simple function that is dependent on the distance.

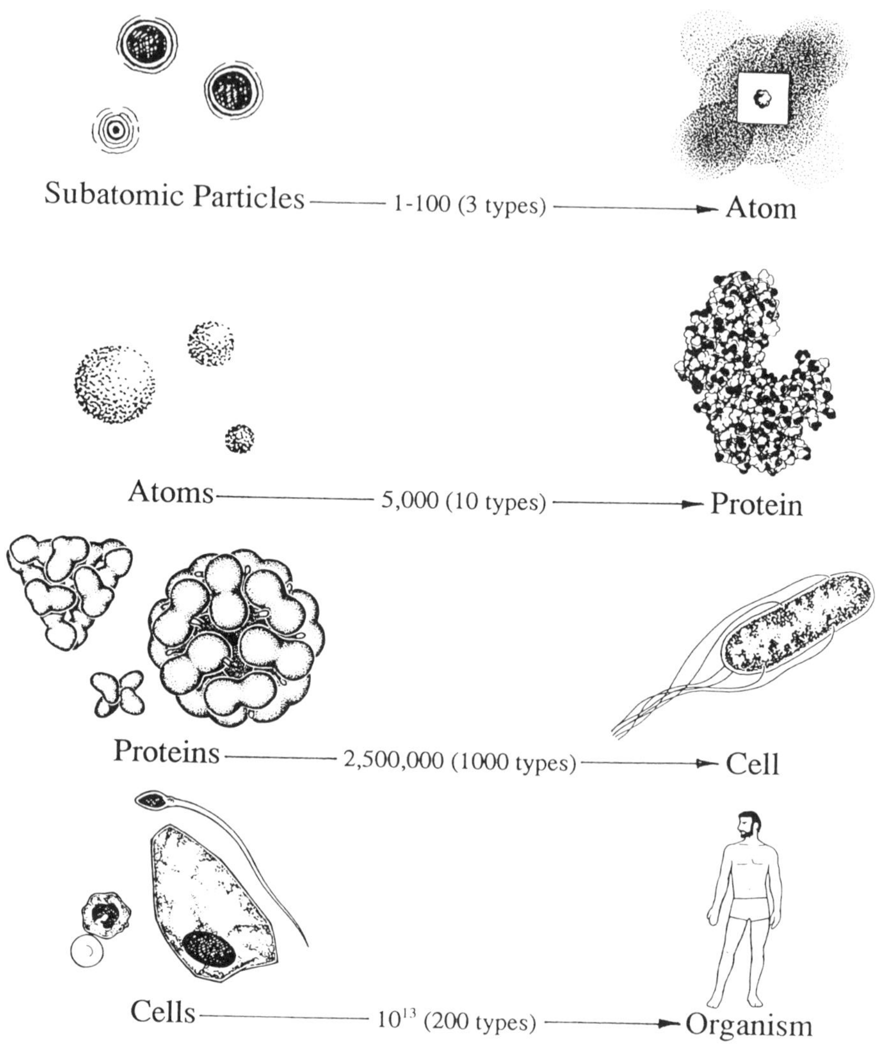

Figure 1. Biological Scale Hierarchy. In the size range from subatomic particles to organisms, four scale domains are traversed. In each domain, an atomistic representation is useful at the lower end and continuous representations are useful at the higher end, as the number of atomistic entities becomes too large for useful representation. Entities used for atomistic representation within each domain are shown at left: subatomic particles, atoms, molecules, and cells. Ensembles of these entities (of the approximate quantities shown) then form atoms, proteins, cells, and organisms, respectively, which are often well studied using continuous representations of the component atomistic entities.

I will not attempt a rigorous definition of the terms "atomistic" and "continuous" here; the current presentation will be more anecdotal, describing the methods in current use in molecular and cell biology. There are many representations that appear to fall in a gray area between perfectly atomistic and smoothly continuous, or representations that combine both elements. In one case, at least, this gray area between atomistic and continuous extends to the physical nature of the system: at the level of quantum mechanics, we think of electrons as being, at least in as much as we can experimentally probe them, a continuous probability distribution of an atomistic particle.

Representations from Atoms to Molecules

Given the intrinsically 'atomistic' nature of molecules, it perhaps comes as a surprise that so many continuous models are in current use in molecular biology. Modern chemists rarely think of molecules in anything but atomistic terms: each molecule has a defined atomic structure, with a defined arrangement of atoms interacting through well-characterized bonding and non-bonding interactions. Molecular biology, however, often makes use of more abstracted representations, both in analysis of data and in the dissemination of results. This may be due, in part, to the provenance of structural molecular biology. Early views of proteins at low resolution did not reveal the location of each atom, but instead showed a richly organic form. Many of the basic principles of macromolecular interaction, oligomerization, and allosteric regulation were proposed based solely on these views, before atomic structures were known.

Atomic structures have added a wealth of new information to these low-resolution, continuous views. A typical protein molecule contains about 5400 atoms [1], about half of which are hydrogen atoms. Each of these atoms have a defined position relative to the rest, a position that is often critical to the stability or function of the entire molecule. The sheer complexity of biological molecules makes their representation a daunting task (Figure 2). Typically, atomistic models are used in computer simulations of molecules, because accuracy is paramount. Continuous models are then used for analysis and presentation of the structures, providing simplified representations that display and highlight the properties of interest.

Atomistic Models of Molecules

Atomistic models of biological molecules are widely used for computational simulation of biomolecular structure and function, and for the utilization of this information in biotechnology and medicine. The Protein Data Bank, a remarkable resource currently containing over 8000 macromolecular structures, is freely available on the internet. Each file contains the three-dimensional coordinates of each atom in a given macromolecule. A variety of methods then allow the user to display the structure, analyze its structural and functional features, and use it for molecular design.

Perhaps the most common method that makes use of atomic structures is *molecular mechanics*. In this technique, the forces between each atom in the structure are defined, parameterizing the distance-dependence of bonding, bond angle bending, torsional rotation about bonds and various non-bonded forces. Based on the starting positions of the atoms and this description of forces between the atoms, a trajectory is then simulated through time, typically adding a random component to the motion dependent on the temperature. These simulations provide insights into the dynamics and energetics of molecular function and interaction. Current computational resources typically allow simulations of 10-1000 picoseconds, which is sufficient for analysis of chemical catalysis and the stability of complexes.

Processes such as the diffusion and association of substrates to enzymes, or the formation of protein complexes, occur over much longer time scales, and are thus largely inaccessible to molecular dynamics simulation. Many modifications and simplifications of this process have been developed to address these problems. The two interacting molecules may be treated as rigid bodies, reducing the conformational space that must be searched. For very large problems, even the atomistic representation may be discarded, using an abstracted surface to define the molecules.

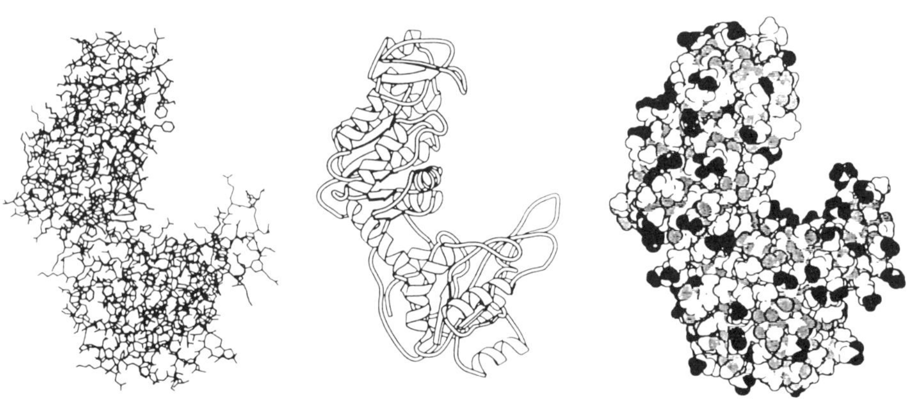

Figure 2. Common Molecular Representations. A typical protein contains over 5000 atoms, making representation a challenge. Three types of representation are commonly used for analysis and presentation of macromolecular structure. A bond diagram (left) depicts every covalent bond in the molecule; atom centers are understood to be placed at the ends of each line. A ribbon diagram (center) simplifies the structure, depicting only the location of one atom in each amino acid. Ribbons and arrows are used to depict the local structure of the chain. Spacefilling diagrams (right) are arguably the best representation of what a protein might "look" like. A sphere is used for each atom, representing the space from which other atoms are excluded. Bond diagrams and spacefilling diagrams are atomistic representations, and ribbon diagrams have a continuous character. The molecule depicted is phosphoglycerate kinase, an enzyme used by all organisms for the mobilization of energy from glucose.

Continuous Models of Molecules

Atomistic models of molecules are used for simulation and prediction of molecular function and interaction, whereas continuous models find more use in the analysis and presentation of biomolecular structures. Typically, much of the atomic detail is stripped away, and a simplified representation is used to highlight a given feature.

Ribbon diagrams (Figure 2 center) are a case-in-point for the power of these representations to clarify complex biostructural concepts. These diagrams are a simple schematic of the polypeptide chain. Conventions for secondary structure elements—a helical tape for α-helices, an arrow for β-strands, and a cord for random coil—were codified in Richardson's review of protein anatomy [2]. Since that review, the ribbon diagram has been unflaggingly popular. Ribbon diagrams are unparalleled for the clear way they present the folding of the polypeptide chain. They are widely used to classify protein folds, and to provide insights into the mechanisms of protein folding.

A variety of molecular surfaces have also shown great utility. The solvent accessible surface is created by rolling a probe sphere, which simulates a water molecule, over the entire surface of the protein, and saving the points at which the sphere touches [3]. This surface approximates the area that is in contact with the surrounding solvent: the outer "skin" of the molecule. Solvent accessible surfaces have been used to analyze complementarity at protein surfaces, and to evaluate the magnitude of the hydrophobic effect.

Three-dimensional fields and potentials are useful both for their methodological applications, and for the conceptual insights they provide. The most familiar is the electrostatic field and potential. For this, one imagines placing a probe with a unit charge at each point in space around the molecule, and evaluating the electrostatic force and the electrostatic potential energy. From this volume of data, one can construct field lines, which follow the direction by which a charge might be pulled or pushed, or one can construct equipotential surfaces, showing regions of space at which a charge will have equivalent potential energy. These properties have found wide use in physics, as is familiar to any high school physics student, and in the analysis of biomolecular interaction.

Representations from Molecules to Cells

At the next level in the scale hierarchy, we look at the range from molecules to cells. A plethora of data is available at the two extremes: techniques of x-ray crystallography and NMR spectroscopy have revealed the detailed form of individual molecules, and electron and light microscopy have revealed the complex inner structure of cells and their organelles. However, the intermediate level, where the continuous opacities and densities seen in micrographs are interpreted as collections of individual molecules, is largely unexplored. Experimental limitations place the study of cells at the molecular level largely beyond reach. Light microscopy cannot resolve single molecules, so micrographs typically yield a 'fuzzy' picture of the cell, in which the position and behavior of individual molecules must be inferred. Electron microscopy can provide the necessary resolution, but the strictures of sample preservation and radiation damage often make observation of intact cells impossible, at least at the molecular level. Currently, an experimental image of molecules within a living cell is beyond reach.

Many clever experiments have been devised to break this experimental barrier. For instance, antibodies have been created with fluorescent probes attached, as described in the paper by Rice and coworkers in this volume. These have proven useful for study of the cytoskeleton. An antibody that recognizes and binds to actin is perfused into a living cell, and under ultraviolet light, the delicate network of fibers then shows up as fluorescent tendrils. By attaching different fluorescent probes to different antibodies, the location of intermediate filaments, microtubules, actin, and other elements may be observed in the same cell, revealing their complex inter-relationships. But note that these experiments are not resolving individual molecules: each glowing line is in reality a narrow filament decorated with antibodies, much like an antenna atop a building may be decorated with flashing lights in order to make it visible to passing airplanes.

Simulation of Molecules in Cells

There have been several attempts to treat individual molecules as the discrete units in an atomistic representation, bridging the scale domain from molecules to cells. One attempt seeks to model the effects of macromolecular 'crowding.' Living cells contain highly concentrated solutions of macromolecules: muscle cells contain approximately 23% protein by weight, typical cells contain from about 17% to 26% protein by weight, and red blood cells, at 35% protein, approach the value of 40% found in typical protein crystals [4]. Macromolecular crowding can have a significant effect on the function of proteins [5]: for instance, a crowded solution will favor the association of two large proteins relative to association of a large and a small molecules, and crowded solutions enhance the binding of large ligands relative to small ligands to protein active sites [6].

The effects of crowding have been analyzed theoretically by use of models that treat individual molecules as hard, non-overlapping spheres. These models are able to reproduce many of the observed experimental properties of crowded molecular ensembles. For instance, Guttman and coworkers [7] tested two similar methods (treating the surrounding water differently), and were able to predict the enhanced aggregation of sickle cell hemoglobin caused by increased concentration of a second protein.

Illustrations of the molecular structure of cells are also feasible, given current biological and biochemical knowledge. The Escherichia coli cell is perhaps the best understood cell, providing a wealth of data for the construction of a detailed molecular model. A full genome sequence is known, and with it, knowledge of the proteins that may be synthesized [8]. Results from 2D PAGE, in which the proteins from whole-cell homogenates are separated electrophoretically, allow the concentrations of molecules to be analyzed under different physiological states [9]. Structural information is also available for most of the common molecules in the cell. By combining this information, accurate illustrations of the molecular structure of the entire cell may be simulated [10], as shown in Figure 3.

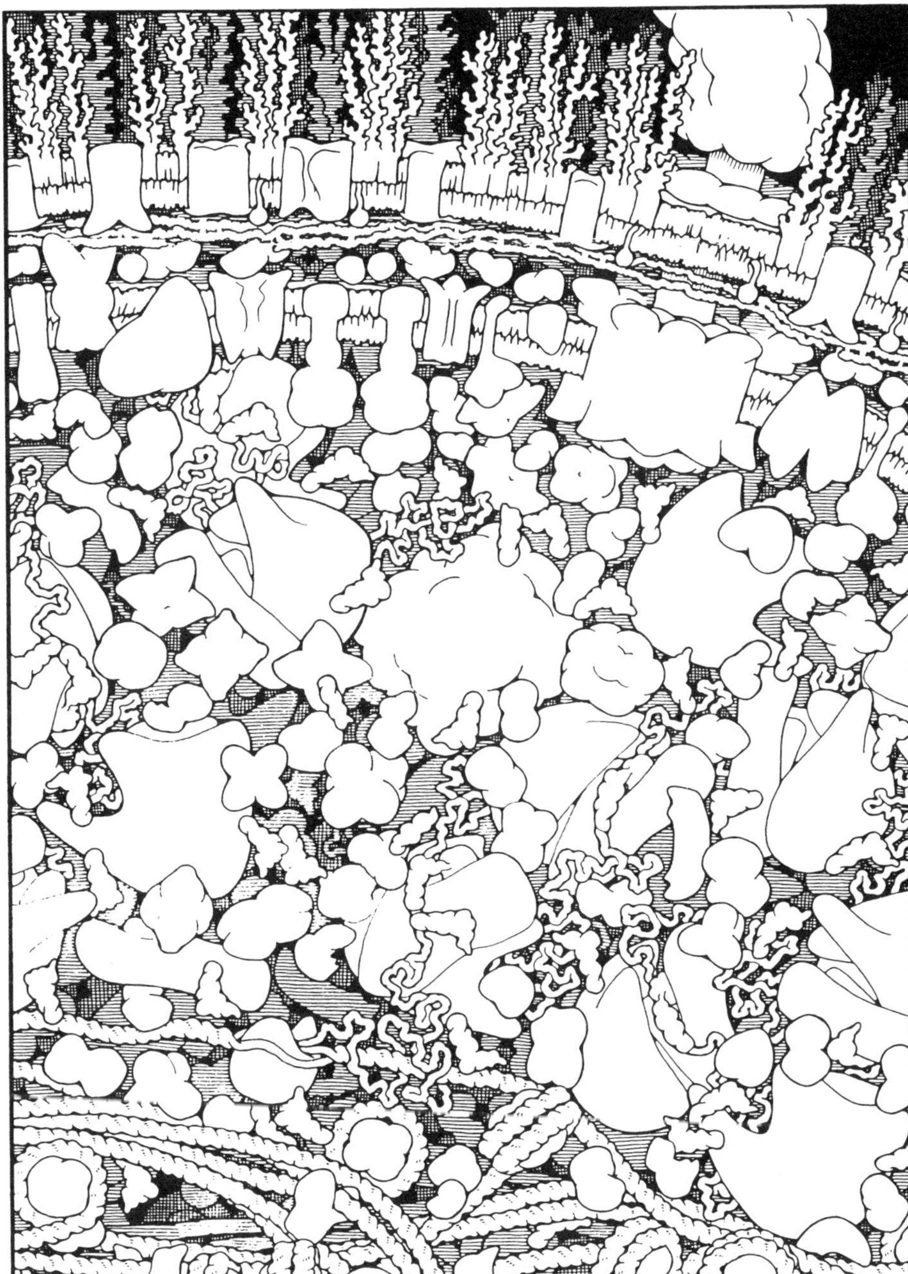

Figure 3. Molecules in a Bacterial Cell. A portion of an Escherichia coli cell is enlarged by 1,000,000 times, revealing the location of all macromolecules. The cell wall is shown at the top, with a large flagellar motor extending entirely through the two membranes. At center is the cytoplasm, dominated by large ribosomes synthesizing new proteins. At bottom is the nuclear region, crisscrossed by strands of DNA. In this atomistic representation, individual molecules are the atomistic entities.

Three-dimensional simulation of these complex cellular environments is an exciting new prospect, just becoming feasible. By adopting a multi-resolution approach, whereby the representation of each molecule is adjusted according to both the size of the image and the actual experimental resolution at which the molecule has been characterized, the problem is becoming computationally tractable.

Conclusions

The development of representations in the scale range from atoms to cells has been driven primarily by scientists, and their need to analyze scientific data and present the results to colleagues and the lay audience. This has not been done in any systematic way: each new type of data carries with it the need to apply an existing representation, or to develop a new one. For example, when atomic structures for biological molecules became available, a diverse collection of new representations were devised to deal with their complexity.

A more systematic approach, however, may yield fruits. Given a quantitative method to classify existing representations, one might identify scale domains that are under-represented in current representations. The images of molecules within cells are one example of an under-represented scale domain, and the image in Figure 3 was created to begin to fill that void. Of course, the quantitative classification of representational modes carries with it grave difficulties, as much of power and utility of representation, particularly visual representation, is subjective. The simple distinction of atomistic from continuous representations, described anecdotally in this paper, may provide one quantitative axis for such an analysis.

Acknowledgements

I thank Arthur J. Olson for helpful comments. This work was supported by grant DEFG03 96ER2272 from the Department of Energy, entitled "From Atoms to Cells: Multi-Scale Computational Integration of Sequence, Structure and Assembly." This is publication 12007-MB from the Scripps Research Institute.

References

1. Goodsell DS and Olson AJ. Soluble proteins: size, shape and function. *Trends Biochem. Sci.* 1993; 18:65-68.
2. Richardson JS. The anatomy and taxonomy of protein structure. *Adv. Protein Chem.* 1981; 34:167-339.
3. Lee B and Richards FM. The interpretation of protein structures: estimation of static accessibility. *J. Mol. Biol.* 1971; 55:379-400.
4. Fulton AB. How crowded is the cytoplasm? *Cell* 1982; 30:345-347.
5. Zimmerman SB and Minton AP. Macromolecular crowding: biochemical, biophysical, and physiological consequences. *Annu. Rev. Biophys. Biomol. Struct.* 1993; 22:27-65.
6. Minton AP. Macromolecular crowding and molecular recognition. *J. Mol. Recognition* 1993; 6:211-214.
7. Guttman HJ, Anderson CF and Record MT. Analysis of thermodynamic data

for concentrated hemoglobin solutions using scaled particle theory: implications for a simple two-state model of water in thermodynamic analyses of crowding in vitro and in vivo. *Biophys. J.* 1995; 68:835-846.
8. Blattner FR, Plunkett G, Bloch CA, *et al.* The complete genome sequence of Escherichia coli K-12. *Science* 1997; 277:1453-1462.
9. VanBogelen RA, Sankar P, Clark RL, Bogan JA and Neidhardt FC. The gene-protein database of Escherichia coli: edition 5. *Electrophoresis* 1992; 13:1014-1054.
10. Goodsell DS. Inside a living cell. *Trends in Biochem. Sci.* 1991; 16(6):203-206.

NetWork: a Tool for Visualization of Genetic Network Structure and Dynamics

Vassili N. Serov, Olga V. Kirillova and Maria G. Samsonova
Institute for High-Performance Computing and Databases,
St.Petersburg , 194291 Russia

Abstract.

We design the Java applet NetWork which enables a user to construct interactively and visualize the genetic network of interest, to work with a genetic network and to evaluate its dynamics in framework of Boolean network model. NetWork displays the mechanism of genes interactions and enables visualization of large genetic networks. Using NetWork it is possible to model the effects of the mutations in the network, as well as to reveal gene interactions compensating for these mutations.

1 Introduction

Understanding the mechanisms of cell functioning requires the investigation of complex behavior of ensembles of interacting genes and therefore calls for novel approaches, which go beyond the traditional experimental methods.
One of these approaches is to consider the ensembles of interacting genes as genetic networks. Genetic networks have been used to model biological systems for several decades. The simplest and the most computational effective model system that gives insight into the overall behavior of large genetic networks is the Boolean network [1]. In this model genes are represented as the elements of the Boolean net, and the wiring of the elements to one another corresponds to the functional links between genes. The state of each gene is determined by its inputs and Boolean function (mechanism of genes interaction). For a particular set of elements, wiring, rules given, a particular trajectory of a network can be calculated. Such a trajectory must reach a final steady state or the repeating cycle named as attractor, that may be envisioned as the "final state" of organism, e.g. cell types at the end of development [2].
Despite the obvious limitations, Boolean networks can be efficiently used to build models for to clarify the mechanisms underlying organism development, the nature of changes causing diseases and therapeutic strategies against these diseases.

The visualization and user interaction are the important tools and techniques which assist scientists in evaluation, absorption navigation and correlation of data. The genetic networks consist of tens or hundreds of genes involved in complex regulatory interactions. Therefore the deciphering of their logic and complex behavior requires the special purpose computational tools for their visualization. These tools should enable the user to simulate interactively the dynamics of genetic networks in frame of different models.
We have designed a tool of this kind using the Java programming language [3]. Java's independence from any particular hardware platform or operating system as well as its object-oriented approach have caused it to be widely used in wide variety of scientific applications, including many developed for visualization of biological data [4].

Here we describe a Java applet that permits a user interactively to construct a genetic network of interest, to work with a genetic network (as user-defined, so specified by the data provider) and to evaluate the network dynamics in framework of Boolean network model.

2 Methods

2.1 The applet architecture

The applet NetWork (http://www.csa.ru:81/ Inst/gorb_dep/inbios/Dyn_bool/Dyn.htm) is written in Java. For a presentation of genes and gene interactions, we modified the Nodes and Edges classes developed by Sun Mocrosystems Inc [3]. A new class DYNAMICS was developed which contains the method for simulation of network dynamics based on the Boolean algebra technique. The applet can be accessed through any World Wide Web browser conforming to the Java standards. The source code is available upon request to the authors.
In the current implementation the NetWork operates with objects and propagates events (e.g. mouse clicks) on them. Currently, the object types that can be displayed by this applet include genes and arrows, which reflect genes interactions. Data presentation and display functionality are controlled by a data provider via parameters (applet tags) in the HTML file containing the applet. The applet takes a number of parameters following HTML 3.2 and Java applet tag specifications: AllNetNames, NetN and NetName.

The AllNetNames tag **<param name=AllNetNames value= "Name1;Name2; Name3; ...">** dictates the name of the genetic network, which can be choosen by the user from the set specified by the data provider.

The NetN parameter (tag) defines the number of genetic networks available in the set.

The structure of each genetic network present in the set is defined by the NetName parameter as follows **<param name=NetName value="gene1-**

gene2/k, ...,genei-genej/k....">. In each pair of genes the first one is the regulator, the second gene is the target, **k** is +1 if the regulator activates the target and -1 otherwise.

This architecture gives great flexibility for displaying various genetic networks, as defined by the data provider, so specified by the user. For the developer it also means that new genetic network can be added easily and any existing network can be modified or replaced without affecting the functionality of others.

2.2 Method for simulation of network dynamics

We describe the dynamics of genetic network by the matrix equation:

$$A(t+1) = \Theta\big(A(t) * M\big); \quad A = \{a_i\}_{i=1}^{N},$$

where A is a vector of the network state in the moment t. i is a gene number, N is the size of system. Assume $a_i = 0$ when the gene is switched off and $a_i = 1$ when the gene is switched on. We assume that the presence of at least one repressor among regulators of the given gene turns it off regardless of the other genes action. In this case the matrix of genes interactions $M = \{m_{i,j}\}_{i,j=1}^{N}$ contains $m_{i,j} = 0$, if genes do not interact; $m_{i,j} = 1$, if gene i activates gene j and $m_{i,j} = -N$, if gene i represses gene j.

As the final state of the gene should be 0 or 1, we use $\Theta(x) = 0$, if $x < 0$ and $\Theta(x) = 1$ otherwise.

As attractor we consider the finite set of network states $\{A(t_i)\}_{i=1}^{k}$, where k is a number of states in the attractor. Once the system reaches attractor it is described by the following equation $A(t_{i+k}) = A(t_i)$, $i > I$, where t_I - is the moment when the attractor is reached.

3 Results

The applet NetWork (see Figure 1) subdivides the browser window into two panels: "GraphPanel" and "CtrlPanel". The former displays the information on genetic network, while the later contains the control elements. These elements are: the input and selection windows, buttons INPUT , ALL, ATTRACTOR, DYNAMICS and HELP, as well as lists DIST and FONT. The size of the GraphPanel is specified automatically depending on the number of network genes. The vertical scrollbar is provided for easy navigation in the network.

The basic elements displayed by NetWork are genes, represented as rectangles, and their interactions, shown as arrows. A given gene may be selected by clicking with the mouse. Regulatory interactions with regulators and targets of the selected gene become displayed in one window and highlighted. Red arrows connect a gene with the upstream genes of network, and blue arrows with downstream genes. Filled and hollow arrows reflect the mode of gene action - activation and repression correspondingly.

The gene may be dragged to a new place. This is sometimes required for better visualization of links between genes in cases where the network is large.

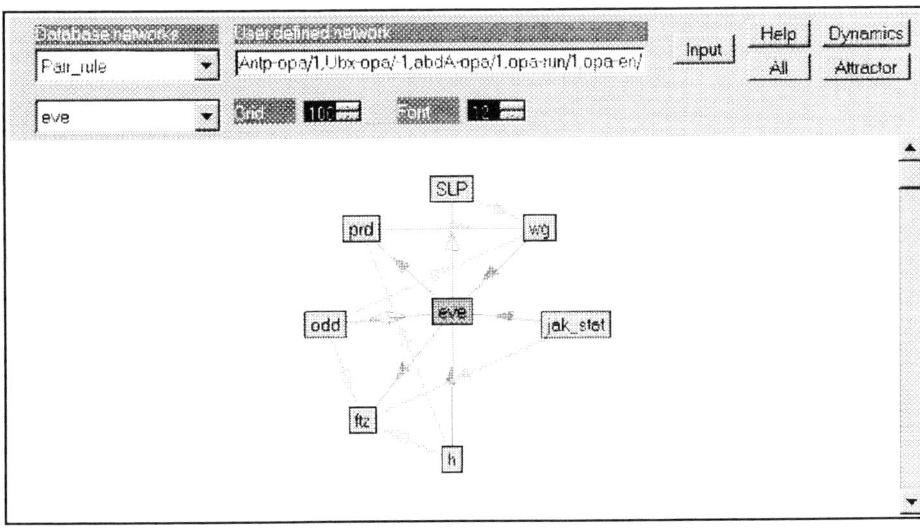

Figure 1. NetWork displaying the pair-rule genetic network in which the eve gene is selected.

The user is provided with the possibility to vary the size of the network region displayed in the browser window. To do so the user can change the dimension of the rectangles representing the genes, as well as the distance between genes by the selection of the desired value in the FONT and GRID lists correspondingly. By this means it is possible to see in the browser window the whole network or only part of it.

For interactive construction of genetic network of interest the user first enters in the input window the information on genes and mechanisms of their interactions in the following format **gene1-gene2/k, gene3-gene2/k,....,** where **k** is +1 in case of activation and -1 in case of repression; **gene1, gene2 and gene3** are genes names, in each pair of interacting genes the first gene is regulator, while the second gene is target. After completion of the input the user presses the INPUT button which enables the visualization of input data as a genetic network.

The user can work with a genetic network defined by the data provider. To do this would require the selection of the genetic network from the selection window containing the list of genetic networks available.

In the course of work the user can perform the interactive editing of the genetic network by deletion or addition of genes or links in the input window. This procedure enables the user to model the effect of mutations in the network.

To perform a simulation of genetic network dynamics the user selects the genes switched on in network initially by clicking on them while pressing Shift key and afterwards presses the DYNAMICS button. As the result the attractor is generated and the genes which are switched on in it are displayed. When more than one state make up the attractor cycle it is possible to see all these states by clicking sequentially the DYNAMICS button.

The user can hide all genes except those, which are switched on in the attractor by click on ATTRACTOR button. Click with the mouse on ALL button restores the display of all network genes.

It is possible to run the dynamics of genetic network several times by selecting interactively different group of initially turned on genes or modifying the genetic network structure.

4 Conclusions

The NetWork applet presented here permits the visualization of a genetic network structure. It displays the mechanism of genes interactions in the network, as the arrows connecting genes differ in shape and color depending on the mechanism of genes interactions. Large genetic networks can be easily visualized with NetWork due to the applet features, which enable to drug a gene to the new place and to display the interactions of the selected gene in one browser window.

Network enables a user to construct the genetic network of interest by interactive filling in the information about genes interactions in the input window in accordance with simple rules..

Our applet allows the rapid evaluation of network dynamics in the framework of Boolean network model. Using NetWork it is possible to model the effects of the mutations in the network, as well as to reveal gene interactions compensating for these mutations.

References

1. Kauffman S.A., The Origin of Order, Self-Organization and Selection in Evolution. Oxford University Press, New York, 1993
2. Somogyi R. and Sniegoski C. Modeling the complexity of genetic networks: understanding multigenic and pleiotropic regulation. Complexity 1996; 1: 45-63
3. Gosling G. and McGilton H. The Java language environment. it Sun Microsystems White Paper (http://www.javasoft.com/whitePaper/java-whitepaper-1.html), 1995
4. Stein L. Web applets: Java, Javascript and ActiveX. Trends Genet 1996; 12: 484-485

THEME 3

Articulating the Design Process

G. Malcolm and J.A. Goguen

M. Treglown

D. England

S.J. Sloane

C.F. Earl

H. Carlisle, P. Phillips and G. Bunce

T. Fernando, P. Wimalaratne and K. Tan

P.J. Stappers and J.M. Hennessey

J. Mcfadzean

C. Tweed

Signs and Representations: Semiotics for User Interface Design

Grant Malcolm
Connect, Dept. of Computer Science
University of Liverpool, UK

Joseph A. Goguen
Dept. of Computer Science and Engineering
University of California at San Diego, USA

Abstract

Goguen has proposed the use of semiotics to study the ways in which information is mediated in computer systems, particularly in user interfaces. His *algebraic semiotics* provides a formal tool for studying the systematic use of signs in computer systems, and for presenting formal comparisons of different interface designs. The formal elements of algebraic semiotics make it a kind of algebraic engineering for sign systems, and introduces an engineering rigour to interface design.

This paper presents some applications of algebraic semiotics to the design of user interfaces. In particular, we study the kinds of signs used in interfaces, and how they work as signs. We present some basic notions from algebraic semiotics, namely *sign systems* and *semiotic morphisms*, and apply these concepts to the sign systems of user interfaces, which allows us to give rigorous argumentation why some representations are better than others.

1 Introduction

Computer technology has been advancing at an astonishing rate, and now in the late twentieth century has reached a point where radical changes are beginning to be precipitated into society. These changes include the enormous growth of email, intranets, the world-wide web and chatrooms, so that both long-distance interpersonal communication and information access have achieved an unprecedented scale of deployment and ease of use. Entities and institutions of all kinds are increasingly being seen from an informational perspective as aquiring, processing, storing, disseminating and controlling data. For example, money has become increasingly abstract, not based on a physical commodity such as gold, but rather transmitted and received across the globe through secure protocols as long strings of bits. As a result of such changes, the productivity of individuals and institutions is often determined by how effectively they can control the information at their disposal.

Information is always mediated: it comes in a particular form or representation, through some medium, and is conveyed through signs. One way of facilitating effective control is to make this mediation *transparent*, so that information can be used as easily as a bird's wings use the air to control its flight. In computer science, such transparency is an explicit goal in user interface design: users should be able to manage complex tasks on a computer with as little overhead cost as possible spent on mastering the particular application program they are using; they should feel as if they are *simply doing the work* [9].

Goguen [2] proposes the use of semiotics to study the ways in which information is mediated in computer systems, particularly in user interfaces. His *algebraic semiotics* provides a formal tool for studying the systematic use of signs in computer systems (although it is of much broader applicablity), and for presenting formal comparisons of different interface designs. The formal elements of algebraic semiotics make it a kind of algebraic engineering for sign systems, and introduces an engineering rigour to interface design.

This paper presents some applications of algebraic semiotics to the design of user interfaces, a programme begun in Goguen (*op. cit.*) and further developed in the area of Computer Supported Cooperative Work by Goguen *et al.* in [3, 5]. In particular, we study the kinds of signs used in interfaces, and how they work as signs. The end goal of this study is to examine user interface design for software systems, especially operating systems, the most basic means by which users interact with computer systems. In Section 2 we present some basic notions from Goguen's algebraic semiotics, namely *sign systems* and *semiotic morphisms*. For reasons of space, the account of these notions is very brief, so we recommend consulting the original paper [2] for the motivation behind the technical definitions. In Section 3 we examine the sign systems of user interfaces, and apply some considerations from algebraic semiotics in comparing different user interfaces, giving rigorous argumentation why some representations can be confusing.

2 Algebraic Semiotics

Semiotics began with the philosopher Charles Sanders Pierce [8], who emphasized that the relationship between signs and their meanings is one of mediation, through a process of semiosis, involving what is called the *semiotic triad*: a *signifier*, or sign that conveys information, a *signified*, i.e., an object or idea that the sign is related to through the third element of the triad, an *interpretant*. This gives a relational, rather than a denotational, theory of meaning.

An important insight in semiotics is due to the Swiss linguist Ferdinand de Saussure, who argued that signs come in *systems*, and it is only through differences between elements of systems, rather than through inherent properties of signs themselves, that meaning can be conveyed. This provides one of the motivations for Goguen's definition of *sign system*. Essentially, these consist of sets of signs that are partially ordered in various ways, together with operations (called 'constructors') that allow signs to be built up from other signs. In addition, sign systems contain relations and axioms that constrain the ways in which signs can be constructed.

In more detail, a **sign system** consists of:

- a set S of **sorts** for signs;
- a partial ordering on S, called the **subsort** ordering;
- a set V of **data sorts**, for information about signs, such as colours, locations, and truth values;
- a partial ordering of sorts by **level**;
- for each level n, a set C_n of **constructors** used to build level n signs from data and signs at level n or less (**constants** take zero arguments);
- a (partial) **priority ordering** on each C_n;
- some relations and functions on signs; and
- a set of **axioms**, constraining the possible signs.

Mathematicians and computer scientists may recognise the similarities between sign systems and logical theories. As we will see below, these similarities are useful for modelling sign systems for the kind of structured data used in computer systems, which can be usefully described as logical (or algebraic) theories (see for example [4]).

Following a relatively recent tradition in mathematics, namely *category theory* [6], which provides a setting for the abstract study of structure, Goguen [2] observes that structure preserving morphisms (or 'translations' in this setting) are often at least as important as the structures themselves. This is part of the motivation for the definition of *semiotic morphism*, which is essentially a partial mapping of signs to signs preserving some of the structure of the source sign system.

More formally, a **semiotic morphism** from a sign system S_1 to a sign system S_2 consists of partial functions mapping

- sorts of S_1 to sorts of S_2,
- constructors of S_1 to constructors of S_2,
- predicates and functions of S_1 to predicates and functions of S_2,

such that the mapping of sorts to sorts preserves the subsort ordering and does not change data sorts, and arguments and result sorts of constructors and predicates are preserved (modulo the sort mapping).

Computer scientists may recognise in this definition a notion of translation or representation that allows meanings related to signs in one system (the target system) to be related to signs in the other system.

The definition above only requires a semiotic morphism to preserve a certain amount of structure. For example, it is not required that semiotic morphisms preserve the level of constructors, or their priorities. However, the more structure that is preserved by a morphism, the more the target system can be viewed as a truer translation or representation of the source system. In the following section, we consider interface designs as corresponding to semiotic morphisms from a *domain* sign system to the sign system presented to the user, and we argue that better designs often involve morphisms that preserve more structure.

3 The Semiotics of User Interfaces

In this section we look at algebraic semiotics applied to user interface design. The subsection below sets out some background detail, and the following subsection looks at the semiotics of operating systems; the next two subsections look at more detailed examples: a simple educational applet, and a presentaion of a formal proof in a cooperative proof system. These last two examples, and more, can be seen in the 'World Famous' UC San Diego Semiotic Zoo at `http://www-cse.ucsd.edu/users/goguen/zoo`, a web site that contains more details on algebraic semiotics.

3.1 Interfaces, Signs and Conventions

Pierce identified three kinds of signs: **icons**, **indices** and **symbols**. An icon is a sign that suggests a signifier through some quality of its own, for example a drawn line representing a geometrical line. An index is a sign that is regularly associated in some way with its signifier, for example smoke is an index of fire. A symbol is a sign that has a signifier simply because it is used and understood as such, for example, the numeral '6' denotes the quantity six simply by convention (a convention not shared, for example by the early Romans, who used the sign 'VI').

Examples of these kinds of sign in user interfaces include:

icons: in a document editor display, a configuration of pixels that resembles the letter 'a' represents the letter 'a' (note that a document editor will want to represent letters rather than *words*);

indices: 'icons' (in the computing sense of the word) representing applications or files, buttons, scrollbars;

symbols: numerals, symbols on icons such as the large 'e' for Microsoft Explorer or the ship's wheel for Netscape Navigator, hypertext links.

It is not always possible to distinguish clearly between these three kinds of sign: for example, the numeral '1' is mainly symbolic, but partly indexical, as it consists of just one stroke.

Iconic representations can be thought of as more immediate, in that their appearance points the way to their interpretation, while symbolic representations are less immediate, in that the association between signifier and signified is arbitrary. For example, there is no quality of the word 'cat' that suggests its meaning.

Symbolic representations, however, sometimes rely on some conventions for their interpretation. For example, certain browsers render hypertext links in a conventional way, for example as blue underlined text, while visited links are rendered as dark blue underlined text. For this reason, it can be confusing if a web page uses coloured fonts in a way that flouts these conventions: users might not recognise active links, or might believe that ordinary text is a link.

Many indexical representations rely on metaphors for their interpretative force. For example, buttons are partly iconic graphical representations of real buttons, to enforce or suggest that clicking on them will produce some action (there may also be a suggestion of the button *affording* clicking, in the sense of Gibson [1]). Similarly scrollbars in their appearance (and their name) suggest a metaphor involving a window that can move up and down a long document. Many document editors display a button with a picture of scissors on it. Its resemblance to a button is indexical, suggesting that clicking on it will produce some action, in this case removing a part of the document, while the image of scissors is both iconic and indexical, relying for its force on a metaphor of the document as a physical paper manuscript that can be cut with scissors. Another standard button displaying a pot of glue extends this metaphor by suggesting that scraps cut out of the manuscript can be pasted back in a different place.

The following subsections present examples of the algebraic semiotics of interface design. Section 3.2 briefly discusses the sign systems of operating systems, and Sections 3.3 and 3.4 apply algebric semiotics to interface design, discussing 'design' morphisms that preserve or don't preserve the structure of their sign systems, and lead to good or bad designs, respectively.

3.2 Operating Systems

Command-line operating systems, such as Unix or DOS are relatively poor in signs presented to users. The main signs include a prompt inviting the user to enter commands, the commands themselves with their options and arguments, and the display of the results of these commands, for example, a directory listing if the user enters the command `ls`.

Windows-based operating systems tend to be much richer in both the signs presented to the user and in the complexity of these signs. Typically, the presentation is less centralised: rather than a single prompt controlling all interaction, various applications and files will have their own space on a virtual desktop.

Command-line operating systems typically display only the prompt sign when they start up, so the user is required to know and remember many signs (commands and their options), while windows-based operating systems usually present graphical access to many commands and files on the system. Windows-based operating systems are more decentralised: they offer a set of conventions to the user and an area in which individual applications and files can display their own signs (for example, icons and interfaces). The conventions typically include the fact that double-clicking the right mouse button will produce some effect, that interfaces appear in windows with buttons to iconize or close the window, menus have a standard appearance, and so on.

Command-line operating systems have relatively small sign systems, and signs generally tend to be symbolic, whereas windows use many more indexical signs, such as the buttons and scrollbars described above. Again, many of these indices rely on metaphor for their effectiveness. The predominant metaphor is of the computer as workplace: the graphical area is called a *desktop*, files are stored in *folders*, and organized by a file manager application whose icon displays a filing cabinet.

Note that there are dangers to using metaphors in designing interfaces, the most notorious example being the use of the Apple Mac trashcan to eject floppy disks from the drive [7, 10].

3.3 A Slightly Confused Applet

Signs are arranged in levels in a sign system, and "good" semiotic morphisms map signs to signs in a way that preserves the ordering on levels. Software systems are often implicitly designed around a semiotic morphism; when this morphism confuses levels, the result is usually a confused design.

Figure 1 shows an applet that illustrates a stack and an array with a pointer. The user can push values onto and pop values off of the stack by means of two

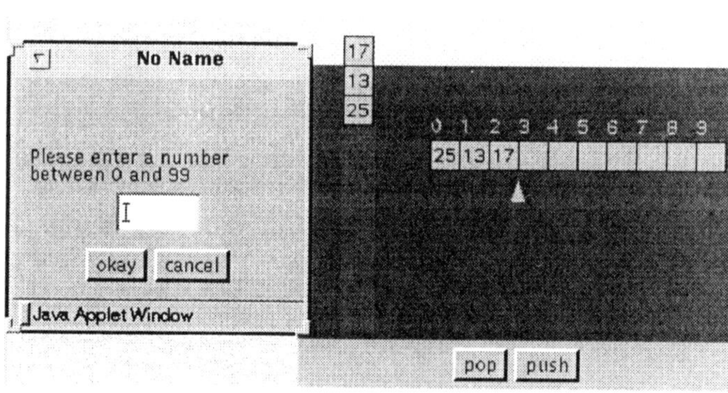

Figure 1: An applet illustrating stacks and arrays.

buttons. The applet can be viewed as the image of a semiotic morphism from a sign system whose signs include stacks and push and pop operations. The target sign system has signs for windows, applets, graphical areas, buttons, and so on. Because of the applet's rectangular visual display, there is a natural ordering of containment on signs, suggesting that window signs are on a higher level than applet signs, which are on a higher level than buttons. However, clicking the push button causes a new window to open up, shown in Figure 1, asking for a value to be pushed onto the stack. One low-level sign in the source system (the push operation) is mapped to a complex sign in the target system that involves signs from different levels (a button and a window). The semiotic morphism therefore confuses sign levels.

An improved version of this applet is shown in Figure 2. The interface

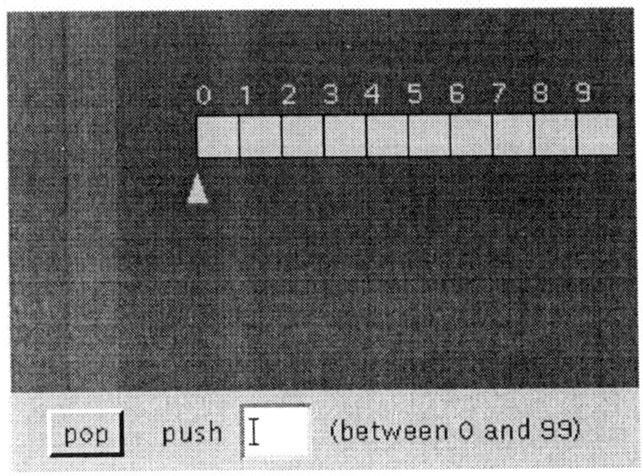

Figure 2: An improved interface.

in this version has a text area beside the push button; clicking the button pushes the value entered in the text area onto the stack. Thus the signs that allow values to be pushed onto the applet's stack are all contained within one graphical region, and one layer of the sign system.

3.4 The Tatami Proof Browser

In this section we look at an example of a semiotic morphism that doesn't preserve priorities of constructors. The extract below is from a description of a proof in the 'Tatami' system [3, 5]. This system allows workers to collaborate on constructing proofs, parts of which can be constructed by individuals, and the results published to colleagues on web pages. The following is from such a web page, and details the proof of some property that is not important for our purposes: the reader will almost certainly not follow the details of the proof; we are merely interested in the form of the proof description:

> We show that R is preserved by all operations in Γ.
>
> We use 1. quantifier elimination, 2. case analysis, 3. implication elimination, 4. conjunction elimination, 5. lemma introduction, and 6. reduction to show that

```
( I1,I2,N : Nat,  A1,A2 : Arr)
    (I1 || A1) R (I2 || A2)   implies
     pop(I1 || A1)  R   pop(I2 || A2)   and
     push(N, I1 || A1)  R  push(N, I2 || A2) .
```

This involves the following steps:

1. introduce new constants `i1`, `i2`, `n` of sort `Nat`, and `a1`, `a2` of sort `Arr`;

2. 3. 4. 6. in case that `i1 = 0`; assume `i2 = 0`, then show

```
pop(0 || a1)  R  top(i2 || a2) = true ,
push(n, 0 || a1)  R  push(n, i2 || a2) = true ,
```

separately by reduction.

A Tatami page is a complex sign that summarises some (part of a) proof. To understand this complex sign, the reader must recognise its component signs and the constructors that were used to combine these into the whole. Constructors have priorities, and ambiguities are often resolved by choosing the highest priority constructor as default. This will give the wrong result if the constructor actually used had a lower priority.

A Tatami page describes a proof by stating the goal and then listing the steps involved in proving that goal. A list is a complex sign whose constructor takes the list items as arguments; the list items are generally preceded by some label, such as a number or a bullet. The primary constructor for ordered lists uses numbers to order the items in sequence. For example, the following list describes how to find the UCSD Semiotic Zoo home page:

1. Start a web browser from the command line.
2. From the "File" menu, select "Open Page".
3. Type "www-cse.ucsd.edu/users/goguen/zoo/" in the dialog box.
4. Click the "Open" button.

The list gives a number of steps to be performed in the order given by the numbers labelling each item. Labels may be used to give different kinds of information; for example, the same list may be labelled by whether the step involves keyboard or mouse actions:

Keyboard Start a web browser from the command line.

Mouse From the "File" menu, select "Open Page".

Keyboard Type "www-cse.ucsd.edu/users/goguen/zoo/" in the dialog box.

Mouse Click the "Open" button.

This kind of list constructor has a lower priority than the enumerated list constructor, so when the reader sees

This involves the following steps:

1. introduce new constants ....

it is natural to assume that the list of proof steps is enumerated. It only becomes clear from the second item in the list that the numerical labels actually refer to the proof tactics listed near the top of the page. (Even then, the labels look confusingly like a subsection-style enumeration.)

The confusion arises because of an ambiguity in the constructor for the list of proof steps. The text preceding the proof steps suggests an enumerated list constructor, but the list is actually built using a lower priority constructor. The effect is rather like a 'garden path' sentence: the reader is forced to backtrack and construct a different understanding of how some complex sign was constructed.

4 Conclusions

We have given a very brief account of algebraic semiotics, and sketched how it applies to user interface design. In particular, Section 3.3 shows that algebraic semiotics can be used to reason about why one interface design is better than another. This represents a first step in introducing some of the rigour of engineering disciplines to user interface design. However, this paper is more a statement of intent of our research programme than a publication of achieved results, and we recognise that more examples are needed in order to present a convincing case.

The main points that we wish to stress are that interaction with computer systems is mediated through signs, and that certain design features are encapsulated by semiotic morphisms from some domain-specific sign system (e.g., the 'stack' sign system in the example of Section 3.3) to the sign system of the user interface (e.g., the appearance of the applet in Section 3.3):

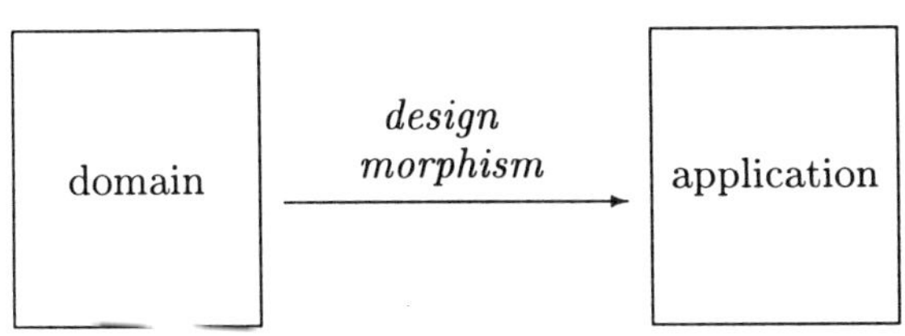

The more structure this *design morphism* preserves, we argue, the closer the interface reflects the underlying structure of the application domain. We might also argue that structure-preserving design morphisms aid intelligibility. For example, the reader of the Tatami proof in Section 3.4 has to recover the structure of the described proof, reconstructing as it were the semiotic morphism represented by the structure of the proof description.

As we said above, more work remains to be done. As well as more examples, it would be useful to try to capture basic design principles in terms of semiotic morphisms, and to test the approach on the adaptive nature of signs and communication in computer supported cooperative work.

References

[1] James J. Gibson. The theory of affordances. In Roberts Shaw John Bransford, editor, *Perceiving, Acting, and Knowing: Toward an Ecological Psychology*. Lawrence Earlbaum Associates, 1977.

[2] Joseph A. Goguen. An introduction to algebraic semiotics, with applications to user interface design. In Chrystopher Nehaniv, editor, *Proceedings, Computation for Metaphors, Analogy and Agents*, pages 54–79, 1998.

[3] Joseph A. Goguen, Kai Lin, Akira Mori, Grigore Rosu, and Akiyoshi Sato. Distributed cooperative formal methods tools. In *Proc. Automated Software Engineering*. IEEE, 1997.

[4] Joseph A. Goguen and Grant Malcolm. *Algebraic Semantics of Imperative Programs*. MIT Press, 1996.

[5] Joseph A. Goguen, Akira Mori, and Kai Lin. Algebraic semiotics, proofwebs and distributed cooperative proving. In *Proc. User Interfaces for Theorem Provers*, 1997.

[6] Saunders Mac Lane. *Categories for the Working Mathematician*, volume 5 of *Graduate Texts in Mathematics*. Springer Verlag, 1971.

[7] John M. Lawler. Metaphors we compute by. Lecture notes available at http://www.ling.lsa.umich.edu/jlawler/, 1987.

[8] Charles Saunders Pierce. *Collected Papers*. Harvard, 1965. 6 volumes.

[9] Ben Shneiderman. *Designing the User Interface: Strategies for Effective Human-Computer Interaction*. Addison Wesley, 1986.

[10] Mark Treglown. Is the trashcan being ironic? Applying a contemporary theory of metaphor to HCI. This volume, 1998.

Is the Trashcan Being Ironic? Analysing Direct Manipulation User Interfaces Using a Contemporary Theory of Metaphor

Mark Treglown
Institute of Educational Technology, The Open University,
Milton Keynes, UK.

1 Analogy Recommended but Also Considered Harmful

One approach adopted in the design of graphical user interfaces is to create icons and dialogue structures, and to consider the tasks supported by interactive systems, according to a consistent theme. By making the theme some aspect of the real world, or a task domain with which the user is assumed to be familiar, it is said that some metaphor or analogy has been adopted in the design of the user interface's model world. It is also suggested that by adopting an analogy in the appearance and behaviour of the on-screen objects that make up the model world, users' existing knowledge can be carried over and the novel interactive system will be easier to learn and use than if new knowledge structures have to be acquired.

Designing user interfaces according to a metaphor is an approach promoted by many best-selling and influential texts, however the reality of learning and using metaphor-based systems is often not as successful as hoped or intended. Halasz and Moran [1] suggest that analogies and metaphors should be avoided as they are said to inhibit a complete conceptual model of the system being developed by users, there possibly being aspects of the system that no mapping between the source domain of the analogy and the target domain of the computing system can account for. Smith [2] suggests that the pragmatics of implementing metaphor-based model worlds on hardware which is always likely to be subject to uncertain delays and unpredictable temporal behaviour means that user interface software will always give rise to behaviour of the on-screen objects that cannot be accounted for by analogies. Studies of users learning to use metaphor-based systems, in addition, often reveal that the metaphor is a source of confusion and difficulty rather than a source of resolution of difficulties

While many articles, as Anderson et al [3] note, offer discussions of the advantages and disadvantages of the use of metaphor in general, some attempts to apply and support psychological theories of metaphor may be found. Typically though, studies of metaphor and analogy in disciplines other than human-computer interaction (HCI) show that HCI can still benefit from greater understanding of these forms of communication and understanding the world, and that work developed in disciplines other than HCI can impact on the design of user interfaces.

2 Can User Interfaces be Understood Through Metaphor?

French [4] surveys many theories of metaphor comprehension arising from a number of disciplines, including cognitive psychology, linguistics and artificial intelligence. Many of these theories and models, while applicable to varying extents to the problem of user interface design, have to date provided little that can be used to suggest or evaluate particular user interface metaphors. The theories surveyed by French can all be described as adopting the Objectivist world view. This view of reality, meaning and reference, long-standing in Western science and philosophy, adopts the following assumptions, that thought is the mechanical manipulation of abstract symbols, that symbols obtain their meaning via correspondences with things in the external world, and that symbols that correspond to the external world are internal representations of external reality.

This model of the world is not one that has gone without criticism, however. Attacks by some authors [5, 6] are having a growing influence on how task domains are understood and on the user interface design process. Other criticisms [7, 8,], are of particular interest when considering the role of metaphor in user interface design and comprehension. In particular the place of user actions in task performance, and user actions suggested by the user interface metaphor and the widgets used in an interface design must be addressed. While it is appreciated in HCI that eventually the user will have to press keys or buttons, or make use of other input devices in order to perform tasks, the need to take into account proprioception, motor skills, and the fact that cognition is embodied, within an account of user interface understanding and use has largely been ignored. The difficulty of providing an account of proprioception within the Objectivist framework has been noted by some of the critical texts cited above. Criticisms of the Objectivist world view will need to be taken into account as further work in examining the roles of metaphor and analogy in HCI is undertaken.

The severest criticism of the Objectivist world view has been provided by Hilary Putnam [9] who has provided a well-known theorem that refutes many of the assumptions of Objectivism. Putnam's result in formal semantics serves to break the claim that symbols in the mind being mirror objects in external reality. Lakoff [10], builds on Putnam's Theorem to claim that the Objectivist paradigm forces a distinction between what is literal and what is figurative. If figurative expressions are to have any meaning, then they must have some related literal meaning, thus metaphor and metonymy are deemed to be subjects not accounted for by an Objectivist semantics, and metaphor cannot be any part of a human's conceptual system since concepts are required by an Objectivist semantics to have a direct correspondence to entities and categories in the real, or a possible, world.

Metaphors require independent access to the domains between which a mapping is to be made. This independent access, the God's eye view as Putnam [9] terms it, is what Putnam's theorem states can never be available. Certainly it is hard to tell how the novice user will have a full understanding of the computing system with which they are unfamiliar. It is a difficult task, sometimes impossible, with existing modelling techniques to provide a complete account of the behaviour of an interactive graphical user interface. The conclusion drawn, therefore, is that metaphor will never allow users to understand the systems they use if concepts and models of the system are to be formed to a large extent by metaphorical mappings between domains modelled in a set-theoretic, Objectivist, way. However, to draw this conclusion would be to reject the pervasive nature of metaphor and analogy in understanding the world [11]. We are therefore required to explore further the role that metaphor will play in user interface design. In doing so, we continue a programme advocated by Rohrer [12] and examine a contemporary, non-Objectivist theory of metaphor and its application in HCI.

3 Towards a Contemporary Theory of Interface Metaphor

3.1 Image Schemata

Putnam's Theorem gives rise to the conclusion that metaphor can play no part in our understanding of concepts assuming an Objectivist world view. Mappings between domains, as assumed in existing work on metaphorical understanding of user interface model worlds, according to the theorem, teach us little about the quality of a user interface metaphor as the concepts and representations of the external world modelled have no connection to mind-independent things. We must therefore confront how meaning is obtained and what role metaphor can play in the world. The conclusion drawn by Lakoff [10] and Johnson [13] is that meaning is grounded in terms of image schemata, and that the world can be understood in terms of these schema and metaphorical mappings or extensions from these schemata to describe a situation or statement. Johnson [13; Pages 28-29] provides the following definition of image schemata:

> "On the one hand, they are not Objectivist propositions that specify abstract relations between symbols and objective reality. There might be conditions of satisfaction for schemata of a special sort (for which we would need a new account), but not in the sense required for traditional treatments of propositions. On the other hand, they do not have the specificity of rich images or mental pictures. They operate at one level of generality and abstraction above concrete rich images. A schema consists of a small number of parts, images, and events. In sum, image schemata operate at a level of mental organisation that falls between abstract propositional structures, on the one side, and particular concrete images, on the other.
>
> The view I am proposing is this: in order for us to have meaningful, connected experiences that we can comprehend and reason about, there must be pattern and order to our actions, perceptions, and conceptions. *A schema is a recurrent pattern, shape,*

and regularity in, or of, these ongoing ordering activities. These patterns emerge as meaningful structures for us chiefly at the level of our bodily movements through space, our manipulation of objects, and our perceptual interactions." (Original italics)

This notion of how meaning is grounded, while radical compared to the Objectivist world view it opposes, is similar to that derived in other disciplines [8, 14].

3.2 Understanding Metaphors

The human conceptual system is said to employ many image schemata, all of which provide structure to our embodied interaction with the world. The examples shown in Figure 1 shows how an OUT schema captures the underlying meaning of a number of utterances and situations. Image-schematic representations of IN-OUT relationships are said to ground large amounts of meaning, perhaps not surprisingly as IN-OUT patterns of interaction with the world are so common.

John went out of the room.
Pump out the air.
Let out your anger.
Pick out the best theory.
Drown out the music.
Harry weaseled out of the contract.

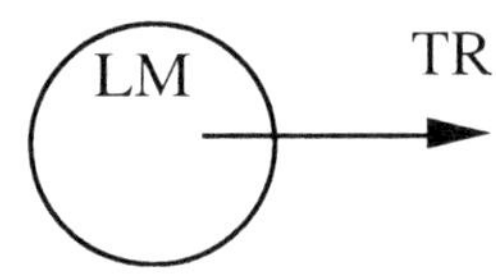

Figure 1 The OUT_1 schema [13; Page 32]

It should be noted that the depiction of an image schema in Figure 1 is only a *depiction*, but it serves to illustrate the bodily experiences captured in and described by the schema. In the schema shown, LM is the "landmark" in relation to which TR, the "trajector", moves. Considering the schema OUT_1 and the sentence "John went out of the room", the circle (LM) represents the room as a container, and John moves along the arrow (as TR) out of the room. The diagram does not represent much information, such as the shape of the room (which may not be circular), or the vector along which John moves, but "gives only one idealized image of the actual schema...It is, rather, a continuous, active, dynamic recurring structure of experiences of similar spatial movements of a certain kind." [13; Page 36].

The intention of the Lakoff/Johnson theory of metaphor is to be able to account for human understanding of concepts and language, in order to do so it must be able to describe the non-physical as well as the physical. To this end, understanding is achieved by metaphorical extensions from image schemata. An example given by Johnson [13; Page 35] is the sentence "I don't want to leave any relevant data out of my argument", this relies upon the OUT schema in order to be understood, but also relies upon the ARGUMENT IS A CONTAINER metaphor, claimed to be a very common metaphor in Western culture [11]. There are, obviously, more schema in addition to IN-

OUT used to ground our comprehension of the world. Johnson [13; Page 126] presents a partial list of schema, which he claims are "*...pervasive, well-defined, and full of sufficient internal structure to constrain our understanding and reasoning*" (original italics). Many more examples of how concepts, including categories, time and causality, are grounded in image schema are given by Lakoff in [15]. Many of the schema that Lakoff and Johnson claim are pervasive in our understanding of the world are applicable, and prove to be useful, when trying to employ their theory to understand metaphor-based user interfaces.

4 Is The Trashcan Being Ironic?

The user interface that most computer users are likely to be familiar with is the desktop metaphor, which has been implemented to a greater or lesser extent in the most influential and best selling graphical user interfaces to the functionality provided by a number of operating systems. In the desktop metaphor, data files are depicted by icons that resemble documents, folders which can contain files denote directories, application software supports tasks that are typically performed on documents and in an office setting.

The file deletion mechanism employed within the implementation of the desktop metaphor on the Apple Macintosh, the trashcan, is notorious for the problems it causes users. Benyon et al [16] note that "..it is common practice to include an icon of the dustbin on the 'desk'. Not only does this contravene our expectations as to where to find dustbins (on the floor), but also the interface dustbin has other functions apart from its conventional use as a container for discarded objects." They [16] note an additional difficulty that is considered further below, that "..the dustbin is often the place where disk icons are put in order to eject the disk from the disk drive. This implies that one has to 'throw away' a disk in order to retrieve it! Such an apparent contradiction can cause conceptual problems to first-time users since it is easy to think that the contents of the disk will be discarded when the disk is placed in the dustbin." While many anecdotal reports tell of the distress felt by users when learning of the task sequence that must be performed in order to achieve the goal of ejecting a floppy disk, in empirical studies we also found that the task was not suggested to users by the desktop metaphor employed by the system examined. We are unaware of any explanation as to why this task should cause users particular difficulties, but by applying the Lakoff/Johnson theory of metaphor understanding, it is possible to offer such an explanation.

Rohrer [12], in an effort to understand the failure of the trashcan, adopts Smith's [2] distinction between literal and magical features in user interface metaphors. He suggests that "The magic of a trash can has to do with its being a portal to the beyond in the PHYSICAL WORLD metaphor - the beyond of the landfill, the beyond of the electronic bit bucket, and the beyond of the world outside of the computer." This statement hints at an explanation as to why the trashcan fails, there is a confusion as to which domains the mapping is made between, and the image schema underlying understanding of the system. Dragging a disk icon into the trashcan appeals directly to the IN schema, an object is placed within a container and according to the schema should remain within the container. Within the domain of the computing functionality and hardware, however, which following Laurel [17] and Treglown [18] should be the target domain considered, the floppy disk is ejected from the disk drive, which can be understood directly by the OUT_1 schema.

The Macintosh trashcan requires the user to construct a mapping between two opposite actions, the schema that explains the disk being ejected has no metaphorical mapping in the desktop model world, and is unlikely to occur to users. By requiring an OUT schema to be realised by performing actions that make up an IN schema, the meaning of the operation is the opposite of the way in which it is articulated, it is possible to claim that the task and the trashcan are being ironic. Irony being "...traditionally seen as referring to situations that postulate a double audience, one of which is 'in the know' and aware of the actor's intention, whereas the other is naive enough to take the situation or utterance at its face value." [19; Page 262]. Furthermore, it is possible to say that the trashcan is an example of an aspect of a user interface metaphor that breaks the *Invariance Principle* [15; Page 219] which states that "Metaphorical mappings preserve the cognitive topology (that is, the image-schema structure) of the source domain, in a way consistent with the inherent structure of the target domain."

5 Conclusions

We are seeking to determine the range of systems that can be described in terms of the Lakoff/Johnson theory. They claim that much of understanding of the world is through metaphor comprehension, therefore much understanding of the model worlds provided on-screen by interactive systems should also be through metaphor comprehension. In addition to the system discussed above, we have elsewhere shown that the Lakoff/Johnson theory of metaphor comprehension can be used to account for the usability, and improved usability in comparison with rival user interface designs, of an immersive virtual reality, and a computer aided design tool, respectively. To judge the extent to which metaphor is important in understanding interactive systems, we are currently attempting to provide accounts of far smaller aspects of direct manipulation systems, in particular the windows, scroll-bars, and icons that are the building blocks of most user interfaces in use today. Previous accounts of features of direct manipulation user interfaces have employed the notion of affordances to explain the actions that users perform when interacting with them, our immediate task is to determine whether metaphorical accounts based upon image schema can also explain these features.

Acknowledgments

I am grateful to Tim O'Shea, Thomas Green, and the anonymous reviewers for their comments.

References

1. Halasz F, Moran TP. Analogy Considered Harmful. In: Proceedings of the Conference on Human-Computer Interaction. ACM, New York, 1982
2. Smith RB. Experiences with the Alternate Reality Kit: An Example of the Tension Between Literalism and Magic. In: Proceedings of CHI'87 Human Factors in Computing Systems. ACM, New York, 1987
3. Anderson B, Smyth M, Knott RP, Bergan M, Bergan J, Alty JL. Minimising Conceptual Baggage: Making Choices about Metaphor. In: Cockton G, Draper SW, Weir GRS (eds) People and Computers IX. Cambridge University Press, Cambridge, 1994
4. French RM. The Suability of Sameness: A Theory and Computer Model of Analogy-Making. The MIT Press, Cambridge, Massachusetts, 1995
5. Winograd T, Flores F. Understanding Computers and Cognition: A New Foundation for Design. Addison-Wesley, Reading, Massachusetts., 1986
6. Suchman, LA. Plans and Situated Actions. Cambridge University Press, Cambridge, 1987
7. Agre PE. Computation and Human Experience. Cambridge University Press, Cambridge, 1997
8. Clancey WR. Situated Cognition. Cambridge University Press, Cambridge, 1997
9. Putnam H. Reason, Truth and History. Cambridge University Press, Cambridge, 1981
10. Lakoff G. Women, Fire and Dangerous Things: What Categories Reveal about the Mind. University of Chicago Press, London, 1987
11. Lakoff G, Johnson, M. Metaphors We Live By. University of Chicago Press, Chicago, 1980
12. Rohrer T. Feeling Stuck in a GUI Web: Metaphors, Image-schemas and Designing the Human Computer Interface. Available from University of Oregon WWW Site, http://darkwing.uoregon.edu/~rohrer/gui4web.htm
13. Johnson M. The Body in the Mind: The Bodily Basis of Meaning, Imagination and Reason. University of Chicago Press, Chicago, 1987
14. Harnad S. The Symbol Grounding Problem. Physica D 1990; 42:335-346
15. Lakoff G. What is Metaphor? In: Barnden JA, Holyoak KJ (eds) Advances in Connectionist and Neural Computation Theory Volume 3 Analogy, Metaphor, and Reminding. Ablex, Norwood, New Jersey, 1994
16. Benyon D, Davies G, Keller L, Preece J, Rogers Y. A Guide to Usability, Open University Press, Milton Keynes, 1990
17. Laurel B. Computers as Theater. Addison-Wesley, Reading, Massachusetts, 1993.
18. Treglown M. Qualitative Models of User Interfaces. In: Cockton G, Draper SW, Weir GRS (eds) People and Computers IX. Cambridge University Press, Cambridge, 1994
19. Gibbs RW. Process and Products in Making Sense of Tropes. In: Ortony A (ed) Metaphor and Thought 2nd edition, Cambridge University Press, Cambridge, 1993

Visualisation of Data Landscapes for Collaborative Virtual Environments

David England

School of Computing and Mathematical Sciences
Liverpool John Moores University
Liverpool UK

d.england@livjm.ac.uk

1.0 Introduction

Collaborative Virtual Environments provide a place to meet for co-workers who are physically distributed from each other. The presentation of the environment may be a simple textual interface or it may be a sophisticated multimedia interface involving video conferencing, electronic white-boards and so on. In our work we are interested in virtual reality as the medium of communication. This means that co-workers meet in a 3-dimensional, virtual world and are visible to each other as figures, or *avatars*, in that world. The world itself may have scenery and devices that represent some model of a real-world office. Now representing a virtual office is an interesting first step but it does not exploit the full potential of virtual reality. The true power of virtual reality lies in combining the real and the abstract. Thus in our worlds we wish the users to inhabit a landscape that is created from some set of information that they share as a working group.

For example, a group of knowledge workers may be creating a set of documents together. Each person is responsible for editing one or more sections of each document. We might choose to show the documents by providing a visualisation of the user, showing objects close to them which represent document sections and then positioning each user according to how their sections relate to the work of their colleagues. A user arriving in this landscape would then see how the different workers and documents are connected to each other, and to their own work. Alternatively we might make the individual documents our main focus of attention and locate them according to which sub-group of users are working on them. One could extend this example to many other domains where distributed groups of workers are working together on some shared artefacts, i.e. in engineering design (of photocopiers, motor vehicles, etc.), building design and architecture, urban planning, group-based distance learning, software design, even to the design of virtual worlds themselves.

In this paper we wish to review our approach to building shared virtual worlds. We firstly review the background for our work and then re-examine our work in the context of new issues of realism in presentation, subjectivity and similarity-based location of data.

2. Review

Previous work in collaborative virtual environments has brought together three separate areas of human-computer interaction,

- CSCW (Computer-Supported Collaborative Work)
- Virtual Reality via networks
- Information Visualisation

CSCW takes a multi-disciplinary approach to collaborative computer systems and ranges from the technology of networking to the social study of distributed groups. CSCW has in the past attempted to classify collaborative systems according to the following matrix. That is we can classify a system by whether the users are in the same location or remote from each other, and by whether communication takes place in real-time or is delayed.

	Immediate Communication	**Delayed Communication**
Same Location	*Electronic white board*	*Post-it notes*
Remote Location	*Video Conference*	*Electronic Mail*

The promise of shared virtual reality is to break this artificial distinction of collaborative systems. Firstly the distinction between same/remote location becomes blurred as the virtual world is *the* place for communication. Secondly virtual reality can be the medium for both immediate and delayed communications, by, for example, chatting in the first case and by using a representative landscape in the second.

The first virtual reality systems grew out of computer-based flight simulators and were both expensive and cumbersome. We now have the technological capabilities to provide networked virtual reality on a user's workstation. For example, the DIVE system [1] offers a shared virtual environment that can be used on UNIX workstations across the Internet. Sony's Community Place browser uses VRML 2.0, the Virtual Reality Modelling Language [2], to provide a similar facility on personal computers. In [3] we provide a critique of virtual reality across networks and suggest future directions for supporting multi-user worlds.

Information visualisation is our third supporting technology. Most work on this area has concentrated on visualising information for single users, from existing information sources. These sources can be divided into two broad areas; databases and information retrieval systems. Databases hold structured information divided into fields whereas information retrieval systems hold unstructured information such as free-text. For example, the Q-PIT system [4] shows the results of a text retrieval query as a 3d pyramid in virtual reality. Benford and Ingram [5] attempts to improve the comprehensibility of information visualisation by basing the visualisation techniques on the architectural principles of Lynch [6].

Much of the preceding work on visualisation ignores the shared and collaborative nature of information. In previous work we have taken a different approach and taken shared work spaces as our information source for visualisation. Shared workspaces not only hold information about documents but also, the actions and events that those documents undergo, and the users who initiate those actions. For example, BSCW [7] keeps a log of events that happen in a shared workspace. In [8] we showed how this log could be used to produce a virtual landscape indicating the relative activeness of different workspaces. Similarly in [9] we have shown how a set of virtual office cabinets could be generated from a shared workspace, to provide a virtual meeting place for distributed government administrators.

3. The Quest for Reality ?

One of the chief goals of research into computer graphics is to produce ever more photo-realistic images. There is an assumption amongst some commentators [10] that this is also the chief goal of virtual reality. In some domains of application visual fidelity is an important aspect of the virtual environment, for example, flight simulators, battlefield simulators and so on. However, the experience of our work is that attempting to model the real in the virtual world is unnecessary and can be a positive hindrance to clear visual representation. For example, in our work [8] with BSCW [7] we used an abstract view of the workspaces of BSCW in order to give an overview of the patterns of group behaviour. There were several hundred objects in the world, representing shared files and folders. However, in the POLITeam project [9] we attempted to locate the same kinds and number of objects in a mock virtual office using cabinets and shelves. This caused two main problems; firstly, parts of the furniture objects obscured the data objects and thus reduce the usefulness of any pattern arrangement we were attempting; secondly, the furniture objects added many extra polygons to the scene thus slowing down rendering. We agree with Manley [11] who argues that, rather than trying to achieve realism, virtual reality should try to achieve believability. He bases his argument on a theatre metaphor. In a theatre we willingly suspend our disbelief and believe in the acts on the stage; a stage with a limited space and limited number of props. The question for researchers is what set of minimal features of design are necessary to populate a virtual world of information and still make it believable and useful to its inhabitants? The initial investigations can obviously be based around such issues as visual appearance of objects in terms of colour, shape, lighting and texture. We can reduce and distort these visual attributes of real world objects so that the objects add to and annotate information in a scene. We can go further and ask questions about the behaviour of objects, and how it can represent information about the shared nature of scene artefacts. This behaviour can be expressed both as responses to user actions and also autonomous actions scripted for objects.

3.1 Subjectivity: breaking the reality link between users?

Another way in which virtual worlds mimic the real world is in the presentation of the same image to all viewers. Now each viewer may have several viewpoints in a virtual world but traditionally each viewer would see the same scene as another at the same viewpoint. Snowdon et al. [12] proposed the breaking of this convention using the mechanism of subjectivity. In this approach each viewer would see a world that meets their individual requirements. For example, I might see only the documents to which I have authorised access. Another viewer in the same world and at the same viewpoint would see documents accessible to them only. Now the question arises: does this break the link of shared information between the inhabitants of the virtual world? I start to discuss the red object and my fellow cybernaughts cannot see it. Does this present a communications barrier? Would my private objects have to be visually marked in some way, would I have the opportunity to reveal them to other users? Or would we limit the application of subjectivity to changing aspects of the appearance of objects to different users? But that would again raise the question of whether some common ground is lost between users because of the differences in appearance of shared objects.

4. Similarity-based landscapes

If subjectivity might break the communication potential of a virtual landscape how might we restore it? In our work with POLITeam and BSCW we have attempt to analyse the similarities between workspaces as a means of locating their visual representation in the virtual landscape. For example, POLITeam keeps a log the initial creator of a document and subsequent editors. From this we can create virtual groups of users who are interested in this document. Documents can then be located in the virtual landscape according to the group of users to which they belong. We could extend this by also including the readers of documents. In fact, we could create a number of different grouping scenarios and allow the user to view the virtual world from a particular grouping. Thus users can see our their work relates to that of their colleagues.

BSCW is more explicit about group membership of workspaces and keeps a log of all operations by users. In this case we analyse cross-memberships between workspaces and can then arrange the workspaces according to their degree of joint user membership. The log of operations is also used to control the geometry of workspace representation. The number of operations is used to set the height of a central workspace cylinder. Thus users can ascertain the relative activity between workspaces, with more active workspaces being taller than other. We can also apply the same rule to document objects themselves so that more frequently used objects are more visible than other. We have used height in our examples so far but we could exploit the techniques described by Munro [13] and make busy objects look physically more used like a well-read book.

5. Future Work

We will now take our work further by exploring further prototype landscape generators for shared virtual worlds. We will again base our work on generating landscapes from BSCW workspaces. Now, however, we wish to take a more general approach by allowing the interactive design of worlds by users. We wish to allow users to pick common features of an underlying set of shared workspaces and then drive landscape creation from those features. These features might include; sets and subsets of artefact authors, time-dependant attributes, common operations and so forth. We also wish to explore the effects of overlaying workflows over a set of workspaces so we can illustrate the process(es) by which artefacts are built. More generally we wish to explore more interactive and dynamic landscapes than previously. We close with the following questions;

- What algorithms do we need to develop viewable and navigable virtual worlds?
- What data filtering methods might be appropriate to control complexity?
- How do we evaluate such worlds?
- What design features and guidelines are needed for believable shared worlds?
- What issues does our work raise for the areas of awareness and workspace design?
- What questions does our work pose for the designers and researchers of virtual environments?

Acknowledgements

This work initially began at GMD, Sankt Augustin and is now further supported by the School of Computing and Mathematical Sciences, Liverpool John Moores University. The author is grateful to the organisers of VRI '98 for the chance to present and discuss these issues with fellow delegates at the conference.

References

[1] Carlsson C and Hagsand O, (1993), "DIVE - A Platform for Multi-User Virtual Environments", Computers & Graphics, pp. 663-669, Vol. 17, No. 6

[2] VRML (1997), The VRML 2.0 (VRML97) Draft International Standard, ISO/IEC DIS 14772.

[3] Broll W, England D (1995), "Bringing Worlds Together: Adding Multi-User Support to VRML", *Proceedings of VRML 95 Symposium*, ACM, New York, 1995.

[4] Mariani, J. A., Benford, S. and Rodden, T. (1995) "Populated Information Terrains", Fadiva 1 Workshop, Seeheim, Arbeitspapiere der GMD 909, GMD Sankt Augustin.

[5] Ingram, R. and Benford S. (1995) "Improving the legibility of virtual Environments" in Proceedings of the 2nd Eurographics Conference on Virtual Environments, Monte-Carlo, Jan/Feb. 1995.

[6] Lynch, K, (1960) "Image of the City", MIT Press.

[7] Bentley, R., Appelt, W., Busbach. U., Hinrichs, E., Kerr, D., Sikkel, S., Trevor, J. and Woetzel, G., (1997) Basic Support for Cooperative Work on the World Wide Web, in International Journal of Human-Computer Studies 46(6): Special issue on Innovative Applications of the World Wide Web, pp. 827-846.

[8] England D (1995), Virtual Places of Real Work, workshop at E-CSCW '95, Stockholm., http://lister.cms.livjm.ac.uk/homepage/staff/cmsdengl/Research/

[9] England D, Prinz W, Simarian K, Stahl O, (1998)"A Virtual Environment for Collaborative Administration", *Proceedings of the International Conference on Virtual Environments on the*

Internet, WWW and Networks, (Earnshaw and Vince eds.), IEEE Computer Society Press, New York.

[10] P Every, Slipping through the net: theories of realism in virtual space?, Visual Representation and Interpretation '98, Springer Verlag 1998

[11] D K Manley, Theatricality and levels of believabilty in graphical virtual environments, Visual Representation and Interpretation '98, Springer Verlag 1998

[12] Dave Snowdon, Chris Greenhalgh & Steve Benford (1995) "What You See is Not What I See: Subjectivity in Virtual Environments". In Framework for Immersive Virtual Enviroments (FIVE'95) 18-19th December, 1995, QMW University of London, UK

[13] A Munro, Judging books by their covers: remarks on information representation in real world information space Visual Representation and Interpretation '98, Springer Verlag 1998

Interpreting Computer-Based Fictional Characters, a Reader's Manifesto: Or, Remarks in Favour of the Accommodating Text

S. J. Sloane
Department of English
University of Puget Sound
Tacoma, WA USA
sloane@ups.edu

Abstract

Close examination of two sets of computer-based characters and analysis of the ways in which those characters evoke strong, affective responses in their "readers" leads this researcher to speculate that many other computer-based stories are missing an opportunity to accommodate the purposes of individual readers. This researcher posits that University of Washington's HIT-Lab project, "SpiderWorld", and Carnegie Mellon University's Oz Project's "Woggles" provide two excellent models for how computer-based characters might better accommodate their "readers" and offer absorbing narratives.

1. Introduction

As narrative theorists already know all too well, contemporary models of the reading-writing relationship usually emphasize one point on the rhetorical triangle and ignore the others. That is, New Critics tend to focus on the text itself, nit-picking about the internal coherencies, patterns of metaphors, or how a particular rhyme scheme underscores an inherent soulfulness, for example. They pay little attention to the provenance of the author, and note hardly at all the living biographies of participants in the reading and writing transaction: a story's readers and authors are largely forgotten. This admittedly reductive portrait of the New Critic is intended to demonstrate how that theoretical stance demands a method in reading the text that obscures the important contributions of readers and forgets the important contributions of writers to the creative enterprise of making meanings. In this paper, I intend to suggest that contemporary programmers and designers of computer-based stories often forget likewise: they fail to note and account for the purposes and personal histories that particular readers are bringing to their computer-based story experiences. (In fact, to a fault, today's collaborative writing teams are likewise obscured by this focus on text or "product"; e.g., programmers and content providers are rarely mentioned by name, and the physical packaging of computer fictions highlights the commercial sponsor of the effort and almost never the writer. That, however, is the subject of another paper.)

The central question this paper will address is the following one: How important are the *readers* (or interactants, participants, users, or players, to use some of the loaded terms from disciplines including psychology, sociology, computer science, and game theory) to the virtual worlds, or stories, we build using computers? Related questions include some of the following ones: What might happen if programmers and designers were to construct virtual worlds that they no longer visualized as neutral spaces in which stories "happened", unfettered by authorial intention and unconcerned with readerly response? What might happen if designers recognized the extent to which a reader's identification with a fictional character might depend upon the purposes she brings to that reading? or the motives with which he approaches that text? How might the quality of an on-line story be improved if world builders were to recognize the variety of readers that will roam those worlds, readers who will alter the landscape in ways slight or major, leaving footprints in the virtual sands faint or deep? What might happen if the world actually responded to different readers' needs, if not only the narrative progression were interactively scripted, but the world itself accommodated itself to the needs and purposes of its visitors? In short, what does it matter who the reader might be?

1.1. Post-structuralist Theories and Reader-Response Criticism

"What Is an Author", Michel Foucault's post-structuralist essay on the author-function ultimately raises the important question, *What matters who's speaking* [1]? Foucault's essay ultimately echoes the post-structuralist commonplace that the author is dead, God is dead, that "God and man [have] died a common death" [2]. Foucault seeks to reconstitute an "author-function", a critical term meant to designate whatever traces of author's self that might remain in text and context, within the vacuum left by the author's disappearance. In my remarks today, I intend to raise the natural counterpart to such a query: *What matters who's reading?*

Like most reader-response critics (Tompkins; Rosenblatt; Iser) and many post-structural theorists (Fish; Bleich; Foucault; Derrida), I see a story's meaning as one (or some) that are created by its reader—in response to the implicit reading strategies and gaps embedded within the text. As Tompkins states simply, a poem or story releases meaning that "has no effective existence outside of its realization in the mind of a reader [3]." Further, I would argue that meanings accrue as a reader discovers a narrative progression offered both explicitly (in the order of the pages, the tables of contents and indices, the chapter headings, the book jacket flaps, the prefaces and end notes) and implicitly (within the gaps in the narrative, the places where partial information is given, in the flawed monologues of unreliable narrators, and so on).

In short, I subscribe to the point of view that readers may draw vastly different conclusions and proffer immensely creative interpretations of any text under study; in particular, I argue that any text worth its salt can accommodate these multiple valid interpretations. However, in the world designs and story generator systems that I have so far seen in late twentieth-century America and at this conference, I have rarely seen sufficient attention given to the ways in which a reader's purpose and a computer-based fictive world might creatively interact and create an absorbing tale.

Critical theorists including J. David Bolter, Roger Chartier, Richard Lanham, and George Landow have identified in numerous essays some of the ways in which computer-mediated textuality realizes many post-structuralist notions of a text's native *jouissance,* its playfulness, its slippery meanings, its algorithmically-driven ability to lumber on in the absence of its programmers, to make mock of an author's intentions altogether. However, in establishing that the relationships between language and world are always tenuous, that rhetoric and reality only occasionally cohere, and that computers offer us an almost impossibly idealistic tool with which to explore some of the more egregious slipperiness between world and word, these theorists have failed to offer us an alternative vision of an ascendant reader. In other words, while many literary critics today recognize the distance between word and world—and can easily see the seams splitting between language and thing described—none has sufficiently shaken off the cognitivist bias that affects much research and design of virtual worlds. The poet William Stafford offers us the simile that avoiding the tricks, traps and misleading terms of language is as hard as taking off a rubber glove with one hand [4]. I posit here that the occasional strengths of post-structuralist theory have not sufficiently been appreciated by computer programmers and designers; in general, the virtual worlds these able people have designed do not anticipate, register, and change to accommodate their many readers and the many narrative progressions in which they participate. They do not go the extra step to build worlds that realize the potential of readers to invent the meanings of stories. Post-structuralist ideas have insufficiently come to terms with some of the insights of reader-response criticism. Computer-based stories are one place to accommodate better some reader-response ideas.

Looking closely at two computer-based fictional worlds will allow us to see how knowledge of one's audience, how implicitly acknowledging a reader's purpose, motives, and compulsions, helps designers shape successful computer-based stories. Finally, in my position today as a narrative theorist, I should note clearly that I find the creation of "absorbing tales" to be one of the greatest strengths of any successful storyteller or story-generating system.

2. Spiders, SpiderWorld, and Spider Phobia

I was delighted to see the headline in the *Daily Mail* yesterday that alerted readers to the "spider plague spinning a web around Britain". The following excerpt captures the gist of the article:

> Step by silent step, an invasion of the nation's lounges, kitchens and bathrooms is under way.
>
> House spiders are on the march as never before . . . 'Thankfully for the terrified, the spiders have some unpleasant habits,' said Mr. Burgess [entomologist at Cambridge University]. 'They are not averse to cannibalism.'
>
> That will be no comfort for spider-haters such as Michelle Collins, 32, from Darlington.
>
> 'I'm spending more time trying to wash them down the bath than actually bathing,' she said [5].

Clearly, fear of spiders is a condition that afflicts citizens of Britain—as it afflicts people in the United States, as well. Hunter Hoffman, Research Engineer and Affiliate Faculty member of the University of Washington Department of Psychology has been collaborating with clinical psychologist Albert Carlin at the University of Washington Outpatient clinic, exploring the use of "Virtual Reality exposure therapy" to systematically desensitize "spider phobics." To date, this use of virtual spiders has been quite effective in the treatment of people who claim a very strong fear of spiders.

2.1 The Human Interface Technology Laboratory's SpiderWorld at University of Washington

The 1997 issue of *Behavioral Research Therapy* offers a description of a virtual world called "SpiderWorld" under the title, "Virtual Reality and Tactile Augmentation in the Treatment of Spider Phobia: A Case Report" [6]. The report details the experiences of an extremely phobic young woman as she encountered the spiders she feared in a controlled, immersive virtual world over a period of twelve one-hour sessions. That immersive virtual world, SpiderWorld, is a virtual reality representation of a kitchen that is home to two virtual spiders, a large furry brown one, and a smaller black widow with a white 3-D spiderweb. Subjects encountering SpiderWorld report that their VR therapy using virtual spiders generalizes quite well to real spiders. I read the set of experiences described in that journal article as an example of how user-character relations might be exploited and heightened in building strong computer-based narratives. The following description of SpiderWorld is based on this article, on my discussions of SpiderWorld with Hunter Hoffman, and my own experiences in SpiderWorld.

Preliminary results of SpiderWorld's effectiveness demonstrate that systematic desensitization using virtual spiders is a powerful new tool for clinical therapists. According to Carlin, et al.:

> Spider phobia is characterized by persistent fear of spiders, an immediate anxiety response upon exposure to spiders, and avoidance of spiders. Fear of phobic proportions can interfere with the patient's normal social routines, activities, and interpersonal relationships, and can produce marked distress about having the fear. [6]

Hoffman and his co-authors hypothesize that placing phobic subjects in a virtual world helped desensitize them to spiders in the real world. Further, they speculate that being able to touch a stand-in for a virtual spider, a patch of hair pasted to the back of a plastic spider, helped "blur" the distinction between the real and the virtual. The authors state: "Touching virtual spiders was an important symbolic gesture (like shaking hands with the enemy) and may have helped transfer of training from the virtual spiders to the real world"[7].

2.2 A Subject in SpiderWorld

Hoffman and his collaborators offer a description of one subject, M.M., who is an example of a spider phobic desensitized successfully by VR immersion therapy. M.M. (Ms. Muffet) was a 37-year-old single woman who had been afraid of spiders for the last twenty years. Any encounter with a spider was likely to cause panic in her as well as fits of weeping, waves of anxiety, and shame. A vivid description of the subject's symptoms is offered:

> [Ms. Muffet] chose to work a 'graveyard' shift of her job to reduce contact with spiders. Prior to going to work, she thoroughly washed and vacuumed her car every day, to wash off any spiders. She frequently fumigated her vehicle with pesticides, and also left cigarettes burning in the ashtray with the windows closed, after hearing from a friend that spiders avoid smoke. Ms. Muffet wore special 'spider gloves' while driving, in case it was necessary to sweep spider webs out of the car window on the way to work [8].

In addition, Ms. Muffet sealed her bedroom windows with duct tape every night, placed folded towels against doors, and ironed each piece of newly washed clothing before she placed it in a sealed plastic bag (to keep spiders out).

2.2.1 The Treatment of Ms. Muffet

In her virtual reality immersion therapy, over a period of three months, Ms. Muffet was exposed to 12 weekly sessions approximately 50 minutes long in SpiderWorld. According to Hoffman, spiders were placed in cupboards, the sink, and in various places in the kitchen space of SpiderWorld. The virtual spiders were made to jump unpredictably, to climb and drop on walls, ceiling, and floor, and to spin webs. In three months, researchers noted a dramatic reduction in dysfunctional behavior as well as a clear drop in the subject's self-ratings of fear of spiders. For example, Ms. Muffet was so desensitized to spiders that after treatment she was able to go on her first camping trip in sixteen years.

2.2.2 Interpretations of the Treatment of Ms. Muffet

Colourful as these descriptions may be, I would like to narrow our focus to two aspects of Ms. Muffet's experience of SpiderWorld: (1) her degree of absorption in the experience; and (2) her clear purpose in her "readings" of

SpiderWorld. I suspect these two aspects are closely related, and if virtual worlds can be designed with the needs of particular kinds of readers in mind, we will be on our way to creating exhilarating, responsive narrative experiences in VR. The authors of the journal article describing SpiderWorld wonder whether "the level of presence experienced [by the subject] can be predicted beforehand based on reported personality characteristics such as absorption" [9]. I would speculate that "the level of presence" experienced by a subject or user relates directly to the intensity of motive she brings to the virtual world, as well as to how well that virtual world is responsive to her needs, wishes, and prior actions within the world. Ms. Muffet was absorbed in the narrative of SpiderWorld because she was a highly motivated participant in a world tailored to her needs.

3. Carnegie Mellon University's Oz Project

The Oz Project at Carnegie Mellon University is another intriguing long-term project, one directed by Principal Researcher Joseph Bates, a member of the Computer Science Faculty at Carnegie Mellon. The Woggles, described in more detail below, were designed by members of the Oz Project who were assisted by the Computer Animation group at Carnegie Mellon. According to the materials posted on the Oz Project Website [10], "there are currently 2 versions of the Oz system" under development. One version of the Oz system is a text system that uses the Lisp programming language to create real-time interactive fictions like the old text adventures published by Infocom [11]. (Scott Reilly at Carnegie Mellon University has built three small demonstration worlds using this system, worlds with the colourful names of "Robbery World, "Office Politics", and "The Playground.") The other version of the Oz system is "a real-time animation version which is built on top of C and RAL (a C preprocessor with built-in Rete matcher)" [12]. Using this second version of the Oz system, the group has built a small and simple world called *The Edge of Intention,* discussed below.

3.1 The Edge of Intention

The designers of *The Edge of Intention* conceive of the world as "an interactive animated art piece." They say that the world "looks like something out of a Dr. Seuss book" and they are right. The background of the world looks like a colourful cliff with a few uneven platforms scattered about in front of it. Those platforms are inhabited by four small creatures nicknamed Woggles, which are ellipsoidal shapes with expressive eyes. Put more simply, the Woggles are stretchy circles that bounce around the platforms and emote via cartoonish eyes expressing happiness, sadness, grumpiness, and so on. Nicknamed Wolf, Shrimp, and Bear, the three primary Woggles are always joined by a fourth one, one who represents the user or interactant.

The Edge of Intention was first shown at the 1992 American Association of Artificial Intelligence's Art Exhibition.

3.1.2 Commentary on the Woggles

I was lucky enough to observe interactants at that first 1992 Art Exhibition as they approached the simple sketches of the Woggles on a computer screen and gradually became engrossed in their world. In particular, as people interacted with the Woggles, they invariably grew excited as it became clear that the Woggles were reacting to their movements and actions. It appeared that the Woggles were looking right at the interactant, for example, and that interactant often would mutter under her breath or talk in half-sentences at the Woggles. The level of absorption I observed among people at the conference was very high. Again, I would speculate that the responsiveness of the "text" to "readers," a responsiveness that felt real because it changed according to what the reader did, is what made *The Edge of Intention* such an absorbing world for its participants. Participants approached the Woggles with the goal of being entertained (cued in part by the canisters of jelly beans and the brightly-coloured Woggles and scenery). They were not disappointed.

When designers of virtual worlds consider the question of how to make their spaces more engaging, they might turn their attention to the ways in which characters engross readers with which they identify or to which they are attracted or repulsed.

4. Inventing Believable Characters in Virtual Worlds

The history of inventing characters to represent various types of real people is very long. Aristotle gave his students a typology of character traits, virtues and vices, and suggested examples of behavior ranging from cowardly to courageous, in his lectures on ethics. His student, Theophrastus, is justly famous for his own long list of character flaws and descriptions of people who might embody them. The rhetorical treatises of Hermogenes and others on this subject enabled the survival of lists of character types well into the Middle Ages. In 1614, Sir Thomas Overbury extended the tradition to include not just a character's vices and virtues, but a list of character traits divided by occupations and national origins. That is, his lists described characters like "the shoemaker" or "the Dutchman". And as any student of rhetoric knows, a close look at the history of lists of characters spans 2300 years and extends from Aristotle's treatises to the lists of caricatures and stereotypes included in eighteenth-century coffeehouse periodicals like *The Tatler* and *The Spectator*, straight through contemporary revivals of the tradition such as Elias Canetti's *Der Ohrenzeuge: Funfzig Caraktere (The Eyewitness: Fifty Characters)*, 1974.

However, no comparable, explicit list of kinds of readers exists, to my knowledge. We might infer such a list from some postmodern literary experiments like Italo Calvino's *If On a Winter's Night a Traveler* [13], but none exists in an explicit typology of which I am aware. Such a list might be valuable to designers of virtual worlds.

4.1 A Taxonomy of Readers

We might think about complementing the long history of work on characters, that work which in contemporary versions offers advice on how to make characters believable or "round" (Forster [14]), with work on framing another set of types—Readers. Further, by building virtual worlds that invite particular kinds of readers, we might be inventing, in a backhanded way, genres of virtual worlds. And the way to create distinctive genres might be to create worlds that best accommodate certain interpretations of visual phenomena, that best suggest or produce the quality of absorption in the experience of particular images.

4.1.2 Absorbing Readings

Absorption of this kind springs from an interaction between the *materials* of the story's characters (in this case, the interactive, multimedial, computer-based creatures in an immersive VR), and the *location* of the reader herself within the microworld. By location here, I mean more than attending to just a person's phobias, valuable though Hoffman's work may be; I mean the person's location in a richer sense. We need stories and characters that attend to a reader's location in terms of his or her experiences, schooling, purposes, motivations, desires, attractions, repulsions, class, historical position, religious affiliation, regional bias, and so on. Designers of VR worlds might do well to consider who we are and who this particular virtual world might be inviting us to become for the duration of the immersion.

Further, instead of genres of fiction, we might start talking about a typology of worlds, worlds that would offer customized, absorbing readings.

5. Computing Fictions

In *Computing Fictions,* a book I am currently working on, I develop the categories of *materials, processes,* and *locations* as critical terms intended to capture some of the dynamics of readers and writers, or viewer-users and author-programmers, content providers, and so on, as they connect via computers. Participating in SpiderWorld and watching The Woggles has helped me understand in particular the connections between the material properties of computer-based fiction and the locations of users, readers, viewers, or interactants. Paralleling the recent claims of researchers from Cynthia Selfe [15] to Richard Lanham [16] that computers provide a window into the writing process, that the computer screen makes visible those revisions and false starts, the zigs and zags that Linda Flower [17] likens to how a porpoise swims underwater between surfacings, I would like to make the claim here that immersive virtual worlds like *SpiderWorld* and *The Edge of Intentions* reveal part of the processes by which readers might be absorbed by stories.

The degree of a reader's presence and absorption may well be the most important category in our interpretations of computer-based fictional characters. The quality of the line, the visual dimensions of character, the cocked eyebrow or half-smile, may be important only insofar as they are cues to readings. The materiality of the interactions may be important insofar as it sustains or ruptures the illusion of being in someone else's world, a world that tailors itself to your needs and desires, that accommodates multiple readers as well as various readings.

5.1 Some More Speculations about Absorption and Interpretation

SpiderWorld users and researchers often discuss the quality of "in vivo" experiences, those encounters, for example, with real-world spiders that are changed or coloured by what happened in the immersive virtual world. Many virtual world designers are acutely interested in the links, blurrings, and overlaps between real-world and virtual world experiences. I join them in their interest and speculate here that virtual worlds can aid us in our understandings of the real world; further, I speculate that the stories and characters we encounter in the virtual world help us see our own lives as narratives and help us build connections between who we are, what we have done, and where we are headed.

Virtual worlds show us that it is possible to shape the often chaotic material of experience, material we call life, and indicates paths through that material, paths that probably have some kinship with stories, those dominant, compelling narratives of the late twentieth century. Virtual worlds implicitly echo real worlds, sometimes in ways cartoonish or ineffective, sometimes non-responsive or incoherent, sometimes in ways slant, or, to borrow Federico Garcia Lorca, "sometimes the piano is out of tune" [18].

But one thing is certain. When we look at the construction of virtual characters such as the Woggles, when we are immersed in the kitchen of SpiderWorld, flailing away at spiders big and small, we have clear examples that images need not be deeply complex nor fully realistic to evoke strong responses and absorption in their participants. We need not labor at realism in physical detail or setting; we need not seek verisimilitude in the characters or places we visit in VR. We need only offer absorbing experiences to different kinds of readers.

I will offer an example. If there are any gardeners among my readers, you might remember Sir Frank Crisp, who clearly subscribed to the opposite point of view and relished in the *trompe l'oeil.* Crisp, an amateur gardener and 'alpine aficionado' tried to recreate the Matterhorn on his four-acre Henley estate. Why not? Various gardening texts recount the 7,000 tons of millstone grit used in this gigantic folly, how its entire surface clad in a mottled, shiny alabaster to represent snow. (One cannot help but wonder whether a photograph or a stone from the actual Matterhorn might not have sufficed to prompt Crisp's nostalgia.) Or as the travel writer Jan Morris tells us in his book *Spain* about another folly, this one more human, at the chapel of Santismo Cristo in Spain, where is suspended the Christ of Burgos, an effigy fashioned of soft buffalo hide and real hair, so lifelike in its presence that residents thought that its fingernails had to be pared periodically.

Sometimes just the thought is enough, and scarecrows, effigies, and models of the Matterhorn need not so explicitly echo the real thing. The efforts of Crisp are as misplaced as the expectations of that congregation of Santismo Cristo. And any gardener who has ever stuffed old clothes with straw and positioned a crude but effective scarecrow in the center of a newly planted field understands, at least implicitly, the evocative power of the crude model, the rough brush stroke, the creative shorthand of children's drawings.

SpiderWorld and The Edge of Intentions both show that realism is not necessary for a satisfying narrative experience. A cartoon, implausible chains of events, and the most simple visual shorthand for characters can absorb their readers endlessly.

6. Conclusion

Many questions remain as we consider the means for making computer-based characters more absorbing or engaging, and as we consider strategies for interpreting the narratives which characters propel for individual readers. We might consider inventing lists of kinds of readers or users, or, perhaps, to train readers and users in a set of genre conventions (the VR equivalents of tables of contents, indices, chapter headings, pick-a-plot cues) that will help them choose the readings that are most satisfying. I am sure that all of us agree on the goal of creating virtual worlds that are the most absorbing and engaging possible for their interactants. Training readers and simultaneously exploring the scaffolding that underlies virtual worlds will start to make those worlds more accommodating and more responsive to their readers or participants. SpiderWorld and The Edge of Intention offer us a promising model for paying attention to what readers need.

Among the questions that we might also entertain while we tackle the goal of building the more accommodating virtual world are the following four:

> (1) If we were to make a taxonomy of readers, would distinguishing them according to the purposes they bring to the world be most useful? Or what might be some other useful ways to distinguish them?
>
> (2) Would reader-virtual world connections be usefully distinguished according to the interpretive strategies a user might bring to the world? Or should the terms of distinguishing among kinds be linked to occupations, physical needs, what the reader overtly wishes?
>
> (3) What parts of a virtual world connect most easily or snugly with particular kinds of readers? where should the hinges be?
>
> (4) What is the difference between presence and absorption from the point of view or participants in a virtual world?

And finally, I would like to thank again Hunter Hoffman of SpiderWorld and Joseph Bates of the Oz Project for the great privilege of hanging around as they play with the scripts and narratives of the past and the future.

References

1. Foucault, M. What is an author? Reprt. in Professing the new rhetorics: A sourcebook. T. Enos and S.C. Brown, Eds. Englewood Cliffs, New Jersey, Prentice Hall, 1992.

2. Ibid.

3. Tompkins, J. P., Ed. Reader-response criticism: from formalism to post-structuralism. Baltimore, Johns Hopkins Press, rpt. 1992, p. ix.

4. Stafford, W. Some arguments against good diction. In Poetics: essays on the art of poetry, Tendril, Inc., 1984, pp. 227-230.

5. Oldfield, S. Spider plague spinning a web around Britain. Daily Mail, September 22, 1998.

6. Carlin, A.S., Hoffman, H.G., and Weghorst, S. Virtual reality and tactile augmentation in the treatment of spider phobia: a case report. Behav. Res. Ther. 35 (2), 1997, pp. 153-158.

7. Ibid., p. 153.

8. Ibid., p. 154.

9. See Spider Project Description (as of august 9, 1998) at http://www.hitl.washington.edu/people/hunter/

10. See Project description at: http://www-cgi.cs.cmu.edu/afs/cs.cmu.edu/project/oz/web/overview2.html

11. Edited trace of a text-based interaction with Lyotard, a virtual cat, available at the following website: http://www.lb.cs.cmu.edu/afs/cs.cmu.edu/project/oz/web/lyotard2.html

12. See Project Description at http://www-cgi.cs.cmu.edu/afs/cs.cmu.edu/project/oz/web/oz.html

13. Calvino, I. If on a winter's night a traveler . . . W. Weaver, Trans., Harcourt Brace Jovanovich, 1981.

14. Forster, E.M. Aspects of the novel, rpt. Harcourt Brace, 1985..

15. Selfe, C. Literacy and computers: the complications of teaching and learning with technology. Modern Language Association, 1994.

16. Lanham, R. The electronic word: democracy, technology, and the arts. Rpt. University of Chicago Press, 1995.

17. Flower, L. Problem-solving strategies for writing. 4th ed., Harcourt Brace Jovanovich, 1993.

18. Lorca, F.G. Antología Poética. 3rd ed., Granada, 1998.

The Boundaries of a Shape and the Shape of Boundaries

C F Earl
Faculty of Engineering, Newcastle University,
Newcastle upon Tyne, NE1 7RU, UK

Abstract
Shapes and shape grammars use algebras of subshapes in the description, redescription and generation of designs. Characteristic features of boundaries in different shape descriptions are identified, including element boundaries, closure boundaries and explicit boundary shapes. All these boundaries are derived from selecting parts to describe a shape

1. Introduction

Shapes and boundaries, in Euclidean point set representations of space, are manipulated computationally in design, through geometric models in CAD systems. Point set representations are used as the basis for higher level descriptions of lines, surfaces and volumes. Spatial elements are restricted to the regular point subsets so that the algebraic requirements of a Boolean Algebra are satisfied [1]. CAD manipulations include unbounded subsets such as half planes although this is a convenience rather than a necessity. The bounded regular sets do not quite constitute a Boolean algebra as they lack a universal element [2]. The shapes with which I am concerned correspond to regular point sets restricted to be bounded and composed of finite connected components. Thus we reach, although in a roundabout way, a pictorial and perceptual idea of a shape which comprises our starting point.

2. Boundaries

Boundaries can distinguish parts of shapes. The circle in Figure 1(a) distinguishes a part of the rectangle. However, the circle and rectangle (as plane area) are different geometric types. In more complex cases the precise parts distinguished may require convention or interpretation to identify them. Conversely, if parts of a shape are distinguished then boundaries emerge. Consider a shape (Figure 1(b)) with parts a black spot and a white background inside a rectangle. The shape has

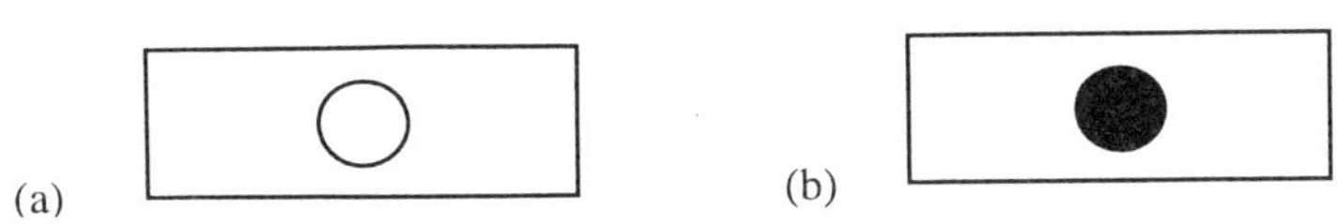

Figure 1 (a) Parts distinguished by boundary and (b) parts distinguished by property

parts distinguished visually by a property (colour) of the spot. Charles Sanders Peirce [3] asked whether the boundary of the spot is black or white? There is no satisfactory answer. Parts are distinguished in Figure 1(b) but the boundary that can be used to make this distinction is problematic. We observe that explicit boundary shapes are not needed to distinguish parts. From a shape point of view no explicit boundary is defined in Figure 1(b) as there is no circle distinguished as part of the shape. However, from a perceptual viewpoint the distinction between parts appears to induce a boundary shape. An extensive discussion of this and other issues relating to surfaces and holes is given by Casati and Varzi [4].

The point set Euclidean representation of a shape, as a continuum of points with regularity properties, allows boundaries to be derived directly from the point set structure of the underlying space. Each subshape of a shape has an associated boundary. Thus in Figure 1(b) any part of the spot or the rectangle has a boundary which does not reflect the structure of the distinguished parts. The underlying point set structure dominates.

This paper explores an alternative to point set descriptions in which parts rather than points are given primacy in describing shape. Stiny [5] considers how shape computations in design lead to this representation. I will examine the consequences of this view for identifying boundaries and analysing their properties.

The philosophical and logical literature on wholes, parts and points in shapes extends from Whitehead [6], through connection based approaches by Clarke [7], to recent treatments [8] comparing the logical scope of different representations. Although I concentrate on the requirements for shape computation and visualisation in design applications, understanding the logic and structure of these representations is vital to their use. In the development of solid modelling for CAD, creating shape representations consistent with the logical and topological structures of point sets, was a major component in establishing the foundations of the subject [1].

When shapes are described by their parts, boundaries will be seen to reflect the structure of the design in terms of its parts. Some of the technical features of these representations are covered in earlier papers [9,10]. Three types of boundary will be considered. First, a descriptive boundary is constructed from point set boundaries of selected subshapes. Second topological or closure boundaries [11] are derived from the structure of selected subshapes. Third, the discrete topology of an acquired visual image [12,13] leads to consideration of distinct boundary shapes to represent discontinuities. The paper shows that as shapes are described by their parts then boundaries emerge. These boundary shapes represent the spatial relationships among the selected subshapes

3. Design

The context of this research is the use of shapes in engineering design. Sketches, drawings and CAD geometric models are key descriptions used in developing products from concept to manufacture. Descriptions are used in transactions between participants at different stages in the product development process. Redescriptions are commonly required before a recipient can apply specific knowledge to develop the design by transformation. For example, a functional description may identify one set of shape features whilst a manufacturing description will identify another. If the manufacturing description creates a costly and complex production method then it may be appropriate to transform the description, creating a new design. The topologies of these descriptions and mappings between them [14,10] allow an insight into how one description influences another in product development.

Two key features emerge. First shape descriptions are used both in perception and generation. Second, multiple descriptions should be easily available and transformations act naturally on them. A computational framework meeting these requirements has shapes described by parts and shape rules acting on parts [5]. The ways that rules change (or preserve) the structure of parts can be used to characterise redescription or transformation. The primacy of a part description in design was noted by William Blake [15], in 1827, whose engraved lines create boundary, form and texture. “A line is a line in its Minutest Subdivisions; Strait or Crooked It is itself and Not Intermeasurable with or by anything Else."

4. Shape representation

A shape representation requires an algebraic component to operate on parts and a topological component to describe relations. The algebra distinguishes types of spatial element such as points, lines and planes. Conditions are put on the elements (such as regular point sets) to define sum, product (intersection) and complement operations. Finally, there needs to be a mechanism for forming product algebras across different types of shape element. The topology represents relations among spatial elements, characterises surfaces (such as by the presence of holes) and provides definitions for boundary, interior, closure and connection. I will outline algebra and topology for subshape descriptions.

Consider the simple shape in Figure 2(a) composed of an orthogonally shaped plane segment, shown shaded, together with four lines creating a square in the centre. There are five maximal shape elements [16], one plane segment and four lines. However, there are many ways to view this shape in terms of elements. Figure 2(b) shows three elements in which the plane segment is decomposed into squares and the lines are aggregated as a complex. Figure 2(c) depicts possible boundary shapes for these elements. Note that the particular boundary of the complex of lines which is identified does not obey the usual nilpotency of the boundary operator in a complex [11]. In a sense, the structure of the shape in terms of simple elements is preserved in the boundary. The boundary of the shape is the shape sum of the boundaries of the shape elements. The canonical description by maximal elements provides a minimal boundary. The boundaries associated with different sets of elements exhibit a partial order [9]. Shapes are represented by elements which are in turn represented by their boundaries. These are also shapes, again represented by their boundaries. For example a plane polygonal segment is represented by its boundary polygon. The lines in the polygon are represented by their endpoints.

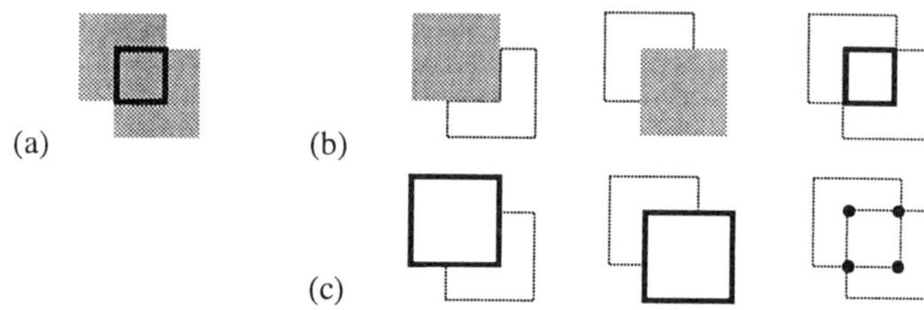

Figure 2: (a) Shape, (b) elements describing the shape and (c) boundaries of elements

The shape *S* in Figure 3(a) can be described by the simple elements in Figure 3(b). In these diagrams the outlines of the shape are indicated by dashed lines which are not part of the shape. From this other decriptions can be derived, such as that composed of the simple elements which are the shape sums and products (intersections) shown in Figure 3(c).

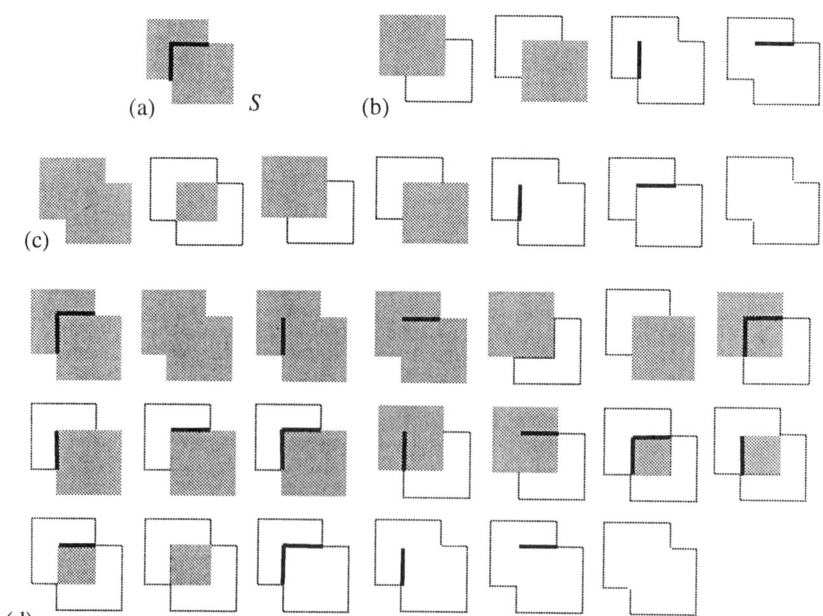

Figure 3: (a) Shape *S* (b) elements (c) extended elements and (d) closed set of subshapes

Arguments based on the representation of designs by parts and relations [10] lead to special consideration of closed (with respect to shape sum and product) sets of subshapes as descriptions. A closed set of subshapes is shown in Figure 3(d), created by finite sum and product of shape elements.

5. Closure boundaries

A closure $c(x)$ can be defined for any subshape x as the smallest closed shape containing x, as illustrated in Figure 4. A topology of subshapes is associated with the closure. The closure boundary of subshape $x \leq S$ is defined as the product (intersection) of shapes $c(x)$ and $c(S\text{-}x)$ where $S\text{-}x$ is the shape complement of subshape $x \leq S$ (Figure 4).

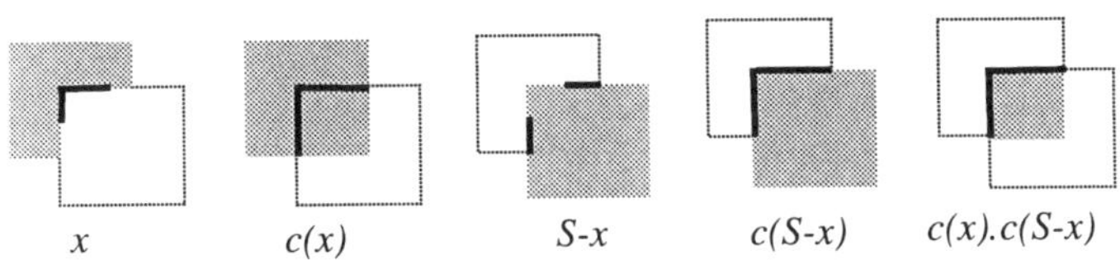

Figure 4: (a) Derivation of closure boundary of subshape of shape S in Figure 3

These closure boundaries reflect the description of the shape by parts. In the underlying subshape representation a topology associated with the Boolean Algebra of subshapes, is disconnected, fragmented and has no 'structural' boundaries [9]. As subshapes are selected for a description the associated topology becomes connected with the boundaries acting as the connections among parts. One way to recover an algebra of closed subshapes is to redefine the complement of a shape as the closure of the shape complement (Figure 5).

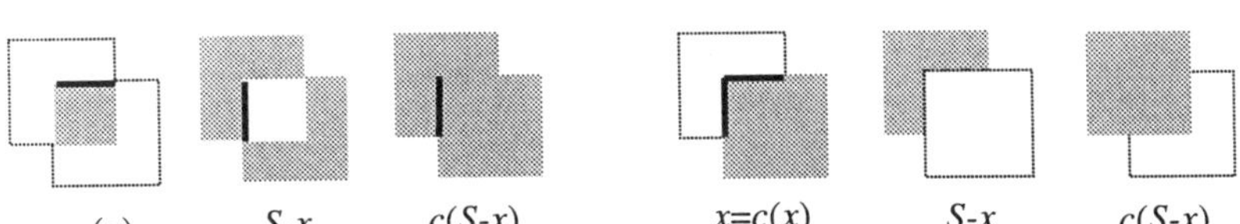

Figure 5: Examples, using the shape S in Figure 3, of a redefined shape complement for an algebra of closed shapes

With this definition of complement the closed shapes form an algebra in which entities and their complements are not disjoint. Shapes are not always clearly distinguished but flow into each other. The shapes of boundaries express these spatial relations among shapes.

Boundaries not only emerge from shape description but are used to construct descriptions. A typical application is image processing in computer vision [13]. The image may be analysed for discontinuities, corresponding boundaries constructed, and a description in terms of shape elements derived. The generalisation of an edge or boundary to be a region is consistent with description by subshapes and the ideas of redescription and transformation introduced earlier.

6. Conclusion

Constructive processes in design require description, redescription and transformation. With rules acting on parts or subshapes of a design it is important to examine the consequences of basing shape description on subshapes. Boundaries are significant not only as cues to subshape selection but also as structural components of the shape, serving to represent relations among subshapes. This paper outlined three types of boundary. As designers perceive and generate shapes they are dealing with rich and fluid structures constantly open to the possibilities of redescription and transformation. The variety of boundary structures touched on briefly in this paper gives a glimpse of the complexity and scope of visualisation.

7. References

1. Requicha AAG. Representations of rigid solids: theory, methods and systems, ACM Computer Surveys 1980; 12: 437-464
2. Stiny G. The algebras of design, Research in Engineering Design 1991; 2(3): 171-181
3. Peirce CS. The logic of quantity. In C Hartshorne P Weiss (ed), Collected Papers of Charles Sanders Peirce, Volume IV, Harvard, Cambridge, MA, 1933
4. Casati R, Varzi A. Holes and other superficialities, MIT Press, Cambridge, MA, 1994
5. Stiny G. Shape rules: closure, continuity and emergence, Planning and Design 1994; 21: s49-s78
6. Whitehead AN. Process and Reality, Cambridge University Press, Cambridge, 1927
7. Clarke BL. Individuals and points, Notre Dame J Formal Logic 1985; 26(1): 61-75
8. Pratt I, Lemon O. Ontologies for Plane, Polygonal Mereotopology, Notre Dame Journal of Formal Logic 1997; 38: 225-245
9. Earl CF. Shape boundaries, Planning and Design 1997; 24: 669-687
10. Earl CF. The structure of designs. In, Proceedings (CD) 10th International Design Theory and Methodology Conference, Atlanta, GA, 13-16 September 1998, Paper DETC/DTM 5656, ASME International, New York
11. Kuratowski K. Introduction to Set Theory and Topology, Pergamon, Oxford, 1972
12. Serra J-P. Image Analysis and Spatial Morphology, Academic Press, London, 1982
13. Fleck MM. Topology of boundaries, Artificial Intelligence 1996; 80(1): 1-28
14. Peters TJ, Rosen DW, Shapiro V. A topological model of the limitations in design for manufacturing, Research in Engineering Design 1994; 6: 223-233
15. Blake W. Letter to George Cumberland Letter 878. In G Keynes (ed) Complete Writings of William Blake, Oxford University Press, Oxford, 1972
16. Krishnamurti R. The arithmetic of maximal planes, Planning and Design 1992; 19: 431-464

Breaking the Monotony: Using Randomisation Techniques in Computer-Aided Textile Design

Hilary Carlisle, Peter Phillips, Gillian Bunce
Department of Fashion & Textiles,
The Nottingham Trent University, UK

Abstract

Most designs on fabric are of a repeating nature due to the mechanical processes involved in weaving, knitting and printing. This paper examines the possibilities of engaging with new technology to produce non-repeating designs for printed fabric.

Background

Mass-produced fabrics almost always contain a repeating element to their pattern design. The mechanisation processes of weaving, knitting and printing patterns have made this a necessity for the majority of textile production.
Whereas the warp and weft structure of a woven fabric, and the stitch structure of knitted fabric lend themselves perfectly to geometric-style repeating patterns, there are no such concrete boundaries for printed fabric. Economically, however, repeating patterns have been favoured, to reduce the number of screens or rollers required, and the amount of skill and time to produce the fabric.
In the last century, much emphasis was placed on the pattern repeat, and producing a pleasing pattern was highly regarded. A motif that appears attractive in isolation may become unattractive in repeating formation. If a block repeat is used, as shown in figure 1, unintentional horizontal or vertical stripes, or even checks, can appear. The half-drop repeat, as shown in figure 2, is commonly used to disguise the repeat and overcome the problems associated with the block repeat, but this sometimes produces undesirable diagonal stripes.

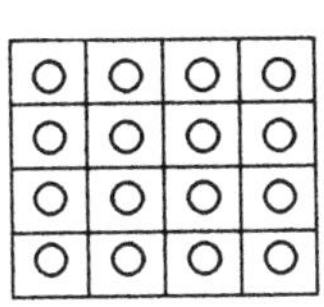

Figure 1

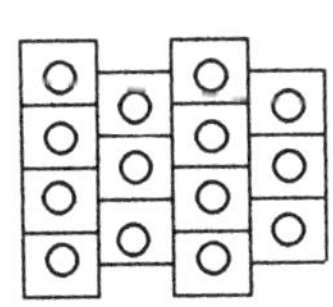

Figure 2

Obviously, stripes, checks, and rigidly structured designs are sometimes in demand. The advantage of a bold repeat is that it can be incorporated into the design of the garment. For example, a striped fabric could be used horizontally on the sleeves and vertically on the body of the garment, or diagonally to produce a chevron effect. Garments produced this way are distinctive and quite different in appearance to ones made from the same pattern pieces in a plain fabric, or one without a heavily repetitive design. The disadvantages of this technique are twofold: more skill is required by the pattern cutter to align the pattern pieces to the fabric and there is more wastage in the fabric itself.

Time and economy have become more and more valuable in the textile industry, as with most industry, as this century has progressed. This has led to a move away from obviously repeating patterns to ones in which the pattern is disguised or inconsequential. A pattern of this nature allows pattern pieces to be placed in any direction on the fabric, cutting down on wastage. If a motif is scattered across the repeating unit, in seemingly random directions, there is less chance that the repeat will be obvious [1]. Similarly, if a large repeat unit is used with large, but similar motifs covering most of the fabric's surface, the repeat can be hidden. This is a consequence of the pattern pieces within the garment not incorporating more than one repeat of the pattern while the similar motifs provide an overall uniformity which prevent the garment seams being obvious, however the fabric is cut.

The latter part of this century has also seen a backlash against the perfection made available through the use of technology and high-level mechanisation. Whereas in the early days of mass-produced printed fabric, the most sought after prints were those which appeared most perfectly printed, we now have manufacturers who deliberately incorporate faults to give fabric a 'hand-crafted', and hence desirable, look.

Project Motivation

This research is inspired by the idea of producing printed textiles, which while satisfying the current commercial criteria outlined above, are also inspirational and interesting to wear. Generally speaking, non-repeating designs on printed clothing are currently only seen at the couture end of the market, due to their handcrafted nature.

At present mass-produced printed fabric is produced by separately printing each colour, via rotary or flatbed screens, on to the fabric. The development of ink-jet printers, similar in principle to those used for colour printing on to paper, has been slow, due to the additional requirements of handling different cloth types and a necessity to use inks which can be made colourfast. Currently, machines capable of printing single metres of fabric are available, making them only suitable for sampling. However, commercial printers capable of several hundred metre lengths, should be available in the next ten years. This would enable the commercial production of non-repeating textile designs, fed directly from computer to printer, to become a reality.

Though there are commercial considerations for producing fabric designs in which the repeat is disguised, there are also aesthetic ones. As Gombrich states 'The monotonous may fail to register while the intricate may confuse' [2]. In general, patterns intrigue us, but a balance between boring and over-complicated needs to be found.

Design Methods

The designs illustrated below have no repeating pattern. They are developed using various manipulations of motifs dependant on a series of random numbers. The concept is to produce designs that look as though they may repeat, providing a degree of continuity that is normally associated with textile patterns. The elements of the design are carefully chosen to assist this. The designs are not computer generated. Once the random numbers have been produced, their effects are manually interpreted using Adobe PhotoShop software.
The first series of designs are based on a square grid. Figure 3 shows an example in which six different motifs are each assigned a number from one to six. A grid was then generated using Microsoft's Excel spreadsheet, in which the numbers one to six appeared randomly, provided by the RANDBETWEEN function. The motifs are then placed according to where their numbers fall on the grid. The negative spaces in this design, i.e. those between the motifs, appear as horizontal and vertical lines, clearly showing the grid structure.

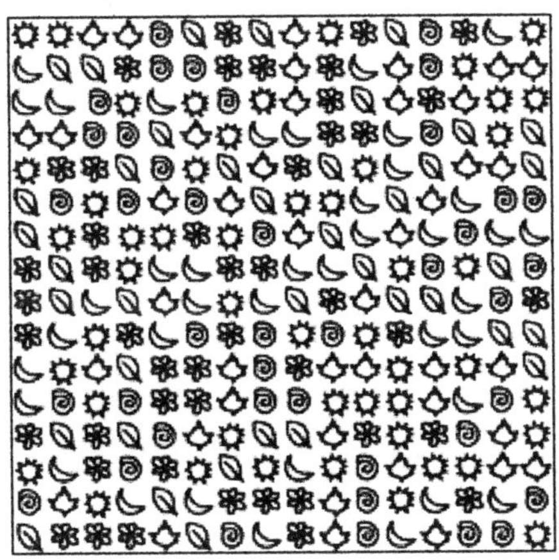

Figure 3

To combat this problem, another series of designs were produced in which the motifs deliberately linked with each other, regardless of their position. Figure 5 demonstates this. This is a three element design, developed in the same way as figure 1. Each motif, shown in figure 4, has a protrusion at the midpoints of each side of the grid square it fills. The square grid is still observable in this design, in both the negative spaces and in places where the same motif appears together several times.

Figure 4

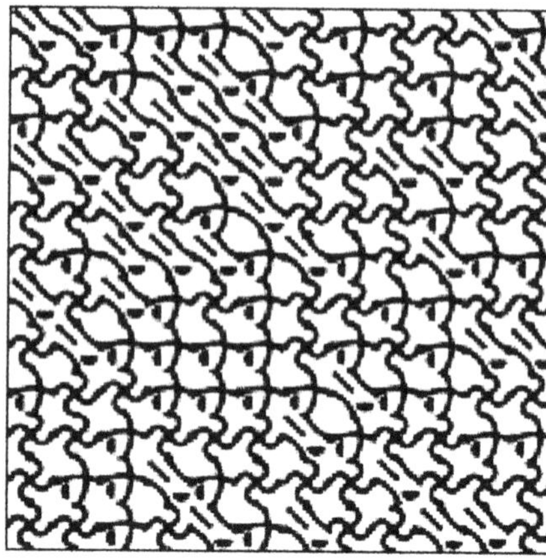

Figure 5

By using a hexagonal grid, rather than a square one, the repeat effect becomes akin to a half-drop, rather than a block repeat. The intention is to further disguise the grid, which, as mentioned earlier, the half-drop normally does.

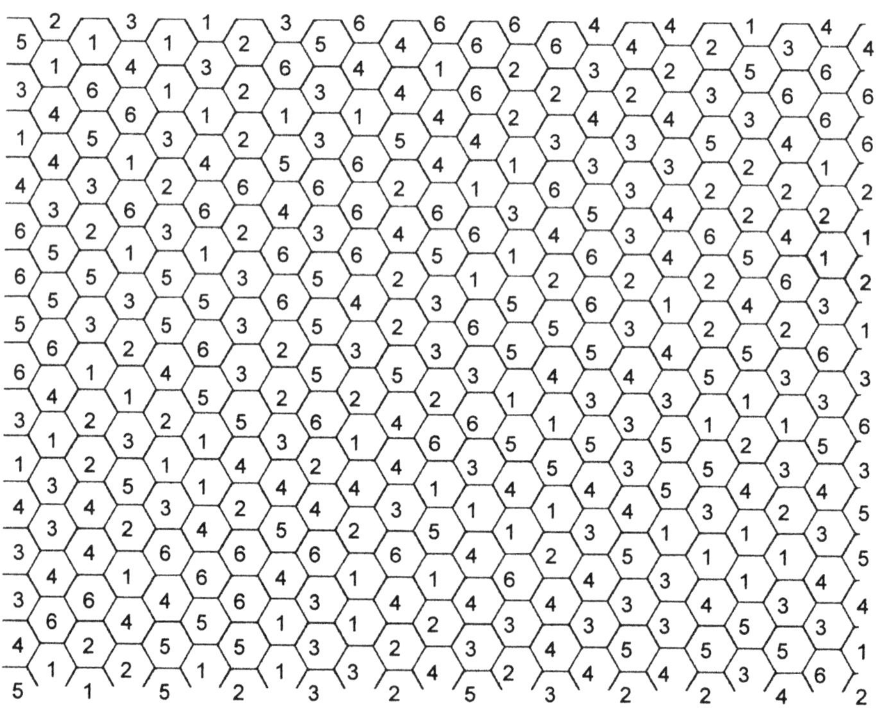

Figure 6

The number placement for a hexagonal grid design is shown in figure 6. In this example a single motif was constructed representing leaves and stems, as shown in Figure 7. The motif has protrusions at each of the hexagon's six vertices, ensuring that the resultant design has continuity and an organic feel. Figure 8 shows how this single motif would appear if placed in a standard half-drop repeat on the hexagonal grid.

Figure 7

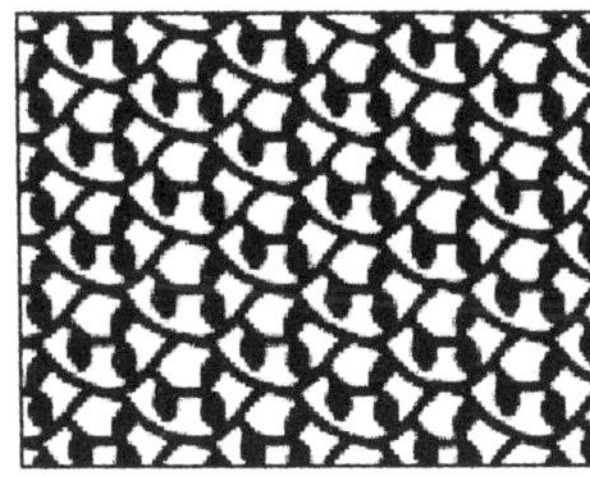

Figure 8

Though the original single motif had a creeping organic feel, this is lost when placed in the half-drop formation. The pattern has a uniform appearance akin to fish scales and, indeed, appears similar to a traditional type of design, known as a scale pattern. Obviously, if the motif were rotated in several different ways and locked together to form a larger repeating unit, this problem could be alleviated. However, figure 9 shows the finished random design, in which the motif is rotated in multiples of sixty degrees, according to numbers shown on the hexagonal grid displayed in figure 6. This design has an overall continuity, and retains the feel of a repeating pattern, without the rigidity of figure 8. The erratically recurring shapes and formations cause fascination to the viewer.

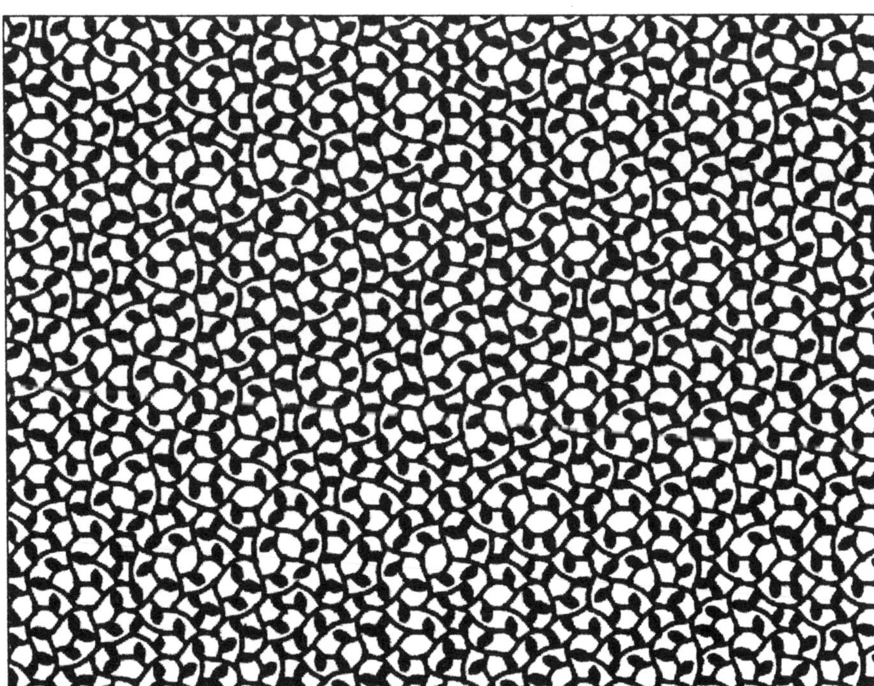

Figure 9

Figure 10 and Figure 11 provide further examples of methods to eliminate the rigidity imposed by a grid structure, in fact neither example is built on a grid. Figure 10 uses a table of random numbers from 1 to 3, each representing the size of a circle. The circles are then placed in the design filling from left to right, top to bottom, the circles are allowed to move up as far as possible, so as to touch the circles above and to the left of them. The identification of a single row or column becomes more difficult as the design grows. In Figure 11 co-ordinates are produced from random numbers, with an extra number to denote the circle diameter. Circles are then placed on the design according to the size and location given by the spreadsheet.

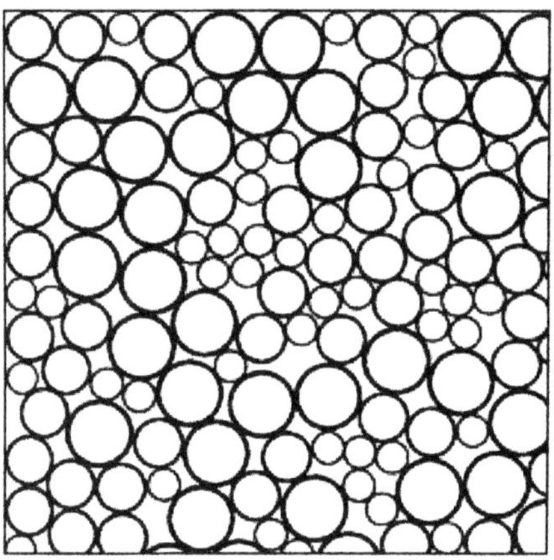

Figure 10

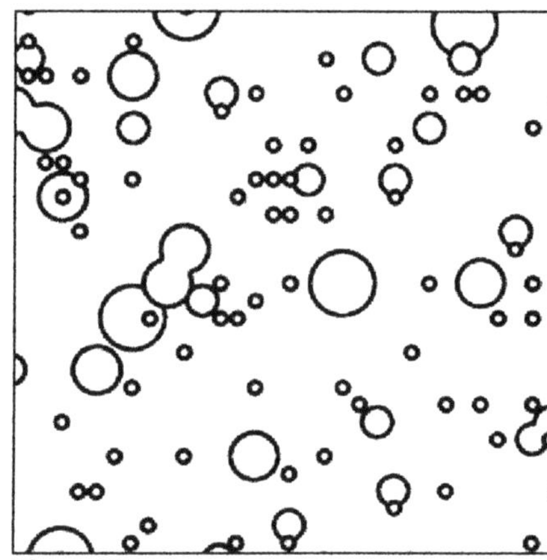

Figure 11

Conclusion

Historically, repeating designs for textiles have been a commercial, and mechanical neccessity, and have provided the framework in which most textile designers work. The production of individual, non-repeating designs has remained a luxury only found at the top end of the market. Within the next ten years it is possible that ink-jet printers for fabric will be developed for the production market. When this becomes a reality, the limitation of the repeating design is removed.

This work looks towards a future of textile design which enables the spontaneous creation and printing of designs such as those illustrated above, on to fabric. It can be hoped the utilisation of technology in this way will lead to innovation in textile design without the usual commercial overheads.

References

1. Bunce G. Point Art & Design Research Journal, Number 2, Summer 1996, pp 33-36
2. Gombrich, E.H. The Sense of Order, Phaidon, UK, 1979, p11

Virtual World Representation Issues for Supporting Assembly and Maintainability Assessment Tasks

Terrence Fernando, Prasad Wimalaratne and Kevin Tan
The Centre for Virtual Environments University of Salford,
Salford, Manchester, M5 4WT, U.K.

1. Introduction

The pressure on manufacturing companies to remain competitive in today's world markets has led many to adopt concurrent engineering in an attempt to reduce the lead time for new products and improve their quality. Concurrent engineering is a systematic approach to the integrated concurrent design of products and related processes, including manufacture and support. It encourages the manufacturing companies to consider all product life cycle issues such as manufacturability and maintainability during design. This reduces unforeseen problems creeping into the design as it progresses through its life cycle, consequently saving both time and money while improving product quality.

Much research and development work is currently being conducted to develop data exchange standards (STEP) and computer support for managing and co-ordinating cross-disciplinary teams to support concurrent engineering. However, very little research has been carried out to develop software environments for assessing human factor issues during product design, such as ease of assembly and maintenance. The consideration of these issues requires support for assessing physical access, part handling, mobility around the product, difficulty in removing and replacing parts etc. Such human factor issues are typically assessed using physical prototypes. However, the building of physical prototypes is extremely expensive and time consuming, increasing the time to market the product. Furthermore, once a physical prototype has been built, there is usually so much inertia in the design that major changes are very difficult to incorporate. Therefore, there is a need for better software environments for assessing human factors issues early in the design phase.

A research programme referred to as IPSEAM (Interactive Product Simulation Environment for Assessing Assembly and Maintainability) has been established at the Centre for Virtual Environment to investigate the development of such a software environment to support the assessment of human factor issues during design. This research is being focused through a industrial case study from Rolls-Royce Aero-engine Ltd.

2.1. Case Study

The maintenance of the main fuel pump from Trent 800 engine has been taken as the main case study for this research. At present, physical representation is used to assess the maintenance issues of the main fuel pump of the Trent 800 engine and therefore it presents a genuine industrial case study for this research. This maintenance task involves removal of adjacent components around the fuel pump, use of spanners within a constrained space, removal of loose items by hand, dis-engagement of the pump by hand within a constrained space etc. Figure 1 shows the some of the main components of the Trent 800 engine.

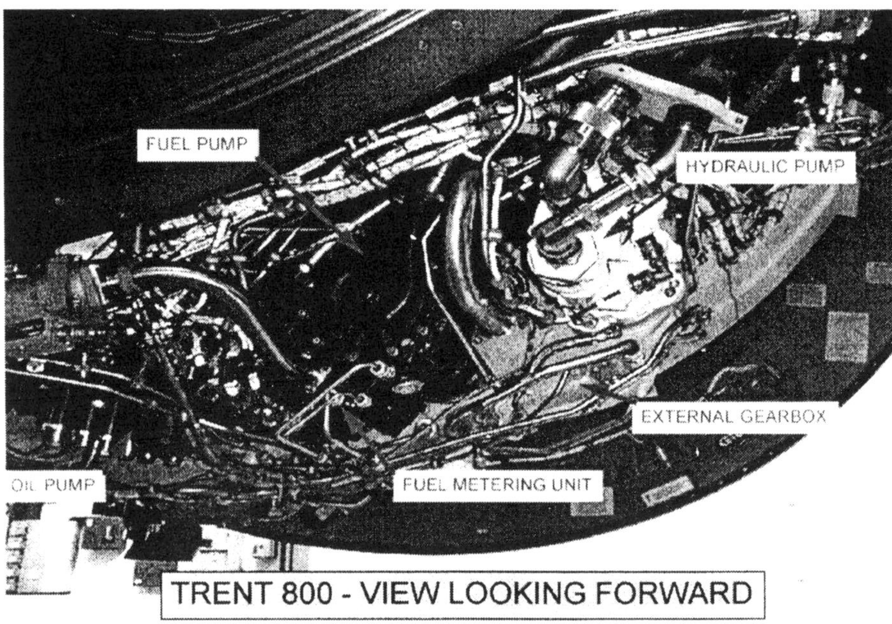

Figure 1 : Physical Prototype of the Trent 800 Engine

2.2. Scope of the Paper

This paper describes the virtual world representations employed within the IPSEAM system. In particular we will discuss the following representations in this paper :

1. **CAD Data Representation within IPSEAM :** At present most of the virtual worlds are based on polygons and therefore through away the rich geometric surface descriptions and dimensional data of CAD models, which are essential for engineering tasks. This paper will explain how this issue has been addressed within the IPSEAM system using the new Optimizer API from Silicon Graphics.

2. **Constraint Representations within IPSEAM :** At present, current commercial virtual environments do not support run-time specification or management of assembly relationships between engineering parts. Hence 3D assembly operations using direct manipulation are not feasible in current virtual environments. This paper explains the techniques and the representations used for establishing and maintaining assembly relationships between engineering parts.

2. Interactive Product Simulation Environment

This section presents the system architecture and the internal data representations of the Interactive Product Simulation Environment IPSEAM. The IPSEAM system architecture builds upon the first author's previous research on constraint-based modelling work [4],[5],[2],[3] and the other relavant state-of-the-art technologies.

There are two main components to this system architecture : baseline virtual environment and the constraint manager.

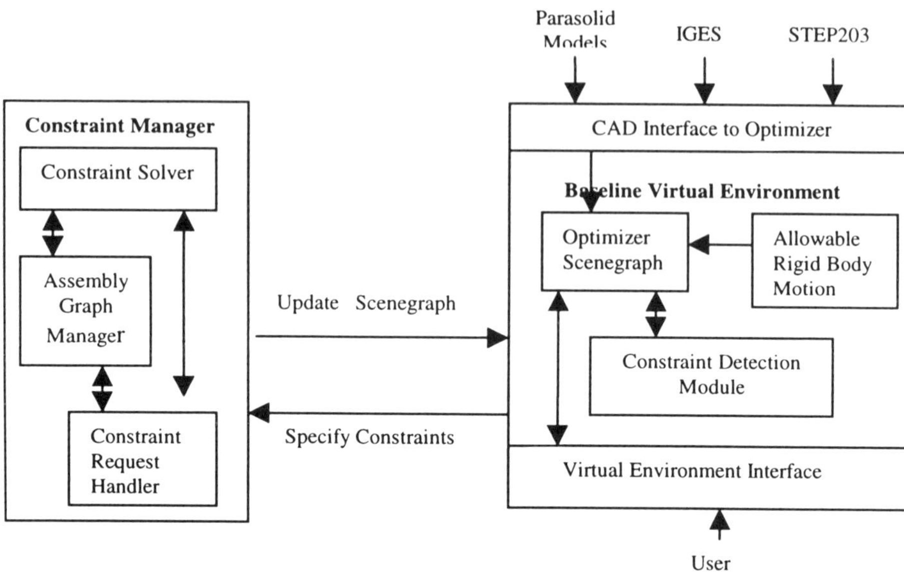

Figure 2 : Software Architecture of IPSEAM

2.1. Baseline Virtual Environment

Most of the present commercial virtual environments are based on polygonal data. When importing CAD data, these virtual environments throw away important geometric information of the CAD models and convert all the geomtric surfaces into a set of polygons. As a result, current virtual environments lack the semantic information necessary for supporting engineering operations such as assembly modelling.

The recent introduction of OpenGL Optimizer from Silicon Graphics has overcome this limitation by implementing a rich scenegraph which is capable of maintaining both surface representations and polygonal data of CAD models. Furthermore, the OpenGL Optimizer provides important features such as efficient occlusion and frustrum culling, built-in algorithms for simplifying level of detail (LOD) of models, efficient surface tessellators without surface cracks and multi-threaded scenegraph operations. This graphics engine has been designed by SGI to support large CAD applications. Due to the improved funtionality, OpenGL Optimizer has been chosen as the baseline virtual environment for developing the IPSEAM system.

However, the optimizer is still going through its development phase and lacks CAD interfaces to import data into the Scenegraph. Therefore a CAD interface was developed as a part of the IPSEAM project for importing CAD data into the optimizer scnegraph. This CAD interface is now capable of importing Parasolid part

files, IGES and STEP 203 models into the scenegraph while preserving the integrity of the CAD data.
Figure 3 shows how main node types of the optimizer graph are being used to represent the geometric information and the polygonal information of assemblies.

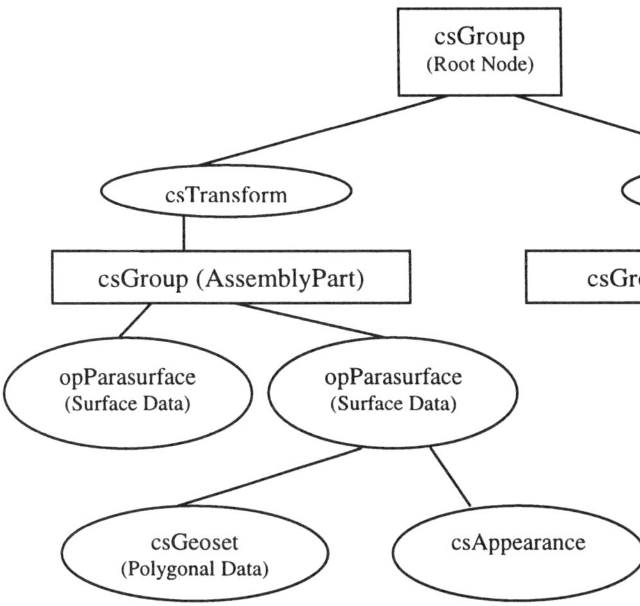

Figure 3 : Optimizer Scenegraph

Once the assembly parts are loaded into the scenegraph via the CAD interface, the virtual environment interface allows the user to grab and manipulate objects in the 3D space. Such manipulations are monitored by the constraint detection module. When the objects collide, the contacting surfaces are identified through the Scenegraph. The surface description of the mating faces and the type of constraint to be satisfied are then sent to the constraint manager. The recognised constraints are satisfied by the constraint manager and the accurate position of the collided assembly part and its allowable rigid body motions are sent back to the scenegraph. This information is used by the scenegraph to define the precise position of the collided assembly part. The purpose of maintaining allowable rigid body motions are to allow only the valid manipulations on the assembly models without breaking the existing constraints. This is done by converting the 3D manipulation data received from the 3D input device into allowable rigid body motions. A particular manipulation of an assembly model is not allowed if it is not supported by its allowable rigid body motion. Constraints such as against, coincident, concentric, tangency, spherical fit, cylindrical fit are supported at present.

2.2. Constraint Management Facilties

2.2.1. Internal Representations

The assembly process consists of a succession of tasks, each of which consists of joining assembly parts (components) to form the final assembly. Parts are considered joined when the necessary contacts and alignments between parts are established. These contacts and alignments are refered to as assembly relationships.

Several researchers have proposed techniques [7],[6],[8],[9],[2] for representing assembly relationships in terms of the relative motion (DOF) permitted in each of the mating pairs. This approach is more efficient for simulating the interactive constrained motion of assemblies and hence is being used within the IPSEAM system. One important feature in this line of research is that assembly constraints are described as a kinematic problem. In [2], Turner describes three classes of constraint relations : lower kinematic pairs, upper kinematic pairs and assembly dimensions. Assembly dimensions are typically used to specify the location and orientation of a part with respect to other geometric entities, for purposes such as welding.

2.2.1.1. Lower Kinematic Pairs

A lower kinematic pair arises when two parts are connected to remain in contact along a common surface. A set of common lower kinematic paris and their relative motion are shown in Figure 4.

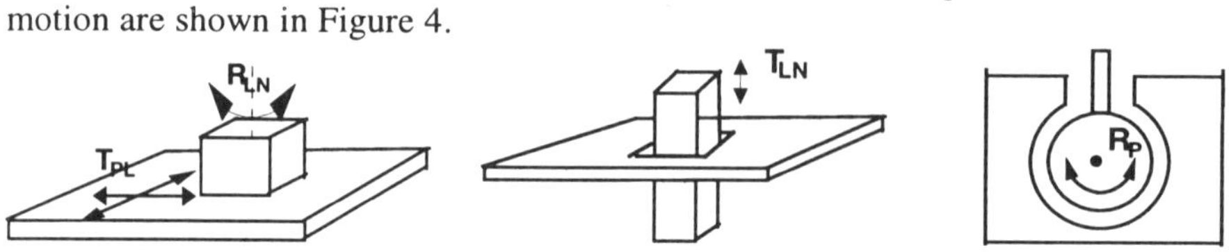

(a) **Planar Pair** : The surface of contact is a plane. The relative motion permitted for the top block is translation on plane (T_{PL}) and rotation about any axis (R_{LN}) in the direction of the plane normal.

(b) **Prismatic Pair** : The surface of contact has a constant cross section in a given direction and is not a round cylinder. The relative motion permitted is only the translation along a line (T_{LN}) .

(c) **Sperical Pair** : The surface of contact is a sphere. The relative motion permitted for the sphere is rotation about it's centre point (R_P).

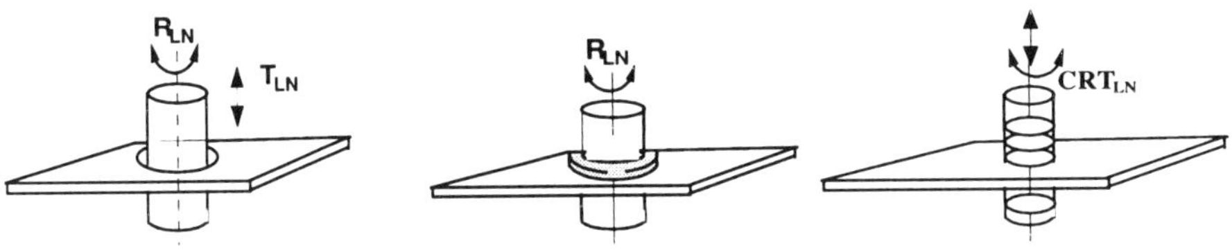

(d) Cylindrical Pair : The surface of contact is a round cylinder. The relative motion permitted for the cylinder is rotation (R_{LN}) and translation (T_{LN}) about its axis.

(e) Revolute Pair : The surface of contact is a surface of revolution. Only rotation about the axis (R_{LN})is permitted.

(f) Screw Pair : The screw pair restricts the motion to a combined rotation and translation along a common axis.

Figure 4 : Lower Kinematic Pairs

2.2.1.2. Upper Kinematic Pairs

The upper kinematic pairs are formed when two surfaces are constrained to remain in contact along a common line or at a common point. There is a large number of upper kinematic pairs. Some examples of upper kinematic pairs are shown in Figure 5.

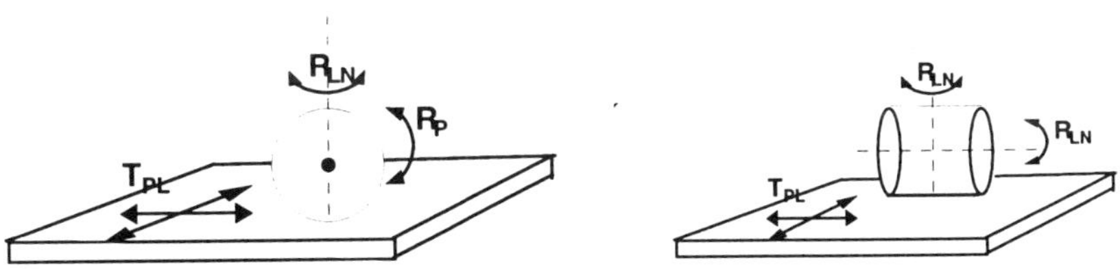

(a) Tangent Between a Sphere and a Plane : The surface of contact is a point. The relative motion permitted for the sphere is translation on the plane (T_{PL}), rotation about its centre (R_P)and rotation about the axis (R_{LN}) parallel to the normal of the plane.

(b) Tangent Between a Cylinder and a Plane : The surface of contact is a line. The relative motions permitted for the cylinder are translation on the plane (T_{PL}), rotation about its axis (R_{LN}) and rotation about a axis (R_{LN}) parallel to the normal of the plane.

Figure 5 : Some Upper Kinematic Pairs (continued overleaf)

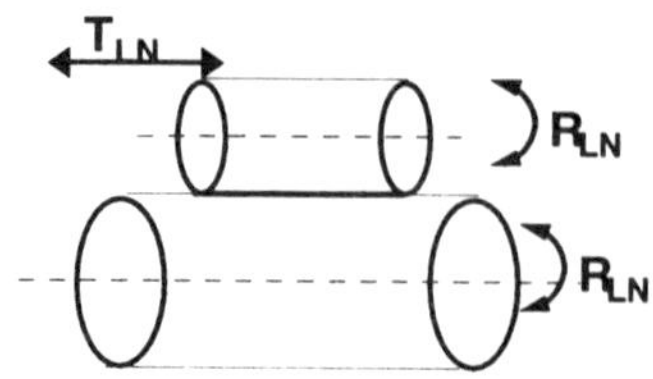

(c) Line Contact Between two Cylinders:
The relative motion permitted for the top cylinder is translation on a line colinear with the line contact (T_{LN}), rotation about its axis (R_{LN})and rotation about the axis of the bottom cylinder (R_{LN}).

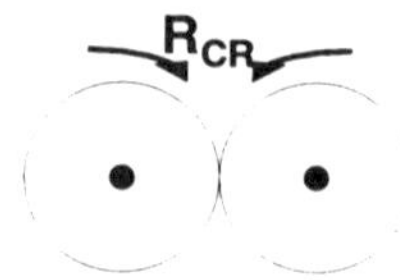

(d) Gear Contact :
The relative motions is a coupled rotation for a gear contact. Each gear is permitted to rotate about its own axis. However, the rotation of the follower gear is opposite to the rotation of the driver gear.

Figure 5 : Some Upper Kinematic Pairs

2.2.1.3. Representation of Multiple Constraints

When several constraints are associated with a assembly part, the resulting rigid body motion can be found by intersecting the rigid body motion of each constraint. In [2],[4], technique called allowable motion intersection is presented to represent multiple constraints. Turner [9] proposes similar concepts through constraint reduction techniques. Effectively, the resultant rigid body motion of two constraints is the intersection of the two sets of rigid-body motions of the original constraints. Intersections are performed for translation and rotational freedom independently. Refer to [2],[4],[9] for more information.

2.2.2. Implementation of Constraint Management Facilities

The constraint manager comprises of three main modules : constraint solver, assembly relationship graph and constraint request handler. The constraint request handler is the interface between the constraint manager and the baseline virtual environment. It processes the requests and directs the action to the constraint solver or the assembly graph.

2.2.2.1. Assembly Relationship Graph (ARG)

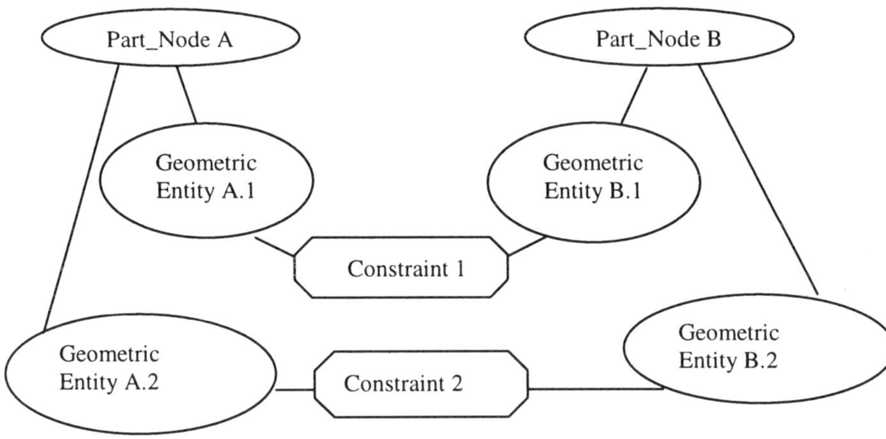

Figure 6 : Abstract View of the Assembly Relationship Graph

The Assembly Relationship Graph (ARG) maintains assembly relationships between the mating surfaces of assembly parts. The Assembly Relationship Graph is an undirected graph where each node represents either a geometric entity (mating surface) or a constraint. The nodes representing geometric entities are connected to constraint nodes using arcs to represent their assembly relationships. The geometric entities which belong to the same assembly part (same rigid body) are maintained within a supernode called Part_Node. An abstract view of the assembly graph is represented in Figure 6.

The RG described above is not a solid representation scheme but is concerned with maintaining the relationship between assembly parts. However, the geometric information for each mating surface is maintained within corresponding entity node. This geometric information is used by the constraint solver when evaluating and solving constraints.

2.2.2.2. Constraint Solver

The task of the constraint solver is to satisfy the specified constraints specified by the system in response to user interaction. The constraint solver satisfies a given set of constraints and produces relative rigid body motion for assembly relationships as specified in Section 2.2.1. These motions are locally stored in the Optimizer scenegraph to speed up the interactive response.

2.2.2.3. Interactive Assembly Constraint Specification

Two dimensional auto-constraint techniques are increasingly being used by CAD systems to build 2D constraint-based models. Bier [1] proposed a 3D snapping technique for building 3D models. These concepts were further extended by Fa [2] and Fernando [4] to support interactive assembly modelling. In their approach constraints were recognised between geometric elements when the assembly parts were coming together. Such auto-constraint recognition techniques are being explored within the IPSEAM system to support complex assembly disassembly operations.

3. Conclusions and Future Work

This paper presented the virtual world representations employed in developing an Interactive Product Simulation Environment called IPSEAM. The main data representations within IPSEAM such such as the Optimizer scenegraph, assembly constraints and rigid body motions were presented. The development of such a sophisticated environment involves bringing together many technologies such as virtual environments, constraint-based modelling, assembly modelling, CAD data representation and 3D direct manipulation techniques.

The basic framework of the Interactive Product Simulation Environment has been implemented and tested using a series of small assemblies. The current system runs on a Onyx2 Infinite Reality machine. All the program development has been written using C++ language.

The research presented in this paper is driven by a realistic industrial problem from the aero-engine industry. The assembly and maintainability assessment of the Trent 800 engine has been taken as the case study for focusing this research. Our future research work will study the maintainability issues of the Trent 800. During this research, techniques used within the physically-based simulation approach will be exploited to simulate forces such as gravity and friction. Further attention will be given to the development of a intuitive VR interface for supporting maintenance operations. Human factor experiments will be conducted to evaluate the final system using end users.

4. Acknowledgements

Thanks goes to Rolls-Royce for providing case study material and support for this project. Dr. Fernando wishes to thank the School of Computer Studies at the University of Leeds and Prof. Dew for supporting this research while he was working at the University of Leeds. Thanks also goes to previous PhD students M. Fa, M.Munlin, E.Lamounier, T.Tsai and John Maxfield who worked hard to realise the initial constraint-based modelling work.

References

1. Bier, A. (1990), Snap-Dragging in Three Dimensions, 1990 Symposium on Interactive 3D Graphics, pages 193-204, 1990.

2. Fa, M., Fernando, T., and Dew, P.M. (1993a) Interactive Constraint-based Solid Modelling using Allowable Motion, ACM/SIGGRAPH Symposium on Solid Modelling and Applications, May 1993, pp. 243-252.

3. Fa, M., Fernando, T., and Dew, P.M. (1993b) Direct 3D Manipulation Techniques for Interactive Constraint-based Solid Modelling, Computer Graphics Forum : Conference Issue, Vol.12,No. 3, September 1993, pp 237-248, ISSN 0167-7055.

4. Fernando, T., Fa, M., Dew, P.M. and Munlin M. (1995a), Constraint-based 3D Manipulation Techniques for Virtual Environments, Proceedings of International State of the Art Conference (BCS) on Virtual Reality Applications, Leeds, June 1994. This was also published in Virtual Reality Applications (et al. Earnshaw), Academic Press, 1995, pp. 71-89, ISBN 0-12-227755-4.

5. Fernando, T., and Dew, P.M. (1995b) Constraint-based Interaction Techniques for Supporting A Distributed Collaborative Engineering Environment, Proceedings of the First Workshop on Simulation and Interaction in Virtual Environments (SIVE'95), July 1995, Iowa City, pp. 265 - 270.

6. Kim, S.H. and Lee, K. (1989) Assembly modelling system for dynamic and kinematic analysis, Computer-Aided Design, vol.21, pp 2-12, Jan 1989.

7. Morris, G.H. and Haynes, L.S. (1987) Robotic assembly by constraints, in Proc. IEEE Conf. Robotics Automation, pp. 1507-1515, 1987.

8. Mullin, S.H. & Anderson, D.C. (1993). A Positioning Algorithm for Mechanical Assemblies with Closed Kinematic Chains in Three Dimensions, In Proceedings of Symposium on Solid Modelling and Applications, ACM Press, New York, 271-282.

9. Turner, J., Subramaniam, S. and Gupta, S. (1992) Constraint Representation and Reduction in Assembly Modeling and Analysis, IEEE Transaction on Robotics and Automation, Vol.8, No.6, December 1992.

Toward Electronic Napkins and Beermats: Computer Support for Visual Ideation Skills

Pieter Jan Stappers & James M. Hennessey
Delft University of Technology,
Jaffalaan 9, NL-2628 BX, Delft, The Netherlands
(p.j.stappers@io.tudelft.nl, j.m.hennessey@io.tudelft.nl)

Abstract

Designers still use traditional tools, such as pen and paper sketching, for the early, conceptual phases of idea generation and exploration of solutions. This paper compares benefits of the archetypal traditional tool, a napkin or beermat, to the way current CAD tools force their users to work. Some trends in research and technology point toward better support for the creative activities of skilled professionals. Finally some projects integrating those findings into design tools are discussed.

1 Introduction: Visual Ideation in Conceptual Design

Product designers make extensive use of visual representations. From early rough sketches to final detailed renderings, they make visualisations to communicate and analyse solutions, but also to be inspired and form new ideas.

In the conceptualisation phase (the early stages) of a design project, three types of visualisation activities are common: sketching, modelling, and collage-making [1],[3]. Sketching is done to visualise forms as partial or whole solutions to the design problem. Modelling serves to probe three-dimensional relations and proportions of such solutions. Collage-making helps to clarify abstract concepts by visualisation, and to solve conceptual paradoxes in the design goal.

Sketching, modelling, and collage-making are highly explorative and creative activities. They are goal-directed (toward solving the design problem), but not target-directed (as in creating a faithful reproduction of a painting). The end-visualisation is not just a copy of a pre-existing idea in the designer's head. In the process of drawing the sketches, searching and composing the visual materials for the collages, or putting together the foam model parts, design solutions emerge from the interaction between the designer and the visualisations. For a tool to be an effective support for visual ideation it is not enough that it enables the designer to make something which looks like a sketch, model, or collage. The effective tool must support the process and actions leading to those results.

2 The Computer in the Design Process

Modern computer technology has had a great impact on how we work with visualisations. Developments in automation, computer graphics and their applications in Computer Aided Design (CAD) have especially changed the designer's workplace. For communication, the designer used to work days to get renderings done, and had to start over if a small change was needed. Now painting and 3D rendering software make it easier to produce nearly photorealistic renderings of different variants, at different scales, and in different media. For analysis, the designer used to make scaled technical drawings, and compare these to numerical tables of human proportions in order to determine if these fit. Now databases of 3D models of anthropometric data can quickly provide information about required sizes for comfortable, efficient, or safe operation. For early idea generation, the designer used to scribble away sketches on paper, or beermats, or napkins. Now the computer... hasn't helped. Designers still work the same way, preferring pen and paper over the advanced CAD systems.

Why hasn't the computer replaced the pencil in idea generation? All CAD manufacturers claim flexibility and power for their systems. Yet even in the automotive industry, where designers have the most advanced machines at their disposal, car stylists don't use computers until their ideas have settled down to a precise form [11],[14].

2.1 Napkins and Beermats versus CAD Systems

A number of studies [1],[7],[14] have commented on the disadvantages of current CAD systems for creative idea generation. Often the informal way in which we can sketch on an odd scrap of paper has been suggested as an ideal to strive for. In this section we'll briskly pace through a rough comparison between the CAD system and the archetype of sketching tools: the napkin or, in Holland at least, the beermat. The emphasis of this comparison is on the way these support skilled, fluent, activities and thought, and the way current CAD systems fail to do that.

It is very easy to start using a beermat. A pen and moderate drawing skills suffice. With a CAD system, the user needs to learn the syntax of actions, operate through an interface of menus, naming conventions, coordinate systems, transformations, and units. Minutes will have passed before the first line hits the display.

You interact directly with the sketch on the beermat or napkin. To focus attention, you lift it or move it. Direct manipulation in CAD is not as direct as its name suggests. You interact with the representation, a hidden mathematical model, by moving a pointer over a derived visual representation, and choosing appropriate actions from a menu or toolbar. Often menus or scrollbars must be manipulated before you can see all parts of the visual representation, and you have to operate these with the same hand, or rather: mouse, that you use for drawing. Most of the shapes that appear on the screen are not even part of the represented design itself. For example, to place an annotation to a view of a 3D model, you have to place the annotation in 3 rather than 2 dimensions, otherwise it will appear in the wrong position when another viewpoint is chosen. The viewpoint you used for drawing is not kept with the 3D model, and as a result the interaction is more complicated than with the traditional media.

Creative ideas often arise away from the drawingboard, in a bar, a bathroom, or in bed. Napkins and beermats allow you to start right away. You do not have to travel to the computer room, but can catch and get the flow of ideas. If you didn't stain the napkin with food, you can take it with you in your shirt pocket.

Early sketches, models, and collages employ 'controlled vagueness' [1],[9],[11],[12],[14]. The designer can focus on some aspects of form and shape and leave out others. For instance, she can concentrate on the relative positioning of objects without specifying details of the rounding and detailing of the surfaces. CAD systems allow no vagueness: you have to indicate precisely the beginning, end, weight and curvature of every line. This distracts the designer, forcing her to focus on choices she isn't thinking about. The resulting images are 'overprecise', suggesting a much higher degree of finishedness and making no visual difference between what is important and what is not. Moreover, CAD models lack the expressiveness of sketches, showing only bare and 'dead' geometry. Sketches carry much more information than mere geometrical shape. One special kind of vagueness refers to the 'mode' of the visual representation. Sketches can be two-dimensional or three-dimensional, or something inbetween; they can be plan views, diagrams or perspective views, and combinations of these. Much sketching activity never hits the paper. During conversation or just drawing, a finger or pen can hover and move over part of the sketch to roughly indicate a position or form of something thought of or spoken about. Current computer interfaces force every user action to be precise, unambiguous, definitive, and completely error-free, i.e., a long sequence of perfect steps toward a prespecified target (for a criticism, see [10]).

Sketching is not the production of a single drawing, but the interaction with a family of partial solutions. Different solutions are compared, merged, or interpolated. Research suggests this diffuse, spread-out, focus is essential to forming new ideas. You can make different sketches on one or more beermats, lay them about, rearrange them, and even retain the ones you discarded somewhere in the background. With computers, you have to explicitly and sequentially save, retrieve, name, open, move, zoom in or out on each of your drawings, all actions which disturb the continuity of your work-flow.

2.2 Advantages of the Computer

The above list may suggest that CAD systems are utterly useless. They are not. It is just that their purposes and strengths, such as exact 3D modelling and photorealistic rendering, do not fit the designer's needs in early concept generation. They were optimized toward other tasks (which were probably selected to match the strengths of the computer technology, instead of vice versa). Computer-based systems hold advantages for supporting early idea generation, but as yet these have not been utilized in a manner which serves the designer. Modern computer systems are powerful with animation and video, 3D modelling and depiction, and information management. It can record the development of a design, and make its history accessible for later reference. Representations can be shared for collaborative work: technically, it is now possible to have many people working at the same sketch at the same time without their elbows getting in each other's way. But the fruitful use depends on developing tools which support the user's skills, rather than enabling the user to access the computer power. Until now, most CAD development has been technology-driven. In order to make useful tools, it has to be task-driven.

3 Developments toward Computer Support for Visual Ideation

Several research lines are emerging which hold promise for the development of computerized tools for conceptual design.

Methodological research looks at how designers work, what methods, techniques, and tools they use, and how they use them. We already mentioned the designer's use of families of solutions, mixed media, controlled vagueness, working in different environments, and tentative, gestural operation. Further important findings are that designers, as do many artists, often draw sketches in a standing posture, as opposed to sitting at a desk in a flatly lit room, adorn their working environment with other sketches, pictures, models, and music, in order to 'immerse' themselves into their problem matter, as opposed to sitting at a desk in a flatly lit room, and use both their hands for different functions as opposed to a single hand clutching over a mouse, trackball, or digitizer pen [7].

Virtual Reality research has generated a broader awareness of the need to support articulated, skilled, spatial actions by computer tools in general. Current computer input tools make a very poor match for the expressive, motor, skills of expert users. An expert craftsman has families of tools, such as pens, hammers, chisels, knives, in different shapes and proportions. These differences are not only there to produce different effects, but also to allow different ways of performing the action. A specific hammer or scalpel is chosen for its weight and balance also, so that its user can the better make use of his body, his motor skills. The computer typically channels all input through a single, small bandwidth device: the mouse; any nuance or change must be made through software, but all these software tools 'feel' the same to the user's hand [8].

Research aimed towards widening the spectrum of input devices to match the expressive capabilities of their user, has shown dramatic improvements on creative tasks. Research on two-handed interaction [3],[8] illustrates how small technical enhancements can greatly improve the intuitiveness and performance of an interface, provided the enhancements are chosen to match the user's skills. One crucial element in developing bimanual computer tools is the realisation that the cooperative tasks of the two hands can be (and sometimes need to be) different.

Increasing the computer's sensitivity beyond mouse-clicks is found in gestural input. In Hummels' experiment the user on the right tries to create a 3D shape by gesturing in front of a computer display [6]. His gestures, but no sound, are displayed to a trained artist, who acts out the role of the computer, i.e., interprets the gestures and produces graphical feedback. The models created in this dialogue indicate that this visual, gestural dialogue suffices as an input language, but also that gestural input needs to be sensitive to a range of dialogue styles, instead of the simple symbol sets used by most current gesture recognition systems.

A move to more sketch-like output is 'expressive rendering'. Whereas the mainstream of computer graphics has been aimed at producing photorealistic images, or purely geometrical CAD drawings, recent research has yielded a variety of non-realistic, sketchlike techniques for visualising geometrical models. Although the underlying geometries are still 'hard' their appearance can be made 'soft', fuzzy, or vague [9],[12].

4 Prototypes of computer-supported tools

The different trends and research studies outlined above need to be integrated and translated to concrete tool designs before their actual merits for supporting ideation in the conceptual phase of design can be assessed. In this section we indicate three different projects that do this integration. All three of them are design tools based on the way designers work rather than on the geometrical algorithms that computer science has produced. They are also different in scope, field, and principle of operation, illustrating the importance of further differentiating between the needs of different applications. The variability in approaches also suggests that these tools are still much in their infancy.

In a series of convincing proof-of-concept implementations and experiments, Gross and Do's work on 'the electronic cocktail napkin' demonstrates the usability of sketches as input objects for architectural CAD [2],[4]. The work exploits the constraints of the highly uniform visual language the authors find among architectural designers, who make extensive use of plan views and conventional perspective choices. It may be hard to extend this approach to other designers, such as automotive and industrial designer, because these vary more in range of perspectives, rendering, and use of graphical elements in sketches [11].

The IDEATOR tablet was designed on the basis of [7] to be portable, allow freedom of posture, detailed and coarse two-handed operation, and to support sketching, presentation, annotation and simple animation [13]. It consists of a portable sketch tablet, a separate device specialised for operation with the non-dominant hand. The tablet has a flat computer display which is at the same time the graphical tablet. Separate physical pens are used to set up contours, detail, and annotate the sketches. At the time of its conception, the required technology was not yet there. Now, pen-sensitive LCD screens, such as the WACOM PL400, are commercially available, and a working prototype appears within reach.

The European BRITE-EURAM III project INSTANCE for CAD for automotive styling, decided not to replace the traditional sketching tools at all, but to optimize the connection between the 2D paper sketches and 3D computer representations [11]. Surfaces are then 'sketched in 3D' over a wireframe model using a VR system, and the sketch is then projected over this model. The added spatial quality of the resulting sketch is a new step inbetween rough 2D sketching and detailed 3D modelling, which allows some design choices to be made before the concept moves on to detailing phases. This shows an interesting hybrid coming out of a linkage between traditional media and computer supported tools.

5 Conclusions

Currently, Computer Aided Design systems are useful only for the later stages of the design process, when ideas have sufficiently crystallized. For explorative, creative actitivites in the early design stages, CAD is still not useful. Recent developments in research and implementation, however, suggest that before long (in a few years?), computer-supported tools may be effective for early design also. Integrated prototype tools exhibit a range of possible operational principles, based on sketches as objects, sketching as an activity, and computer-enhanced hybrid 3D sketch models. In the future, such principles may be merged into productive and unconventional tools which still do justice to the creative skills of designers.

References

1. Coyne, R, Snodgrass, A. Rescuing CAD from rationalism. Design Studies 1993; 14:100-123.
2. Do, E. Computability of design diagrams-an empirical study of diagram conventions in design, In: Junge, R (ed) Proceedings CAAD Futures'97, München, August 1997, pp 171-176
3. Gribnau, MW, Hennessey, JM. Comparing single- and two-handed 3D input for a 3D object assembly task. In: Karat, CM, Lund, A. (eds) Proceedings ACM-CHI'98: Human factors in computing, Addison-Wesley, Reading, MA, 1998, pp 233-234.
4. Gross, M. The electronic cocktail napkin - a computational environment for working with design diagrams. Design Studies 1996; 17:53-69.
5. Hennessey, JM. Exploring computer enhancements for conceptualising. In: White, T, Tzonis, A, (eds) Automation based creative design. Elsevier Science, Amsterdam, 1994, pp 349-362.
6. Hummels, CJ, Stappers, PJ. Meaningful gestures for human computer interaction: beyond hand postures. In: Proceedings of the 3rd International Conference on Automatic Face & Gesture Recognition (FG'98), Nara, Japan, April 14-16. IEEE Computer Society Press, Los Alamitos, CA, 1998, pp 591-596.
7. Kolli, R, Stuyver, R., Hennessey, JM. Deriving the functional requirements for a concept sketching device: A case study. In: Grechenig, T, Tscheligi, M (ed) Proceedings of HCI: Vienna conference, VCHCI93, september 1993, pp 184-195 (Lecture notes in computer science no. 733)
8. Kurtenbach, G, Fitzmaurice, G, Baudel, T, Buxton, W. The design of a GUI paradigm based on tablets, two-hands, and transparency. In: Pemberton, S (ed) Proceedings ACM-CHI'97: Human factors in computing, Addison-Wesley, Reading, MA, 1997, pp 35-42.
9. Lansdown, J, Schofield, S. Expressive rendering: A review of nonphotorealistic techniques, IEEE Computer Graphics and Applications, 1995(May): 29-37.
10. Laurel, B. Computers as theatre. Addison-Wesley, Reading, MA, 1992.
11. Overbeeke, CJ, Kehler, T, Hummels, CCM, Stappers, PJ. Exploiting the expressive: rapid entry of car designers' conceptual sketches into the CAD environment. In: Roller, D (ed) Proceedings of ISATA-2, 1997, pp 243-250.
12. Schumann, J, Strothotte, T, Raab, A, Laser, S. Assessing the effect of non-photorealistic rendered images in CAD. In: Tauber, MJ (ed) Proceedings ACM-CHI'96: Human factors in computing, Addison-Wesley, Reading, MA, 1996, pp 35-41.
13. Stuyver, R and Hennessey, JM. A support tool for the conceptual phase of design. In: Kirby, M.A.R., Dix, AJ, Finlay, JE (eds) People and Computers Vol. X, Cambridge University Press, 1995, pp 235-245
14. Tovey, M. Intuitive and objective processes in automotive design. Design Studies 1992, 13(1):23-41.
15. Weiser, M. The computer for the 21st century. Scientific American 1991, 265(3):94-104.

Computational Support for Conceptual Sketching

Analysis and Interpretation of the Graphical Notation of Visual Representations

Jeanette Mcfadzean
Department of Design & Innovation, Open University,
Milton Keynes

Abstract

The research investigates *how* designers sketch specifically analysing the physical details of mark-making. It contrasts the physical representations with the abstract cognitive processes of architectural design. A new form of protocol analysis has been developed using video and computer records of designers' sketching activity. The research compares the designer's post-hoc commentary and interpretations of the sketching activity with the computer's record of that activity. This process will lead to a greater understanding of the relationships between *design events* and *graphical events*.

1 Introduction

Protocol studies have been successfully used to analyse some aspects of design activity [1], but little research has been done to examine empirically the use of sketches during conceptual designing. Do [2] carried out three protocol analysis studies, which examined the verbal activity and more fundamentally the graphical notation of sketches. In the same vein Suwa and Tversky [3] [4] carried out protocol studies, with retrospective analysis. Both studies were instigated in order to elicit information about the graphical notation used by architectural designers during conceptual sketching. The current research brings together this empirical evidence with studies from design science [1], and cognitive psychology [5] [6] [7]. The current study differs from the preceding research because its main interest is in understanding how the construction of external representations aids problem resolving in conceptual design. The questions addressed in the current research are;

1. How can representations produced by the graphical notational language of sketching be understood in computational terms?
2. What cognitive reasoning strategies does the graphical notation facilitate?
3. How does this enable us to understand the early stages of design?

2. Pilot Study

A protocol analysis pilot study was conducted. Each designer was given a one-hour conceptual engineering design task. The sessions were videotaped, and based on observations a time series analysis of the design activity was conducted. Building on previous encoding systems, such as the activity based model [8], the analysis of the design activity was given three distinct classifications of conceptual design activity; writing, drawing and physical inactivity. It was hypothesised that there would be a measured difference in frequency between the physical acts of writing and drawing. The objective of the pilot study was to determine if the physical acts of the drawing and writing were very different even when the marks look similar. The differences in sketching activity have allowed the classification of a graphical text mark and a line drawing mark, permitting the separation of these marks from each other.

3. Aims of Computational Sketching Analysis

Whilst the use and analysis of video and audio protocols is considered to be a valuable method for understanding the complex interaction of many different variables during a design task, it is not always ideal when analysing the use of graphical notation. The pilot study highlighted possible inconsistencies that may arise when analysing graphical notation using video recordings.

From this it was found that a more extensive and reliable data set could be extracted from a more extensive set of experimental procedures. 'Computational Sketch Analysis' (CSA) for conceptual design has been developed in order to elicit information at the micro level of conceptual sketching. CSA consists of two functional pieces of software a *Data Collector* and a *Sketch Analyser*.

The pilot study revealed that it is only by having a detailed computational representation of the design session that analysis can be carried out with objectivity and consistency. For example, algorithms can be applied to the recorded design session which will extract quantitative data regarding the time spent drawing and the time spent on each pencil mark, the pressure of the pencil strokes and the speed at which the marks are created.

The Sketch Analyser serves two functions. Firstly it acts as a record of the graphical notational activity which can be replayed to the designer retrospectively, for comments and analysis. Secondly the software is an analytical tool which builds structures in a hierarchical manner. The lowest level captures all the graphical notation of the visual representations that are generated during a design session. The next layer extracts the lines of the graphical notation. The Sketch Analyser uses the representational schema derived in the pilot study, in order to determine how sketches are constructed. The new method of collecting data allows a rigorous and consistent analysis of the graphical notation used by designers. CSA records the generation of graphical notation used by designers created in a conceptual design session. CSA is a more appropriate method of data collection and analysis than any present methods of data collection in the discipline of design. This is because a stream of time-stamped stroke co-ordinate data allows graphical events to be abstracted automatically.

4. Representation of a Graphical Notation

At present there is no formal description of the graphical notation in conceptual designing. This makes it difficult to analyse 'How and what do designers draw?' In the pilot study the analysis of the graphical notational data pursues this line of thought, through the use of Van Sommers' executive constraints [7]. Van Sommers suggested that drawings are construction and constrained by executive constraints, such as the preferred starting position and preferred stroke direction of a line.

Executive constraints were applied in the pilot study to the non-symbolic data, in order to identify the elements and sets that define the designers graphical notation of sketching. The simplest form of information was proposed to be a pencil mark[1]. All marks are extracted from the design session and time stamped. Attributes of the marks were then calculated, for example the length of a line and the estimated speed of creation. Figure 1 shows the analytical process in action.

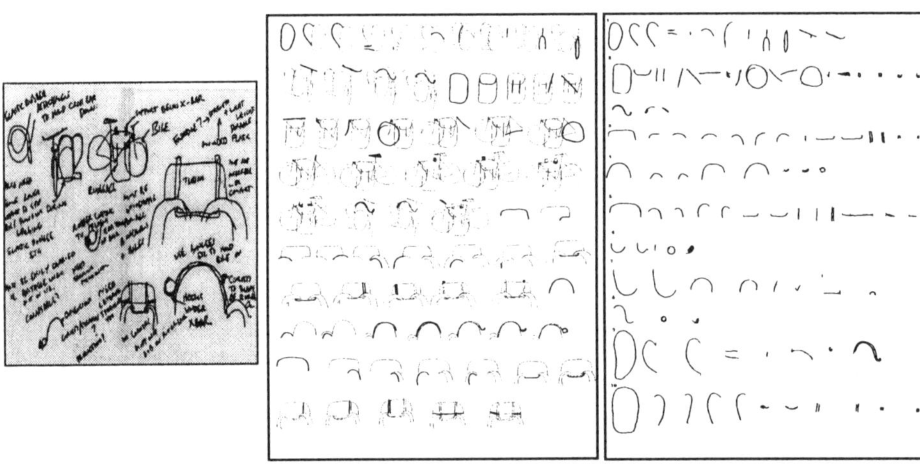

Figure 1 Sketches by a designer, the extraction of the order and context of the graphical notation and the extraction of single marks.

The results of the pilot study show that analysis of the graphical notation and the use of the defined sketch representation allow the analyser's perception of similar representations to be identified through rigorous analysis. Van Sommers' executive constraints can be used to form a representation of the graphical notational language of sketching which is unambiguous.

---

[1] *Mark* is defined as moving the pencil on the paper between points (A) and (B)

5. CSA Experiment

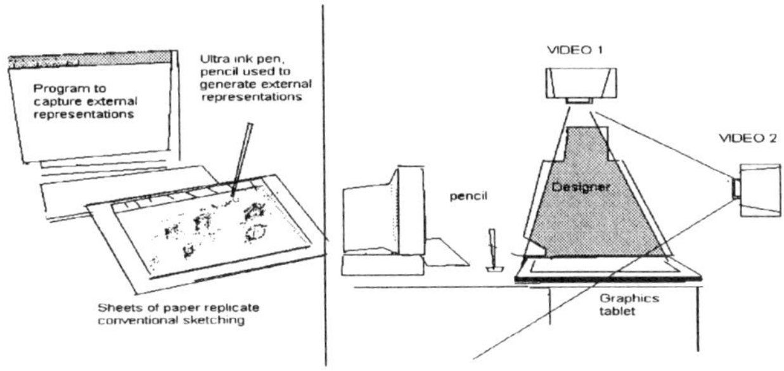

Figure 2 Apparatus set up

The experimental set up, shown in figure 2 is proposed to replicate a conventional sketching environment. Two forms of data capture techniques are carried out to extract the graphical notational information. (i) The graphical data generated in a design session is collected and time-stamped by the data capture program. (ii) Video recorders capture the context of the design actions and verbalisations. The data capture techniques and the use of the recording and analysis of information throughout the design session is shown in Table 1.

Computer	**Video 1**	**Video 2**	**Video 3**
(Data Collector) Record graphical notation during designing i	Record drawing	Record physical activity	
(Sketch Analyser) Designer reviews the graphical notation			Record retrospective analysis
Experimenter Investigate the graphical data for graphical events		Transcribe the video tape	Transcribe the video tape
(Sketch Analyser) Automatic generation of graphical events[2] ii iii		Investigate the tape for design events	Investigate the tape for design events

Table 1 The data capture and analysis procedures

i Ambiguitics may arise in the data extracted via the data capture program. Video1 and the Data Collector allow analysis of ambiguous events that arise in the graphical notation. **ii**. Video 2 and the Sketch Analyser, allows us to ask 'Is there a relationship between graphical events and the designers actions?' **iii**. Identification of important concepts in the external representations may be investigating by analysis of the graphical and design events.

6. Experimental Research

The research has undertaken three experiments consisting of two tasks; a design task and a retrospective report task. The first asked the participants to design a smokers

[2] Graphical Events are 'chunks' of notation that emerge out of a lower-level data set.

lodge for a University campus. Participants were given a brief, after which they were taken to a site that would house the lodge. On returning they were asked to produce designs on the paper provided using the graphics tablet and a lead pencil. The design sessions lasted 1hour 10 minutes and 45 minutes respectively. The task was recorded using the Computational Data Collector. Following the design task, the designers reviewed the sketching activities using the Sketch Analyser and reported on what they were thinking when generating the graphical notation.

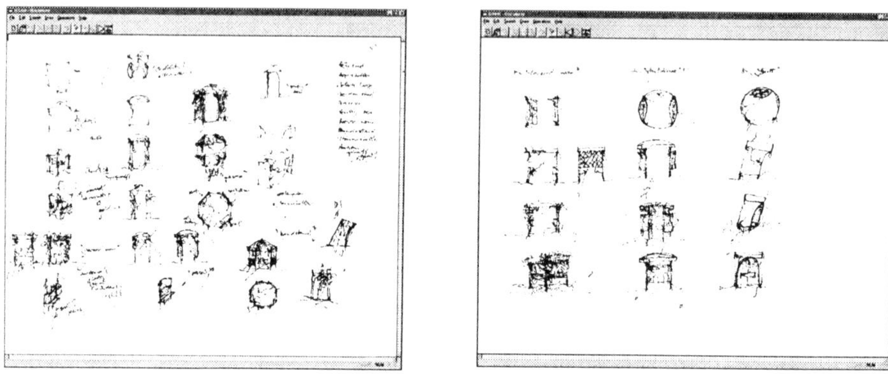

Figure 3 Graphical representations generated during a designer's conceptual design session.

'Design Events' are defined to be important incidents that are recognised as occurring during the process of designing. Twelve types of Design Events have been designated provisionally to classify these events from chunks of information that arise from the retrospective reports of the participants. From the design literature [1] [3] [9], and the initial interpretation of the retrospective report task; the contents of the participant's transcripts have been categorised based on the idea of 'Design Events'. Design events are not considered to be mutually exclusive thus a chunk of information may have more than one Design Event attached to it.

In order to conform to standards of protocol analysis; completeness of vocabulary, increased reliability [10], five transcript analysts were selected based on their knowledge of the design literature and their experience of examining verbal protocols. The analysts' task was to read the transcript and classify the retrospective reports in accordance with the descriptions of the twelve Design Events and their sub-categories. Cohen's Kappa analysis on the analysts' encoding suggests that the classifications of twelve design events; can be applied consistently and the analysts' agree that the classification accounts for a high percentage of the important Design Events' identified in the transcripts.

The next step of analysis and interpretation is based on the graphical notational activity being associated with the design events. This research hypothesises that there is a measurable difference in the physical activity of the graphical notation and that these differences can be mapped to the design events. It is expected that mappings will allow the extraction of denotational sub-systems that relate the designers' mode of problem solving with the syntactic structure of the external representations. The objective is to understand how graphical notation is utilised as a problem resolution device and how it is used to define a design problem space. A longer-term objective is to facilitate the development of computational support tools.

7. Conclusions

The pilot study demonstrated the need for notational languages to be applied to graphical, drawn representations. The Data Collector and the Sketch Analyser address the following issues;

1. The extraction of non-symbolic information and the classification of this information into graphical units, based on the understanding of an expert's knowledge of graphical notation and cognitive processing of the information.

2. The appropriate development of a representation that can deal with;
   - The represented sketch,
   - The graphical notation of the sketch,
   - The relationship between the perceived concepts of the sketch and the facts inferred by the graphical notation.

The research indicates that the new method of data collection gives essential information enabling new methods of sketch representations to be developed.

References

1. Cross N, Christiaans H, Dorst K. Analysing Design Activity. John Wiley & Sons Ltd, Chichester, 1996
2. Do E. Protocol Analysis of 3 designers. Personal communication, The Sundance Lab, University of Colorado, Boulder, 1998
3. Suwa M, Tversky B. What do architects and students perceive in their design sketches? A protocol analysis. Design Studies, 1997; 18(4):385 - 403.
4. Suwa, M., Purcell T, Gero J. Macroscopic analysis of design processes based on a scheme for coding designers' cognitive actions. Design Studies (to appear), 1998.
5. Finke RA, Ward TB, Smith SM. Creative Cognition: Theory, Research and applications. MIT Press, Massachusetts, 1996
6. Karniloff-Smith A. Beyond Modularity: A Developmental Perspective on Cognitive Science. MIT Press, Massachusetts, 1995
7. van Sommers P. Drawing and Cognition. Drawing ability. Cambridge University Press, New York, 1984
8. Akin O, Lin C. Design Protocol Data and Novel Design Decisions. In: Cross N et al (ed) Analysing Design Activity, John Wiley & Sons Ltd. Chichester, 1996 pp 35-62
9. Oxman R. Design by Re-representations: A Model of Visual Reasoning in Design. Design Studies, 1997; 18(4):329-347.
10. Ericsson KA, Simon HA. Protocol Analysis: verbal reports as data. The MIT Press, Massachusetts, 1993

Learning to See Architecturally

Christopher Tweed
School of Architecture, The Queen's University of Belfast
Belfast, N. Ireland

Abstract

The development of computer-based techniques for generating photorealistic renderings of designs promises to overcome difficulties many lay people have in understanding conventional architectural drawings. Greater 'realism', however, does not necessarily lead to converging interpretations. Existing studies of perception have shown that architects 'see' in quite specific ways. This paper examines 'architectural seeing' from a phenomenological perspective, using examples from previous studies of perception in design representation and from recent fieldwork carried out at Queen's University. The paper suggests that a combination of phenomenological *homeworlds* and canonically defined *appreciative communities* offers a new approach to understanding differences in perception among architects and non-architects.

1 Introduction

Considerable research effort has been expended on developing greater realism in the representation of architectural space in computers. Some have even claimed that once virtual reality has been refined, most architectural debate will centre on virtual rather than physical buildings [1]. Greater 'realism', however, will not necessarily lead to a convergence of interpretations between architects and their clients. Experienced architects see more than mere form [2]. They 'see' the sound, warmth or coolness, light and shade of the spaces they are manipulating on a page. Recent research at Queen's supports the view, held by Ihde [3], that the availability of different interpretations of visual phenomena is dependent on the sedimented associations of different subjects. For any given representation there can be many different interpretations, even among architects. And these may change as individuals gather more experience. The central purpose of this paper, therefore, is to identify the influences on the *development* of perceptions and interpretations of architectural information and how new visualisation techniques impinge upon this.

The paper begins by summarising different accounts of perception in the phenomenological tradition [4]. It then describes how 'objects' of perception are thrown into "affective relief" based on an individual's sedimented associations and practical orientation towards the lifeworld [5]. Existing studies of the perception of design representations are discussed before presenting recent research at Queen's into the perception of architecture by non-architects, students of architecture and practising architects. The penultimate section introduces the notion of "appreciative communities" to explain how architects with different "appreciative systems" converge on similar evaluations of design. The final part of the paper offers a critique of attempts to treat visual experience in isolation from other sensory modalities, using architecture as an example.

2 Phenomenology and architecture

The phenomenological tradition in twentieth century philosophy has direct appeal to architectural critics and practitioners because it provides methods of addressing phenomena, such as our experiencing of space, that lie at the heart of architectural concerns [6, 7, 8]. This has also led some philosophers to address architectural problems from a phenomenological perspective [9, 10, 11]. But phenomenology is such a broad discipline that it is entirely possible for two people to call themselves phenomenologists and yet hold opposing views. There is a need, therefore, to clarify how phenomenology can inform a study of perception of architecture.

2.1. Perception

Edmund Husserl is often credited as the founder of modern phenomenology. For Husserl, perception is central to our way of being in the world and his view of perception may be summarised as follows:

- perception is the primary mode around which most other experiences revolve
- perception is multi-modal and complex—the separation of perception into independent modalities of sight, sound, and touch takes place *after* the experience
- the form visual perception takes is that of a gestalt, or figure against a ground, with every object situated in a context—it was Husserl's insight that inspired the Gestalt movement in psychology
- there is a "depth" to all perceptions with both manifest and meant characteristics—objects present profiles, but profiles carry significance

Maurice Merleau-Ponty took on board much of what Husserl had developed within phenomenology [12]. However, Merleau-Ponty rejected the strong foundationalism of Husserl and placed much greater emphasis on the role of the body in perception. To the above, therefore, the following points can be added:

- the body is the primary means of access to the world—it is only through having a body than we can be aware of such fundamental phenomena as space
- the body knows the world, above all, through its practical engagement with it
- perception is ambiguous or polymorphic and is informed by cultural context

In cognitive approaches to perception, the perceiving subject is distinct from the perceived object. The external world provides the subject with sensory information which is operated on by cognitive processes that bring to bear knowledge of the objective world to interpret what has been perceived. According to Ingold, this "knowing consists in the organization of sensations impinging upon the passively receptive human subject into progressively higher-order structures or 'representations'" [13]. For Merleau-Ponty, and others such as Sartre and Bergson, "perception is not a 'function of knowledge' but a sketch of what I can do; it expresses a possible action" [14]. Gibson has arrived at similar conclusions encapsulated in his notion of "affordances" which reflects his view that knowledge gained through perception is knowledge of what an object affords, what it "offers the animal, what it *provides* or *furnishes*, either for good or ill" [15]. Common to Gibson and Merleau-Ponty is the view that the lived body and the world are correlatives, such that world and body together constitute a system in which their interaction is driven largely by practical concerns.

2.2. Variational method

Central to Husserl's method was the idea that we can explore the contents of consciousness through use of a variational method, primarily through developing variants in imagination or 'phantasy' as he called it. Later phenomenologists have found sufficient ambiguity in perception without needing to consider 'phantasy' variants [4]. Figure 1 shows perceptual variants found in the Necker cube.

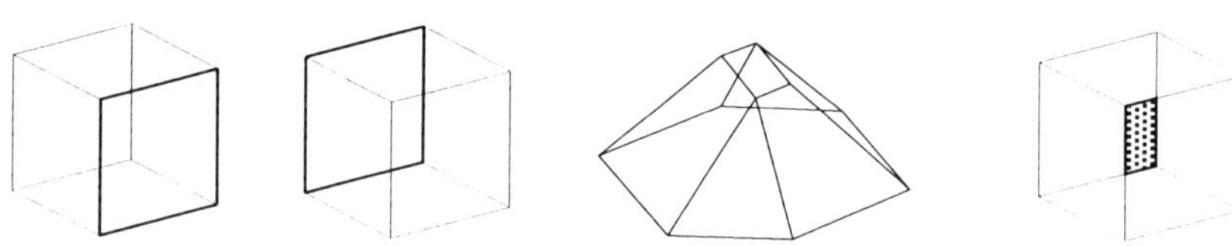

(a) (b) (c) (d)

Figure 1: variants of the Necker cube (after Ihde [4]).

The 'cubes' in (a) and (b) are probably the most easily retrieved, but (c) and (d) can also be seen. For (d) a prompt might be 'a six-legged insect in a hexagonal rainpipe.' Two important points need to be mentioned even about these simple line figures: first, it is impossible to see more than one variant at the same time—the viewer must 'flip' between them; and second, switching between them implies a change of viewing (body) position—the change in perception can be 'felt'

Ihde's concludes that the ability of different individuals to see these variants and the order in which they are found is significant [3]. To ask what a diagram 'really' depicts, therefore, is misleading. The answer depends on context, and the purposes and cultural background of the observer.

2.3. Three dimensions of phenomenology

The inability of phenomenology to address the socio-cultural world has been seen as a major deficiency in Husserl's philosophy. However, Anthony Steinbock has rehabilitated Husserl's work to address the wider contexts of perception and interpretation [5]. Steinbock posits three dimensions of phenomenological analysis: static, genetic and generative. These are explained with reference to figure 2 below.

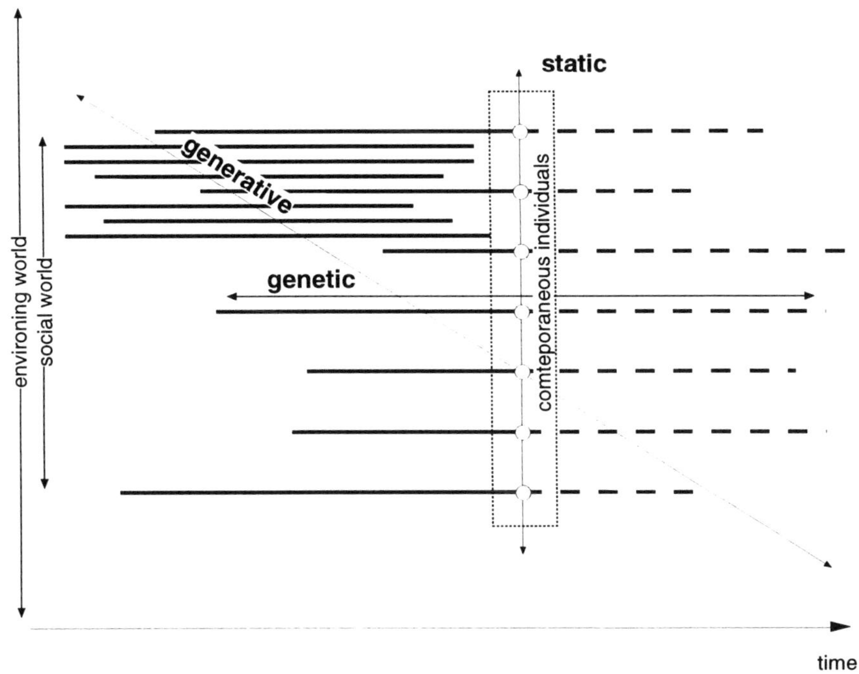

Figure 2: three dimensions of phenomenological analysis.

The horizontal lines in the figure represent the lives of individuals along a time line. They are of different lengths, indicating varied lifespans, and overlap to greater or lesser extents. Circles on these lines represent individuals at a specific point in their biographical development. The vertical arrangement of lines is not intended to represent except that individuals live alongside others who share a social world. The environing world is the larger context that includes not just social, but physical, cultural and even spiritual aspects of experience. The environing world is all that we can possibly experience.

Static analysis focuses only on the present time and on a range of contemporaneous individuals. Neither the developmental history of the individual, nor the historico-cultural context surrounding his or her personal development, are taken into consideration. The main concern of a static analysis is to describe *how* something is given to consciousness rather than inquire into *what* something is. At the core of static analysis is the fundamental phenomenological insight that all experience is experience of something.

Genetic analyses are primarily concerned with the genesis, or becoming, of individual subjectivities. A genetic analysis, therefore, embraces the biographical development of contemporaneous individuals to account for differences in the constitution of meaning, which exist across them. A genetic analysis must concern itself with how the sedimented associations of past experience bring certain 'objects' into "affective relief" such that what we perceive is never a "flat" world but is instead a world with "depth". Our perceptual experience is structured around figure-ground relations, that bring to the fore one set of meanings rather than another. Silverman, in reconciling conflicting accounts of genetic development posited by Sartre, on the one hand, and Piaget, on the other, borrows the painting term 'pentimento', which is used to describe how earlier elements within a painting show through later layers of paint long after the artist has changed the composition of the work [16]. Past experience may 'print through' on to the present.

The third dimension of analysis is generative. Generative, in this context, has two related meanings. First, it refers to the generation of norms, values, systems of belief; and second, it refers to generations of individuals and the enduring sense of tradition and community that crosses the boundaries of individual lives and biographies. Generativity is, at the same time, the handing down of traditions *and* the generation of new traditions for future generations. Steinbock underlines the role of the cultural context in the constitution of meanings: "[g]enerative phenomenology treats phenomena that are *historical, geological, cultural, intersubjective, and normative* from the very start" [5]. Generative matters and methods are intersubjective rather than subjective. They are concerned with how normative behaviour is shaped and modified by successive generations through a process of critique and renewal. A key concern of generative phenomenology is how the norms, values and belief systems of one particular tradition are defined in relation to another. To investigate this, Steinbock makes use of Husserl's homeworld/alienworld structure.

A homeworld is that with which we are typically familiar. Our homeworld embodies the norms against which individual behaviour and beliefs are measured. Steinbock goes to some length to dispel the notion that 'our' homeworld is in any sense superior to others. It is, for us—but only for us. The homeworld/alienworld structure is co-generative in the sense that our typically familiar beliefs, norms etc. are ours only because there is a realm of beliefs that is not ours. It is this liminal relation between home and alien that defines each: "home and alien are [not merely] formed by positing limits, but ... are *mutually delimited* as home and alien, normal and abnormal. ... they are *co-relative* and *co-constitutive*" [5].

It is impossible to define the limits of either homeworld or alienworld in any final or stable sense because they are constantly undergoing redefinition through encounter. Nor are homeworlds homogeneous collections of individuals who think the same thoughts and agree on everything. The limits of the homeworld are changing continually not just through encounters with the alien but also through critical renewal and appropriation by 'homecomrades'.

3 Seeing while designing

An underlying aim of many studies of visual perception in design is to develop an understanding of human perception, particularly in design sketching, that will inform the development of computational tools to support design. They often assume it is possible to identify universal characteristics of perception that are independent of historical or cultural influence and which, therefore, provide immutable foundations for a computational approach. Not surprisingly, such studies tend to adopt a cognitivist approach, in which it is broadly assumed that seeing involves two stages: first, the perception of a particular representation, whether it be lines on paper or on a computer screen, and the subsequent interpretation of the meaning of sensory data.

In Goldschmidt's study of design sketching, a novice designer begins a design project with random 'doodling' of his signature. The signature serves as a stimulus for a plan which retains the 'essential' characteristics of the signature—a curvilinear form with spaces defined by enclosing loops. In response to the question of whether any starting shape would have worked, it is argued that only the signature "hit on the desire to liberate [the student] from straight lines and angles" [17]. The only choice considered is between the designer's own sketch and ready-made images prepared by others, e.g. photographs. But there are other possible explanations as to why a self-drawn sketch is preferable to an existing image. One is that the act of drawing as a bodily activity is important to the evolution of the design. As Lawson notes, some designers find it difficult to think without a pencil in their hands [18]. Certainly, if one attends closely to what designers do when they sketch one can see that the movement of the drawing tool on the medium is important; designers frequently retrace the outline of parts of a sketch, as if they were training their hands to experience the space.

Suwa and Tversky have analysed conceptual dependencies between segments of design exercises [19]. In contrast to Goldschmidt's study, theirs recognises the link between form and other qualities of the design, such as the functions that elements of a design are likely to fulfil. Hence, there is an explicit recognition that when architects look at design sketches they read into them much more than visual qualities. They conclude that longer architectural experience leads to deeper thought processes and better understanding of the functional relations implicit in externally visual representations. Experienced architects were found to be able to 'read-off' more than fledgling designers.

Liu's study narrows the scope, focusing on just one design skill: the ability to recognise emergent shapes in drawings [20]. Experienced designers were able to find more emergent shapes than inexperienced designers. Moreover, experienced designers were able to find implicit emergent shapes that remained unavailable to inexperienced designers. Design ability, as gauged by these studies, improves along the genetic dimension of the framework in figure 2.

Schön and Wiggins have also conducted detailed studies of design in which they explicitly recognise the importance of generatively, as well as genetically, constituted norms [2]. In the session involving the design student (Petra) and the studio master (Quist), the influence of cultural context is foregrounded when Petra, after having made a change to her design, describes the layout as being 'more significant.' Schön and Wiggins are keenly aware that "Petra's designing depends on her ability to make just such normative judgements of quality." However, they also recognise that normative statements may be limited to the individual—the genetic dimension of normativity—or to larger groups. They cite Geoffrey Vickers as positing "systems of beliefs, values, norms, prizings ... possessed by individuals, sometimes shared by groups or by whole cultures, on the basis of which we make our positive and negative judgements of phenomena" [21]. What Schön and Wiggins acknowledge is that the evaluation of design moves is shaped by the generative critique and renewal of values embedded in a particular design community's (homeworld) traditions as well as in the genetic development of individual designers. The central importance of this assessment of design moves is underlined by their observation that "how one develops a particular appreciative system seems to have a great deal to do with the process by which one learns to become an architectural designer" [2]."

4 Spatialisation and affective recall

As a supplement to the work described previously, this section describes recent fieldwork carried out at the author's institution. The purpose of the fieldwork was to test some inchoate ideas that could be investigated in greater detail at a later date.

Postgraduate students in the School of Architecture at Queen's University carried out some basic fieldwork to establish differences in perception between architects and non-architects. The aims of the survey were:

(1) to investigate the extent to which simple line drawings (Necker cubes) are perceived as 3D representations by people from different backgrounds

(2) to identify which buildings "stand out" (for whatever reasons) for people from different backgrounds

(3) to determine whether subjects are able to identify a recent building in Belfast (the Waterfront Concert Hall) from a quote and from an image

Discussion here is restricted to (1) and (2), but it should be noted that the choice of subjects was heavily influenced by the third aim.

Forty subjects were interviewed in random locations over a two-week period in December 1997. The breakdown was: four full-time tutors in a school of architecture; four practising architects; five people who had been involved in the design or construction of the Waterfront Hall; six staff employed in the Waterfront Hall; six 'users' of the Waterfront Hall; eight members of the general public; and six architecture students—one from each year of the course at Queen's. From the obvious criterion of 'having experienced a formal architectural education,' 19 were classified as architects, 21 as non-architects.

Each subject was shown two versions of a Necker cube, as depicted in figure 3, and asked to say what they thought each one was.

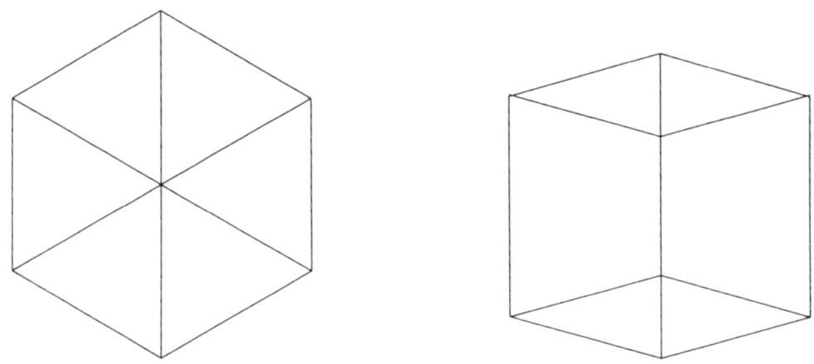

(a) (b)

Figure 3: diagrams shown to respondents.

Figure 3(a) was chosen because it appeared to be neutral, in the sense that it offered more or less equal opportunities for interpretation as a 2D or 3D element. In the responses, 12 out of the 19 (63%) architects offered a 3D interpretation as their first response, as opposed to 5 out of the 21 (24%) non-architects. On the surface it would appear that those engaged on, or having previously undertaken, a formal course in architecture offer a 3D interpretation more readily than others. Of course, there are many possible explanations for this, none of which can be conclusively be excluded on the basis of this simple experiment. It could be, for example, that those drawn to a career in architecture are predisposed to yield 3D interpretations, regardless of the formal education they subsequently receive.

Figure 3(b), the second diagram shown to subjects, was judged to be more readily seen as a 3D element by virtue of the separation of previously coincident 'corners.' In Liu's terms it contains fewer 'nameable' shapes and so should require more interpretational effort [20]. All respondents offered a 3D interpretation of this figure as their first response.

The second part of the survey broadened the scope of the inquiry to look at which buildings "stand out" for different people. Survey respondents were asked to name any three buildings and then to provide three words to describe their choices. Of the architects, only 5 (26%) named buildings in N Ireland, whereas 17 non-architects (86%) named buildings in Belfast. Of these, Belfast City Hall featured most frequently. The words used to describe buildings were also revealing. Architects often used words which have a specifically architectural interpretation: "Classical", "functional", even "Palladian". Non-architects tended to use words which feature in everyday usage: "old", "ugly", "big". Nearly all of the buildings named by non-architects were designed and built pre-1960—the word "old" appeared frequently (5 times) in descriptions. Non-architects were the only ones to offer specifically non-architectural words or phrases for buildings: "good food" was used by one respondent to describe a named pub/restaurant, and "upper class" was used by another to describe the Europa Hotel in Belfast.

Results from this brief study are clearly inconclusive but serve a useful purpose by suggesting areas where future research might concentrate its efforts. It was noted in the previous section that the evaluation of designs in the midst of designing calls on an implicit set of norms and values that designers routinely and unselfconsciously apply to their own efforts. Until this generative dimension is explored there seems to be little chance of understanding architectural seeing in any depth. The next section outlines a possible direction for pursuing this topic that will complement the earlier framework of homeworld/alienworld.

5 Appreciative communities in architecture

For Schön and Wiggins, values are embedded in "appreciative systems" [2]; in phenomenological terms, they are embedded in homeworlds. However, the granularity of the homeworld/alienworld structure is too coarse to account for groups of individuals who, in spite of sharing normative behaviours, often disagree on specific judgements of architectural merit. We need to make finer distinctions to get a better understanding of evaluative phenomena in architecture.

There are close similarities between the homeworld/alienworld structure and other approaches to understanding the situatedness of individuals within specific cultural perspectives. For example, the anthropologist Clifford Geertz uses Boyle's term to refer to 'invisible colleges' as consisting of people who think along the same lines within an academic discipline [22]. But it is perhaps Stanley Fish's notion of "interpretive communities," which best describes how critical groups form within the broader cultural context of a homeworld [23].

An interpretive community is a group of people who read along similar lines in literary criticism. Interpretive communities are not so much collections of individuals who share the same theories or ideas, but ideas who share the same subscribers. Interpretive communities, therefore, are not monolithic. To distinguish interpretive communities in literary criticism from the appreciative systems operating in architecture we will use the term "appreciative community". Architecture has relatively few such communities. Modernism is still taught as the mainstay of twentieth century design. Postmodernism and deconstruction often seem to be tolerated rather than actively encouraged. In these, form and geometry remain central to debate, with a concomitant reification of the visual. Perhaps the strongest challenge to these has come from the environmental movement where the invisible consequences of designs, e.g. embodied energy, can become more prominent than what is visible.

The juxtaposition of the homeworld/alienworld structure and the notion of appreciative communities in architecture opens up interesting avenues to explore. We may ask how the norms and values of a homeworld interact with the evaluative practices of an appreciative community. For example, how does an architect in N Ireland appropriate the values of architectural precedents from remote geographical and cultural locations? What influence, if any, do the traditions of the homeworld exert on an individual's perceptions? If there is little or no interaction or influence, then, why? And, how does change occur in appreciative communities? Is it generational, as the generative description of a homeworld implies?

6 Technology and the new visualism

Different appreciative communities privilege different aspects of architecture. Often it is geometry and form that matter most; for others, it is the invisible impact of buildings on world resources. Privileging of aesthetics is common to many appreciative communities. New technological advances in the depiction and representation of designs foreground visual aspects at the expense of others. This final main section will try to apply some of the points raised above in the light of this growing emphasis on the visual, visualism.

In an earlier paper the author presented the results of a phenomenological 'experiment' designed to identify some of the differences between perception and imaging in design [24]. An essential difference between these two modes is that perception requires considerably less effort to sustain than imaging. Recording design ideas externally allows a designer to reduce the cognitive effort of holding on to an image in the mind. As the earlier studies have shown, it allows the designer to 'play' with features of the representation which 'emerge' from the re-interpretation of a drawing. For the early stages of design a key property of the external representation is its vagueness. It has also been argued that the more detailed and less ambiguous a drawing is, the more it constrains possible interpretations or variants. Thus the move towards greater photorealism in the rendering of designs limits the scope for imagination. Invoking the literary analogy again, we might say that the more 'literal' the representation the less room there is for poetic readings. At the final stages of design this may be desirable, if only to admit greater honesty to the client-architect relationship. Negatively, however, enhanced visual realism only serves to privilege the visual mode of experience at the expense of other important modes.

7 Conclusions

Architects see differently to others. They notice features of the world that others, in many cases, do not; and architectural seeing becomes more differentiated from other ways with greater experience. The paper has proposed the static-genetic-generative framework as a tool for exploring how differences in perception and interpretation might be addressed. Most existing studies have focused on the genesis of seeing within individual designers, though there is often an implied recognition of the generative dimension. We are often blind to the influences which the norms and values of our homeworld, precisely because they are *our* values. In the Western architectural tradition form-giving in design is prioritised over others, and this is evident from the examples of design analysis referred to in this paper. The paper has also highlighted the influences of appreciative communities in shaping our approach to design and in deciding what are good and bad design moves.

Much of the knowledge a designer possesses is gained through understanding what it is like to be in buildings. It can only be acquired through the bodily-sensory experience. The importance of the body as a means to interacting with the world has been neglected and the increasing realism of CAD techniques is distancing us further from the total experience of architecture by reducing opportunities for greater use of the imagination. It is the development of these tools more than anything else which underlines the need for a better understanding of architectural seeing changes across the generations.

8 Acknowledgements

The author wishes to acknowledge and thank the following postgraduate students in the School of Architecture at Queen's for their contribution to the fieldwork: Robert Jamison, Dermott McMeel, Lisa McVeigh, Anne Melly, Dominic Morris and Aoibheann Reilly.

References

1. Novak, M., Liquid Architectures in Cyberspace. In Cyberspace: First Steps, M. Benedikt (ed), MIT Press, Cambridge MA, 1991.
2. Schön, DA. and Wiggins, G. Kinds of seeing and their functions in designing, Design Studies, Butterworth-Heinemann Ltd, London, 13, 2, 1992; pp 135-156.
3. Ihde, D. Experimental Phenomenology, SUNY, New York, 1986.
4. Ihde, D. Postphenomenology: Essays in the Postmodern Context, Northwestern University Studies in Phenomenology and Existential Philosophy, Northwestern University Press, Evanston, Illinois, 1993.
5. Steinbock, AJ. Home and Beyond: Generative Phenomenology after Husserl, Northwestern University Press, Evanston, Illinois, 1995.
6. Norberg-Schulz, C. Genius Loci: towards a phenomenology of architecture, Academy Editions, London, 1980.
7. Holl, S, Pallasmaa, J and Pérez-Gómez, A. Questions of Perception: Phenomenology of Architecture, A+U, Architecture and Urbanism, Special Issue, Tokyo, Japan, 1994, July.
8. Pallasmaa, J. The Eyes of the Skin: Architecture and the Senses, Polemics, Academy Editions, London, 1996.
9. Heidegger, M. Building Dwelling Thinking. In DF. Krell (ed) Basic Writings: Martin Heidegger, trans. from the German by A. Hofstader, Routledge, London, 1993.
10. Bachelard, G. The Poetics of Space: the classic look at how we experience intimate places, trans. from the French by Jolas, Maria, Beacon Press, Boston, 1994 edition, 1964.
11. Casey, ES. Getting Back into Place, Studies in Continental Thought, Indiana University Press, Bloomington, 1993.
12. Merleau-Ponty, M. Phenomenology of Perception, trans. from the French by Colin Smith, Routledge and Kegan Paul Ltd, 1962.
13. Ingold, T. Culture and the perception of the environment. In E. Croll and D. Parkin (eds) Bush Base: Forest Farm – Culture, Environment and Development, Routledge, London, 1992; pp 39-56.
14. Madison, GB. The Phenomenology of Merleau-Ponty: A Search for the Limits of Consciousness, Ohio University Press Series in Continental Thought, Ohio University Press, Athens, USA, 1981.

15. Gibson, JJ. The Ecological Approach to Visual Perception, Houghton Mifflin, Boston, 1979.
16. Silverman, HJ. Inscriptions: After Phenomenology and Structuralism, Northwestern University Studies in Phenomenology and Existential Philosophy, Northwestern University Press, Evanston, Ill., retitled 1997 edition, 1987.
17. Goldschmidt, G. On visual design thinking: the vis kids of architecture, Design Studies, Butterworth-Heinmann Ltd, 15, 2, 1994; pp 158-174.
18. Lawson, B. Design in Mind, Butterworth-Heinemann Ltd, London, 1994.
19. Suwa, M and Tversky, B. What do architects and students perceive in their design sketches? A protocol analysis, Design Studies, Elsevier Science Ltd, 18, 4, 1997; pp 385-403.
20. Liu, Y-T. Some phenomena of seeing shapes in design, Design Studies, Elsevier Science Ltd, 16, 3, 1995; pp 367-385.
21. Vickers, G. The Art of Judgement, Basic Books, New York, 1965.
22. Geertz, C. Local Knowledge, Fontana Press, London, 1993.
23. Fish, S. Doing What Comes Naturally. Change, Rhetoric, and the Practice of Theory in Literary and Legal Studies, Clarendon Press, Oxford, 1989.
24. Tweed, C. The predominance of the visual in computer-aided architectural design. In A. Asanowicz and A. Jakimowicz (eds) CAAD—Towards New Design Conventions, Technical University of Bialystok, Bialystok, Poland, 1997; pp 269-285.

THEME 4

Psychological and Philosophical Perspectives

A.E. Welchman and J.M. Harris

T. Marsh and P. Wright

R. Kovordányi

T. Schubert, F. Friedmann and H. Regenbrecht

C. Dormann

B.C. Buckley and C.J. Boulter

S.R. Edwards

D.K. Manley

H. Clapin

M.A.R Biggs

Studying 'Holes' to Understand Visual Representation

Andrew E. Welchman & Julie M. Harris
Psychology Department, University of Newcastle,
Newcastle upon Tyne, NE1 7RU, UK

Abstract

To examine the nature of perceptual representation this paper addresses how the presence of holes in the visual field affects human visual perception. The holes in question are due to a lack of visual information which could result from damage to the eye or brain, the underlying biological structure of the visual system, or experimental procedures designed to simulate blind spots. We review evidence for how the brain copes with missing information, and discuss the philosophical debate surrounding the 'filling-in' of this information.

1. Introduction

The naïve conception of the eye "as camera", although much derided, provides two important insights into our understanding of the visual system. Primarily, it outlines the importance placed on pictures in conceptualising the outside world. Secondly, it highlights just how simple vision could be were it a camera, avoiding the problems of: ① a biological retina organised in back-to-front fashion which contains an uneven array of photoreceptors and ② a highly mobile and fast moving eye which is periodically shuttered by eye blinks. Examining why, unlike a camera, there is not a perfect pictorial representation in human vision, allows insight into the purpose and processes of a visual brain that is able to internalise and act upon its environment. In this paper we examine one barrier to a perfect pictorial representation: the presence of holes in the visual world.

2. What are these Holes?

In order to understand how the brain treats an absence of information we must first define what we mean by *missing* information. This is not as trivial as it may seem: to identify such information requires that we first have a complete understanding of the normal perceptual representation. Rather than engage in tautology, we provide a working definition of a hole as: an area corresponding to missing information.

In discussing holes in perception we typically refer to *scotomas*: regions of the visual field that are blanked out due to a gap in the photoreceptor cells of the retina, a gap in the visual cortex resultant from brain injury, or a gap in conscious perception. These holes might subsequently disrupt the brain's ability to represent all of space. It is worth noting the many similarities that exist between having *no information* and having *low information*. For instance, there are fewer cone photoreceptors in the central 2° of vision than in the retinal periphery. This reduces the ability of the visual system to detect high-resolution information in the periphery. However, despite this *low information* situation, we are unaware of any reduced acuity, perceiving uniform surfaces extending into the periphery as similarly textured.

An example of a *no information* situation is a complete retinal scotoma. This will ensure that no visual information from one region of space can be mapped directly onto the brain. The inputs to primary visual cortex are thus strongly affected. However, higher up the processing pathway, where neurones are able to respond to more extensive regions of space, the scotoma will have effectively changed the spatial distribution of the information reaching the cell. In other words, a neurone that responds to a sufficiently large region of space will be able to subsume a hole, given signals from neighbouring locations. This is analogous to the way in which the whole cognitive system is able to represent regions outside the field of view (e.g. behind the head) on the basis of other sources of information (e.g. memory, audition, proprioception etc.).

In this paper we review two methodologies for studying holes in normal visual perception: the first concerns retinal scotomas and the second "Artificial Scotomas"[1] which attempt to simulate the effects of a region of missing information in normal observers.

3. Retinal Scotomas

A convenient way to examine the processes ensuing from missing retinal information is to examine the Blind Spot, present in all human eyes, corresponding to the optic nerve head. This area, completely devoid of photoreceptors and thus insensitive to light, is surprising large (7° high by 5° wide at an eccentricity of 13°). Despite its presence there is no phenomenological experience of missing information. (The blind spot is simply demonstrated by clenching your fists with your thumbs exposed and lining them up at arms length. With one eye closed, fixate one whilst you move the other slowly away. At around 20cm apart you will hit the blind spot and the thumb that was moved should disappear, being replaced by information from the background). This in itself is not that surprising given that vision is largely binocular and the Blind Spots in each eye never concurrently view the same portions of space. However, careful examination of the Blind Spot reveals that, under monocular viewing, the processes involved in providing continuous visual perception can be quite complex. A series of demonstrations by Ramachandran and colleagues [2,3] suggests that complex line patterns, colour boundaries, illusory contours and even rich textures such as typewritten text, can be 'extrapolated' across the Blind Spot. Even more impressive is the visual system's apparent ability to integrate information over considerable portions of space to perform the 'extrapolation' process, and to seemingly do this instantaneously.

One might question the usefulness of observations based on examining a design quirk that the human visual system evolved with. However, the Blind Spot provides a useful retinal scotoma with which to investigate holes in perception and most of the available evidence suggests that there is no special cortical mechanism for it. For example, work by Tripathy et al. [4,5] suggests that cortical organisation around the blind spot is monocular, but essentially normal. Further support for the normality of cortical processing around the Blind Spot comes from Murakami [6] who demonstrated a normal inter-ocular transfer of a motion aftereffect following adaptation to a moving stimulus that covered the Blind Spot.

Komatsu & Murakami [7] assessed perception around the Blind Spot in monkeys through an ingenious behavioural paradigm; they report that monkeys, like humans, appear not to be aware of a hole in perception at the Blind Spot. Murakami et al. [8] followed this work up by comparing these results with those produced following experimentally induced retinal scotomas in monkeys. Their results again suggested that the monkeys are not aware of a small hole in their visual field. By making electrophysiological recordings of primary visual cortex (V1) neurones that represent the scotomal and peri-scotomal regions, they determined that no cortical reorganisation was necessary for monkeys to experience a continuous visual scene. They suggest that primary visual cortex has a mechanism able to compensate for missing information situations.

4. Artificial Scotomas

The importance of phenomena relating to the blind spot for normal perception has been questioned due to: the eccentricity of the blind spot (detailed vision is performed in the central 2°) and the ready availability of binocular input. In an attempt to study less peripheral effects, and to investigate the temporal dynamics of the effects, Ramachandran & Gregory [1] developed a paradigm aiming to induce an "Artificial Scotoma". They used a temporally and spatially varying white noise pattern displayed on a monitor within which there was a small, uniformly grey region at around 6° eccentricity. (This can be approximated by a de-tuned television with a piece of card stuck on the screen). With steady fixation, the grey area (or Artificial Scotoma) disappears, being replaced by the pattern from the surround. The time course of this perceptual "filling-in" is dependent on retinal eccentricity and scotomal size; a sufficiently large movement of the scotomal patch (either by eye movement or experimental displacement) restores the perception of the grey patch. If the noise is turned off after viewing the stimulus for 10-20 seconds, observers frequently report perceiving a dynamic "twinkling" aftereffect at the scotomal location. Ramachandran & Gregory suggest that a neural representation of the dynamic noise is created within the scotoma and that the aftereffect might result from the persistence of this representation. However, other evidence [9] suggests that the mechanisms underlying the filling-in of the scotoma and those responsible for the dynamic aftereffect are discrete.

What might the underlying physiological mechanism be for the observed perceptual filling-in? It would seem that retinal adaptation is unlikely as the dynamic nature of the stimulus ensures that the luminance edges of the scotoma are continually replaced. It therefore seems that the locus of the filling-in effects is cortical. Explanations have been posited in terms of neural fatigue and lateral inhibition and excitation between early visual neurones [10, 11; but see 12]. However, despite the close correspondence between physiological recordings and psychophysical results, it is a brave (or foolish) scientist who claims to have discovered a *bridge locus* between neural activity and perception (see 13 & below).

5. The Philosophy of "Filling-in"

In the above review of the literature, we have been careful to avoid putting excessive weight on the idea that active filling-in of holes in perception takes place. The reason for such caution results from the philosophical debate surrounding what we mean by perception in, and around, gaps in the image, a debate that we believe strikes at the heart of the nature of perceptual representation.

Dennett [14] strongly rejects the idea that active filling-in in the cognitive system takes place because of its implications for a view of consciousness that depends on *Cartesian Materialism*. He argues that to invoke explanations in terms of filling-in suggests that there is some "Cartesian Theatre" in the head: a place where a model of the external world is built and acted upon by some all-important Homunculus. Dennett argues that rather than filling-in the missing information, the cognitive system simply ignores the absence of that information: "The fundamental flaw in the idea of 'filling in' is that it suggests that the brain is providing something when in fact the brain is ignoring something" (14, p. 356). Thus holes in perception need not be filled-in as the visual system is able to ignore the missing information.

But what of the evidence for the modulation in activity of cortical neurones on being presented with scotomal stimuli [10,11, & above]? Such results must be interpreted with extreme care. Pessoa et al. [13] discuss the dangers of this approach in producing *Analytic Isomorphism*, which entails that neural filling-in is *necessary* to ensure that there is equivalence between how things are and how they are perceived to be. Further, the link between neuronal activity and perception is far from clear; hence to identify neuronal responses gives a poor indication of the quality of the perceptual content.

Ramachandran's work [1-3] clearly suggests that perceptual filling-in processes are complex: such complexity, according to current models of the visual system, would necessitate the activity of large portions of extra-striate cortex to compensate for a hole in perception at 13° eccentricity. We question the usefulness of such a filling-in mechanism in a visual system that has evolved to sample a rich environment through a series of eye, head and body movements. Provided that a hole in perception provides no misleading information (and the likelihood of this is reduced in a dynamic system) there is little point in expending precious resources to "touch up the paint job".

Another reason to question the notion of active filling-in is the recent work conducted on Change Blindness [15] which has investigated the ability of observers to detect changes in two temporally sequenced images separated by a very brief intervening interval. This work demonstrates the dramatic *inability* of observers to detect changes in two images presented in rapid succession when observers are not cued to attend the items that are changed, pointing to the very fragile nature of the perceptual representation. Indeed, O'Regan [16] turns the notion of the perceptual process on its head, arguing that, rather than constructing a complex representation of the external world in our heads, "seeing constitutes an active process of probing the external environment as though it were a continuously available *external memory*." (p.484, emphasis original). Within such a framework, propositions of an active filling-in process are difficult to sustain: the brain makes little enough long-term effort with information that *is* there, so to actively spend effort representing things that *are not* there would seem unlikely.

We do not argue that the visual system has *no* long-term or spatially extensive representations; clearly that observers are unable to report changes in pictures does not imply that the visual system does not make use of information unavailable to conscious report. Indeed, Milner & Goodale observe a number of interesting dissociations between the conscious perceptual process and automatic action processes in brain-damaged patients and normal observers alike [17]. However, we believe it unlikely that the visual system represents the world to the extent suggested by phenomenological experience.

Having articulated these doubts about the richness of the perceptual representation, it should be clear that we are sceptical about the utility of a visual mechanism that actively fills-in information missing from holes, whether these are retinal, cortical or artificial. We argue that holes in perception are not *actively filled-in* nor *actively ignored*, rather, holes in perception simply are not noticed because they are not significant. The visual system has evolved to detect changes in the environment, not to generate perfect pictorial representations.

6. Some Unanswered Questions

Having now expressed our views on the subject of filling-in we finally outline some of the many issues that need resolving before our objections to an active filling-in mechanism can be either substantiated or rejected.

One of the most pressing questions in filling-in is the role that attention might play in the generation of the phenomenological percept. How might the specific allocation of attention to a particular region help or hinder the perceptual filling-in process? How might unattended information within a scotoma (retinal or artificial) be used by the visual system, and how might such information affect subsequent performance in an experimental task? Are there stimulus dimensions that prevent filling-in by providing sufficiently strong attentional object markers?

Why should perceptual filling-in take the time it does in the Artificial Scotoma paradigm? If the Artificial Scotoma technique truly taps a process important in everyday vision, why should it take around six seconds to occur?

Finally, if active filling-in does in fact occur around holes in perception, how detailed and explicit is the representation, and how might the information generated for the scotomal patched be used in higher stages of processing?

7. Summary

In this paper we have examined what the presence of holes in perception might tell us about the underlying perceptual representation of the environment. We principally argued against a strong representational view of human vision, and suggested that the visual brain is sufficiently plastic to be able to cope with the noisy visual signals that the retina supplies. We finally set out a number of issues that need to be disambiguated for a fuller understanding of the visual representations underlying vision and which we hope to examine in forthcoming work.

Acknowledgements: Thanks to S. Rushton & J. Sumnall for helpful comments on this paper.

References:

1. Ramachandran VS, Gregory RL. Perceptual Filling in of Artificially Induced Scotomas in Human Vision. Nature 1991; 350: 699-702
2. Ramachandran VS. Filling in gaps in perception: 1. Curr Dir Psychol Sci 1992; 1: 119-205
3. Ramachandran VS. Blind Spots. Sci Amer 1992; 266: 86-91
4. Durgin FH, Tripathy SP, Levi DM. On the Filling in of the Visual Blind Spot - Some Rules of Thumb. Perception 1995; 24: 827-840
5. Tripathy SP, Levi DM. Long-Range Dichoptic Interactions in the Human Visual-Cortex in the Region Corresponding to the Blind Spot. Vis Res 1994; 34: 1127-1138
6. Murakami I. Motion Aftereffect after Monocular Adaptation to Filled-in Motion at the Blind Spot. Vis Res 1995; 35: 1041-1045
7. Komatsu H, Murakami I. Behavioral Evidence of Filling-in at the Blind Spot of the Monkey. Visual Neurosci 1994; 11: 1103-1113
8. Murakami I, Komatsu H, Kinoshita M. Perceptual filling-in at the scotoma following a monocular retinal lesion in the monkey. Visual Neurosci 1997; 14: 89-101
9. Hardage L, Tyler CW. Induced Twinkle Aftereffect as a Probe of Dynamic Visual Processing Mechanisms. Vis Res 1995; 35: 757-766
10. Deweerd P, Gattass R, Desimone R, Ungerleider LG. Responses of Cells in Monkey Visual-Cortex during Perceptual Filling-in of an Artificial Scotoma. Nature 1995; 377: 731-734
11. Pettet MW, Gilbert CD. Dynamic Changes in Receptive-Field Size in Cat Primary Visual-Cortex. Proc Natl Acad Sci USA 1992; 89: 8366-8370
12. Deangelis GC, Anzai A, Ohzawa I, Freeman RD. Receptive-Field Structure in the Visual-Cortex - Does Selective Stimulation Induce Plasticity. Proc Natl Acad Sci USA 1995; 92: 9682-9686
13. Pessoa L, Thompson E, Noe A. Finding Out about Filling In: A Guide to Perceptual Completion for Visual Science and the Philosophy of Perception. Behav Brain Sci 1998; In press
14. Dennett DC. Consciousness Explained. Little Brown, Boston, 1991
15. Rensink RA, O'Regan JK, Clark JJ. To See or Not to See: The Need for Attention to Perceive Changes in Scenes. Psychol Sci 1997; 8: 368-373
16. O'Regan JK. Solving the "real" mysteries of visual perception: The world as an outside memory. Can J Psychol 1992; 46: 461-488
17. Milner AD, Goodale MA. The Visual Brain in Action. Oxford University Press, Oxford, 1995

Articulation of Spatial Information: 3D Shapes

Timothy Marsh
Peter Wright
Human Computer Interaction Group,
Department of Computer Science,
University of York, YO10 5DD, UK.
tmarsh@cs.york.ac.uk
pcw@cs.york.ac.uk

Abstract

Attempting to evaluate 3D virtual interfaces is difficult. It has been argued that this is because we lack a natural and coherent spatial language. If this is true, then the only effective way to convey spatial information would appear to be through specialized mathematically-based geometric modelling techniques, and this may disadvantage general users employed in the evaluation of 3D virtual interfaces. In an attempt to find out if users posses a so-called '3D language', and also, to increase the expressive capabilities of the user, this paper describes the preliminary work and details of an empirical study to find ways to articulate spatial information. Three articulation methods are compared: verbal, pictorial and iconic hand gestures, to determine their effectiveness to articulate spatial information about 3D shapes in a natural and intuitive way. The results from the study may be helpful in empirical evaluations of 3D virtual interfaces.

1 Introduction

The adoption of 3D virtual or graphical human-computer interfaces is becoming more widespread. 3D virtual interfaces are composed of 3D computer generated graphical representations of real, abstract or imaginary objects and environments. Evaluation of virtual interfaces and environments should be carried out with users. Without users it may be difficult to determine the effectiveness of a virtual interface [1]. However, a recent study suggests that traditional HCI usability evaluation techniques may be inappropriate to evaluate virtual environments [2]. Johnson (1998) states that it may be difficult to gain direct feedback through a 'think aloud' verbal protocol. This is because many users find it difficult to explain what contributes to a successful virtual interface. He suggests that one of the main problems is that users have difficulty in trying to articulate a '3D language'. For these reasons, alternative ways to articulate spatial information are investigated. In particular, verbal and non-verbal communication: pictorial and iconic hand gestures are explored. The studies contained in this paper are concerned with the articulation of 3D shapes. A follow on study concerned with the navigation and exploration, and object manipulation in 3D virtual environments is currently being planned.

2 Background

Evaluation is a way to measure or judge the usability of a computer-based system. Usability is the ability to carry out tasks: efficiently, effectively and with satisfaction [3]. That is, the more successfully users can accomplish their tasks or objectives and the more satisfied they feel in carrying out their objectives, the more usable a user interface is judged to be. A myriad of traditional usability evaluation tools, methods, and techniques, exist for the evaluation of 2D Graphical User Interfaces (GUI). The GUI made the desktop metaphor standard for user-computer interaction. Tasks with GUIs are carried out using input interactive devices: keyboard and mouse, interacting with 2D graphical objects, such as, tools, widgets and icons, performed in a windowing environment. The criteria by which we measure or evaluate a GUI is concerned with [4]:

1. the performance and behaviour of the computer-based system
2. human performance and behaviour with the application

Tasks are devised that will allow us to judge, measure or evaluate, these criteria. In contrast, Virtual Reality (VR) systems come in many guises for which there is no dominant paradigm. The central component of all VR systems (with the exception of text-based VR: MUD and MOO) is the 3D computer generated graphical models of real, abstract or imaginary objects and environments. This additional dimension creates a 3 dimensional space in which all tasks are performed. Tasks in VR fall in one of two main groups:

a) navigation and exploration *within* a 3D virtual environment
b) interaction and manipulation of 3D virtual objects *within* a 3D virtual environment

The additional dimension means that tasks with VR systems are not only performed *with* the VR application, but also, *within or inside* the Virtual Environment (VE). This is the main difference between the evaluation of tasks with GUIs and virtual reality systems. Therefore, in addition to the evaluation criteria for conventional GUI applications, as outlined in (2) above, the evaluation of tasks performed with VR applications is also concerned with [4]:

1. the performance and behaviour of the computer-based system
2i. human performance and behaviour *with* the application
2ii. the human performance and behaviour *within* the VE

This is what seems to set 3D virtual interfaces apart from 2D GUIs, and introduces issues such as, awareness, presence and immersion within the VEs.

3 3D Language Supporting VR Evaluation

Evaluation is carried out with or without users, depending on the evaluation method employed. Kalawski (1998) states that usability evaluation of 3D virtual interfaces should be carried out with users. Without users it may be difficult to determine the effectiveness of a virtual interface [1]. Considering the highly interactive capabilities within a 3D VE: navigation and exploration, and object manipulation, a usability evaluation employing the use of users would seem to be a highly effective way to determine the usability of VR systems.

User evaluation can take the form of an interview, questionnaire, or observation. The most effective way to obtain direct feedback from users, is to get users to verbalize their thoughts whilst performing a task. This is known as 'think-aloud' verbal protocol. Proposed by Clayton Lewis (1992), the 'think-aloud' verbal protocol is effectively giving a kind of running commentary [5]. The feedback from users is used to highlight good or bad features of a computer interface for possible system redesign. That is, users' comments are used to indicate usability problems, sometimes suggesting an alternative design or even a solution to a design problem. However, a recent study suggests that traditional formative evaluation, incorporating a 'think-aloud' verbal protocol may be an inappropriate technique for the evaluation of 3D virtual environments [2]. Johnson (1998) states that it maybe difficult to gain direct feedback through a 'think-aloud' verbal protocol. This is because many users find it difficult to explain what contributes to a successful 3D virtual interface. Johnson suggests that one of the main problems is that users have difficulty in trying to articulate a '3D language' [2].

The main advantages of graphical environments are that they represent data as meaningful information, promote exploration and the understanding of complex domains [6]. Another very important reason, is that they support creative non-verbal thought [7]. In our minds, we have the facility to think visually. Mental images are either depictive using pictorial representations [8], descriptive using propositions [9], or perhaps a mix of the two. Although we can think visually, it is however, difficult to articulate mental imagery. Johnson (1998) cites Gibson (1971), "there is no vocabulary of picturing as there is of saying" [10]. The language of mental imagery is non-verbal, it is an object, or a picture, or a visual image [7]. If this is true, then the only effective way to convey spatial information would appear to be through specialized mathematically-based geometric modelling techniques, and this may disadvantage general users employed in the evaluation of 3D virtual interfaces.

Our inability to externalise spatial information may well be further compounded by the dynamic nature of virtual reality. The images in VR are not static, VR is a real-time experience. Users are permitted to explore or navigate through the virtual environment and interact or manipulate virtual objects contained within it. With each interaction and movement in the virtual environment there is a corresponding update in 3D graphics.

If effective empirical usability studies of 3D virtual interfaces are to be performed, then users will be required to articulate a language to describe the 3D environment and tasks performed within virtual environments. However, we may well already possess an effective way to describe 3 dimensional objects and environments that would be helpful in evaluations of virtual environments. Therefore, to find out if users posses an effective '3D language' an empirical study has been carried out. The study is concerned with the articulation of 3D spatial information about 3D objects. Finding ways to support the dynamic nature of 3D objects and navigation and exploration within a 3D virtual environment will be the topic of a follow on paper.

4 Study

A study was conducted to test the ability to communicate spatial information using verbal and non-verbal techniques: pictorial and iconic hand gestures. The following are the research questions that the study attempts to answer:

- do users have an effective way of articulating or describing 3D information about shapes and objects, that is, do we have a 3D language?
- what is the simplest and most effective way to convey spatial information about 3D objects (using: verbal, iconic hand gestures, and drawings)?
- is there a problem using a 'think-aloud' verbal protocol to evaluate VR systems?

4.1 Subjects

Twelve subjects volunteered to participate in the study. These consisted of 9 males and 3 females. Half the subjects had experience of computer graphics programming and/or modelling experience. Subjects were divided into 2 groups. The first group consisting of 9 subjects, described the stimuli (see 4.3) through verbal, iconic hand gestures, and drawings (see 4.2), whilst the second group of 3 subjects attempted to identify the stimuli through these descriptions.

The first group of articulators were seated in a quiet room. The stimuli consisting of nine 3 dimensional computer generated graphical shapes (see figure 1 overleaf) were presented on a display monitor in the same order, to each subject for a short duration (~15 seconds). After each shape was shown, subjects were asked to articulate the 3D shape, using just one of the articulation methods. For example, say the first of the 3D shapes was articulated using verbalizations; the second 3D shape articulated using iconic hand gestures; the third with pencil drawings on paper; the forth again using verbalizations, and so on, until all nine of the 3D shapes had been articulated. The order of articulation method was changed for each subject, to ensure that each of the 3D stimuli were articulated equally using all three methods. Subjects' verbalizations and iconic hand gestures were captured on video.

The second group consisting of 3 subjects acted as adjudicators or independent referees, were shown the video recording of the verbal and iconic articulations, and pencil drawings produced by the first group. They were asked to match these to the original 3D computer generated graphical shapes.

4.2 Articulation Methods

Three articulation methods were compared: verbal, pictorial and iconic hand gestures, to determine their effectiveness to articulate 3D spatial information.

i. Verbal: subjects are simply asked to provide a verbal description of the 3 dimensional computer generated graphical shapes that they are presented with.

ii. Pictorial: this is simply drawing with pencil and paper. Subjects sketch a representation of the 3 dimensional computer generated graphical shape on paper.

iii. Iconic Hand Gestures: iconic hand gestures involve a geometric similarity between a hand gesture and its meaning [11]. They are formed by either, drawing or tracing an outline of a picture of a shape or object in space (virtual depiction), or by forming the hand(s) to represent the shape or object itself (substitutive depiction) [12]. Research from sign language [12] and natural gestures [13] has shown that iconic gestures are used to express shapes and objects.

    Research has investigated the possibility of employing iconic hand gestures as a human computer interaction technique for the input of shapes and objects, and as a drawing and visualization technique in computer generated graphical environments [14][15]. A study to support this, showed that subjects used iconic hand gestures (100%) to articulate 2D and 3D geometric objects during non-verbal communication [14].

4.3 Stimuli: 3D Shapes

The nine 3 dimensional computer generated graphical shapes were produced using OpenGL (see figure 1. overleaf). These were constructed using primitive 3D shapes that are the basic building blocks found in most computer graphics modelling systems. The 3D shapes were created to be as abstract as possible, and not resemble anything in the real world. Each shape could be rotated positively and negatively around the y-axis (vertical).

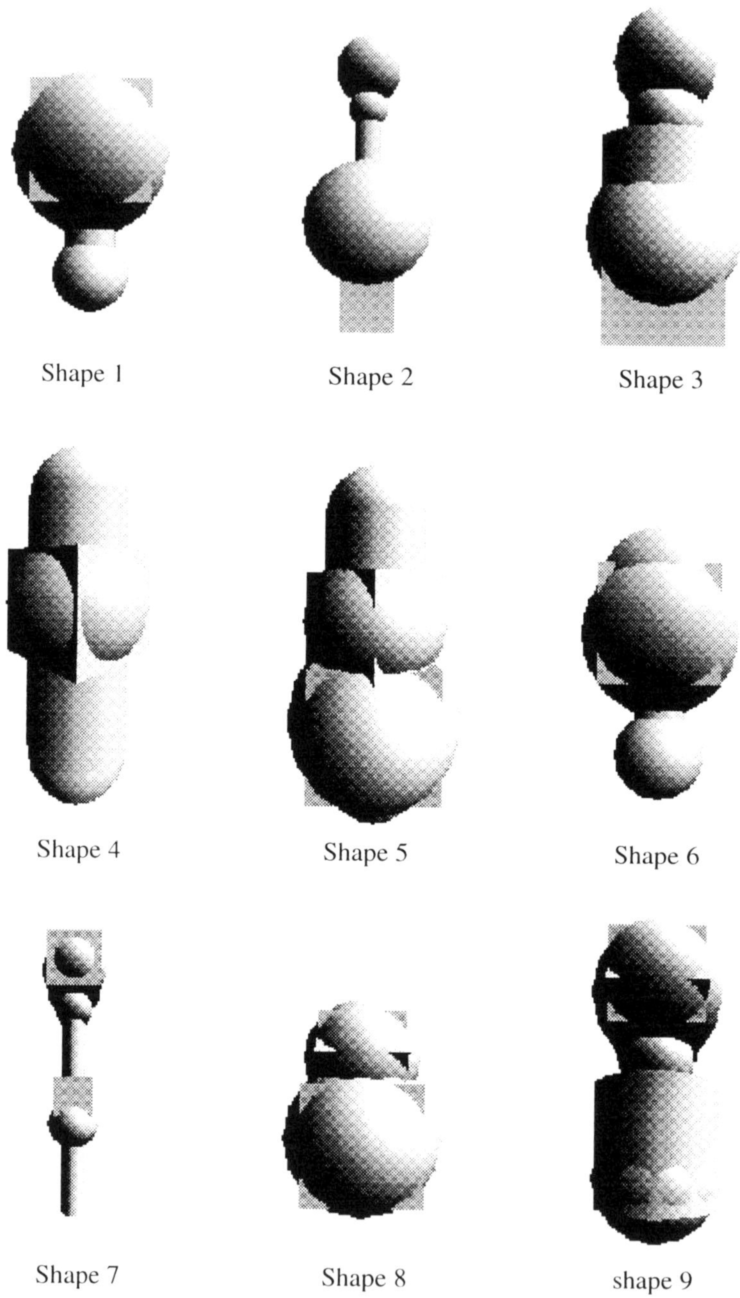

Figure 1. 3D Shapes

5 Results

Overall, a total of 81 verbal, iconic and pictorial articulations were made, and of these, 60 articulations were matched correctly to the original 3D shape. That is, complex abstract 3 dimensional shapes were articulated or described quite effectively 74%. Refer to table 1 below. Along each row is shown the effectively articulated and identified 3D shape for each subject (the articulation methods are indicated by the letters: v = verbal, i = iconic hand gesture, p = pictorial); each vertical column indicates the number of times each 3D shape was effectively articulated and identified by articulation method. Pictorial was articulated most effectively 81% (22 out of 27), next verbal 78% (21 out of 27), and finally, iconic 63% (17 out of 27). The articulation times for pictorial varied between 15 to 110 seconds; all verbalizations were under 60 seconds; and all iconic hand gestures were under 30 seconds.

	3D shape									
subject	**1**	**2**	**3**	**4**	**5**	**6**	**7**	**8**	**9**	**total**
1	v	i		v	i		v	i	p	7
2	i	p		i	p	v	i	p	v	8
3	p	v		p				v		4
4			p	v	i	p	v	i	p	7
5	i	p	v	i	p	v	i	p	v	9
6	p	v	i	p			p	v		6
7	v	i		v	i		v	i	p	7
8		p		i	p	v	i	p	v	7
9	p	v		p			p	v		5
total	7	8	3	9	6	4	8	9	6	60

Table 1. Effectively articulated 3D shapes (v = verbal, i = iconic, p = pictorial)

Pictorial was the most effective of the three articulation methods used in the study. The original 3D shapes were matched to the subjects' drawings, 22 out of 27 times (81%). Subjects' drawings used to convey the 3 dimensional computer generated graphical shapes ranged from 2D or silhouette line drawings to elaborate sketches with perspective and shading. In a post study questionnaire, subjects stated that, of the three articulation methods used in the study, drawing was the simplest and most effective. Some suggested that this is because drawing had a well defined or standard language to describe the 3 dimensional form of the shapes through techniques such as, perspective and shading. Additionally, subjects stated that the pictorial method supported the articulation of 3D shapes by allowing one to fix or record a portion, part or section of the whole shape before moving on to draw the next part, and so on. Thus, freeing the memory and perhaps supporting the natural flow of ones thoughts.

The verbal articulation method effectively described, and was then correctly matched to the original 3D shape, 21 out of 27 times (78%). Wherever possible subjects used analogies or similarities with real world objects to reflect an overall feature/shape that would capture the main or central part of the 3D shape. For example, shape 4 was described by most subjects as sausage or cigar shaped. Refer to figure 1. Failing this, the 3D shapes were invariably described through the deconstruction of the whole shape into its primitive component parts, such as, cube, sphere or cylinder, that go to make up the whole. Verbalizations began either at the top or the bottom of the 3D shape, proceeding down/up, describing the next shape with reference to the size and position of the proceeding shape, and so on. For example, at the top is a sphere, connected to bottom of the sphere is a cube slightly larger in size. Inside the cube is a sphere, its curved edges protruding out of the sides of the cube. Attached to the bottom of the cube is a cylinder with a diameter about a third the size of the cube. The length of the cylinder is about one and a half times larger than that of the cube. In a post study questionnaire some subjects suggested that a hybrid technique incorporating verbal and iconic hand gestures would enable them to provide a more precise description of the 3D shapes.

Subjects used both virtual (drawing or tracing a picture of the shape in space) and substitutive (the hand(s) form the shape of the object itself) iconic hand gestures [12] to articulate the 3D shapes. Iconic hand gestures were not as effective at describing the 3D shapes, as were the pictorial and verbal techniques; 17 out 27 (63%) iconic hand gestures were matched to their original 3D shapes. Although, all hand gestures were articulated in under 30 seconds, and therefore, was the quickest articulation method of the three. In a post study questionnaire, subjects suggested that hand gesturing was simple, although, the main difficulties that they had encountered was trying to articulate a hand gesture that could effectively communicate the 3D shape. That is, iconic hand gestures do not have a commonly accepted or standard language with which one can communicate 3D shapes and objects. As previously mentioned, subjects suggested that a hybrid technique incorporating iconic hand gestures with verbalizations would increase the effectiveness to articulate 3D shapes.

6 Discussion

For the 3D shapes used in this study, pictorial articulation was the most effective method. Although, only one more 3D shape was effectively articulated and identified to the original using pictorial articulation than using verbal articulation. There is some suggestion that some of the 3D shapes were better suited to certain articulation methods. For example, shape 5 was articulated effectively by all subjects drawing or using iconic hand gestures, although, no subjects effectively described shape 5 verbally. Refer to figure 1. Similarly, shape 9 was described effectively by all subjects verbalizing and drawing, although, no subjects effectively described shape 9 using iconic hand gestures. Articulating 3D shapes using iconic hand gestures was the least effective of the three methods. In a post study questionnaire, subjects suggested that whilst hand gesturing was simple, trying to establish or decide upon a representative hand trace or hand shape to communicate the 3D shape was difficult. That is, iconic hand gestures do not have a commonly accepted or standard language which one can communicate 3D shapes. The use of an input device to track the position and orientation of the hand(s) may increase the effectiveness to articulate 3D shapes. For instance, employing say, VR gloves or computer vision techniques to echo or display the movements or traces of the hand(s) in space. This can be represented on a display monitor in the form of a line drawing or a more sophisticated 3D modelling system. For example, see [15][16]. The advantages of this are similar to those of the pictorial technique. That is, drawing supported the articulation of 3D shapes by allowing one to fix or record a portion, part or section of the whole shape before moving on to draw the next part, and so on. Thus, freeing the memory and perhaps supporting the natural flow of ones thoughts. Subjects suggested that a hybrid articulation method of verbal and iconic would be more effective in the articulation of 3D shapes. This may also be true of a hybrid articulation method incorporating pictorial with verbal or iconic, or a mix of the three. The 3D shapes used as stimuli in the study were constructed using primitive 3D shapes: cube, sphere and cylinder, that are the basic building blocks found in most 3D computer graphics modelling systems. The 3D shapes were created to be as abstract as possible, and not resemble anything in the real world. However, because we have names for these primitive component shapes, the verbal articulation method may well have had an unfair advantage over the iconic and pictorial methods. Therefore, it may be interesting to repeat the study using 3D shapes that are constructed from just one totally abstract or deformed shape, that is, having no component parts, and make a comparison with the results of this study.

It has been shown in this empirical study that users have little problems articulating spatial information about 3 dimensional shapes. Although, these results specifically apply to the 3D shapes and the subject used in the study. However, whilst the study was confined to just the articulation of spatial information about 3D shapes, there was no indication in the study to suggest that the articulation of spatial information about 3D object manipulation and navigation and exploration in 3D VEs would cause any major problems. Whether there are any further difficulties in the articulation of 3D spatial information remains to be seen and this will be explored in a further supporting study outlined within the paper. Finally, is there a problem using a 'think-aloud' verbal protocol to evaluate VR systems? In this study it has been shown that there appears to be quite effective ways to articulate 3 dimensional information about 3D shapes. Although, to move a step closer to answering this question additional follow-on supporting studies need to be carried out to test that tasks can be performed and then articulated with a virtual reality system. Therefore, follow-on studies are currently under way that will test whether we have a '3D language' to describe: objects manipulations of virtual objects, and navigation and exploration within 3 dimensional environments. Only then can we be sure that we have a '3D language' that will allow us to contribute effectively to the evaluation of virtual reality systems using a 'think-aloud' verbal protocol.

Acknowledgements

Supported by, UK EPSRC: INQUISITIVE, Grant GR/L53199.

References

[1] R. S. Kalawsky, New Methodologies And Technologies For Evaluating User Performance, In: Advanced 3D Virtual Interfaces, D. F. A. Leevers, I. D. Benests, (eds)., The 3D Interface For The Information Worker (IEE), London, 1998.

[2] Johnson C., Why 'Traditional' HCI Techniques Fail to Support Desktop VR, In: Advanced 3D Virtual Interfaces, D. F. A. Leevers, I. D. Benests, (eds)., The 3D Interface For The Information Worker (IEE), London, 1998.

[3] International Standards Organization, DIS 9241-11, Ergonomic requirements for office work with visual display terminals (VDTS), 1997.

[4] Tromp, G. J, Methodology for Distributed Usability Evaluation in Collaborative Virtual Environments, In: Proceedings of 4th UK VR-SIG, 1997.

[5] Lewis C, Using the "Thinking-Aloud" Method in Cognitive Interface Design, IBM Research Report: RC 9265(#40713), 1982.

[6] Hix D. and Hartson R. H., Developing User Interfaces Ensuring Usability, Wiley, New York, 1993.

[7] Ferguson E. S., The Mind's Eye: Nonverbal Thought in Technology, Science, 1977: 197, 4306, 827-836.

[8] Shepard, R. N. and J Metzler, Mental rotation of three-dimensional objects, Science, 1971: 171, 3972, 701-706.

[9] Pylyshyn, Z. W., The imagery debate: Analogue media versus tacit knowledge, Psychological Review, 1981: 88, 16-45.

[10] Gibson J. J., The information available in pictures, Leonardo, 1971: 4:27-35.

[11] Hockett, C. F., A Course in Modern Linguistics, Macmillan, New York, 1958.

[12] Mandel, M., Iconic devices in American Sign Language, In: Friedman, L. A. (ed.), On the Other Hand. New Perspectives on American Sign Language, Academic Press, New York, 1977, pp 57-107.

[13] Rime, B. and L Schiaratura, Gesture and Speech, In: Feldman R. S and B. Rime (eds), Fundamentals of nonverbal behavior, Cambridge University Press, New York, 1991, pp 238-281.

[14] Marsh, T. and A Watt, Shape Your Imagination: Iconic Gestural-Based Interaction, In: Proceedings of IEEE Virtual Reality Annual International Symposium (VRAIS98), 1998, pp 122-125.

[15] Marsh T, An Iconic Gesture Is Worth More Than A Thousand Words, In: Proceedings of Information Visualisation '98, IEEE, 1998, pp 222-223.

Mental Image Reinterpretation in the Intersection of Conceptual and Visual Constraints

Rita Kovordányi
Department of Computer and Information Science, Linköping University, Linköping, Sweden

Abstract

Psychological experiments indicate that mental images are more difficult to reinterpret than physical drawings. This difficulty is often attributed to various limitations of the mental image and/or mental image fading. However, experiments indicate that additional, non-visual factors might be involved. In view of this, we propose a model of mental image reinterpretation which focuses on the interaction between conceptual and visual information in the cognitive system. Simulations of this model support our hypothesis that reinterpretations are inhibited when the presently held interpretation is kept within focus of attention. Also, it appears that the mental image itself can inhibit the reinterpretation process in cases when potential new interpretations do not match well with the mental image.

1 Introduction

Mental imagery in general, and mental image reinterpretation in particular, has attracted much attention in the field of cognitive science, as it involves a highly debated phenomenon, namely that of seeing a visual image in the mind's eye. Alternative accounts for this mental experience range from the descriptive view that mental images are non-visual and non-functional [1,2], and the claim that mental images are by definition overspecified and therefore unambiguous [3], to the depictive view stating that mental images constitute *rich* repositories of visual information which can support alternative interpretations [4,5,6]. These views take opposite sides in what is called the imagery debate, and offer different accounts for how mental images are represented in the cognitive system, and whether they constitute a pregnant sounding board for non-visual processes or are non-functional by-products of these. Psychological experiments are far from conclusive: Mental images are pregnant enough to provide a basis for reinterpretation. Yet, alternative interpretations are discovered less frequently in a mental image than in the same drawing [7]. The issue is further complicated by the findings of Finke and colleagues, who report of cases when mental image reinterpretation is *not* difficult [8].

The long term objective of the present project is to suggest ways in which mental image reinterpretation could be facilitated, and thereby contribute to the design of computer systems which support the creative use of visual images. To this end, we need to map out the constraining mechanisms of mental image reinterpretation.

Much of the debate around mental imagery is focused on the alleged shortcomings of the mental image as such. We believe instead that successful reinterpretations arise through an interaction between previously stored conceptual knowledge *and* temporarily evoked visual information. To uncover the implications of this idea, we have developed a cognitive model of mental image reinterpretation. By varying central aspects of this model in a computer simulation, we hope to distinguish between model properties which propel cognitive processing towards the discovery of new interpretations, and those which obstruct the reinterpretation process.

2 A Model of Mental Image Reinterpretation

Among the psychological experiments conducted in this area, perhaps the most astonishing findings are those of Finke and colleagues, who report that the ease with which a mental image is reinterpreted depends on what type of interpretation is produced [8]. They found that in mental imagery, 'geometric' patterns were easier to discover than 'symbolic' concepts (Fig. 1). What is more, geometric patterns were detected as frequently in a mental image as in the same drawing. Symbolic interpretations occurred less frequently in mental imagery than during perception.

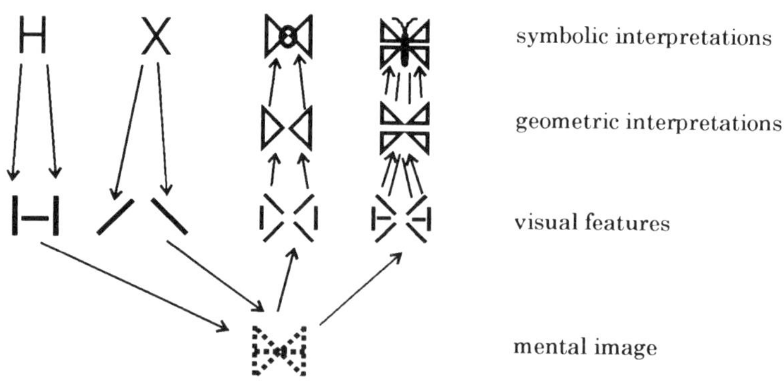

Figure 1. Alternative interpretations of a mental image generated from an upper case 'X' *mentally* superimposed on an upper case 'H'. The two interpretations in the upper right corner of the figure denote "bow tie" and "butterfly", and exemplify symbolic interpretations (using the terminology of Finke and colleagues, [8]). Alternative geometric interpretations would be, for example, "two large triangles" or "four small triangles pointing towards each other".

In general, reinterpreting a mental image, such as that in Fig. 1, involves the projection of long term memory structures into a visual medium, followed by a subsequent inspection of the image, and a re-association of the information contained in the image with new long term memory structures [5]. Based on a broad range of empirical evidence, we propose a model of mental image reinterpretation which centres on the interactive aspect of visual processing [9]. With a late selection view on selective attention as its central component, our model makes the following assumptions:

- Reinterpretations of a mental image arise in the abstract space defined by both conceptual and visual information.
- Focusing selective attention on the current interpretation has the effect of "cementing" the presently held interpretation. Symbolic interpretations are mutually more competitive than geometric interpretations, and are more exposed to suppression by currently focused competing interpretation.

According to the late selection view we propose [9], new interpretations will thus be suppressed by the current interpretation as long as a mental image is in use. This would be the case, for example, if the image is verbally described or mentally manipulated. Since a mental image is maintained via its present interpretation, reinterpretations will be suppressed as long as the mental image is maintained. It is therefore not clear whether mental image maintenance will improve reinterpretation probabilities or instead have a negative effect. A related issue is that of mental image fading: We expect this mechanism to have a negative effect on reinterpretation probabilities.

By simulating our model, we would thus like to answer the following questions:

1. How is reinterpretation probability affected when a currently held interpretation is attended to, in other words when the currently held interpretation is within the focus of selective attention?
2. How is reinterpretation probability affected by mental image fading?

Our model centres around the view that successful reinterpretations hinge on a balancing act between not getting stuck on the present interpretation, on the one hand, and not letting the mental image fade, on the other hand. This insight can be expressed within a model framework which captures the interplay between conceptual and visual information flow in the visual system. Our model is inspired by the comprehensive neurocognitive architecture for mental imagery which has been proposed by Kosslyn [5,10], and embodies the following set of basic assumptions:

- Processing in the visual system proceeds along reciprocally connected stages. The basic computational step which underlies visual processing involves the updating of neuron activation levels in accordance with the momentary activation level of connecting neurons. Unless actively sustained, neural activation throughout the visual system will decay.
- Image inspection and interpretation—be the image mentally or perceptually created—corresponds to a step-by-step propagation of activation levels from lower towards higher levels of processing. Mental image generation and maintenance, on the other hand, corresponds to long term memory structures being activated at a high level and this activation propelled towards lower levels of processing.

- Finally, we assume that geometric interpretations are based on a successful match with geometric patterns stored in visual long term memory, what we call the 'pattern recognition subsystem' (Fig. 2). In contrast, symbolic interpretations require that a mapping can be established between visual features in the mental image, on the one hand, and abstract conceptual structures stored in the associative long term memory, on the other hand.

3 The Simulations

In order to map out the causal relationships of individual model components to reinterpretation probabilities, we chose to work with variations of the original model. In these alternative models, central aspects of the proposed model were set to take on their "opposite" value. The simulations were run in a full two-level factorial design, which allowed every design decision to be cross-combined [11]. Although this simulation design is computationally expensive, it made it possible to trace the effect of individual model components in the resulting reinterpretation probabilities.

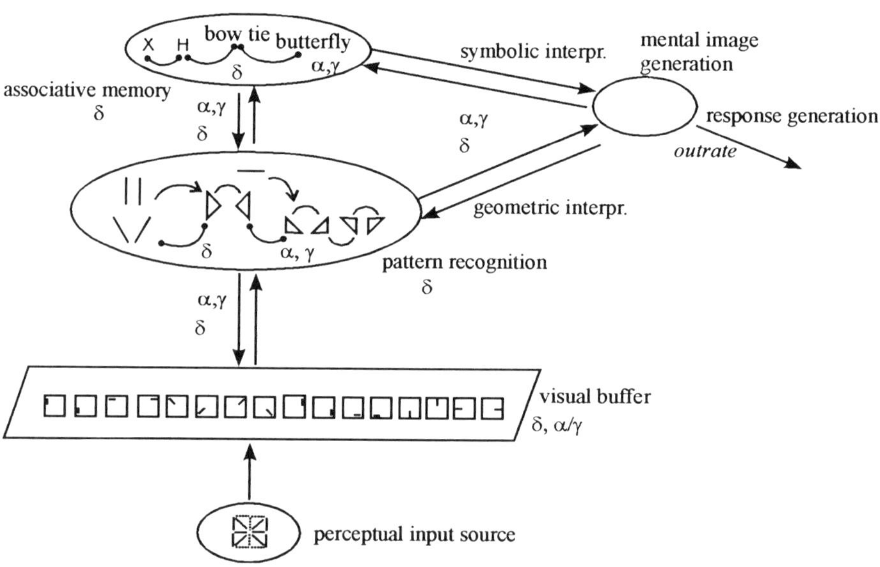

Figure 2. Subsystems and communication structure of the simulated system. The dynamic behavior of each subsystem is controlled via an activation decay parameter, and lateral connection properties. Connections of the same type, going in the same direction between the same subsystems are modulated by excitatory and inhibitory weights, α, γ, and a decay parameter, δ. Depending on whether a symbolic or depictive view on mental imagery is adopted, lateral connections within the two memory subsystems, associative memory and pattern recognition, are used to model either mutual competition or logical implication between interpretations.

To provide an unbiased basis for comparison between alternative models, a priori hypotheses about the underlying system structure were kept to a minimum. Alternative models were embedded in this system framework, and evaluated with respect to the reinterpretation probabilities reported by Finke and colleagues [8].

3.1 System Structure

The system framework is an interactive activation model [12,13,14], which is in essence a local connectionist network, written in Matlab (ver. 5.2). The system comprises of five subsystems organized into reciprocally connected stages of processing (Fig. 2). Two of the five subsystems, 'perceptual input source' and 'mental image generation' are used to initiate the system when the simulation is run in perceptual and mental mode, respectively. Each subsystem contains a number of internal nodes representing visual features, geometric patterns and symbolic concepts which can be evoked during processing. In the two higher level subsystems, pattern recognition and associative long term memory, the internal nodes are organized into a one-layer, lateral network of inhibitory or excitatory connections which reflects mutual competition or inferential implication between long term memory units.

Simulation proceeds in discrete steps, whereby the system's activation levels are updated from their previous state (for a detailed description of the underlying calculations refer to [14]). Activation levels of memory units were measured at predetermined points in time. Reinterpretation probabilities were calculated from the relative activation level of competing interpretations.

4 Results and Conclusions

Finke and colleagues [8] have shown that variables not directly related to the mental image, as such, must be involved in the general mental reinterpretation difficulties which has been previously observed by others. In particular, the fact that symbolic interpretations are more difficult to discover than geometric interpretations seems to suggest the presence of non-visual inhibitory factors.

We have theorized that one additional reason for why symbolic interpretations are more difficult to discover could be that they are more exposed to suppression when late attentional selection fixates the presently held interpretation. This notion seems to supported by our simulation results. In particular, simulated reinterpretation probability for symbolic interpretations decreased when these interpretations were modelled to be mutually more competitive than geometric interpretations. On the other hand, suppressing the presently focused interpretation has a positive effect on reinterpretation probabilities, and this effect is more pronounced for symbolic interpretations.

In addition to these findings, our simulations show that reinterpretation can, in some cases, be inhibited by the presence of a mental image. Depending on how well a particular image matches the set of alternative interpretations, it will evoke some of these interpretations, and inhibit others. Similarly, the role of mental image fading seems not as clear-cut as we have hypothesized: It appears that mental image fading can have a positive effect on reinterpretation probabilities when the image does not match well with potential new interpretations. In conclusion, mental image reinterpretation seems to rely on *both* a good match with the mental image *and* the relinquishment of old conceptual structures.

Acknowledgments

This project was conceived during a visit at S. Kosslyn's laboratory at Harvard University. We would like to thank S. Kosslyn for his inspiration and engagement in the project. We would also like to thank S. Hägglund, Y. Wærn, and J. Barklund for their insightful comments, and for fruitful discussions, as well as D. Carr for proofreading, and an anonymous reviewer for valuable hints.

References

1. Pylyshyn, Z W. What the mind's eye tells the mind's brain: A critique of mental imagery. Psychological Bulletin, 1973; 80:1-24
2. Pylyshyn, Z W. The imagery debate: Analogue media versus tacit knowledge. Psychological Review, 1981; 87:16-45
3. Reisberg, D, Chambers, D. Neither pictures nor propositions: What can we learn from a mental image? Canadian Journal of Psychology, 1991; 45:336-352
4. Kosslyn, S M, Ball, T M, Reiser, B J. Visual images preserve metric spatial information: Evidence from studies of image scanning. Journal of Experimental Psychology: Human Perception and Performance, 1978; 4(1):47-60
5. Kosslyn, S M. Image and Brain: The resolution of the imagery debate. MIT Press, Cambridge, MA, 1994
6. Farah, M J. Is visual imagery really visual? Overlooked evidence from neuropsychology. Psychological Review 1988; 95:307-317
7. Peterson, M A, Kihlstrom, J F, Rose, P M, Glisky M L. Mental images can be ambiguous: Reconstruals and reference-frame reversals. Memory and Cognition, 1992; 20:107-123
8. Finke, R A, Pinker, S, Farah, M J. Reinterpreting visual patterns in mental imagery. Cognitive Science 1989; 13:51-78
9. Kovordanyi, R. An interactive activation model of mental image reinterpretation, manuscript, in prep., Linköping University.
10. Kosslyn, S M. Image and mind. MIT Press, Cambridge, MA, 1980
11. Law, A M, Kelton, W D. Simulation modeling and analysis. McGraw-Hill, New York, 1991
12. McClelland, J L, Rumelhart, D E. An interactive activation model of context effects in letter perception: Part 1. An account of basic findings. Psychological Review, 1981; 88(5):375-407
13. Rumelhart D E, McClelland, J L. An interactive activation model of context effects in letter perception: Part 2. The contextual enhancement effect and some tests and extensions of the model. Psychological Review, 1982; 89(1):60-94
14. McClelland, J L, Rumelhart, D E. Explorations in parallel distributed processing: A handbook of models, programs and exercises. MIT Press, Cambridge, MA, 1994

Embodied Presence in Virtual Environments

Thomas Schubert
Frank Friedmann
Friedrich-Schiller-University
Jena, Germany

Holger Regenbrecht
Bauhaus University
Weimar, Germany

Abstract

Presence, the sense of being in a virtual environment (VE), is analysed in an embodied cognition framework. We propose that VEs are mentally represented as meshed sets of patterns of actions and that presence is experienced when these actions include the perceived possibility to navigate and move the own body in the VE. A factor analyses of survey data shows 3 different presence components: spatial presence, involvement, and judgement of realness. A path analysis shows that spatial presence is mostly determined by sources of meshed patterns of actions: interaction with the VE, understanding of dynamics, and perception of dramatic meaning.

1 The role of psychology in virtual environments

When we use virtual environments (VEs), we often experience *presence*, the subjective *sense of being in the virtual place*. Presence is observable when people interact in and with a virtual world as if they were there, when they grasp for virtual objects or develop fear of virtual cliffs [1]. The presence phenomenon is at the centre of psychological research in VEs. Applications of VEs for psychological research and applications of psychological findings for hardware and software design need an understanding of what presence is, how it develops, and how we can measure it. It has been said that psychology "determines what is and what is not virtually 'real'" [2, p. 244] If this is so, what can psychological theories tell us about when and how we experience presence and construct virtual environments as our reality?

In fact, already in the 60's the radical constructivist Heinz von Foerster used an early stereoscopic virtual reality system to display four-dimensional virtual objects

---

We thank Gabi and Hartmut for their hospitality during our stay at Pfuhlsborn, where we developed the ideas for this paper.

[3]. He showed in his experiment that only those participants who were allowed to interact with the objects via two joysticks were able to understand the forth dimension, as opposed to those who merely watched the interaction. Thus, acting in an environment led to a perceived reality of this environment .

In this vein, we want to present an approach which frames presence as *embodied cognition* – as the outcome of the active interpretation of a virtual environment. We argue that presence emerges when possibilities of bodily action in the virtual world are mentally represented. The interpretation of the environment through action and how it leads to the attribution of reality and *Wirklichkeit* is the topic of this paper.

2 Psychological concepts of presence

Virtual environments are computer-based three-dimensional spaces presented via various media, such as pictures on head-mounted displays or monitors. They can also be presented via text only, as it is the case in text-based virtual environments. The stimulus field depicting a three-dimensional space and its coupling with the user of a VE lead to what we call *immersion.* Immersion can be described objectively and should be distinguished from presence. Presence, in contrast, is a psychological phenomenon. It has been defined as the "the participant's sense of 'being there' in the virtual environment." [4, p. 131]. Biocca [5, sect. 5.1.1.] has noted that "users experiencing presence report having a compelling sense of being in a mediated space other than where their physical body is located...". Presence is such a central element of virtual reality that it is seen as a part of its definition [6].

Immersion and the content which is presented by it on the one side and presence on the other side describe a dichotomy between presentation of stimuli and psychological experience. It is tempting to see these two in an uni-directional causal relationship, where stimuli govern the psychological experience. We think however that the bodily and cognitive activity of the user - his interaction with the virtual world on various levels - is the true source of presence [6]. It is the interplay of bodily and cognitive processes that needs to be described.

Interestingly, the user's body – although seemingly disappearing in most VE applications – has been at the centre of theoretical concerns since the beginning of presence research, mostly as a result of the application of J. J. Gibson's [7] ideas to the conceptualisation of presence. The emphasis of bodily action and motor processes for perception is an important point of this work and is compatible with new proposals in cognitive science such as that from Varela, Thompson & Rosch [8]: "Sensory and motor processes, perception and action, are fundamentally inseparable in lived cognition.... Perception consists in perceptually guided action." (p. 173). Modern cognitive theories like the mental model theory look promising [1] for an extension of these ideas. Such an approach has been suggested by Biocca [5], who assumes that "users are ... constructing a mental model of the virtual space and responding to and attending to cues in the virtual mediated environment." (sect. 6.1.2). The combination of both ideas, the emphasis on the body and the concept of mental models, is possible in the *embodied cognition framework* [9-11]. The main focus of this approach is memory and its function. To approach this goal, a theory of situational conceptualisation and meaning grounded in embodied cognition has been developed. We will focus on this aspect of the proposal, ignoring the aspect of memory for the moment.

3 Glenberg's framewor k for embodied cognition

Glenberg [11] argues that only a part of the interaction with the environment can be managed without a representational system. Tasks like differentiation, however, require more than is available from an optical flow field. With virtual environments gaining in complexity and richness of possible actions, those tasks will become more and more important. Glenberg proposes that in the service of those needs, a conceptualisation of the situation is created by representing *meshed patterns of actions* possible in this situation.

> Patterns of action derived from the projectable properties of the environment are combined (or meshed...) with patterns of interaction based on memory. The two patterns can combine because they are both embodied, that is, both are constrained by how one's body can move itself and manipulate objects. The resulting pattern of possible actions is a conceptualization: the possible actions for that person in that situation.
>
> Thus meaning of an object or a situation is a pattern of possible action. (p. 4)

The cognitive representation of an environment consists of possible patterns of actions. It thus captures the relation between our body and the objects in our environment, forming the meaning of the situation. At least two steps of interpretation are inherent in the understanding. First, projectable properties are actively created by the individual agent. Second, non-projectable properties retrieved from the memory are meshed with the representation in the search for an understanding of the situation.

Since the conceptualisation is driven by the need to survive in a dangerous environment, the projectable stimuli from the environment have priority for the understanding. This priority is provided by the process of clamping. "Clamping projectable properties ensures that experiences are individuated or situated" [11, p. 6f]. To explain the ability of conscious remembering and understanding of language, Glenberg introduces the concept of suppression, which is central for our own application of the framework on presence: "In the service of prediction, we have developed the ability to, if not ignore, at least to suppress the overriding contribution of the current environment to conceptualization." [11, p. 7] This suppression is easy when the to be represented transformations follow embodied constraints. When however brute force manipulation of perceptual symbols is necessary, the construction of an embodied understanding will be much harder.

As the last point in this overview of some of Glenberg's ideas we want to mention the special *feel of memory* described by him. He explains that this feel of memory is rooted in the fact that we remember our own actions which we have performed with our own bodies.

4 The understanding of virtual worlds: suppression and construction

Understanding of a virtual environment is, just like the understanding of language, the processing of mediated information. The understanding will also result in a meshed set of patterns of actions possible in this situation. "We understand language (that is, it takes on meaning) in the same way we understand a physical situation – in terms of possibilities for action." [11, p. 41] Just like the understanding of language, the understanding of a virtual environment will need the suppression of conflicting projectable features from the real environment – namely the stimuli from the head-mounted display (HMD) or screen, cables, sound from the environment, the constraints of the field of view and so on. Thus, the understanding of a VE is the process of an active suppression of stimuli from the real world and the construction of meshed sets of patterns of action on the basis of mediated stimuli – the visual representation of the VE and, if available, stimuli perceived with other senses.

The resulting meaning of the virtual world consists of the possible actions in it. We assume that the central interaction with an environment is the navigation of the body or at least body parts in it. Further kinds of interaction are the manipulation of objects and the influence on agents (objects in the virtual world which have their own intentions and which perform actions themselves). We can now propose an interpretation of presence as *embodied presence*: Presence develops from the representation of navigation (movement) of the own body (or body parts) as a possible action in the virtual world.

Presence is the outcome of media perception. In the process of developing presence, a mental model of the virtual three-dimensional space is constructed, consisting of the possible actions in this space. The possible actions of the body are central in this model. Stimuli from the real environment must be suppressed for presence to emerge. The more the mediated stimuli follow embodied constraints (e.g., coupling with body movement), the easier is the construction. Because the virtual environment is perceived in terms of embodied action, a feeling equivalent to the feel of memory mentioned above develops: This is what we call the sense of presence.

5 Evidence for embodied presence in self reports

One way to test this model would be to experimentally manipulate the involved processes suppression and construction, probably using a sophisticated VR system. Indeed, most of the presence research took place in VR installations with HMD environments. While this research has told us a lot about the technical factors which contribute to presence, we want to argue for a supplementary research approach. This approach emphasizes two points: First, we concentrate on how users *experience their interactions* with a VE. Second, in order to do this, we investigate a wide range of rich and complex VEs and a wide spectrum of subjective experiences with survey methods. The research questions are then: Which different experiences will be reported by the users, and which presence and immersion components can be found?

On the basis of the presented theoretical model, the following predictions can be made. Presence should involve at least two components: One component related to the suppression of the actual environment and the focusing on the VE, and a second component related to the mental construction of a space out of the VE in which the body can be moved. These two factors were described above as central in the understanding of the VE as being the own environment. Furthermore, the interaction experiences should include those that relate to interactions between body and VE which are the basis for and the topic of meshed patterns of actions.

Data which confirm these predictions and describe additional experiences were presented by Schubert, Regenbrecht and Friedmann [12]. In this study, we surveyed 246 users of different VEs, including VEs using HMDs and CAVEs, text-based MOOs and MUDs, but mainly users of screen-based 3D games. Today's video and PC 3D games present highly developed, complex VEs, incorporating sophisticated visual, aural, spatial and dramatic content. The participants answered a 75 item questionnaire. The questionnaire consisted of items drawn from various presence and immersion scales, including almost all published presence items from the last years. Additionally, we developed items which specifically asked about body-VE relations and construction of the VE as being the own environment.*

The data were analysed in factor analyses. Details are presented elsewhere [12], but we want to describe here the factors and then present additional path analysis on these data which relate to the framework presented above.

5.1 Immersion and Presence Factors

The data were first factor analysed using oblique rotation. Eight factors emerged in the factor analysis. Three of them describe components of presence: (1) the relation between the VE as a space and the own body (*spatial presence*), (2) the awareness devoted to the VE (*involvement*) and (3) the sense of reality attributed to the VE (*realness*). These factors were categorised as presence factors because they included only subjective reports of how the users experienced the environment, rather than descriptions of interactions between user and VE or descriptions of the technical side of the VE.

Factor (1) describes exactly what is commonly included in the presence definition. Interestingly, the formulation "*sense of being in a place*" is actually the item with the highest loading on this factor. This factor confirms that the construction of the VE as being the own environment involves the construction of meshed patterns of navigational actions. Factor (2) isolates the attention side of presence, the

---

* See [12] for a description of the survey.

concentration and focus on the VE and the suppression and forgetting of the real environment, relating to the suppression process described above. Factor (3) was not predicted by us. It combines items which involve the comparison between VE and real world concerning their "realness". We think that this is some kind of judgement elicited by our questions and that it relates closely to presence, but is probably not a part of the actual presence experience itself.
Five additional factors contain items which assess the stimuli presentation and properties of the interaction between user and VE: (4) the sensory quality, describing richness and consistency of the multimodal presentation (*quality of immersion*), (5) perception of dramatic content and structures (*drama*), (6) awareness of interfaces that distract from the VE experience (*interface awareness*), (7) the possiblity to explore and actively search the VE (*exploration*), and (8) the ability to predict and anticipate what will happen next (*predictability*).

Table 1. Factors of experiences in VEs

Presence		**Immersion**			
		Stimuli presentation		**Interaction**	
Spatial Presence	SP	Quality of Immersion	QI	Exploration of VE	EXPL
Involvement	INV	Drama	DRA	Predictability	PRED
Realness	REAL	Interface Awareness	IA		

These findings are highly consistent with presence factors described and predicted by Held and Durlach [13], Sheridan [14] and Witmer and Singer [15]. However, we can extend their analyses in the following way: First, the factor analysis shows that the presence components and the immersion factors are indeed separate constructs. Secondly, presence itself is not a unitary construct, but consists of at least 3 components. Thirdly, using additional exploratory path analysis we can investigate how well the various immersion factors can predict the presence components. This will be the topic of the remainder of this paper.

5.2 Modelling causal relations between Immersion and Presence

Path analyses are commonly used for confirmatory tests of models of causal relations between variables. However, they can also be used for exploratory analyses. In the analyses described here, we investigate if the presence factors can be significantly predicted by the immersion factors in a path model. It is important to note however that the *direction* of the causal flow implied by our model is an *a priori* assumption. That is, the direction of the relations can not be tested with data like ours but must be tested in a controlled experiment.
We started with a model which incorporated the following assumptions: First, the immersion factors determine *spatial presence*, *involvement* and *judgement of*

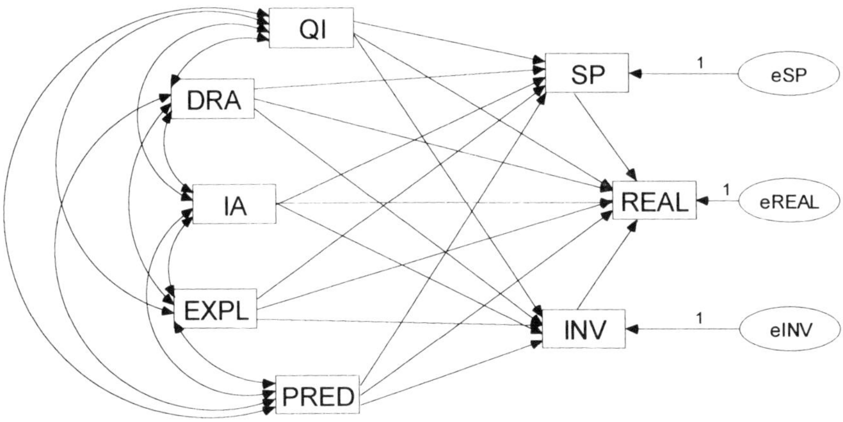

Figure 1. Initial path model.

reality. Second, *spatial presence* and *involvement* also have effects on *judgement of reality*. This model is depicted in Figure 1. The variables used in this model were computed as the mean scores of those items clearly loading on each factor (loadings higher .40). We used the same data set as in the factor analyses (see comment below). This model was tested with the statistical package AMOS.

The model has one degree of freedom; therefore fit and modification indices can be computed. The model does not fit the data ($\chi^2(1, n=246)=39.348$, $p<.001$). Modification indices point to a strong relation between *spatial presence* and *involvement*. To include this relation in the model, it would be possible to either assume a causal flow from SP to INV or one in the other direction. Since we don't know which direction this causation takes, we included a covariance between the error terms of the two variables.

Including this covariance, the model is saturated. In order to get fit statistics, it is necessary to eliminate paths. We deleted all regression paths which were not significant. The resulting model is presented in Figure 2. It shows that the paths from *interface awareness* to *involvement* and from *predictability*, *drama*, *interface awareness* and *quality of immersion* to *realness* did not prove to be significant. They were therefore deleted. Additionally, the covariance between (the error terms of) *spatial presence* and *involvement* is included. This model fits the data very well with a $\chi^2(5, n=246)=2.040$, $p>.80$, RMSEA < 0.001. Note that the figure shows standardised regression weights which can be interpreted like correlations.

Except *exploration*, no variable retains a direct effect on *realness*. Except *interface awareness*, every variable has a significant relation to the two primary presence components *spatial presence* and *involvement*. Out of these regression paths, some show higher and more significant weights, notable the impacts of *drama*, *exploration* and *predictability* on *spatial presence* and the impacts of *quality of immersion* and *predictability* on *involvement*. *Spatial presence* and *involvement* show a highly significant covariation (cov = 0.403, r= 0.385).

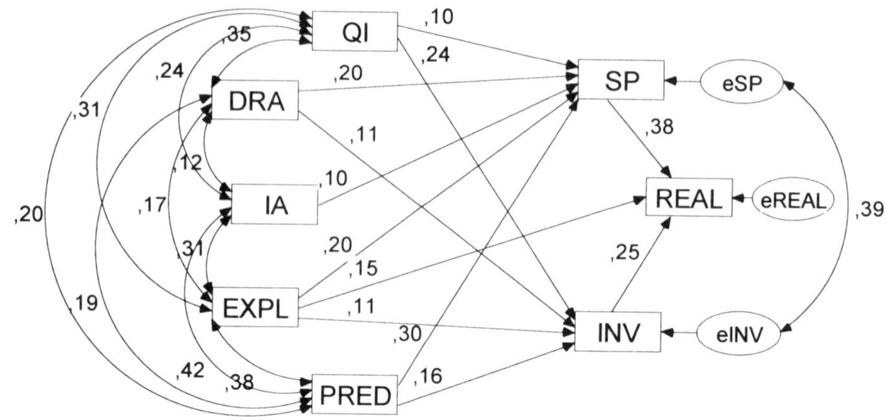

Figure 2. Modified Model.

Table 2 . Regression Weights

Path			Estimate	Standard. Estimate	S.E.
SP	←	QI	0.114†	0.102	0.063
SP	←	DRA	0.215**	0.204	0.058
SP	←	IA	0.136†	0.096	0.076
SP	←	EXPL	0.263**	0.204	0.074
SP	←	PRED	0.441**	0.300	0.086
INV	←	QI	0.236**	0.236	0.064
INV	←	PRED	0.208*	0.157	0.084
INV	←	EXPL	0.128†	0.111	0.075
INV	←	DRA	0.103†	0.109	0.059
REAL	←	EXPL	0.157**	0.151	0.057
REAL	←	INV	0.227**	0.252	0.052
REAL	←	SP	0.305**	0.378	0.050

Note. † indicates $p<.10$; * $p<.05$; ** $p<.01$

5.3 Discussion

What can be concluded from this path analysis? We want to discuss some of the results. First of all, the interaction factors *exploration* of the VE and *predictability* of the VE dynamics have the highest impact on spatial presence. This fits the presented framework very well. Interaction, the mental representation of these interactions and their results determine how much the VE is experienced as being the own environment. Second, the perception of dramatic content has a high impact on spatial presence. It seems that the perception of meaningful spaces contributes to the presence experience [16]. In terms of the framework above, this could be described as the meshing of the space perception with other connotations and action constraints or possibilities based on drama. Since the actions depend on the dramatic meaning, presence is enhanced.

Involvement seems to depend highly on quality of immersion and predictability. Surprisingly, interface awareness does not show a significant impact here. It might be that the characteristics of our sample explain this fact: The majority of our participants played screen-based VR games. It is likely that they mastered the interface very well. We assume that when higher levels of interface awareness are reached, it should also have an impact on involvement.

In the initial model, we included direct and indirect effects of the immersion variables on realness. Only one direct impact remained after the modification: the one of exploration. It seems that the actual bodily activity has a quality that is independent from spatial presence and involvement when it comes to a feeling of realness. In earlier work, we have speculated that the feeling of reality is projected from the real body onto virtual objects when direct interaction is experienced [1]. The dynamics of both involvement and feeling of realness need to be better understood in future research.

Some caveats concerning the path analysis have to be made, though. First of all, we used the same data set for both exploratory factor and path analyses. The resulting modified model should be tested with a second, independent data set. Secondly, the relation between involvement and spatial presence needs to be clarified. In the model, we included a covariance between the two as a compromise. Future research should explore whether the two can be manipulated independently in experiments.

The presented work offers the new possibility to distinguish theoretically and empirically between three facets of presence: spatial presence, involvement and realness. It is not enough to think of presence as if it were a uniform construct. We have to distinguish different phenomenological facets. The cited factor analyses opened the way to measure them independently with questionnaires. The presented path analyses show how these three facets are determined by different immersion and interaction components. The primary lesson learned from this research is: When possibilities to act in a spatial environment are perceived or when dramatic events structure the interaction, presence emerges. Both spatial and dramatic conceptualisation can be framed as *meaning*. Spatial and dramatic meaning determine how present we feel in a virtual environment.

References

1. Regenbrecht H, Schubert T, Friedmann F. Measuring the Sense of Presence and its Relations to Fear of Heights in Virtual Environments. International Journal of Human-Computer Interaction 1998; 10:233-249

2. Woolley B. Virtual Worlds: A Journey in Hype and Hyperreality. Blackwell, Oxford, 1992

3. Foerster Hv: Entdecken oder Erfinden - Wie läßt sich Verstehen verstehen?. In: Glasersfeld Ev (ed) Einführung in den Konstruktivismus. Piper, München, 1992, pp 41-88

4. Slater M, Usoh M, Steed A. Depth of Presence in Virtual Environments. Presence: Teleoperators and Virtual Environments 1994; 3:130-144

5. Biocca F. The Cyborg's Dilemma: Progressive Embodiment in Virtual Environments. Journal of Computer-Mediated Communication 1997; 3: http://207.201.161.120/jcmc/vol3/issue2/

6. Steuer JS. Defining virtual reality: Dimensions determining telepresence. Journal of Communication 1992; 42:73-93

7. Gibson JJ. The Ecological Approach to Visual Perception. Houghton Mifflin, Boston, 1979

8. Varela FJ, Thompson E, Rosch E. The Embodied Mind. MIT Press, Cambridge, MA., 1991

9. Lakoff G, Johnson M. Metaphors We Live By. University of Chicago Press, Chicago, 1980

10. Lakoff G. Women, Fire, and Dangerous Things. University of Chicago Press, Chicago, 1987

11. Glenberg AM. What memory is for. Behavioral and Brain Sciences 1997; 20:1-55

12. Schubert T, Regenbrecht H, Friedmann F. The Experience of Presence: Factor Analytic Insights. 1998 (Unpublished Manuscript)

13. Held R, Durlach N. Telepresence. Presence: Teleoperators and Virtual Environments 1992; 1:109-112

14. Sheridan TB. Musings on Telepresence and Virtual Presence. Presence: Teleoperators and Virtual Environments 1992; 1:120-125

15. Witmer BG, Singer MJ. Measuring Presence in Virtual Environments: A Presence Questionnaire. Presence: Teleoperators and Virtual Environments 1998; 7:225-240

16. Hoffman HG, Prothero JD, Wells MJ, et al. Virtual Chess: Meaning Enhances Users' Sense of Presence in Virtual Environments. International Journal of Human-Computer Interaction 1998; 10:251-263

A taxonomy of visual metaphors

Claire Dormann,
Center for Tele-Information, DTU
Lyngby, Denmark

Abstract

Metaphors are approached from the perspective of visual rhetoric. In this paper, the origin of the rhetorical figures is first briefly outlined. Then, rhetorical figures are described and illustrated in relation with web pages. The rhetorical perspective suggests manners in which to express the most efficient statement. A web design strategy grounded in rhetoric has been initiated which can guide further research in this domain.

1 Introduction

We should also look more closely at the utilisation of metaphors in user interface (UI) design and at metaphors within the classical system of rhetoric.

The most well known example in UI design is the desk top metaphor. The traditional physical media is a natural starting point for metaphoric representations. Metaphor is usually defined as the presentation of one idea in terms of another, belonging to a different category so that either our understanding of the first idea is transformed or that from the fusion of the two ideas a new one is created. Metaphors draw incomplete parallels between unlike things, emphasising some qualities and suppressing others. Thus discussing user interface metaphor in term of direct mapping between the source and target, as is often the case, is a misconception of the role of metaphor. Moreover, in user interface the function of metaphor corresponds primarly to world creation i.e. to palliate a lack of vocabulary, a new word is created by a metaphoric process.

In addition, keeping the discussion of metaphor to this function is far too limited. It does not provide procedures or concepts for explaining precisely how the sign 'knife and fork' represents a restaurant, or why a web designer should use Figure 2 instead of CLOTHING CONNECTION [1]. Nor does it help to characterize differences between Figure 1, 2 and 3.

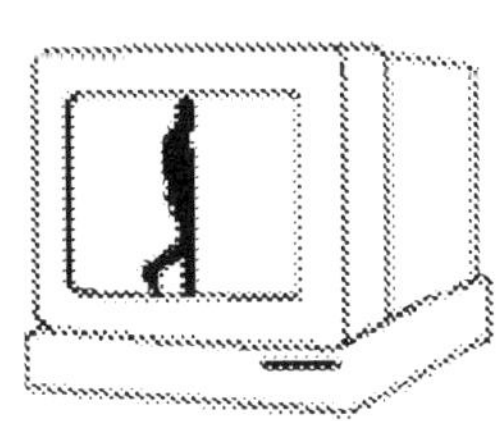

Figure 1: personification   Figure 2: visual pun   Figure 3: anacoluthon

The theory of rhetorical figures accounts for these examples. In anacoluthon the exchange of elements results in the breaking of syntactic rules. It often serves to link one world to another, or of persons embarking in a new discovery journey (as in Figure 3, the computer world). Personification is defined as a comparison whereby human qualities are assigned to inanimate objects. It often has a humorous value (see Figure 1).

The rhetoric system is more attached to the expressiveness of these devices than in the utilisation of metaphors in world creation. When using rhetorical techniques, authors / designers can change the shape of information, these devices can give the message greater vitality and impact by presenting the information in many ways. This paper will focus on that aspect of communication.

2 Rhetoric

Rhetoric is the study of discourse and concerns effective communication. The objectives of rhetoric are the modification of the viewer's conceptions and attitudes toward the object of communication: rhetoric is sometimes considered as 'the art of persuasion'.

2.1 Classical System

Rhetoric originated during antiquity from land disputes and conflicts over civil property. The technique evolved from the work of Aristotle (384-322 BC) and the Institute Oratoria of Quintillion in the First Century AD, to give birth to the classical system of rhetoric.

The figures were seen as an another means of lending credibility to argument, exciting audience's emotion and winning approval for our characters as pleaders. Antithesis, juxtaposing contrasting ideas in balanced phrases, forms an argumentative piece of imagery that sharpens differences significantly. Figures like visual pun or caricature are calculated to work directly on emotions while figures like comprobatio are calculated to establish the ethical image of the speaker or the writer.

There is a choice of three types of arguments which can be adopted to persuade others: the ethical, the emotional, and the rational. Their operational functions are respectively to delight, to move and to inform. To achieve these ends, authors can use rhetorical tools i.e. rhetorical figures. A rhetorical figure is defined as an artful departure from the ordinary mode of speaking [2]. More generally, a rhetorical figure occurs when an expression deviates from expectation. The rhetorical figure is argumentative as its use is meant to change perspective.

This departure can be characterised by four fundamental rhetoric operations: repetition, permutation, suppression, and substitution. For example, the rhetorical operation of repetition combines multiple instances of the same elements. Multitudes of figures such as anaphora (see 3.1.1), or *anadiplosis* (the repetition of the last word of one clause at the beginning of the following clause) are based on this operation. Another subdivision is the distinction between similarities and contrast. Most taxonomies are organised around thes principles. It has to be noted, that metaphor can also be used as a generic term including all the rhetorical figures.

2.2 Visual Rhetoric

In modern rhetoric, rhetoric has been extended to encompass visual discourse. Eco [3] defines the rhetorical code as coming from the conventionalisation of an original iconic solution, which has been assimilated by the social group and has become the model or communication norm.Visual elements are capable of representing concepts, abstractions, actions, metaphors and modifiers, so they can be used in the invention of a complex arguments. There is an ability to guide the order of argumentation via the arrangement of the visual elements. Visual elements must also carry meaningful variation in their manner of delivery, so the selection of style has an intended value.

Rhetorical figures have been discussed in relation to visual discourse in fields such as: advertising [4], graphic design [5], user interfaces [6], and cinema [7]. The aim of Durand [4] studies was to find a visual transposition of rhetorical figures in the advertising image. He developed a taxonomy based on traditional rhetorical. The Rhetorical handbook [5] contains many illustrations of these figures found in student work and in the general design environment.

Clifton [7] discusses numerous examples from hundreds of films. Filmic metaphors have a specific relevance to the WWW. The medium of film enables the expression of figures in new ways. A figure can be expressed in an image but more importantly across shots, scenes, and sequences. Metonymy (i.e. is defined as the substitution of terms suggesting an actual relationship) has a special actualisation in the film chain. In Fritz Lang, M for murder, a brutal murder is suggested by a red balloon floating away (metonymy), made possible by the association of the little girl and the balloon, earlier in the film. The figure of anadiplosis, i.e. is realised in a film by repeating the same shot at the beginning and end of the film. Similarly in the WWW, some figures are expressed across web pages instead of on a single page.

3 Taxonomy of Rhetorical Figures

The examples (around 100) were first collected while browsing through the web, then a closer investigation in electronic commerce was initiated. Because of the convergence between electronic commerce and advertising, it was assumed that a high number of figures would be found in this domain. This explains the type of examples given in this paper. Some of the most frequent figures are presented here. We have also tried to concentrate on figures which have not been discussed previously, in user interface design [6].

3.1 Figures

A figure cannot be met in isolation from other figures. This will remind readers that an image may combine several figures, or be seen as different figures from different viewpoints. Moreover to simplify the discussion, we have not presented the image in relation with text. Some figures are purely visual, while other have to be seen in relation with the text. Moreover some figures are only realised by looking simultaneously at the visual and textual elements.

3.1.1 Repetition

Anaphora is the duplication of a word or a group of words, it is the most elementary figure of repetition. Similarly to textual figures we could classify figures in function of the process and the effect created. Clifton [7] distinguishes further between simultaneous repetition (on the page), repetition with variation and repetition with development (across web page).

Multiple duplications can be created. A specific technique worth mentioning is "mise en abyme": duplication of film in a film, or of a painting in a painting. An example is a page of a book showing a page of a book, etc. There are multiple ways of creating repetition, by varying an element's colours or its size. *Gradation* consists of ordering words by length thus a variation of an object size is a very pure form of graduation.

Paraphrase is described as the most powerful figure of amplification. It consists of developing a central theme through a series of secondary indications which provide many aspects, details or illustrations. This figure is at the heart of guided tour and of many image maps. Key aspects of sites, products or services are condensed in an image.

It seems a simple technique. Suffice to look at a number of commercial sites selling one type of products or another to see the efficiency of this figure. After looking at rows of watches or chocolates over endless web pages, seeing such a simple construction seems refreshing. Three different coloured packs of coffee are depicted in an image [8]; where at one bottom corner beans and at another a cop of coffee are added, slightly breaking the picture frame. Here, a complex visual message is given in a single image. The breadth of the products is suggested by the different pack colours (i.e cultural experience) The cup of coffee and beans relates to the taste and aroma of coffee (i.e. by metonymy) suggesting the pleasurable experience of sampling coffee.

3.1.2 Personification

Personification is defined as a comparison whereby human qualities are assigned to inanimate objects. In advertising, viewers are confronted with a multiplicity of animated objects : talking lawn-mowers, aggressive pepper sausages, smiling car. Similar objects have been found in several web sites: a personified mayonnaise pot [9], animated chocolate bars [10] or a smiling smart disc (i.e in a thumbnail ad placed in the hotwired magazine). Personification serves to express feelings and emotions. With this figure, different parts of the web site can be linked together. Different representations have been found in both [9] and [10]. A small animated pot of mayonnaise parachuting, directs our attention toward visiting the sandwich club. This example functions as "ad into an ad" corresponding to a specific figure "mise en abyme".

3.1.3 Visual Pun

Visual pun is the use of symbols to suggest two or more meanings or different associations. The pun effect happens when a viewer becomes aware of the multiple meanings or associations.

The simplest form of pun is to rearrange letters themselves to form an image reflecting the meaning of the word. On the home page of an astrological site, a list of links has been arranged on dark-blue background to form a moon croissant. This is a very powerful way of arranging the list content. In Lancome, a page inciting consumers to buy (a perfume), words (love, sun, smile etc.) formed a bouquet of flowers, a symbol of romantic love. The design [11] is also a kind of visual poem, poême being the name of the perfume.

In a title, the simplest expression consists in replacing a letter with a graphic element associated with the meaning of the title. The Oneworld news services used Oneworld as a logo, where O has been replaced by an image of earth standing for the letter. In extraordinary Art [12], a company selling art product, the letters A is replaced by drawing tools. Redesigning the letter or adding additional elements create more striking examples as in Figure 2, where the letters themselves have been rearranged to form a zip. There are many other type of examples such as in Voyager [13].

In Voyager, a photograph's objective which contains a small picture of homeless men gives access to a site containing such photos This design successfully captures the essence of the site in a witty way.

We have shown instantiations of pun in different types of designs for different elements of the web pages i.e. title and image map. Pun is the best figure for associating the emotional and functional element of communication. With a pun, a complex visual message is expressed through a single image. Furthermore this device cannot fail to provoke a reaction in the viewers, e.g. a smile in acknowledgment in the cleverness of the designer.

3.1.4 From Irony to Satire

Irony can be defined as any statement that conveys a meaning different than one it professes to give. An example given by Ehses [14] is depicting lady Macbeth and Macbeth as an amiable couple. Irony's importance lies in its ability to evoke an intimate relationship based on a mutually enjoyable moment of shared fun. The pleasure of understanding is boosted by a feeling of intellectual accomplishment, many viewers take pride in correct interpretations.

Satire is based on criticism, parody depends on prior knowledge utilising the familiar in such way that we recognise both the original and the departure of the original. These figures have a similar function to irony as they create a shared relation between an author and viewers. Parody and satire of browsers seem very popular in the WWW. They could be placed in web tutorial, or guidelines design, bringing a lighter tone to the document. Web site can also be based on this design, such as this site [15] selling hot sauce who used a profusion of Horror elements to differentiate between different sauces. Another example is specialised booked shop e.g. science-fiction using "B-movie imagery" as the inspiration for their design.

3.2 Case Study: Parvo

We have discussed, so far mostly single instantiations of these figures. We are now going to look at figures within the whole site design. Parvo [16] is a very small site selling an unique type of products i.e. specially reinforced shoes. The site is constructed around a very clear and strong message. "If you want to appear taller then buy parvo shoes, a shoes with a hidden insole". The visual argument is build very logically in a number of steps (i.e. on each web page).

On the home page, the protagonists are set (e.g. the happy couple). The slogan "want to be taller ?" accompanies the image. Note the utlisation of a male silhouette in the title (i.e standing for the letter A). In the next two pages the mystery is solved. The solution is given by a juxtaposition of two images (antithesis) picturing difference in sizes between the characters. The figure of anthithesis is found in this juxtaposition of images. *Antithesis* is the juxtaposition of contrasting ideas, often in parallel structure (before / after). The expression of characters indicate the right combination. Part of the effect is based on a cultural convention which stipulates that in a couple, a man has to be taller than a woman. Moreover the difference in size is greatly exaggerated in a humorous way (i.e. hyperbol defined as exaggeration for emphasis). The solution to this transformation is given on another page showing how the shoes are made. By then, anyone wanting to appear taller should be convinced of the usefulness of Parvo shoes. Next are pages containing the different shoes models on offer. The silhouette found in the title is repeated on the order page background. We can see here, the figure of anadiplosis, linking the beginning and end of the web site (it is for anyone making an order, this figure happens when the goal of the site has been fulfilled).

3.3 Model of Use

Rhetorical figures can help to set the mood (e.g. irony, personification), enhance information (e.g. ellipsis, hyperbole) or, orient the viewer to the context of the information (e.g. visual pun). We should review in more details the function of rhetorical devices. A model by Whittock [17] is a good starting point for this review.

3.3.1 Emotional

The works of Aristotle and Quintillion express the insight that metaphor is concerned with the communication of thought, emotion, excitement, and an extension of understanding through it. It is this way that its use can help the reader or listener come closer to the insight being expressed.

Emotion and humour are expressed not only through techniques like personification, satire, hyperbole but many other figures can serve this function. Caricature is a special instantiation of hyperbole. It is a well known technique often used to portray celebrities in a humoristic fashion [18]. When using caricature for a political leader instead of its photograph, the author can express comptempt for the leader and his weaknesses. In his turn viewers can react strongly to the caricature (e.g amusement or anger). The figure is thus more expressive and can get people more involved in the communication.

3.3.2 Concision

Metaphor is regarded as contracting a series of complex statements into one brief figures. In *Synecdoche*, a part is substituted for the whole. Synecdoche is very useful in design to represent a larger concept by a single image. An example is using the Eiffel tower for Paris. We have also discussed such function in relation to pun. These devices enhance and enrich the communication.

3.3.3 Cognitive Factors such as Memory and Attention

Clifton describes metaphor as contributing to vividness and *memorability*. The positive effect of rhetorical figures on retention is largely acknowledge by many writers. Many studies have been conducted in advertising (although not in the web) confirming this fact.

One of the main function of these devices is to attract attention. By presenting the information in different ways and using striking images, the information will stand out. Figures such as accent or litote are specifically good for this purpose. *Accent* is a figure that describes the use of colour to highlight objects in a predominantly black and white environment. *Litote* is the deliberate use of understatement, not to deceive someone but to enhance the impressiveness of what we say. Visually it can be expressed by very small images or text figuring in an almost empty web page. It would give a powerful contrast to too many overcrowded web pages. Such solutions might prove a pleasant alternative to the overuse of animation (e.g blinking objects and animated gifs).

3.3.4 Vocabulary Creation

It has already been discussed in relation to user interface where metaphors are used to compensate a deficiency in the vocabulary. Examples for the web include libraries with doors, help desk rooms, collections and shelves or the city of knowledge with gates, streets, buildings and landmarks for interface function and representation [19]. The over-generalisation of similarities between the two systems at the heart of the metaphor, and not the metaphor per say, might explain the confusion experience by users. Users striving to attach one system to the other, thus baffled by inconsistencies between the two models.

It has another very close function. Some experience always fall beyond and can only be expressed with rhetorical figures. What is expressed by a metaphor cannot be expressed otherwise without losing something e.g. some expressiveness, poetic nuances, or specific relation that we want to stress and convey to the viewers in communication).

3.3.5 Eliciting the Reader's Creativity

Readers must figure out the meaning of metaphors. In some case viewers must stress to elucidate the meaning of metaphors. Many visual jokes and visual puzzles are based on this principle. Its function is to challenge viewers. It has a more subtle value, as in film, to engage viewers and insure their participation in the story. The impact of some Fritz Lang and Hitchock movies are unmistakable: many things are hinted or suggested (e.g red balloon). By engaging user intellects we might insure their cooperation and participation in the communication.

3.3.6 *Eliciting the Designer's Creativity*

Ehses [5] has developed a method for teaching graphic design which uses rhetoric, a tool for generating concepts. For a single problem, as many desgins can be produced using these devices. *Metonymy* is the substitution of terms suggesting an actual relationship. Examples of relations are cause instead of effect, instrument instead of agent, container instead of contents, etc. Thus designers can systematically go through all types of metonymic relations in order to find the best design. Metaphors can serve as design techniques to provide different solutions to problems and in assisting in finding the most effective solutions.

Figures can have more than one function. Visual metaphor can also have a humorous purpose. Chaplin films are filled with such examples, in the Dictator, Charlie swallows money like aspirin. Pun has a functional role expressing as much in one image, or a hunoristic role. Hyperbole can make the object more visible thus making the communication more understandable. The dominant function will depend on the goal of the communication.

3 Conclusion

The aim of this paper was to take the first step in defining a grammar of visual rhetoric encompassing different visual phenomena found in the visual world. The proposed framework can be used to guide future research.

Studies could be carried out to compare and distinguish between the effects of different figures rather than focusing on individual figures. It will also be important to examine moderating variables that heighten or limit the efficiency of rhetorical figures.

We have focused here on representation, however we also need to look at how viewers interpret these figures. In advertising, Forceville [20] discussed this topic and showed that subjects do interpret pictorial metaphor as such. An interesting issue mentioned by the author concerns cultural difference.

In WWW, there are many possible ways of expressing information. Music may perform a number of rhetorical tasks: supporting arguments, demonstrating claims, building a ground for mutual confidence, catching and holding attention and providing a vehicle for repetition and remembrance [21] We should also look at how different forms of rhetoric, such as a rhetoric of sound, a rhetoric of text, a rhetoric of image and a rhetoric of film, will work together within a general theory of multimodal rhetoric.

Rhetoric can serve as analytical tool, for example to see if an increased utlisation of these figures is an indication of the WWW maturation. A parallel between utilisation of pun in web title and press, and the use of personification in advertising and e-commerce was found. Until recently human characters were in e-commerce conspicuous by their absence. Stylistic variation between e-commerce sites are appearing leading to a crystalisation into genres e.g. music, bookshop, etc. Contrary to a popular myth "web sites are not cheap and easy", not when you have to hire companies to maintain complex catalogs, periodically refresh your site in function of consumer trends, seasonal variations and timely events (e.g. games, contests and consumer questionnaire). These findings might indicate that e-commerce (and possibly the web) has become, and is acting like any other mass media. A larger investigation in the realm of WWW could be carried out to refine and confirm this fact.

References

1. Shoppersuniverse. http:// Shoppersuniverse.com 1997

2. Corbett, E. (1971) Classical Rhetoric for the Modern Student. Oxford

3. Eco, U. (1970) Sémiologie des messages visuels. Communications, 15, pp. 11-51

4. Durand J. Rhétorique et image publicitaire. Communication, 1970, 15:70-95.

5. Ehses H, Lupton E. Rhetorical Handbook, An Illustrated Manual for Graphic Designers (with Ellen Lupton). Design Papers 1988, 5: 1-39

6. Marcus A. Human Communications Issues in Advanced User Interfaces. Communications of the ACM, 1993, 26: 4, 101-109.

7. Clifton R. The figures in film. University of Delaware Press, Delaware 1983.

8. Majestic Choices http://www.majestic-choices.com/ 1997

9. Hellmanns http://www.mayo.com 1998

10. Hersheys http:// www.hersheys.com 1997

11.Lancome. http://www.lancome.com/_france/cgi-bin/get/ctx=90828849700?/planet-beauty/fragrance/p_poeme.htm 1998

12. Extraordinair Art. http://air-art.com/ 1996

13. Voyager, Fragile Dwelling. http://www.voyagerco.com/fragile/ 1997

14. Ehses H. Representing Macbeth: A Case Study in Visual Rhetorics. In: Margolin V (ed) Design Discourse. Chicago University Press, London,1989, pp. 187-199.

15. HotHotHot. http://www.HotHotHot.com/ 1997

16. Parvo. http://www.sfprestige.com/Parvo/ 1997

17. Whittock T. Metaphor in film. Cambridge University press, Cambridge 1990

18. Rockmine http://www.rockmine.music.co.uk/Char.html 1998

19. Shneirderman B. Designing Information-Abundant Websites: Issues and Recommendations, to be published in International Journal of Human-Computer Studies, July 1997, <http://kmi.open.ac.uk/~simonb/ijhcs-www/>.

20. Forceville C. Pictorial metaphor in Advertising. Routledge, London, 1996

21. Scott L. Understanding Jingles and Needletrop: A rhetorical approach to music in advertising. Journal of consummer research 1995, 21:252-273

Analysis of Representations in Model-Based Teaching and Learning in Science

Dr. Barbara C. Buckley & Dr. Carolyn J. Boulter
School of Education, University of Reading
Reading, England

Abstract

Drawing on our research in science education, we illustrate a method for analysing representations in terms of content, semiotic challenges of particular representations, and the impact of the interface on learning.

1. Introduction

This paper presents an analytical framework we have developed to further our investigations of model-based teaching and learning in science. This complex phenomenon occurs not only in classrooms, but also in a variety of informal learning environments such as museums, zoos, gardens, and activity centres. It also occurs simultaneously on many levels (individuals, groups of various size and composition, in diverse cultures) and for different purposes. Because models are central to science we investigate how models function in science teaching and learning. Representations or expressed models [1] form essential and accessible links among the different levels and across different contexts. A systematic method for characterising, categorising and comparing representations and one that relates logically to the theoretical framework that guides our research was needed. The analytical framework draws most directly on prior research conducted in science classrooms by the authors [2-4] and on research into illustration conducted by Goldsmith [5], but because the phenomena we study are multilevel and complex, we also draw on research in cognitive and social psychology and information technology. This method has evolved as we applied it to discourse-based, object-based, paper-based and screen-based representations of phenomena including the heart, a lunar eclipse, and the greenhouse effect. In this paper we illustrate a method for analysing representations that takes into account the content of the representation, how the particulars of the representation facilitate or hinder sensemaking, and how the interface interacts with both of these issues. We use analysis of a screen-based representation of a living heart beating in an open chest to illustrate the method and conclude with discussion and questions for further study.

2. Background: Model-based Teaching and Learning

As part of the Models in Science and Technology: Research in Education (MISTRE) group at the University of Reading we focus on knowledge construction by individuals, whether in classrooms, museums, or during study of a textbook, screen-based resource, physical model or actual phenomena. We have integrated the frameworks that emerged from earlier studies of model-based learning [4] and collaborative learning [3] in an attempt to create a model of science learning that encompasses both social and cognitive levels. See Figure 1.

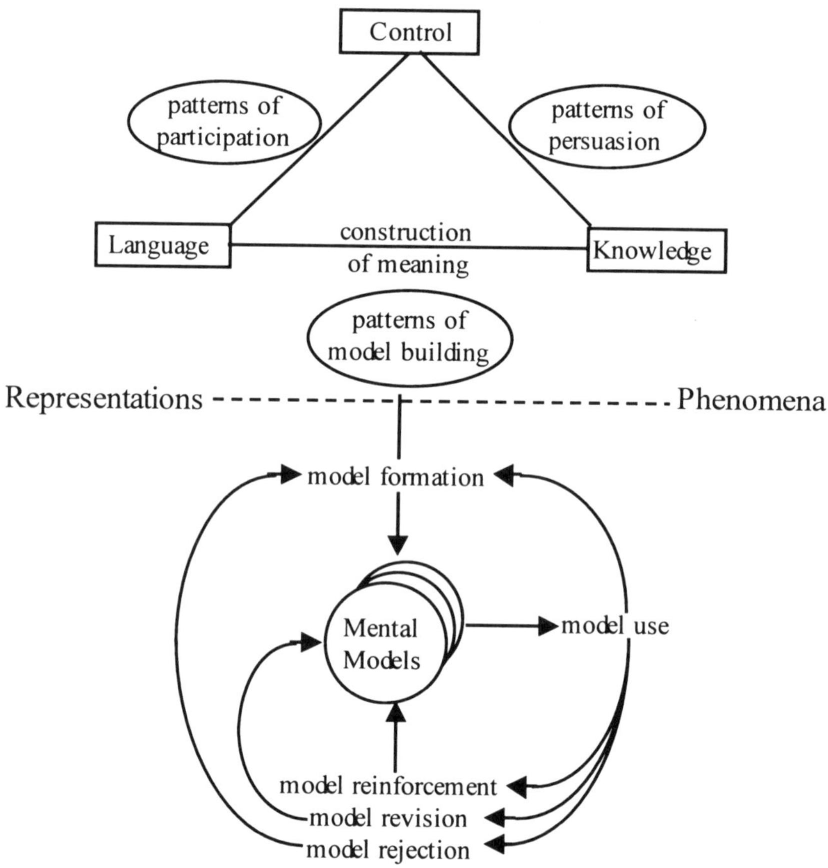

Figure 1. Model-based Teaching and Learning Framework

The top half of the diagram concerns model-based teaching as described by Boulter [3]. It focuses on the patterns of participation, persuasion and model-building in the classroom during which individuals construct their understanding of some phenomenon. This is accomplished through discourse with and about representations, guided by the teacher who facilitates negotiation among the participants in the discourse, including those not present such as the scientists who developed the public knowledge in the domain and the educationists who developed the materials and activities intended to facilitate learners' understanding of the phenomenon.

The bottom half of the diagram concerns model-based learning as described by Buckley [4] and others. [6, 7] It focuses on individuals' construction of mental models of the phenomena under study during which learners form an initial model of some phenomenon either intentionally to meet some learning goal or spontaneously in response to some task. When the model is used successfully, the model is reinforced and may eventually become a precompiled, stable model. [8] If the model is not satisfactory in use, it may be revised or rejected resulting in a progression of mental models. [9, 10]

Phenomena and representations of phenomena link these two levels of learning because they serve as the focus of both goals and discourse while the representations serve also as tools for conducting the discourse and constructing meaning. The relationship between phenomena or reality and representations has been considered from diverse perspectives. For our purposes, we consider representations to be simplifications of the phenomenon constructed for particular purposes; in our case, pedagogical purposes such as communication, exploration, assessment and problem-solving. We do not work at the level of investigating the means by which mental models are represented in the mind, but at the level of inferring what content may be represented in the mind of the teacher or learner as well as what and how learning materials and activities contribute to the process.

3. Analytical Framework

Our focus on model-based learning dictates the first stage of our analysis: What can the user learn about the phenomenon from this representation? Here we focus on the content of the representation. Does it contain information about the structure, function, behaviour and/or mechanism of the phenomenon? *Structure*, in our framework, refers to the components and their spatial relationships. *Function* (useful mostly in biology and technology) refers to the role it plays in the larger system in which it is embedded. *Behaviour* refers to the time-based changes and processes, while *mechanism* refers to the causes of the behaviour. Mechanism is often unpacked by describing the subcomponents of the phenomenon and the interacting (emergent) behaviours that produce the behaviour of the whole.

Analysing video of a living heart beating in an open chest, we would decide that it represents the external structure of the heart and its behaviour. We could observe the different chambers of the heart and the coronary vessels as well as the contraction and relaxation of the chambers. As is often the case with living things, the mechanism or cause of the behaviour is not visible.

However, this analysis of the content of the representation reveals only the potential information conveyed from the perspective of a person who knows something about the heart. What the learner perceives and understands is a function of the learner's goals and prior knowledge. Goals help direct the learner's attention and motivate constructive interaction [11] with the image while prior knowledge may enable the learner to see what is there. Without prior knowledge the learner may have difficulty identifying the parts, recognising or naming them, or understanding what is happening. These represent the semiotic challenges of the representation and indeed of the phenomenon itself. Nature doesn't come with outlines and labels. Goldsmith [5] refers to these as syntactic, semantic, and pragmatic, respectively, where syntactic refers to the perception of the entities represented, semantic to recognition of them, and pragmatic to familiarity with the larger context from which the representation is drawn. In science education part of the larger context is the collection of models and hypotheses that connect them to the real world. [12] Armed with these models experts perceive far more in representations like this video than do novices.

Now imagine an interface that allows the learner to interact with the images. The interface allows the user to click on a portion of the image after which the program highlights that part (showing the boundaries) and displays a text box which names the part and/or describes what is happening. In addition, the user can control the playback of the video to replay it at normal speed, in slow motion or as a static image. Highlighting the part helps overcome the syntactic challenge of the representation (finding the entity) while the text box can be used to address semantic and pragmatic challenges (identifying it or connecting it to the larger system, respectively). The interface also places control of access to information firmly in the hands of the learner.

But providing access to representations and compensating for their inherent semiotic challenges to understanding is insufficient to ensure that learners construct an adequate understanding. In a classroom of 27 students who were at ease with technology and used the information resource containing the heart images and interface described above, only one student engaged in learning that enabled her to outperform her classmates on various measures of knowledge and to reason about a novel illustration, even with incomplete knowledge. What distinguished her learning activities were the goals evident in her project plans and notes, her constructive engagement [11] with all of the media and representations at her disposal, and her integration of the various pieces of information into a hierarchy of embedded dynamic causal models of the circulatory system. [4] This is a case of metacognitive control employed by the learner, as distinguished from control exerted by the teacher in guiding the learner or control imposed by the interface.

4. Discussion

We have completed similar analyses of physical and visual models of a lunar eclipse, seasons, and day and night and their use in classrooms, museums and CD-ROMs and textbook illustrations of the greenhouse effect, as well as in current projects focusing on models of the environment and have found it quite useful. [13, 14] The issues of control are recent additions to our analysis and require further exploration in theoretical discussion, research projects and classroom situations. In particular we plan to examine the parallels among classroom control as practised by teachers, metacognitive control exercised by learners, and control programmed into interfaces to information of all kinds.

5. Conclusion

We have described a method of analysing representations of all kinds that takes into account the content of the representation, the semiotic challenges inherent in the representation, and how an interface may help compensate for those challenges. While this framework is essential to our understanding of model-based teaching and learning in science, we have also pointed out that access to information is only one facet of the complex phenomenon of science learning.

References

1. Gilbert, J.K. The role of models and modelling in some narratives of science learning. Paper presented at the annual meeting of the American Educational Research Association, San Francisco, 1995
2. Boulter, C.J. Language,models and modelling in primary science classroom. In: Exploring models and modelling in science and technology education. J.K. Gilbert, Editor. Faculty of Education and Community Studies, The University of Reading, Reading, 1997, pp 180-200
3. Boulter, C. Collaborating to investigate questions: A model for primary science. PhD thesis, University of Reading, 1992
4. Buckley, B.C. Multimedia, misconceptions and working models of biological phenomena: Learning about the circulatory system. PhD thesis, Stanford University, 1992
5. Goldsmith, E. Research into illustration, Cambridge University Press, Cambridge, 1984
6. Johnson-Laird, P.N. Mental models, Harvard University Press, Cambridge, MA, 1983
7. Stewart, J. and B. Hafner, Extending the conception of problem solving. Science Education 1991; 75(1):105-120

8. Vosniadou, S. and W.F. Brewer, Mental models of the earth: A study of conceptual change in childhood. Cognitive Psychology 1992; 24(4):535-585
9. Clement, J. Learning via model construction and criticism: Protocol evidence on sources of creativity in science. in Handbook of creativity: Assessment, theory and research. J.A. Glover, R.R. Ronning, and C.R. Reynolds, Editors. Plenum Press, New York, 1989, pp 341-381
10. White, B.Y. and J.R. Frederiksen, Causal model progressions as a foundation for intelligent learning environments. Artificial Intelligence 1990; 42(1):99-157
11. Chan, C.K.K., *et al.*, Constructive activity in learning from text. American Educational Research Journal 1992; 29(1):97-118
12. Giere, R.N. Explaining science, University of Chicago Press, Chicago, 1990
13. Buckley, B.C., C.J. Boulter, and J.K. Gilbert Towards a typology of models for science education. In: Exploring models and modelling in science and technology education. J.K. Gilbert, Editor. Faculty of Education and Community Studies, The University of Reading, Reading, 1997, pp 90-105
14. Buckley, B.C. and C.J. Boulter. Taking models apart: Towards a framework for analyzing representations in teaching and learning science. Paper presented at European Science Education Research Association, Rome, Italy, 1997

From Gutenberg to Gates

The creation of the photographic negative, the consequent evolution of a visual language, and its impact on the way societies represent and read their world(s)

Associate Professor S.R.Edwards
Department of Screen and Media Studies, The University of Waikato, Hamilton, New Zealand

Abstract

The photographic negative has been arguably more significant than the invention of moveable type in informing the world's cultures and societies and influencing their world view(s). The presence of recognisable visual representations of our world, and the affirmation of those worlds through multiple identical copies of those images, has at once broadened humanity's knowledge base, and restricted our understanding.

The impetus for this article came a couple of years ago when I was visiting the paper for which I write a screen column. In the foyer of *The Waikato Times* , the biggest evening daily in New Zealand, stands one of its early linotype machines. A commemorative plaque alongside the machine has the entry

Previously assembled by hand from individual metal characters, ...this... tedious method of typesetting had remained almost unaltered since its invention in 1440 by Gutenberg. (1)

Here were the origins of mass produced information.

In a conference devoted to visual representations and interpretations, a conference initiated by a department from a discipline not normally seen by members of the traditional arts communities as dealing with images at anything much more than an immmediate 'iconic' sense, a discipline which appears to have more affinities with the strongly denotative languages of mathematics than the connotative images of the arts, and one in which syntax and semiotics are embedded in rather different semiotic and conceptual fields, there is good reason to consider the historical importance of the advent of moveable type and the photographic negative, and especially the latter.

The thesis of the paper is a simple one. Consequent upon their possession of a sophisticated language, human beings have developed two great capacities, the ability to reason, and the ability to create images. Less explored than reason by philosophers and logicians, the capacity for creating images has nevertheless become an essential element in the definition of humanity. It provides us with systems through which our perceptions may be encoded and transmitted, and at the same time, imposes structures which mediate our selection and understanding of what we perceive. We continually create and receive images which order and contain the universe, and objectify the essence of humanity's ideas or perceptions about that universe. The medium may be aural, or visual, but supported by their verbal signifiers, the essence is the same. The selected or constructed image condenses and generalises information in the priorities the image maker intends.

Images are essentially conceptualising tools. Perceptions are selected and ordered, cross referenced with similar or associated perceptions, and, together with their verbal markers, provide a classification technology for the systematic storage and retrieval of information. Each time an image is constructed by an individual, the view it gives of the world, the way it interprets the world, what it selects from the world to codify in the image, is unique, and novel.

Initially the creation of images was marked by their individuality. Each image was unique, from the elemental images created by cave dwellers to the stunningly representational daguerrotype. (2) Then two events occurred, some four centuries apart in time, but immediately connected by a common characteristic. Both enabled information, in the form of constructed images, to be replicated. Each replication was virtually identical to each other replication. Each was accessible to an unlimited population - unlimited, that is, other than for reasons of learning, or cost, or censorial prohibition.

The two events were the creation of moveable type in the fifteenth century by Johann Gutenberg, and the patenting by Fox Talbot in 1841 of the Calotype, a photographic process incorporating silver nitrate and providing the first negative / positive system, permitting an unlimited number of image replications to be made from the one original. Each provided identical sources of images, images limited in their multiplicity only by the number of users. Access to knowledge was at once hugely expanded, but also codified and structured. Knowledge could now be mediated in identical packages. Instead of music being heard in the cathedral for which it was composed, or paintings seen only in their original - or in near originals as artists produced hand made copies, or words read from individually copied, and extremely rare texts, the world came to be saturated with identical images. While images mediated verbally appeared to demonstrate a higher degree of ambiguity, seemingly identical visual representations came to be characterised by an apparent and increasingly persuasive authenticity.

When, on August 24, 1456, in Mainz, Germany, Heinrich Cremer finished binding the first of the Gutenberg Bibles, he was making practical the invention, by Gutenberg, of what we know as moveable type. Instead of creating each letter by hand, with a pen, and consequently producing, in print, what would only be available to, and read by, a miniscule proportion of the population, those marks on the page could now be reproduced for as long as the ink lasted. The pen had been replaced by **negative** characters which were fitted into place on a flat frame, inked, and then pressed onto paper, which when dry, was even easier to read than the laboriously created, handwritten pages which filled business records and Bibles alike.

Half a century after the appearance of Gutenberg's 42 line Latin Bible, generally reckoned to be the first printed book in the European, modern, sense, there were hundreds of printing shops in cities all over the continent: a map of their distribution shows the heaviest concentrations in Italy and the Low Countries, but there is a general scatter through nearly all the countries in the Western world - the world, that is, of Western Christendom. (3)

It was an invention which was to revolutionise the world, to free knowledge in ways unthinkable before Gutenberg, and which would result in the creation of such diverse phenomena as what we have come to know as the Fourth Estate, of Sunday Schools and oratorios, of revolutions powered by political pamphlets, of poetry on paper instead of the eardrum, of scientific treatises, and that great nineteenth century time stealer, the novel.

What it also did, was to supply people with the same information - or at least identical copies of that information. The way the information was received, of course, was influenced by the way in which we receive any imaged, coded information, information mediated through signs, as opposed to information received through immediate sensory perception. That is, it is influenced by the semiotic trains, those syntactic organisers which present the lexis, the verbal signs, in a preselected and linear fashion. It is influenced by the way we have learned to read or receive those signs, even though the contexts in which we receive them may vary. We do not have the capacity to search outside the signs, except by using prior knowledge and inference. That humans generally are uninformed about the way in which signs function, and the ambiguities which are inherent in the images we create to organise, store, retrieve, and communicate information is grotesquely emphasised in the current turgid rivers of interpretation surrounding the public and private events in the life of President Bill (William) Clinton.

The constructed image, the *representation*, is the ultimate generalisation. Interpretation is the interpretation of generalisations. New Zealand poet Dennis Glover, talking of poetry, commented

Poetry is the generalisation of collective experience. (4)

The same is true of any system of encoded representation, including the apparently transparent and honest visual image.

Thus, in the five hundred and fifty years which have followed the invention of moveable type, human beings have come to receive information, and have learned to view the world, in remarkably new, but remarkably uniform conformist/conforming ways, culminating in the current developments in digital technology, but also enabling Hungarian film maker Istvan Szabo to say,

In the history of human culture every age has an art that expresses best what people feel about life. The most expressive art of our age has been film. The face of the 20th century is preserved by film with a richness hitherto unknown to humanity. Film has become the authentic memory of our times." (5)

While Szabo's 'authenticity' is perfectly valid in its context, it also needs the qualification that film, like any other visual representation, is itself selective generalisation. The images we see moving across the screen are memory in the same way as other stimuli to memory, stimuli connecting us to our actual and vicariously remembered pasts, are memory. What film does, however, is to provide viewers with an identical stimulus to memory, and in its persuasively generalising form, seems to authenticate what we have come to believe to be true.

Significantly, however, there is an inbuilt tension in the development of the replicating technologies. The technology permits the storage and retrieval of information, information derived both from the creative imagination and from the physical world, but the way in which that information is selected, assembled, and used, still is the product of the human mind. That that mind is heavily influenced by the language it uses as its own storage and retrieval system, its sorting and conceptualising process, is a philosophical given, but the link between language systems and imaging processes is central to the creation and use of visual representations and their interpretation.

The pre and early history of cinema in New Zealand is a surprisingly complete, and clear, demonstration of the ways in which New Zealanders, very quickly adapted to the conventions and practices which were imposed by the emerging photographic technologies. Why New Zealand? Because as has been the case with so many other examples, from chilled meat to health and education systems - New Zealand is the world leader in the introduction of required courses in visual representation throughout the formal education process from age five to age eighteen - in this case the small nation provides an accurate and representative example of what occurred with much of the rest of the world.

The most significant of these technological developments culminated in the patenting of William Henry Fox Talbot's Calotype negative to positive process in England in 1841. In 1839, he had detailed his Photogenic Drawing process. This was a technology on which he had been working since 1834 where he used paper soaked in silver nitrate, silver salts, which darkened on exposure to light, to create a negative image. This image could be fixed chemically, then printed onto a new silver salt sensitised paper which gave a positive image. Because the original image was permanently fixed, as many positive images as required could be printed as the negative, on a transparent plate or medium, was simply a medium which reversed the light values sensitising the chemicals on the positive paper. This apparently innocuous development, however, allowed for the first time, virtually unlimited mutiple reproductions of the same photographic image, an advance in visual information technology akin to Gutenberg's printing press. For the first time, mass audiences would be able to see copies of the same image, copies, what is more, which were indistinguishable from the original from which they came. In addition, the copies were replications of what people believed they saw in the 'real' world, limited only by the frame and the position of the camera. These limitations are, of course, significant, but of quite a different order from those imposed on a painter who is creating a thoroughly representative image.

The effect of the multiplication of images, and their apparent authenticity, was to suggest common truths about the world in which we live, truths which are founded on the common experience of the same image. Photographs of New Zealand, whether the ethnographic representations of the Burtons, who recorded 'authentic memories' of Maori life in New Zealand's central North Island, or the architectural recordings of Willie Melhuish who spent more than a decade recording the growth of the city of Dunedin, photographing the same landscapes from the same positions at the same time of the year to accumulate a remarkable architectural record, provide a perspective which viewers accepted as the 'real' New Zealand, a perspective which is confirmed constantly and consistently by others who see the same images. Not just the Burtons and Melhuishes, but the strongly authenticising images of a host of nineteenth century photographers, taken often from the attitude considered most sellable by commercial image makers, were, and are, highly influential in constructing the views of ourselves which were held then, and which we still hold today.

These photographs were not seen by viewers as representations, as generalisations, as products of a trained lens operator, but as accurate images of the world as it is. When viewers received their images, and had their view confirmed by others who had received identical images, the authenticiy oif the information was constantly confirmed. That it was the ultimate in circular argument, that *post hoc* ruled in this kingdom of the same, was simply not an issue. The photographs were real, and consequently seen as presenting, not representing, reality.

Around the middle of the nineteenth century, the first surviving photograph of Maori, a daguerrotype, was taken. Probably recorded in 1852, it shows two young women, Caroline and Sarah Barrett, identical in European dress, with severe Victorian hairstyles, posing rather stiffly and uneasily for an unknown photographer. Apart from facial features, they could be any pair of nineteenth century sisters sitting for a portrait. In a sense indicative of the future, they were the daughters of whaler Dicky Barrett who had married a Maori, Rawinia Waikauia of Ngati Te Whiti, and had come ashore to run a hotel in New Plymouth. The girls demonstrate the readiness with which Maori were willing to adopt European imports, and is a family rather than a commercial portrait, unlike most of the photographs of Maori which appeared later in the century and after.

Photographs record information, but they record it in particular ways. The information is positioned by the camera, by the size of the frame, by the distance of the camera from its subject, by the presence of colour, or shadow, or light, and we have learned to read photographic images using those conventions.

Still photographs then, portray selected subjects, recorded at a selected instant in time, from a selected point of view. Moving pictures add the dimension of time, but even there the time is not real time. It is time which is cropped and adjusted to suit the narrative carried by the images. Moving pictures are selected for what they add to the information, and where the information is not deemed necessary it is deleted. Like a testimonial, often as much is said by what is left out as is said by what we read or see. Thus the process of selection itself, as much as the images in the frame, becomes a continuing and significant commentary on the significant cultural determinants of the period in which the photographs are taken, and on the information which is contained in them. When one examines the images of nineteenth century New Zealand, for example, the partiality for a strongly Eurocentric view of the emergent colony becomes clear, as do predominant attitudes toward children, toward women, toward Maori, and toward the dominant pakeha male.

Learning to see, to accept the conventions, was the intellectual, social, and emotional equivalent of the industrial revolution. The nineteenth century became the century of the multiple visual image, laying the foundation for the image saturated, screen addicted societies of the twentieth. Audiences took what they wanted from what was there in front of them, briefly acknowledging the possible different reception of images, and then, in the twentieth century with moving images, in a constant checking of narrative - 'Did you see when...?' Audiences, too, talk about the ideas contained in the images they absorbed, and for the first time in history, are able to work from what was essentially the same base material, observed under remarkably similar conditions.

We learned, and learn, about the world from the results of Fox Talbot's remarkable discovery. We are able to study the same text, albeit bringing our own ways of intepreting what we see.

The ultimate purveyor of the exotic, as well as the mundane, is the photograph. The advent of the camera with its ability to display the wares of different cultures around the globe, together with the cultural hegemony of the great powers, was to create fundamental changes in the cultural integrity of smaller nations. Images bounded by the camera lens and recorded on film became an essential element in the construction of perception, and hence of history. These images were recorded, however, because they were dramatic, or because they were able to communicate the essence of an idea. They were never a whole culture, or a complete event, only selected and characteristic elements. The selections were, in effect, visual summaries, and because of the ease with which such images could be spread, the camera was to prove even more powerful than the pen as an agent for the global generalisation of cultural images.

Its advent defines the end of traditional verbal histories and the onset of a new age of remarkably compelling historical reconstructions as well as realistically believable fictions. In our contemporary screen driven age, there is a gently anachronistic irony in that, on the front page of each edition of a daily New Zealand newspaper, *The Waikato Times,* there is a logo which shows a quill pen crossing over a sword. It is an image which links the verbal and the visual, and retains the fundamental principle that information is more powerful than military might, but perhaps a more accurate new age logo for the power now wielded by the press would be a movie camera crossing a Stealth bomber.

One has only to note the way in which William Main's visual text illustrates nineteenth century New Zealand (6) to understand how visually documented histories seem to connect readers directly with the historic past. The reproduced images become not just artefacts, but assume the same authority as fact. That powerful folk belief in the sanctity of history conveyed through screen images is exemplified in a letter to the editor of the *New Zealand Herald* in 1925. The writer, praising the excellence of Rudall Hayward's 1925 film, *Rewi's Last Stand*, goes on to claim,

> *Films like this teach history better than any book can do, because they give the spirit of the time and those who lived in an age that is in danger of being forgotten. They inculcate the best type of patriotism by helping to form a living link with the past.* (7)

That same belief in the power of the image is reinforced by lines of dialogue like these which follow. They are transcribed from a sequence in Michael Black's *Pictures,* a film about the Burton brothers, photographers in and of nineteenth century New Zealand. In the film, two bureaucrats, responsible for publicity designed to encourage English immigration to New Zealand, are confronted by a series of photographs taken by one of the brothers. The images show Maori degradingly bound in chains and trudging through mud after they have been defeated in battle with the European colonists and their protecting militia. Told by the bureaucrats, who were preparing a sanitised and attractive package to attract new settlers, that his photographs were 'disgusting' and 'an outrage', Burton replied,

"That's exactly the way it was."

The subsequent bureaucratic response again underlines a belief in the power of the image to influence its viewers,

"Who wants to know that... These pictures show the colony in a very bad light... Have you any idea what people back home in England would think if they saw these?" (8)

Images may be accurate, sanitised for public acceptance, shifted for dramatic emphasis, or even only vaguely connected with historical events, but they are out of all proportion to print in establishing historical 'verities' in the minds of contemporary society.

What gave visual images an ultimate power, however, was the development of photographs in which the subjects appeared to move. The movie camera, and its successor the video camera, became the ultimate in objective record. The image was there on the screen. It was a record of something that had happened. It was real. The willingness to suspend disbelief and accept the truth of screen images which recorded historical verities quickly translated to narratives where truth and fiction could be equally convincing, and where both the ordinary and the most fantastic dreams of audiences could be given an existence on the screen.

But all cinematic dreams, recordings of the historical world, or created fictions, were constructed. The way in which images were selected, the point of view from which they were observed, and the way they were distributed in the frame and along the narrative path, provided information about how subjects and ideas were to be perceived. The new apparatus, Daguerrotype or Cinematographe, and the multiplicity of cameras and projectors which have followed, created visual iconographies in which cultural and gender generalisations were fashioned by the camera operator, not the subject being recorded. It gave overwhelming cultural capital to the group which took control of the construction and distribution of photographic images.

The vast majority of photographers and film makers came to utilise two primary methods of communicating information. Both were based on principles of selection and consistent practice, and worked to render the photographic message both easily accessible and highly efficient. The first, applicable both to still photography and to cinematography, was to provide the shorthand of image identification, leading viewers immediately to the primary meanings of the photographic image by selecting and arranging key elements within the frame.

The process of selection included the placing of iconographic markers which enable viewers to identify subjects quickly and accurately. Such markers were as well known as a vicar's collar, or as obvious as the severe hair style of the Barrett sisters denoting their acceptable social standing, or the *moko* or tattoo which identified the Maori male as a *toa* (warrior) and not simply as male. In New Zealand cinema, early indicators or markers of the setting in which the narrative was taking place included rugged mountain backdrops, empty landscapes, rainforest and tree ferns, Maori *kaainga* (villages), *paa*, (fortified villages), and or *whare* (houses), and only rarely urban scenes, and it is an indication of their power that most still remain to codify New Zealand cinema. In *The Piano*, for example, prize winner at Cannes in 1993, the settings utilising exactly those iconographic elements shout that the film is a New Zealand feature, even though it is marketed as Australian, and financed primarily from France. Together with camera point of view, and the arrangement of images within the frame, iconographic elements, themselves essentially selective generalisations, became vital markers in the system of visual codes through which the new medium communicated.

The second essential element in cinematic communication, consisted of the arrangement of elements, the ordering of events, and the ways in which they were located in relation to other events within the narrative, but was specific to the moving image. As a result, the new discourse of cinema, was to become as powerful a tool in the shaping of ways of seeing as were mise-en-scene or iconographic elements in the still photograph.

Cinema is also about audience and audience size. In the early battles for audience loyalty, the seamless narrative, and its attendant ease of suspension of disbelief, provided Hollywood with an important lead. Audiences leaned towards the narrative codes of Hollywood and learned quickly to measure other narratives against those codes. Their reception of Hollywood narratives was not the result of a conscious critical assessment, however. It was the result of a regular pattern of attendance at cinemas. In New Zealand by 1934, for example, there was a total of 489 theatres and six cinema chains, increasing to 525 theatres in 1943 for a population of just over a million and a half. Regular patterns of attendance showed each person seeing a movie, on average, once a fortnight or twenty four times a year, and two fifths of the population aged between 13 and 18 attended once a week.(9) There was no doubt about the source of films for those theatres. A typical complaint as far back as 1925 was found in another letter to the editor of the *New Zealand Herald*, this time from Nigel Vancouver, who wrote, "We are all "seeing America First" on the screen; let us see a bit of New Zealand now and then!" (10)

Not just America. Photographic images ultimately defined the way in which pakeha New Zealand, and indeed many Maori, were to see the indigenous people of this country. Merata Mita, Maori woman film maker and commentator, talking of her feature film *Mauri*, acknowledges,

"I know a few Maori had difficulty with it because you get so colonised and accept the image that the pakeha throws up at you." (11).

The photograph, that technology which was to become so influential in recording history as it was being made, arrived in New Zealand just too late to record the generation of Maori which was able to bridge the gap between pre-European times and the coming of the pakeha. The photographers were pakeha, their attitudes and points of view were alien to the Maori, and they had no real concept of pre European Maori apart from the contemporary generalisations about Maori made by other pakeha and the paintings and drawings made by earlier explorers and the artists that accompanied them.

Just as with paintings of other New Zealand subjects, paintings of Maori were influenced by European conventions and styles. The eyes of 18th and 19th century painters were unable to perceive the new found race with any ethnographic accuracy apart from recording such clearly identifiable and exotic markers as moko (tattooing) or decoration. The interest in the moko typifies the differences in perception between Maori and pakeha.

"It (the moko *) was a mark of grace dignity and beaut* (by Maori). *And when the European came it wasn't regarded like that at all - it was the face that a savage wore."* (12)

The Maori subjects of early European art provided the first and sometimes the only visual contact for many pakeha. Photographers learned to perceive the Maori often through eyes which were conditioned by the paintings. So did the pakeha interests in England and Europe. Yet "*few if any artists depicted the Maori literally and 'objectively'...European stylistic and thematic conventions constantly came between the artists and any unvarnished recording of the physical and psychological 'realities' of the Maori, and thus played a fundamental role in determining how the Maori was represented.*" (13).

This link, between the Europeans representers of Maori, the viewers of their work, and the way in which subsequent images of Maori are influenced by those visual perceptions, can be traced from the Maori in early European art in New Zealand, through the later record of still photographs, into the feature films of this century. It is a record which reflects a selective view of Maori, and one which appears to have influenced Maori and pakeha alike, to the extent that even in a feature like *Mauri,* written and directed by Merata Mita in 1987 which has been made by a Maori with an intentionally Maori perspective, elements of that early visual conditioning, stemming from the authenticising and confirming character of identical images, persist.

The paradox is that something which accurately portrays a current ethnographic reality nevertheless selects roles which affirm that reality. If the portrayal unconsciously includes pakeha as well as Maori constructs as a result of the image pressures of the past then it not only confirms Mita's concern with cultural colonisation, but also underlines the potentially self fulfilling nature of a visual history which is selective of subject and setting, adjusted to suit the visualisations and beliefs of a particular culture, and offered in a self confirming medium based on the ability to produce infinite numbers of identical visual representations.

End Notes:

1. Wording from a note describing the evolution of the printing press. *The Waikato Times* 1994.
2. See, for example, the whole plate daguerrotype of two Maori rangatira from 1850, cited in Main, William, *The Maori In Focus* Millwood Press, Wellington, 1976. p.7.
3. Small, Christopher *The Printed Word: An Instrument of Popularity* Aberdeen University Press, Aberdeen. 1982 p.2.
4. From the introduction to the film, *The Magpies*, dir. Alistair Taylor, Ripoff Productions, 1974, sd, b&w and col, 16mm, 5mins.
5. Istvan Szabo, quoted following the title page of *The Lumiere Project: European Film Archives at the Crossroads* Ed., Catherina Surowiec, Associacio Projecto Lumiere, Portugal 1996.
6. Main, William, *The Maori In Focus* Millwood Press, Wellington, 1976.
7. *The New Zealand Herald* Letters, 8 May 1925.
8. *Pictures*, directed by Michael Black. Pacific Films Ltd. 1981. Transcript from the film.

9. Dennis Jonathan, and Bieringa, Jan (Eds) *Film In Aotearoa New Zealand* Wellington, Victoria University Press, 1992, p. 204.
10. *The New Zealand Herald* Letters, 8 May 1925.
11. Mita, Merata. *Illusions*, No 9, December 1988 p.24
12. Merata Mita interviewed in *Making Utu*, directed by Gaylene Preston, 1982.
13. Bell, Leonard. The Maori in European Art, Reed, Wellington 1980. p.4.

Theatricality and Levels of Believability in Graphical Virtual Environments

David K. Manley
Liverpool John Moores University,
Liverpool, Merseyside.

Abstract

The experience theatre has in the creation of believable performance environments, could be constructively transferred to the emerging field of computer virtual environments...There seems to me to be little to differentiate between these worlds...other than the medium of delivery.

1 Introduction

I first became aware of a critical link between theatre and computer science when I was given the book, "Computers as Theatre" [1]. Its proposal that theatre could define an underlying philosophy for computer human action was fascinating. But it was the title that had really gripped my imagination. The idea that computer worlds could be linked to theatre worlds made sense of my past subjective experience and my knowledge of the developing world of computer supported virtual environments.

My background of twenty years as a professional theatre technician had given me the opportunity to work in and with many varied performance spaces. All of them 3D, all of them to a greater or lesser degree interactive, and all of them designed using the common collected experience of theatre. A common experience backed up by arguably over a thousands years of development. The similarity between all those performance spaces was that they sought to be, for the watching audience, a believable environment.

2 Foundations

Believability, as a primary design consideration, should not be confused with realistic or naturalistic. The arguments about realism and naturalism have been going on since the 1870's and is evidenced in the work of writers such as August Strindberg and Gerhart Hauptmann [2]. In this area, realism can be thought to destructuralise complex realistic globals into smaller usable entities and then re use those entities overlaid onto other carriers. I.e. an unrealistic cartoon character can show realistic anger. Naturalism in this work is considered as more environmental. A cartoon character is 'natural' to a cartoon world as a human is natural to our human world but we would be unnatural in a cartoon world and vice versa. Believability simply means the ability to accept as true. Theatrical rules governing this believability have been used for thousands of year's [3] within theatre and I believe on the whole to good effect.

Theatricality and its consideration of three-dimensional space make it a candidate for comparison with architectural techniques when addressing the design of virtual environments. Where they differ is in that theatricality also seeks to design the representation of the content of that space. An architect will not seek to tell a user of a building what clothes to wear but a theatre designer will! This designed integration of space and content representation may give it an edge over architectural methods in fields such as the representation of data in virtual CSCW [4] environments, both immersive and desktop.

There is another chain of argument that leads me to believe that theatricality may be an important element in a CSCW environment. It goes as follows.

2.1 Step one

It is a reasonable assumption to say that people working within CSCW structures such as a CALVIN [5] type environment form a community. Community being defined as: *All the people living in a specific locality, including its inhabitants. Fellowship of interests (community of intellect)* [6].
This and other collaborative virtual systems such as DIVE [7], Blaxxsun worlds [8], Viscape worlds [9] and various Mud's [10] support the notion that virtual communities or societies are a real phenomenon.

2.2 Step two

The term's community and society can be interchanged. Society being defined as: *a social community, all societies must have firm laws* [11] Computer based virtual environments are law based in the sense that they obey computational rules. And in the wider sense of social rules, such as found in 'Worlds Away' environments, where they are dealing, at the moment with virtual theft [12].

2.3 Step Three

Overt theatricality seems to have been present in all societies throughout history and as of the present I know of no exceptions to this. I have come to this conclusion after discussion with members of various theatre departments and in particular from talking extensively to Dr Peter Harrop [13] and by consideration of the links between Shamanism and the roots of theatre [14].

2.4 Step four

Virtual communities seem to often lack believability, and it is my view that this believability could be supplied through theatricality. If theatricality is common to all societies why not virtual societies? It could be argued that by their nature virtual societies already contain theatricality but this is not overt. This all leads me to believe that it may be possible to argue that this crucial missing element of believability in many virtual on-line worlds could be supplied through theatricality.

There is a weakness here in that there is a need to identify satisfactorily the elements that constitute believability to a level that provides a defensible workable definition. This could be addressed from two angles. Firstly, to show what it is, by identifying its constituents. Or secondly, by identifying what it is not, and thus reveal what it should be. On the surface this seems a daunting task but becomes less so if you break down believability to the subdivisions of experiential belief structures, cultural belief structures, and rule based belief structures. By breaking down these to other sub levels, it should be possible to arrive at, eventually, a definition by, 'the identification of parts'. Definition by showing what it is not would be no less valid, but would lead to a very large and unwieldy formulation. Though because of the nature of the argument it would be advisable to combine both methods into one definition to give it a robustness of usage.

But most importantly, it is in the use of theatres experience in the creation of believable environments that I see most opportunity. There seems to me to be little to differentiate between the worlds of theatrical performance environments and the developing field of computer virtual environments, other than the medium of delivery. Both work in bounded environments using three dimensional spatial awareness, both use light to illuminate, to colour and to give orientation, both use spatial auditory awareness and both use human psychology.

I am not saying that the rules of theatrical design are unique; only that theatricality has brought together and integrated concepts and ideas from many fields. Consider it a unification point for virtual environment design. It is this ability to absorb and integrate ideas from other sometimes-contrary areas that has given it such strength. It may prove fruitful to revisit these other areas and construct a new unifying theory, (unifying both container design and contained object design) if theatricality proves weaker than I anticipate. Until then it would be a case of trying to reinvent the wheel.

3 Elements of theatricality for design consideration

The following are some of the main considerations for inclusion in the design stage of a virtual environment from a theatrical point of view. These are often not included or are viewed from a different approach. These are in addition to normal considerations such as file size, intention, content etc.

There seem to be two ways to structure these design elements. One is to use a departmental approach where standard theatre departments such as LX dept for lighting, SFX for sound, wardrobe, set design etc. are used with their associated individual design methodologies, but I think this is taking the metaphor too far. Instead I have chosen a series of titled fields. This seems to me to be a more flexible approach to something that is still very much under development.

From now on my use of the word audience is intended to cover, single or multiple agents, both human and computer; intelligent or otherwise.

3.1 Convention

A dramatic convention is something that can be used as a substitute for reality, but is experienced by an audience not as a symbol, but as the reality itself. For example, on stage a tree may be represented by a mere branch, the rest of the tree being inferred. This could be a useful tool in the design of virtual environments, were considerations of the bandwidth usage of an object are important. It is something, I think most computer users are culturally aware of and subconsciously use, to the extent that they often don't realise the huge leaps of credibility they are making. I have a hypothesis that this could be a part of inherited memory, natural to all cultures in so far as they are or have been through an influentially shamanic stage.

This also links into ideas of why symbolism and semiotics can be so powerful in, what is after all, an environment devoted to the manipulation of symbols, as suggested by Steve Dixon [15].

3.2 Focus

It is possible to direct the focus of attention to specific parts of a world using the same tricks as a stage designer. To use light, not just as a prerequisite of vision, but on another more subtle level. If an audience looks onto a new scene in a performance, their view tends to be drawn to the lighter areas and afterwards to darker areas. This could be used as a 'guide' mechanism to order the viewing of a virtual world. Small scintillation's of light will draw attention to an object and thus equally draw attention away from other objects.

There are other methods of focus such as colour response, additive and subtractive colour mixing, and dynamic light changes. These could be useful methods in a CSCW environment to create an awareness of other users by the depth of focus those users have in relation to individual view fields. They could also form the basis of a filter mechanism for changing dynamically the level and quantity of data representation viewed by an individual within a PIT environment [16].

3.3 Set Design

A Set design delineates a performance space necessary for the completion of a theatrical process and can both inform and frame the action. In the same way areas of a virtual environment could be delineated to allow for the completion of a virtual event. To render all the parts of a virtual world up to a true horizon could be a massive computational task and pointless if only a small section was required. So some form of boundary delineation is usually sensible if not actually vital. I think in many virtual worlds, this boundary delineation, though practical, only makes pretty and does not inform. This is not necessarily wrong, but seems a wasted opportunity. For example in a performance environment, a world beyond and integral with the viewed area is normally suggested. The degree to which an audience can visually and mentally associate with this world is carefully controlled via the textural, visual, and theatrical elements that are placed in front of them. In other words the stage set. Within a virtual environment degrees of fogging can limit view distance and thus the amount of the total environment on view. The density of the fog could delineate a boundary area (of variable depth). Inside which an awareness of, but no clear vision of the objects it contained would be allowed. The depth of this area could either be fixed or dynamic. The object content of this area, as opposed to object clarity, could be filtered (as in control of focus) by the use of additive and subtractive colour mixing. Thus the boundary layer could both frame and inform.

3.4 Believability

As I discussed earlier, believability, is a missing element in many virtual worlds and should be considered as a design field. If a virtual environment can be made to be believable then it arguably doesn't need to be realistic and this has implications for the amount of bandwidth used. Less bandwidth would be needed if an object could be represented believably with 80 polygons where previously it was represented using 200 polygons. I also think that a believable world could extrapolate to a world that is comfortable for people to work in. This comfort would lead to ease in assimilation of the working methods of that world. It could be a factor in helping make real world skill sets transferable to virtual worlds and reduce learning curves. Though logical this is however still at present speculation, and needs developing, testing and validating.

3.5 Kinaesthetics

This is the appreciation of movement within space. It is a main consideration of dance and is of vital importance at the blocking stage of theatrical rehearsals. Kinaesthetics can effect focus and can make movements believable by overlaying a chosen aesthetic. The eye picks up on movement within a still field, and this can be used for direct representation of entity values and for present's awareness. A PIT environment object needing to occupy a distant co-ordinate to satisfy its representational function could also be give an oscillatory movement to increase its visibility in comparison to closer objects. Various speeds and axis of spin could be used as representations of other relevant data fields as could the size of orbit. Kinaesthetics could be used to represent not only a change from state A, to state B, but believably reflect the process of the change itself.

3.6 Emotion Transfer

There have been experiments done with trained actors to see what it is that causes transfer of emotion. Experiments such as those carried out by Ekman and

Birdwhistell. [17] They looked into how, a type of gesture called illustrators could be used to reveal information about the speaker's attitudes and emotions. None of these to my mind have been conclusive but they do strongly suggest that the perception of emotion does not need to always be derived from an emotional event. Western actors are often taught to look into their emotional past to create, for example, an expression of sadness. This derives from the teaching of Stanislavski. [18] This is ingrained to the extent that often acting that does not contain felt emotion is derided as 'poor'. Yet performance without the aid of emotion is the basis of Kathakali theatre in India [19]. A performer in this form would be derided if he 'lost control' and allowed emotion into his performance. Yet both seek to control the emotional empathy of an audience. The point of this is that an audience can perceive emotion from a non-emotional event. It should therefore be possible to create a sense of emotion within a virtual environment, without resorting to more bandwidth heavy methods such as video links, facial and postural simulators and all their associated hardware. The fixed expressional face code and postural code of Kathakali theatre applied to avatar representations of collaborative workers in virtual environments could form a model for future work.

3.7 Patterns of sensory phenomena

Brenda Laurel Describes patterns of sensory phenomena from the Aristotelian stand that "they are a source of pleasure to humans". She echo's Aristotle's view that humans seek patterns and structures within all sensory experience and hold those patterns dear. I support this and thus say that it should be possible for certain pre-ordering pattern perceptions to be triggered within a virtual environment. This could be used to complete patterns of visualisation, emotion and possibility using only partial descriptors rather than bandwidth heavy complete descriptors. A simple example is a gradual increase in lighting level and colour spectrum shift, giving a feeling of sunrise and all its associated attributes. Thus vocabularies of sensory phenomenon, culturally coded in the same shamanic way as theatrical convention, could be triggered without the need for all the constituent parts to be present.

4 Observations

At this point of development conclusions may be misleading as they could lead to a false sense of completion; rather I would like to sum up with two comments.

This work describes a possible starting point for the consideration of the design of computer supported virtual environments. It has enough validity to make it worthwhile to develop further and to look at its foundation in greater detail.

Its aim is to formulate an approach that

- is repeatable.
- has a design consistency to allow familiarity of usage in many different types of worlds and on different platforms.

- guides but does not inhibit creativity and originality.
- gives a system for comparative benchmarks for considering other worlds.

References

1. Laurel B. Computers as theatre, Addison-Wesley, Massachusetts, 1996
2. Jacabus L A. The Bedford introduction to drama, Bedford, New York, 1989
3. Aristotle. Poetics, Penguin, London, 1996
4. CSCW. Computer supported collaborative workspace
5. CALVIN. Collaborative Architecture via Immersive Navigation, http://evlweb.eecs.uic.edu/spiff/calvin/ieeecga/index.html
6. Ninth edition of the Concise Oxford Dictionary.
7. DIVE. Distributed Interactive Virtual Environment, http://www.sics.se/dive/dive.html
8. Blaxxun World. http://www.blaxxun.com/vrml/home/ccpro2.html
9. Viscape. http://www.myweb.de/phantasus/aptsec.htm
10. MUD, Multi User Domain
11. See [6]
12. Worldsaway, http://www.worldsaway.com/home.shtml
13. Dr Harrop P. Head of Dance, Drama and Theatre studies, University College Chester, UK.
14. Cardeña E and Beard J, Truthful Trickery: Shamanism, Acting and Reality. Performance Practice, 1996; 3:31-45
15. Dixon S. Digital Performance, Unpublished Talk, University College Chester, 1998.
16. Populated Information Terrain's, http://www.crg.computer-science.nottingham.ac.uk/research/applications/pits/
17. Lynn S, Messing. The Use of Bimodal Communication by Hearing Female Signers, PhD Thesis, University of Delaware, Newark, 1993, chapter 4
18. Stanislavski C. My Life in Art, Translator Robbins J Jeyre, Methuen, London, 1980
19. Barba E. A dictionary of theatre anthropology the secret art of the performer, Routlege, London, 1991

Visual Representation and Taxonomy

Hugh Clapin
School of Philosophy
The University of Sydney
Sydney, Australia

Abstract

How ought we classify visual representation? Is there any reason to suppose that information made available through the eyes is represented in a different kind of way to information made available to the ears, or to touch? In this paper I will explore whether, for the purposes of cognitive science, a useful representational taxonomy will give a special place to visual representation. In particular, I argue that pictures are not a good exemplar of the 'iconic' genus of representation.

1 Introduction

How ought we classify visual representation? I will treat this question as a special case of the more general problem of classifying representation in the cognitive sciences.

Contemporary study of the mind and brain is strongly representational in two ways. First, the domain of explanation – mental phenomena – is widely held to be representational. Secondly, cognitive explanation of mental phenomena typically invoke representations of various types. Thus a computational explanation of learning makes appeal to representations of various sorts – hypotheses to be tested, perceptual data to test the hypotheses and so on.

Thus the cognitive sciences are in sore need of a clear understanding of what representations are, and how they are to be classified.

I take the term 'visual representation' to refer to those representations in the world which we access via our sense of sight, for example pictures, maps, sculptures, film and video images and so on.

It is not obvious that visual representation is a special category. Is there any reason to suppose that information made available through the eyes is represented in a different kind of way to information made available to the ears, or to touch?

2 Canonical Genera

Following John Haugeland in his paper 'Representational Genera' [1], let's say that the received view of representational taxonomy is that there are three genera of representation, and they are defined in terms of the relation which holds between representational vehicle and content. Thus 'logical' representational schemes such as languages and formal symbol systems have compositional semantics – there are clear rules which define the meaning of a complex representation in terms of the meaning of the atomic constituents of that complex representation. 'Iconic' schemes such as scale models and pictures are isomorphic to their contents – the representational vehicle shares structure with the content. 'Distributed' schemes such as holograms and connectionist weight vectors superpose many contents in one vehicle. We will not consider distributed representation in detail here.

It is clear that one distinctive feature of many logical schemes is a fairly complex sort of compositional semantics, like that found in natural languages, rather than the simple compositionality of concatenation found in pictures. For example, a scheme which can distinguish between conjunction and disjunction shows significant complexity in its compositional semantics. The ability to represent negation and complex, abstract combinations of atomic contents is a source of the significant utility of some logical representational schemes. Similarly predication is another compositional form which adds depth and complexity to a representational system.

Necessary for this sophisticated sort of compositionality, it would seem, is the ability to group vehicles according to well-defined types. This is because sophisticated compositionality depends on general rules of composition, and such general rules need a well-defined domain to operate over. And type-identification itself seems to require that the vehicles be discrete (as contrasted with the continuous nature of some iconic vehicles, for example scale models).

Considering the very loose constraint on the range of possible vehicles for logical schemes, and that they can represent pretty much anything, the only thing that can be said, in general, about the relation between vehicles and contents is that it is *arbitrary*.[1] Of course, in a logical scheme with compositional semantics, the relation between complex vehicles and their contents won't be arbitrary because the content of the vehicle will relate in fixed ways to the contents of its component parts.

So a refinement to the canonical account is the idea that the representing relation of logical schemes of representation be arbitrary for *atomic* vehicles. *Sophisticated* compositionality might however be a sufficient condition on a scheme's being logical.

---

[1] Colin McGinn [2] p. 178 makes a similar claim.

Iconic representations represent relations among different properties. So, if the velocity of a car is represented by the height of a rectangle, and the time spent travelling at that velocity by the length of that same rectangle, then the distance travelled by the car in that time will be represented by the area of the rectangle. If the representation of velocity changes, the area *automatically* changes; it does not need to be recalculated because the *relational structures* have been preserved in the representation. (See Figure 1.)

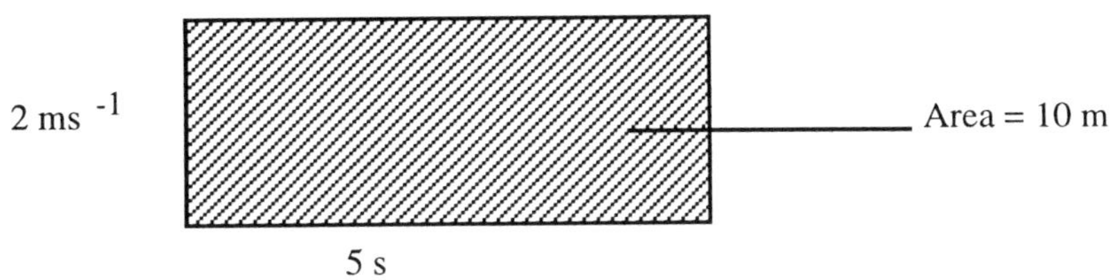

Figure 1

Canonically, isomorphism is the defining relation of iconic schemes. The key notion is that iconic representation obtains when there is a reproduction of structure. Thus a bust of Immanuel Kant represents Kant's head and neck because they share structural features. Mathematically, structure is understood as a set of elements and a set of relations over those elements. So in Figure 1, there is a 1-1 mapping from possible car velocities to possible heights of the rectangle, from possible durations to possible widths, and from possible areas to possible distances.[2] These mappings are trivial because each domain is the real numbers. Critically, there is also a mapping from the relation between time, velocity and distance in the car to the relation between the height, width and area of the rectangle. So a structure in the square is the same as one in the body moving with uniform velocity. Thus the representational relation – the relation between the representational vehicle and the content – is that of identity. The structure of the content is reproduced in the representation.

John Haugeland opposes this canonical account of representational genera by considering the intuitive distinction between translation from one representational scheme to another on the one hand and 'mere recording' on the other. Haugeland defines translation as an act of re-representing which requires understanding of the content translated. Any computational act of re-representation, for example scanning images or digitising electronic signals is mere 'witless' recording in

---

[2] I say 'roughly' because there are a number of idealisations going on here. The rectangle may not be of indefinite size because we don't the have the resources to draw very big rectangles. Note also that we are assuming that the car in question has uniform velocity throughout the associated time period.

Haugeland's terms.[3] Thus describing a photograph in English is a *translation* from an iconic scheme to a logical scheme, whereas digitising a photograph with a scanner is a mere *recording* of an iconic scheme in a logical scheme. Haugeland appears to assume that translation is difficult because it requires a change in essential features of the representational schemes in question. Making use of this stipulation, Haugeland says that an act of re-representation which changes the representational scheme from one genus to another must be an act of translation, rather than a mechanical and simple act of recording.

Haugeland's argument, then, is this: Intuitively, changing a representation from one genus to another requires an act of translation, and could not be done mechanically (i.e. by mere recording). I think the basic intuition here is that to move between genera you need to 'get at' the content directly – simply messing about with the vehicles can't be enough. But, observes Haugeland, you *can* change the representational relation by mere recording (for example by digitising a photograph). Thus changing the representational relation *can't* entail changing the representational genus (because changing genus can't be done by mere recording), hence the representational relation can't be that which identifies representational genus.

I think Haugeland is wrong here. He is right to suggest that digitising a photograph is merely recording, and not an act of translation. Haugeland is also right to say that recording in this instance (and in many others) changes the representational relation. But the change in relation is carried out by applying a new relation which doesn't supersede the old relation. Recording operates on *vehicles*, not on the original content (indeed, this is another way of distinguishing it from translation), and the resultant vehicle represents by virtue now of *two* representational relations: *viz*, the reproduction relation used to create the photograph, and the (particular) arbitrary relation used to create the digitised version of the photograph. So if the photograph relies on relation R_1, and the digitising process relies on R_2, then the digitised picture is related to the original content via the *composition* of R_1 and R_2. Thus reversing the digitising process to recover the content – reading the representation, if you like – requires inverting both R_1 and R_2.[4]

This means that we can maintain the claim that it is the representational relation that determines representational genera, but we need to be more careful about how we specify the representational scheme under consideration. The digitised version of a photograph is a purely logical representation with respect to the photograph,

---

[3] Unless it was as good as a competent human translator, and then I suppose Haugeland would be forced to say that the computer had understanding.

[4] More correctly, it would require a function which is equivalent to the inverse of the composition of R_1 and R_2.

but a hybrid, or composition, of logical and iconic representation with respect to the content of the photograph.

Put another way, in this example there is a primacy to the pictorial nature of the representation which Haugeland's discussion fails to recognise. One way to recognise this primacy is to consider how the representations can be manipulated. Digitising a picture might be useful way of storing the picture, but it is not useful if one wants to *look at* the picture. While this picture has been recorded into a logical representational scheme, it cannot be *viewed* unless it is decoded. The picture itself is a representation, and the digitised version is a representation of a representation.

Haugeland [1] claims that 'the image is not translated or transformed into a logical representation, but only recorded in a logical medium' (p. 68). This misses the point that the digitised image is *both* a logical representation (of a picture) and an iconic representation (of a man). The original representing relation is in some sense still there in the recorded representation. Thus even though recording changes representational genus, nonetheless representational relation could still define genus. Recording doesn't 'undo' the original representation relation, and so while recording does involve a change to the representational genus, it is an additive change. Such acts of re-representation don't require the original representation to be read or understood.

So the canonical account stands. Logical schemes are characterised by the arbitrary nature of the relation between atomic vehicles and content, and they must allow the possibility of compositional semantics. The atomic vehicles of logical schemes can be anything at all that admits of type-identification.

Iconic representational schemes, on the other hand, are distinguished by the *reproduction* of some aspect of the structure of the content of the representation and (aspects of) the structure of the representational vehicle. Therefore identity is the relation which defines iconic schemes. Hence whatever feature of the content is reproduced in the representation constrains the vehicles of iconic schemes. I think this view also suggests that the content of iconic schemes is most obviously the structure being reproduced in the representation, and thus we can say, with the canonical account, that iconic contents are relational.

3 Visual Representation

Where does visual representation fit in to this taxonomy? Let's consider some examples of what might be called 'visual' representations. The primary example is the picture: a two-dimensional rendering of a three-dimensional object - portraits, photographs, etchings, drawings and so on all fit this description. Next we have diagrams. A 'wall-planner' calendar, for example, is a diagrammatic representation of time. An electronic circuit diagram is also a visual representation of the way the circuit is connected. A third kind of diagram is that seen in Figure 1: use of what we might call Galilean geometrical representation. Another kind of visual representation is the hologram. Lastly written language might be thought to be a form of visual representation. (This list is not exhaustive.)

We've seen that one useful way to categorise representation is in terms of the relation that holds between the representational vehicle and its content. On this taxonomy, pictures, and diagrams are members of the same iconic genus as scale models; while sentences – whether spoken or written – are of a kind with formal symbol systems. Holograms are distributed representations like weight-vector representations in connectionist networks. In terms of the basic features of representation (vehicle, content and relation between vehicle and content) visual representations *per se* don't form a distinct kind: photographs are in essence the same kind of representation as the grooves in an LP record, while linguistic tokens can be found in visual, aural and tactile media. Thus visual representations as a class cross-cut the canonical representational taxonomy of logical, iconic and distributed representation.

However further consideration of visual representations is warranted. Consider a picture of Kant. If it is to be an iconic representation, it must represent in virtue of sharing structure with Kant himself. But this two-dimensional pattern of ink shares very little structure with Kant – arguably none of significance. However it is a likeness of him. I take it the likeness arises from the fact that this pattern of ink gives rise to a pattern of light on our retinas which does share significant structural features with the retinal pattern that the man himself would give rise to under particular viewing conditions. Compare this to a sculpture. A sculpture of Kant – say a bust – would also give rise to retinal patterns that share structure with those produced by Kant himself. But crucially, the bust also shares structural features independent of any particular kind of observer. The bust represents Kant because it has the same shape as Kant's head. So pictures don't fit the iconic genus in a straightforward manner. Picture P represents content C not because P shares structure with C, but because effects of P under certain conditions share structure with effects of C under different conditions. Pictures are only derivatively iconic representations, and are not good exemplars of the genus.

In any case, there must be more to iconic representation than sharing structure. Any given representation shares structure, to varying degrees, with many different objects. Thus Kant's bust shares structure with many human heads, although it should share the most structure with Kant himself. But even a poor bust of Kant, which in fact is structurally more similar to me rather than Kant, is nonetheless a representation of Kant. The intentions of the maker and the user of the representation are critical here. When we move inside the head, however, we can't rely on this distinction. Cognitive science requires a notion of representation whereby representations represent independently of anybody's intentions – because it is people's intentions that have to be explained in terms of these inner representations. Robert Cummins' answer here is to lean on the notion of a 'target' [3]. A cognitive system narrows down the relevant content of a given representation by applying it to a target. So just as in computer systems where variables get assigned values, when you apply a representation to a target you get a specific content. An ordinary fuel gauge in a car, or a thermometer, are good examples. To represent that the fuel tank is half full, you might apply a vehicle which is isomorphic to how much fuel is in the tank to a target whose content is the amount of fuel – that is, the function of this particular target is to represent how much fuel there is. In the car, the marks on the fuel gauge fix the target, while the needle is the representational vehicle.

In general, then, the target fixes an intended content, and the representation's accuracy is measured according to how similar it is to the relevant features of the target. So the bust is a good representation of the shape of Kant's head if it shares the same shape. Similarly the engraving of Kant is a representation of how Kant looked. Thinking now of Galilean diagrams, the rectangle in Figure 1 could be a representation of any multiplicative relation - we need to set its target as the velocity/time/distance relation of a particular car to fix its representational content.

So it seems all iconic representations are representations relative to a given target. Sometimes that target is determined by an agent (as is the case with extra-mental representations). This applies equally to pictures, however pictures depend on a second dimension of relativity, discussed above.

Diagrams like Figure 1, however do not differ from scale models in their basic representational character. We said that part of what made it an iconic representation was that the structural relationships in the rectangle track certain relationships in the vehicle (the area of the rectangle automatically tracks the distance travelled by the vehicle). But of course a pattern of ink on a page does no such thing – only with human intervention, or sophisticated additional apparatus, could it do so.

A scale model aeroplane or car in a wind tunnel is a better – more *adequate* – iconic representation than is a Galilean diagram of the relation between wind velocity and stress. The aerodynamic properties of the model aeroplane will track the aerodynamic properties of the real aeroplane without additional apparatus. Degree of adequacy, I suggest, should be measured by the amount of structure shared (or intended to be shared) between the representation and its target. More specifically, we can compare the number of dimensions in the structure, and the range occupied in each dimension. Thus in Figure 1 the only dimensions modelled are velocity, time and distance; and only one point in the state-space is represented by the diagram. A dynamic diagram might represent the same dimensions, but over a range of values on each dimension. Scale models are richer representations again because more dimensions are modelled.

Given this measure of adequacy, let's consider the examples of iconic visual representation we began with. Diagrams are truly iconic representations, but of a less adequate sort than scale models. Pictures and photographs are only derivatively iconic representations because it is their effects under certain circumstances that explain their representational status, not their direct relations with their contents.

Lastly, let's consider holograms. I said earlier that holograms are clearly distributed, rather than iconic, representations. But the visual effect of holograms strongly suggests that they share much in common with pictures. Like a picture, under the right conditions a holographic plate gives rise to a certain effect which shares structure with the effect of its content under certain conditions. This is no different to a picture. We are inclined to classify it as a distributed representation because the manner in which the visual information is stored is superpositional, but the effect is surely a visual representation.

In summary, attention to visual representation assists the general taxonomic project. Pictures are often thought to be paradigm iconic representations – as indicated by the term 'iconic'. This discussion suggests that on the contrary they are poor exemplars of iconic representation.

References

1. Haugeland, J. Representational Genera. In: W. Ramsey, S. P. Stich and D. E. Rumelhart. (eds) Philosophy and Connectionist Theory. Lawrence Erlbaum Associates, Hillsdale, New Jersey, 1991

2. McGinn, C. Mental Content. Blackwell, Oxford, 1989

3. Cummins, R. Representations, Targets and Attitudes. Cambridge, Massachusetts: MIT Press, 1996.

4. Millikan. Language, Thought, and Other Biological Categories. The MIT Press, Cambridge, Massachusetts, 1984

5. Cummins, R. Meaning and Mental Representation. The MIT Press, Cambridge, Massachusetts, 1989

6. Goodman, N. Languages of Art. Hackett Publishing Company, Indianapolis, Indiana, 1976

7. Gregory, R. L. Eye and Brain. 3rd ed. McGraw-Hill, New York, 1978

8. van Gelder, T. Defining 'Distributed Representation'. Connection Science 1992 4: 175-191

9. van Gelder, T. What is the "D" in "PDP"? A Survey of the Concept of Distribution. In: W. Ramsey, S. P. Stich and D. E. Rumelhart. (eds) Philosophy and Connectionist Theory. Lawrence Erlbaum Associates, Hillsdale, New Jersey, 1991

Interpreting Wittgenstein's Graphics

Michael A.R. Biggs
University of Hertfordshire
Hatfield, England

Abstract

The purpose of this paper is to identify a function for some of the graphics which may be found in Wittgenstein's writings. Not all the graphics function in the same way, but so little has been written about them that an outline of the function of even a few would seem to make a useful contribution. I describe the graphics in relation to seven key [lexical] concepts taken from the co-text (criterion, symptom, calculation, proof, explanation, description, paradigm). By adopting a content-model for the interpretation of the graphics, and comparing them to the key lexical concepts it is concluded that graphics function normatively in that they establish the underlying grammatical structure of concepts such as proof.

1 Lexical Concepts

The concept of criteria developed gradually throughout Wittgenstein's middle and later periods. For the purposes of this paper I am concerned only to give *one* reading of the term. Criteria function normatively and are part of the grammatical rules of application for a term. These rules are part of our form of representation. Confusions between criteria and symptoms arise when the form of representation is applicable and supportive of one grammatical proposition, but not supportive of another which appears to have the same structure. For example, first-person assertions of sensations such as "I am in pain" are regarded by Wittgenstein as a symptom of pain for the utterer, because of the lack of criteria. The private language argument discusses why there can be no criteria in this case. On the other hand, third-person assertions such as "she is in pain" are made on the basis of observing pain behaviour, that are regarded as one of many criteria of her pain for us. Another criterion would be her avowal "I am in pain".

The first-person statement is an avowal with no means of sharing the accompanying sensation. We therefore have no way of ascertaining the sincerity of the utterer and thereby the truthfulness of the avowal. Furthermore, it would be nonsense to assert "I thought I was in pain but I was mistaken" because the person making the avowal does not have [Cartesian] privileged access to data which would ensure the consistent application of the term. The avowal cannot therefore be a criterion for the utterer of whether she has a pain. In the case of the third-person assertion, we take it as one criterion of pain that certain behaviour determines the conditions under which we can appropriately say "she is in pain". Manifest behaviour accompanied by first-person avowals are usually our main criteria of third-person pain. Thus there is an unexpected asymmetry between the expressions "I am in pain" and "she is in pain" [1] (§§246-265).

Furthermore, "verifiability" does not offer a simple substitute for the meaning of a proposition. Meaning is determined by the use of the proposition in a framework of application (§353). Thus the meaning of "sameness of number" is not determined by a single act of verifying (counting), but has several context-dependent criteria:

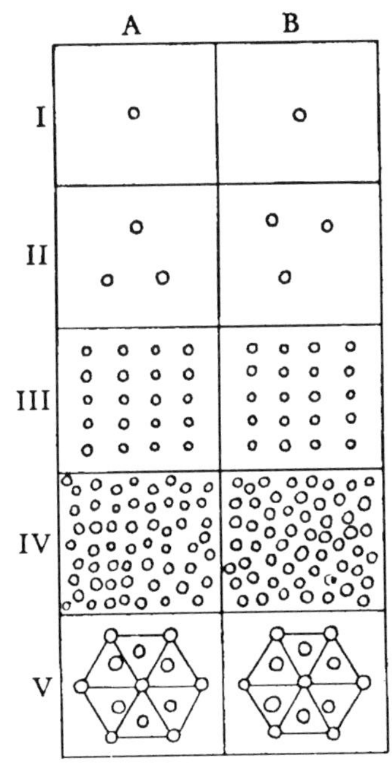

Figure 1

in I and II the number that one immediately recognises; in III the criterion of correlation; in IV we have to count both groups; in V we recognise the same pattern. [2] (p.354)

The term "calculation" is applied by Wittgenstein to non-mathematical concepts, but for the moment I will assume reference to a mathematical calculation. Calculation is a particular operation in which we draw correct inferences. Thus when we say 25x25=625 we calculate with numbers and when we say 25x25=605 we do not calculate [3] (VI §23). When we calculate we do not "discover" something. "A calculation is not an experiment" [1] (p.218). It is a criterion of calculation that we should accept the outcome as a correct inference. What we take as a correct inference cannot therefore be determined by calculation but by the nature of our numerical practice. This appears to leave our numerical practice open to considerable arbitrariness based on eccentricities of implementation. However, the coherence of our numerical system contributes to our notion of correct inference. Thus we can, and do, say (24x25)+(1x25)≡25x25.

Our use of conventions is not arbitrary but discretionary, because the fabric of our conventions is a closely woven one in which we subscribe to many conventions when we subscribe to one. However, at the outset it may be discretionary whether one convention or another is applied. What is discretionary is the sense in which one convention or form of representation may be exchanged for another while remaining useful. Utility is probably a matter of compatibility. The less exchange there is between systems the fewer are the constraints over the form of representation.

What Wittgenstein attacks is the feeling that our grammar is answerable to reality. 7+5 is an "alternative description" of 12 [4] (p.321). 7+5=12 flows from the meaning of these signs. In another system, 7+5 might equal 13 but then 12 and 13 would mean something different.

Correct inference is a criterion by which we test whether calculation has occurred. Likewise proof, being related to calculation with numbers or geometrical proof, is a certain kind of operation which needs some context of practice:

A rectangle can be made of two parallelograms and two triangles. Proof: [3] (I §50)

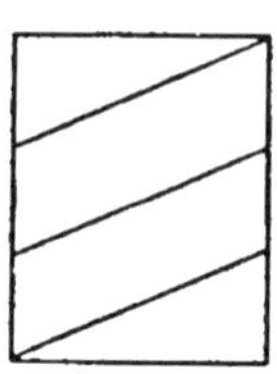

Figure 2

That we take something as a proof is a grammatical move in our game of calculating with numbers or in geometry. This brings us to our third pair of words: explanation and description.

Contrary to our naïve expectations, when we think we are explaining by means of the assertion of criteria, we are most commonly simply describing what constitutes our practice. We take a particular move in our language game as a proper application. Our naïve expectation of the difference between description and explanation is illustrated at the beginning of *Philosophical Investigations* by the Augustinian picture of language learning. Wittgenstein's target is not whether we do in fact learn language by this means, i.e. that we learn words which are names of objects defined by ostension and that operators are learned in the context of speaking and action. What is in question is that we commonly have a view that explaining how language is acquired could be constituted by an account of this kind. On the contrary, Wittgenstein asserts [1] (§30) that this simply describes our practice of responding to the question "how is language learned?" One move in our response-game is description by ostension. In the case of naming we take it as a criterion of correct learning that an appropriate action is performed by the learner in response to a gesture from the teacher. This is "having learned the meaning of a word".

2 Proposed Content-Model

So what part do graphics play in this social construct? In particular, given the considerable number of graphics, are they illustrations which reveal our common misconception of an explanation as a description, or a criterion as a symptom?

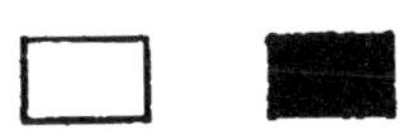

Figure 3

> the picture of a black and white patch serve us simultaneously as a paradigm of what we understand by "lighter" and "darker" and as a paradigm for "white" and "black". [3] (I §105)

In response I shall introduce a seventh term from the quotation above: paradigm. I shall use the term in the following way: that a paradigmatic word or graphic shall (a) have a certain quality so that when we compare it with something it is to that quality that we attend, and (b) that this word or graphic has a role as part of an accepted practice of general reference. Let me give an example: we might take the colour of the British pillar-box as a paradigm of "red".

The pillar-box is normally red, and so meets criterion (a) by virtue of its colour. It may be that in some place a pillar-box has been painted a different colour and so although standardised it must be accepted that the "redness" and not the "pillar-box form" is the quality to which we draw attention. Of course, Wittgenstein discusses at some length the object of reference in ostensive definition, i.e. whether we can draw attention to the colour and not to the form with any reliability [1] (§§28 & 29).

Criterion (b) requires that although the pillar-box has the colour red it does not become a paradigm of red until we use it in ostensive descriptions. We point to the pillar box and say "this is pillar box red". However, there may be atypical examples of pillar boxes that are not red. So we cannot say that "pillar box red" is defined by any pillar box. In fact there are colour samples which define British Standard Colours, amongst which is (perhaps) "pillar box red". It is reference to this sample rather than to a pillar box that defines the colour.

Samples have a particular role. They provide a referent for a definition, e.g. the standard metre is the length of the so-called "standard metre" in Paris. Thus if we ask whether something is one metre in length we can/should compare it with the sample in Paris. In such systems we must be confident that the canonical sample is invariable. More particularly, it becomes meaningless to ask in this case whether the canonical sample itself has a length of one metre.

We use a paradigm as an exemplar but not as a definition. This introduces a certain generality to the content-model that is a feature of concept like "red" but not of the concept "one metre in length". The philosophical, rather than commonplace, problem of generality finds expression in "the problem of the heap" and in everyday concepts such as "noticeably longer" [2] (appendix 8). The problem only becomes a philosophical problem when we seek specific boundaries to the transition from quantity ***a*** to quantity ***b***.

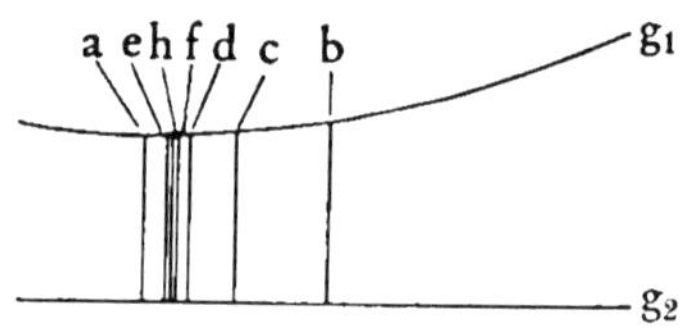

Figure 4

In *Remarks on the Foundations of Mathematics* Wittgenstein discusses a paradigm of counting and calculating up to five in the form of "bracket notation" [3] (I §67):

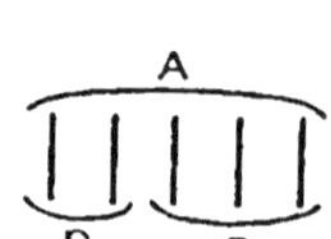

Figure 5

This shows what we mean by addition. If we have this content-model then we are able to correctly infer that 3+2=5. We can also represent the commutativity of arithmetical operations, e.g. 27+16=43, 43-16=27, etc., and other internal relations by showing the sum divided by a line which may be placed anywhere along our total number (the representation in ibid., III §11 is less clear than the corresponding entry in an unpublished manuscript MS 122 p.28r reproduced here):

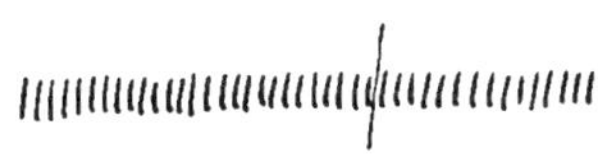

Figure 6

Commutation also applies to our understanding of spatial objects which fit together, e.g. (ibid., I §70):

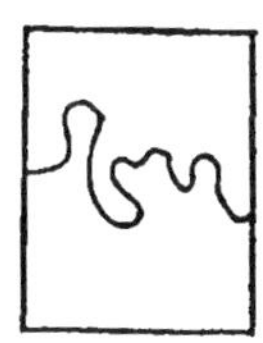

Figure 7

It is not the case that number-concepts are defined by graphics but that these examples show the fundamentally graphical/practical foundations of our mathematical grammar. They show what we mean by correct inference, which is in turn bound up with our concept of the continuity of physical objects.

> This is how our children learn sums; for one makes them put down three beans and then another three beans and then count what is there. If the result at one time were 5, at another 7 then the first thing we said would be that beans were no good for teaching sums. (ibid., I §37)

This comparison with practice is reinforced by Wittgenstein's thought-experiment of the tribe who calculate the price of a heap of wood by the area covered by the heap rather than the volume of wood (ibid., I §149). In other words they ignore the height. We would say they do not calculate consistently, but our concept of accuracy is bound up with our concept of three-dimensionality and value according to quantity.

However, we do not always apply such a framework of calculation to monetary value. For example, we often calculate salaries not on the basis of quantity of work done (e.g. wood stacked), but on the basis of hours consumed or the age or sex of the worker.

So how does this generalised content-model of a paradigm affect our interpretation of the graphics in relation to the text? Appropriately chosen paradigms give us the opportunity of seeing connections, of having perspicuous representations of our concepts. Seeing connections is fundamental [1] (§122). Given the generality of the paradigm: that it is a particularly apposite example but not itself a definiens, it allows us to see beyond the ostensive definition provided by the sample, to the broader way in which this might act normatively for further applications.

References

Graphics reprinted with permission of Wittgenstein's Trustees and Blackwell Publishers.

An earlier, longer version of this paper was published as 'Wittgenstein: graphics, normativity and paradigms' in: Krüger, W. and A. Pichler (eds) *Arbeiten zu Wittgenstein.* Skriftserie fra Wittgensteinarkivet ved Universitetet i Bergen, No.15, 8-22. Bergen, Norway: University of Bergen Press.

1. Wittgenstein, L. Philosophical Investigations. Basil Blackwell, Oxford, 1953

2. Wittgenstein, L. Philosophical Grammar. Basil Blackwell, Oxford, 1974

3. Wittgenstein, L. Remarks on the Foundations of Mathematics. 3rd edition. Basil Blackwell, Oxford, 1978

4. Baker, G. & P. Hacker. Wittgenstein: Rules, Grammar and Necessity. Basil Blackwell, Oxford, 1985

THEME 5

Visual Representations and Computational Processes

M.A. Beaumont, D. Jackson and M. Usher

P. Young and M. Munro

D.S. Neary and M.R. Woodward

C.N. Yap and M. Holcombe

A.G.P. Brown, F.P. Coenen and M.W. Knight

L. Pineda and G. Garza

B.E. Bürdeck, M. Eibl and J. Krause

D. Reid and C. Gittings

Visualising Complex Sequential and Parallel Programs

M A Beaumont, D Jackson & M Usher

Dept. of Computer Science, University of Liverpool,
Chadwick Building, Peach Street, Liverpool L69 7ZF
United Kingdom

Abstract

The authors have addressed two areas of programming that have proved problematical for visual language designers. The first concerns sequential code that does not adhere to the rules of structured programming, and therefore exhibits highly complex control flow; the second concerns parallel execution, where the multiple threads of control can again lead to visualisations that are difficult to comprehend and maintain. A number of techniques have been devised to overcome these problems, and prototype visual systems have been implemented.

1 Introduction

Extensive research into the topic of visual programming [1] has led to the generation of a whole host of languages aimed at a number of problem domains. It has been said before [2] that visual programming languages enjoy most success in domains that are reasonably limited and well-defined; truly general-purpose visual languages are few and far between (perhaps the best known being Prograph [3]). One of the reasons for this lies in the sheer variety and complexity of real world problems, and in the difficulty associated with scaling up visual languages to cope with them.

It must be admitted that most visual language designs avoid tackling the situation head-on. For example, many existing visual languages facilitate coding at the highest, most abstract level, but offer no solution for lower level implementation details. More often than not, the programmer must resort to conventional textual code for the bottom-level modules. For similar reasons, visual languages are often founded upon computational models that are inherently more amenable to visualisation: there are significantly more visual languages based on the purely functional data-flow model [4], for example, than there are based on control-flow. Even when other models are adopted, however, it is noticeable that the language designers often enforce limitations that prevent the creation of overly complex code.

It might be suggested, therefore, that the true test of visual programming is in its ability to deal with naturally complex problem scenarios. In this paper, we describe how we have been addressing two aspects of visual program complexity. The first concerns the representation of program control flow, for which visualisation is recognised as a notoriously difficult problem. Although a number of researchers have proposed graphical systems and environments that can accommodate structured control flow, these techniques cope less well with highly unstructured code. In Section 2, we present our approach to solving this.

A second area of difficulty for visual language design is that of concurrency. It has already been mentioned that many visual languages are based on the data-flow model. Since this is a functional model, parallelism is implicit, and so attempts to incorporate explicit parallel programming operations into such languages often result in constructs that are both highly artificial and cumbersome. An alternative is to employ a computational model that is more suited to explicit concurrent programming, yet is still appropriate for visualisation. In Section 3 we describe how we have used Petri nets as the basis for a concurrent, high-level visual language. Finally, in Section 4, we draw some conclusions and present ideas for further work.

2 Sequential Programs

Nowhere is the abandonment of structured control constructs more apparent than in assembly language and other forms of low-level code. Indeed, one of the primary motivations for programming at such levels is the gain in speed that can only be achieved at the expense of sacrificing good structure. In the following discussion, this section will therefore use assembly language as a means for illustrating the problems associated with visualising poorly structured code, but it should be made clear from the outset that most of what is said here applies equally well to poorly structured code at higher levels of abstraction.

2.1 Deficiencies of Existing Approaches

The primary reason why most existing graphical representations are unable to represent unstructured code is the one to many relationship between jump destinations and jump sources. Nassi-Schneiderman charts and other similar techniques which work so well for highly structured code provide no solution for less well-structured programs. Flowcharts are one of the few diagrammatic techniques that can incorporate the 'one to many' relationship since there is no limit to the number of arrows that can point to a single entity. It follows, therefore, that a simple control flow graph would be one solution to our problem. Figure 1 presents a simple 68000 program that is represented in Figure 2 by a control flow graph. The graph shows the program at a similar level of abstraction to the text; the control flow lines, however, add a sense of context to each node in the graph.

Program Listing			Node	Basic Block
start	move	#start,SP	1	1
	clr.l	D0	2	
	move	#$D,-(SP)	3	
	move	#$A,-(SP)	4	
loop	btst	#0,trmstat	5	2
	beq	loop	6	
	move.b	trmdata,D0	7	3
	cmp	#$D,D0	8	
	beq	out	9	
	move	D0,-(SP)	10	4
	bra	loop	11	
out	btst	#1,trmstat	12	5
	beq	out	13	
	move	(SP)+,D0	14	6
	move.b	D0,trmdata	15	
	cmp	#start,sp	16	
	bne	out	17	
	bra	start	18	7

Figure 1. A Simple 68000 Program

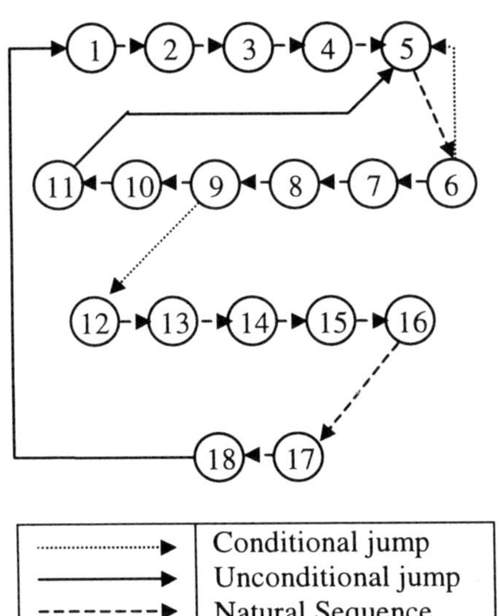

Figure 2. A Simple Control Flow Graph

Within such a graph, the fact that the possible predecessors and successors of each instruction are made visually explicit may be regarded as an advantage for small programs like that of Figure 1. For anything much larger, however, this may be a hindrance: making visible the normally implicit 'down-the-page' sequencing of an assembly language program could be regarded as simply introducing unnecessary clutter. Moreover, the existence of a node for every instruction leads to graphs of horrendous complexity for any substantial programs.

What is needed for sensible visualisation, therefore, is a definition of a graph node which is at a higher level of abstraction, i.e. it encapsulates more than a single program instruction. One possibility is the 'basic block,' defined as a sequence of code through which there can be only one path, and by which control must enter at the start and leave at the end. The rightmost column of Figure 1 shows the basic block structure of the example program. Whilst using this structure greatly simplifies the appearance of the control flow graph, the arcs associated with implicit sequencing are still present. What is worse, however, is that the breakdown of code generated by the approach forms instruction groupings with little coherent semantic meaning, i.e. it is generally quite difficult to describe the program activity associated with a given node. Such a representation produces graphs that are difficult both to document and to comprehend.

2.2 LCSAJ Span Graphs

An *LCSAJ* (Linear Code Sequence And Jump) is a linear sequence of executable code commencing either at the start of the program or at a point to which control flow may jump. It is terminated by either a specific control flow jump or by the end of the program. The linear code sequence of an LCSAJ, therefore, consists of one or more consecutive basic blocks. LCSAJs are characterised by three numbers (A,B,C) where A is the start line, B is the end line and C is the target line for the terminating jump [5].

An *LCSAJ span* [6] is defined as being a minimal partition of the code such that the linear code sequence of any LCSAJ is wholly contained within the span. A consequence of this is that the first line in an LCSAJ span is either the start of the program or a line that cannot be reached by its predecessor. Similarly, the last line in an LCSAJ span is either the end of the program, or a line from which control cannot pass to the next line.

Figure 3 shows our sample program broken into its LCSAJ spans; Figure 4 shows the program represented as a graph. Control can iterate in the first span or pass to the second. Once control has entered the second span it will iterate until control is passed back to the first span.

The representation is now at a level of abstraction that appears to scale up well. Another factor that aids scaling is that the natural flow lines of the linear sequence are no longer necessary. By definition an LCSAJ span must end with an unconditional jump. As control has to progress to the destination of an unconditional jump, natural control flow lines are not necessary.

Program Listing			LCSAJ Spans
start	move	#start,SP	
	clr.l	D0	
	move	#$D,-(SP)	
	move	#$A,-(SP)	
loop	btst	#0,trmstat	1
	beq	loop	
	move.b	trmdata,D0	
	cmp	#$D,D0	
	beq	out	
	move	D0,-(SP)	
	bra	loop	
out	btst	#1,trmstat	
	beq	out	
	move	(SP)+,D0	
	move.b	D0,trmdata	2
	cmp	#start,sp	
	bne	out	
	bra	start	

Figure 3. LCSAJ Spans

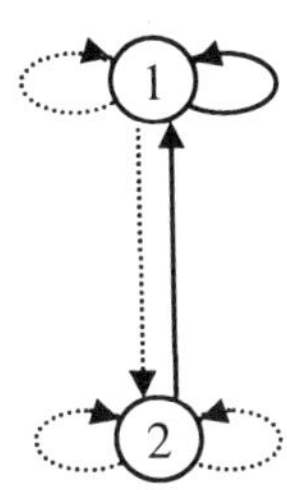

Figure 4. An LCSAJ Span Graph

Perhaps the biggest advantage of the LCSAJ-based approach to visualisation is that the resultant graphs exhibit extremely good cohesive qualities, in that their nodes represent instruction sequences with well-defined and self-contained functionality.

This use of LCSAJs, together with a number of other techniques that have also been devised to assist in visualising complex control flow, have been incorporated into a prototype visualisation system; further details are available elsewhere [7].

3 Parallel Programs

Previous work on Petri nets has concentrated on their use for specification or simulation. However, a program representation must contain a complete definition of system behaviour. As our language is intended for general-purpose programming, we have integrated an object-oriented data model into the design.

Our language [8,9,10] retains the simplicity of the Petri net model. Places represent possible states or conditions, and the presence of a token in a place indicates that state or condition. Typically, a token in a specific place will represent the availability and/or readiness of a piece of data or a resource to those transitions for which the place is an input, although there is no requirement that tokens and data objects are related one-to-one.

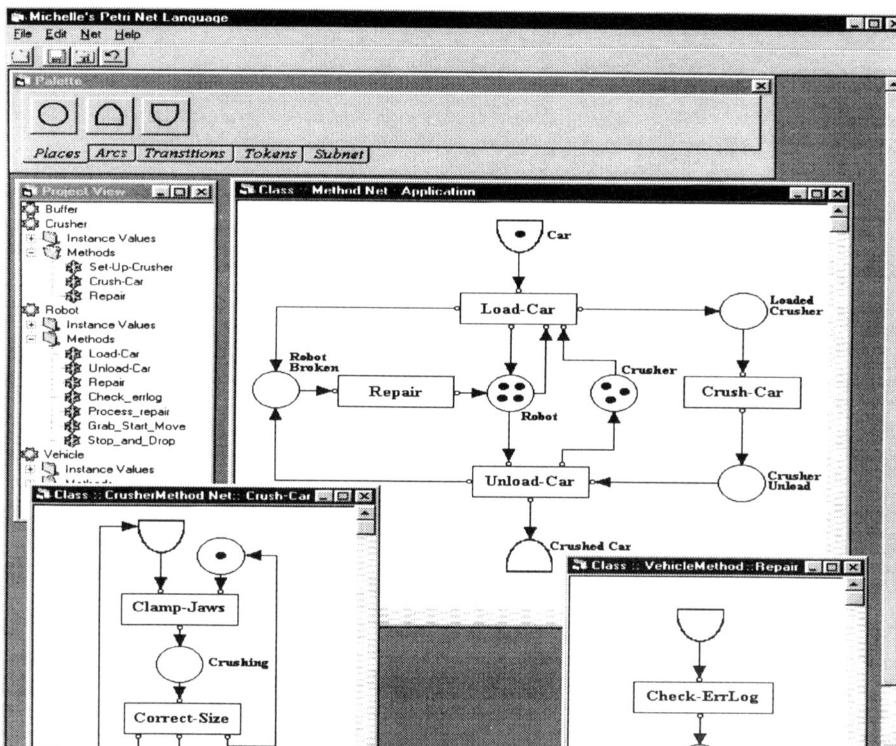

Figure 5. Screen shot of programming environment showing car-crusher example program

Transitions represent actions resulting in a change of program state, as in the basic Petri net model. In our language, these actions are either sub-nets or sections of textual program code which are executed when the transition fires. The data referred to by the tokens in the input places is consumed or manipulated, and tokens are placed into the output places of the transition according to the changes in data or program state effected by the execution of the transition.

The language achieves concurrent program execution in that more than one transition may be executing at once. Not only is this concurrency apparent from the program representation, but the synchronisation is also expressed, without extension of the notation as is required in concurrent dataflow languages. Places and tokens are used to ensure that concurrent threads of execution are blocked until the required data or resources are available. Places and tokens may also be used specifically for the purpose of synchronisation or sequencing, without representing any data or resource.

Figure 5 shows a screen view from our prototype implementation. The largest sub-window shows a simple program for controlling a car-crushing plant. The places are represented by circles, as in the basic Petri net model. Transitions are represented by rectangles rather than bars, to provide space for a name identifying the sub-net or code primitive to be executed. Because program segments have specific input and output requirements, the rectangles are supplemented with circular ports which show the connections available. Places need not be named, but can be annotated to indicate their meaning within the program. Tokens are included in a program graph to indicate the initial marking of a net; in the example, the plant has four robots and three crusher machines available, all of which are initially ready and in working condition.

This program example is highly concurrent and shows how this concurrency is naturally expressed using Petri nets. At any point in time there may be up to seven concurrently executing threads of control, corresponding to the four robots and the three crushers. Robots may be involved in Load-Car, Unload-Car or Repair actions. Crushers may be involved in Load-Car, Crush-Car or Unload-Car actions. As an example of synchronisation, the Load-Car and Unload-Car transitions cannot perform until both a robot and a crusher are ready; a robot may have to wait in an idle state until a crusher is ready to be loaded or unloaded. In a typical concurrent programming language this would involve the robot thread calling a system function which blocks until a semaphore is flagged; in our language, the synchronisation is much more naturally expressed.

3.1 Sub-nets and Hierarchical Abstraction

In common with many other visual programming languages, our language uses hierarchical abstraction both to allow re-use of program segments and to alleviate the problem of screen contention. A single transition within a higher-level net may correspond to a sub-net. A sub-net is a collection of actions which together perform a specific task, rather like a procedure or method. This integrates well with the view of a transition as an action. A single firing of a higher-level transition may invoke multiple concurrent actions within the sub-net, as within any other net.

Each sub-net has a set of entry and exit points. In the calling net these are the places connected as inputs and outputs respectively. In the sub-net implementation a set of exit and entry places correspond to these input and output places in the calling net. These places are distinguished by being a different shape and are annotated with a description of the incoming or outgoing data.

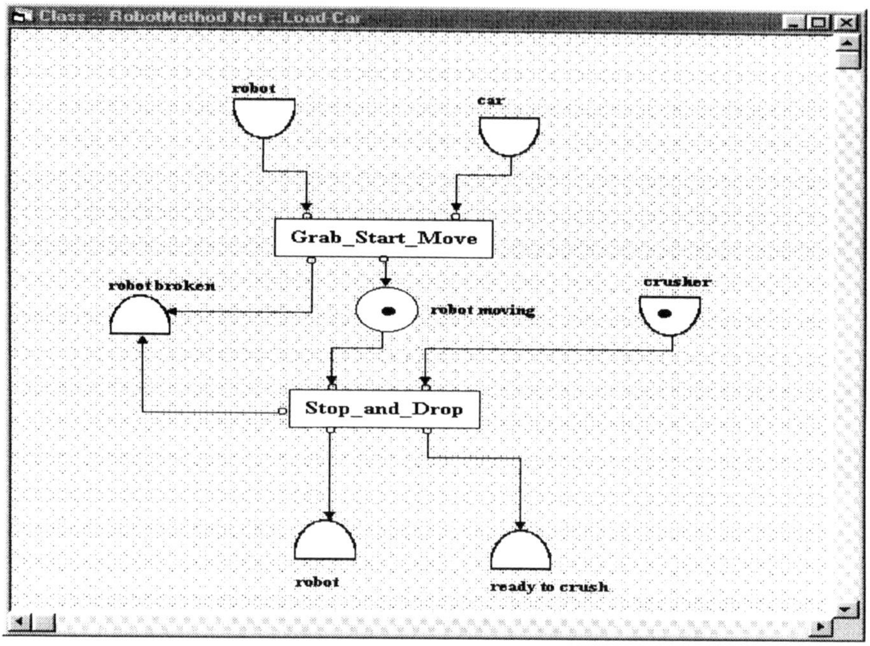

Figure 6. Example sub-net from the car crusher example

Figure 6 shows the sub-net corresponding to the Load-Car transition in the previous example. Input places are shown with flat tops, and output places are shown with flat bottoms. The same sub-net marking is shared by successive firings of the same transition at the same level of recursion, to preserve substitution semantics. However, a sub-net has a separate and independent token marking for each location it is deployed as a higher-level transition and for each level of recursion. This is to prevent independent calls from interfering with each other, which would make code re-use problematic

3.2 Object-Orientation

Using the visual environment, object classes may be defined. A class definition comprises a set of sub-nets which constitute the methods of that class. Method sub-nets may contain special 'shared' places denoted by double circles and labelled with a name. A shared place in one method sub-net and a shared place with the same name in another method sub-net of the same class are effectively the same place. Tokens produced in one net may be consumed within the other. It is helpful to imagine all the method sub-nets of a class combined by superimposing them and drawing the shared places as single places, thereby producing a single Petri net describing the behaviour of an object of the class.

A method is invoked when an object of an appropriate class is passed as a token to a transition which represents a method sub-net. Each object has a single marking that spans all the method sub-nets of its class, and persists for the lifetime of the object. This marking constitutes the object's state. Objects may therefore behave concurrently, because more than one of their methods may be firing at once, and the shared places provide not only a persistent state for the object but also a means of synchronising these concurrent method calls.

Classes are constructed using the project window shown to the left in Figure 5. Each class node has child nodes that represent the instance places and method nets of the class. A method is edited by double-clicking the method node to bring up an editor. An instance place can be dragged from the project view and dropped into the editor, producing a shared place.

The object-oriented approach also provides a convenient way of organising libraries. Classes may be written and distributed as single modules. A set of basic classes provide a variety of services necessary for general-purpose program construction, such as user interface classes. They also allow low-level facilities available through function calls from textual code fragments to be wrapped as objects and manipulated directly using the visual Petri net notation. It is the class library feature which gives the language much of its appeal for general purpose programming, where additional classes may be added to the library as needed (e.g. for communications, mathematics or graphics).

4 Conclusions

We have described a number of techniques aimed at assisting with the visualisation of complex program code. In the case of those devised for purely sequential code, evaluation has been performed on a large number of real-world programs of varying sizes. Results have been encouraging, in that not only have the program graphs been greatly simplified, but also the individual graph nodes exhibit a close correspondence to a natural partitioning of the program code into separate functions or modules. Moreover, the approach has also been applied with success to unstructured programs written in high-level languages. Our intentions are to proceed with the development and further evaluation of the prototype visualisation system, perhaps integrating additional techniques for visualisation of low-level operations [11].

For parallel code, the Petri-net based approach has led to the design and implementation of a visual programming language that has also been applied to several problem domains, and which has been found to possess a number of advantages in comparison with related approaches, including ease of program development, scalability and reduced complexity. Implementation and evaluation of the programming environment is on-going.

References

[1] Shu N.C. Visual Programming. Van Nostrand Reinhold Co., New York, USA, 1988

[2] Bell M.A. and Jackson D. Visual Author Languages for Computer-Aided Learning. Proc. IEEE International Workshop on Visual Languages (VL '92), Seattle, Washington, USA, September 1992, pp 258-260

[3] Cox P.T., Giles F.R. and Pietrzykowski T. PROGRAPH: A Step Towards Liberating Programming from Textual Conditioning. Proc. IEEE Workshop on Visual Languages, Rome, Italy, 1989, pp 150-156

[4] Hils D.D. Visual Languages and Computing Survey: Data Flow Visual Programming Languages. Journal of Visual Languages and Computing, 1992; 3:69-101

[5] Woodward M.R., Hennell M.A. and Hedley D. The Analysis of Control Flow Structure in Computer Programs. Proceedings of Liverpool University Conference on Combinatorial Programming(CP77). Ed. T. B. Boffey, Sept.1977, pp 190-202

[6] Woodward M.R. An Investigation into Program Paths and their Representation. in *Technique et Science Informatiques*, 1984; 3: 273-279

[7] Beaumont M.A. and Jackson D. Visualising Complex Control Flow. Proc. IEEE Int. Symposium on Visual Languages (VL'98), Halifax, Nova Scotia, Canada, Sept. 1998, pp 244-251

[8] Jackson D. and Usher M. Petri Nets as Visual Programs. Proc. IASTED/ISMM Int. Conf. Modelling and Simulation, Pittsburgh PA, April 1996, pp 339-342

[9] Usher M. and Jackson D. A Concurrent Visual Language Based on Petri Nets. Proc. IEEE Int. Symposium on Visual Languages (VL'98), Halifax, Nova Scotia, Canada, Sept. 1998, pp 72-73

[10] Usher M. and Jackson D. A Petri Net Based Visual Programming Language. To appear in Proc. IEEE Int. Conference on Systems, Man and Cybernetics (SMC'98), San Diego, California, USA, Oct. 1998

[11] Beaumont M.A. and Jackson D. Low Level Visual Programming. Proc. IEEE Int. Symposium on Visual Languages (VL'97), Capri, Italy, 1997, pp 410-417

3D Software Visualisation

Peter Young and Malcolm Munro
Visualisation Research Group, Department of Computer Science
University of Durham, UK.

Abstract

Visualisation is arguably one of the most profitable means of communicating information to a user. Software visualisation promises to provide useful techniques for supporting the program comprehension process. This research is investigating the application of 3D graphics and virtual reality technology to software visualisation. This paper identifies the seven key areas of 3D software visualisation which must be addressed. Also described are two prototype visualisation systems.

1 Introduction

Software maintainers are often confronted with very large and complex software systems, which can be completely new and unfamiliar to them. These maintainers will normally have some maintenance task to perform on the software though possibly little indication of where or how to start.

One problem expressed by software engineers is that when confronted by a large, unfamiliar mass of code, they have no notion of what components it consists of, or how it is structured. Only by searching through the source code files, directory structures and (often scant) documentation can any such information be obtained. Essentially, the maintainer needs an overview of the software structure yet requires detail on the specific area they are interested in. The latter can be found by inspecting the source code, but gaining an overview of a software system is a difficult problem, compounded by the sheer scale of modern software. This is an area in which software visualisation can be particularly profitable.

The application of 3D graphics and VR technology to software visualisation has the potential to aid the maintenance process and enhance a user's understanding of a software system; however, this potential has been left largely under-utilised [1]. One area in which visualisation can aid the maintenance process is by producing a picture of the software. By creating a physical (visual) object, which represents the software system, engineers can gain some initial insight into how it is structured and what components it consists of. The goal is to allow the engineers to make full use of their natural perceptual skills in investigating and understanding the software.

2 3D Software Visualisation

The seven key areas of 3D software visualisation have been identified and are listed below. These areas are general in scope but are of a fundamental importance. Careful consideration must be made as to how a new visualisation will address each of these points:

Representation. This is concerned with how the various components of the software system are shown graphically and also how information about those components can be encoded into that graphical representation. This is possibly the most important aspect of a 3D visualisation. The graphical representations used will determine the overall structure and feel of a visualisation. Design factors here will impact on all the other key areas listed below and vice versa.

Abstraction. One of the main goals of software visualisation is to abstract information away from the low-level detail, for example the source code, and present it in a more useful, higher level representation. Determining the level of abstraction to be used involves selecting what information will be presented and at what level of detail. The level of abstraction implemented will greatly affect how, and for what tasks the visualisation tool will be used.

Navigation. Software systems can be considered as extremely large and complex information systems. It follows that a visualisation of such a system will also tend to be large. It is important that users can easily navigate their way through the visualisations without becoming lost or disorientated. Features such as signposts, landmarks, paths and districts all aid in creating a legible environment [2, 3]. Navigation is a wide ranging term including the legibility of the environment, yet it is also concerned with tools which can aid navigation, such as maps, bookmarks or teleports. Such tools fall under the category of *interaction*.

Correlation. Visualisations only constitute another view of a software system or information store. They present additional information on the system, they do not replace the information already available. It is important to be able to link the visualisations in with other forms of information, for example the source code or documentation in the case of software systems. Providing a readily understandable correlation between the visualisation and the underlying information is vital if the visualisation is to be of any use. The actual changes made to software occur at the code level so relationships between the objects in the visualisation and actual points in the source code must be clearly visible or easily accessible.

Automation. An important point to consider when designing information visualisations is to what extent the creation of the visualisation is automated. It is necessary to determine how much of the visualisation is generated automatically and how much control the user has over the process or the result. The goal of software visualisation is to aid the understanding of software systems, often this understanding is best obtained by practical exercises. Allowing the user to 'build' the visualisations while investigating areas of the software system may prove more intellectually profitable than fully automating the process with the user then gaining their understanding from the completed visualisation. Other automation issues include layout algorithms/heuristics, legibility, resilience to change, etc.

Interaction. Creating a suitable visualisation is only one part of the problem. Complex visualisations will inevitably require some form of interaction with the user. This interaction may be no more complex than navigating the visualisation or, in contrast, performing some complex data mining using visual query techniques [4]. Consideration must be made as to how the user will interact with the visualisation and how they can manipulate its contents or build upon it with higher level semantic information, such as domain knowledge. The subject of interaction also covers any virtual tools which could be used in the environment for various purposes. For example, a map, a virtual display screen (for displaying documentation, source code listings, etc.), or editing tools for customising or annotating the visualisation.

Scaling. This concept borders on the subjects covered by *abstraction* and *navigation*. The size and complexity of software systems varies greatly from the simplest of programs to huge multimillion line systems. When creating a 3D software visualisation it is very important to consider how the visualisation will cope with these extremes, or alternatively to specifically target a visualisation with a certain size of system in mind. For example, visualisation of a small program would allow the display of more detail and "at-a-glance" information, whereas visualisation of a very large system would require less immediate detail (to avoid information overload) and more emphasis on navigation and querying techniques.

3 Visualisations and Representations

In order to create or evaluate a 3D visualisation a set of desirable properties, which are important for a visualisation to be effective, must first be derived. In order to derive these desirable properties it was found necessary to divide the notion of a visualisation into two distinct concepts. These have been termed **visualisations** and **representations**. The properties and goals of each vary sufficiently to warrant such a distinction. These two terms can be defined as follows:

> **Representation:** A graphical (and other media) depiction of a single component.
>
> **Visualisation:** A collection or configuration of individual representations (and other information) which comprise a higher level component.

Effectively, representations are the graphical symbols used in a visualisation to depict each of its sub-components. For example, in a typical graph such as a call-graph or control-flow graph, the graph itself is the visualisation while the nodes and arcs are the representations. These terms are, however, interchangeable and they depend greatly on the level of abstraction and amount of detail being presented. A graphical object can be both a representation within one context and a visualisation within another. For example, a node in a function call-graph could provide further information on the structure or qualities of the function that it represented. In the context of the software system (i.e. the graph) it is a representation, whereas in the context of the function (i.e. the node) it is a visualisation of further information on that function. In such cases we must consider carefully the structure and properties of the object both as a visualisation and as a representation and also in the transition between these distinctions.

3.1 Desirable properties of a representation

The following list highlights some important properties which must be considered when creating a representation or evaluating the merits and effectiveness of a given representation. Several of these properties are mutually exclusive, thus a good representation will achieve a suitable compromise between them. These properties are only summarised briefly here, but are described in further detail in [5].

Individuality: Representations of different components should appear differently and identical components, displayed in the same context, should appear identical.

Distinctive Appearance: Differing representations should appear as contrasting as possible. Representations should be easily recognisable as being either identical or dissimilar, even within a large visualisation. A careful balance between distinctive appearance, individuality and low visual complexity must be made.

High information content: Representations should provide as much information as possible about the underlying component. Unfortunately, as the information content is increased then inevitably the visual complexity will also increase.

Low visual complexity: Representations should not be visually over complicated. This is beneficial both to the performance of the visualisation system and also to the user's comprehension of the information encoded in the representation.

Scaleability of visual complexity and information content: Mechanisms would be desirable for reducing or increasing the amount of information presented or the visual complexity of representations as the context in which they are used varies.

Flexibility for integration into visualisations: This is a very important issue which affects both the representations and the visualisations in which they are used. Using up resources such as colour, shape, and particularly size to encode information in a representation reduces the scope for providing information within the visualisation. For example, imagine a representation which uses it's size to encode some information while the visualisation uses the positional depth of the representations to encode other information. Confusion will occur when differentiating between a component being near or big and far or small.

Suitability for automation: Another important aspect of any visualisation or representation is its ability to be automatically generated relatively easily.

3.2 Desirable properties of a visualisation

The following list highlights some important qualities which must be considered when designing a visualisation. As with the representations, many of these desirable properties are mutually exclusive and compromise must be made. Again, these properties are summarised here but are explained further in [5].

Simple navigation with minimum disorientation: Visualisations should be designed with the user in mind. As the user will be 'submerged' within the data, it will be necessary to structure the visualisation and introduce features to aid them in navigating through the visualisation.

High information content: Visualisations should present as much information as possible without overwhelming the user. Again, there must be a trade-off between high information content and a low visual complexity.

Low visual complexity, should be well structured: The structural complexity of a visualisation will undoubtedly be dependent on the complexity of the information presented, however, effort should be made to reduce the visual complexity of the visualisations. A well-structured data terrain should also result in a more understandable layout and easier navigation.

Varying levels of detail: The level of detail, information content and type of information presented should vary to cater for the users' interests. The visualisation should support this change in interest and provide increasing detail and information as the user moves towards a component or expresses an interest in a component.

Resilience to change: Small additions or changes to the information content of the visualisation or shifts in the users interests should not result in major differences in the visualisation. Major changes such as a full repositioning of representations will result in the user becoming disorientated and having to re-learn the structure of the environment.

Good use of visual metaphors: Metaphors introduce familiar concepts to the user of the visualisations and provide a good starting point for gaining an understanding of the visualisation.

Approachable user interface: The user interface to the visualisations should be flexible enough to provide intuitive navigation and control, yet should not discourage the user or introduce any unnecessary overheads.

Integration with other information sources: Visualisations provide a different viewpoint on the information they are presenting, in most cases they cannot entirely replace that information. It is desirable to be able to correlate between the visualisations and the original information, or other views on it. For example, visualisations of a software module structure could be linked to the actual source code of that module.

Good use of interaction: Visualisations can benefit greatly by allowing the users to interact with them in various ways. This provides mechanisms for gaining more information and also helps maintain interest.

Suitability for automation: As with the representations, a good level of automation is required in order to make the visualisations of any practical worth.

4 3D Software visualisations

A number of prototype 3D software visualisations have been created in order to assess how the desirable properties could be applied in a real example. This section will now describe two such prototypes and explain how the desirable properties apply to each, and how they affected the development of the visualisations.

The goal of this research is to develop theories and ideas which will help create useful visualisations of software systems that maximise the additional flexibility and benefits afforded by virtual reality. One of the first obstacles we must overcome is to map the information already available from traditional 2D techniques and visualisations, into 3D. Certain existing 2D visualisations do not transfer well into a 3D environment so we must explore new ways of presenting the same information. One such 2D visualisation is the function call-graph and this is the subject of the first visualisation prototype, *CallStax* [6].

4.1 CallStax

The first challenge sought was to provide an alternative to the directed graphs so evident in software maintenance tools. The most common visualisation used within software maintenance tools is the function call-graph. A call-graph is a directed graph showing the function call relationships between all the functions of a software system. The CallStax visualisation is an attempt to move away from the standard node and arc representations of graphs and to maximise use of the extra dimension afforded by virtual reality.

It is not generally the number of components in a call-graph which complicates the visualisation, rather it is the (typically) much larger set of relationships between these components. CallStax attempts to reduce the complexity overhead which these explicit relationships place on the visualisation by making them implicit. This effectively reduces the complexity of the visualisation, but increases the cognitive load on the user as they then have to reconstruct these relationships mentally. It is hoped the latter will prove less mentally demanding than attempting to decipher the relationships from a complex and less readable visualisation.

CallStax is different from traditional call-graphs in that it visualises the *paths* through the graph rather than the graph as a network. CallStax visualises each possible path through the program as a stack of individual function representations, in the simplest case, as coloured cubes. Each of these cubes represents a particular component or function and identical representations or cubes represent the same component. The base function (e.g. `main`) resides at the bottom of the stack, with the functions called along a particular path stacked above it.

The basic technique used for querying in CallStax allows the user to select a particular function, or cube, as their current focus of interest. Once selected, all of the stacks in the visualisation will move vertically to align all occurrences of that function within all stacks into a horizontal plane. Any stacks which do not contain that function will fall away below the horizontal plane, thus removing them from the immediate attention of the user yet leaving them visible to maintain a notion of context in the results.

The power of the CallStax visualisation lies in its flexibility. The stacks are not explicitly connected in any way, allowing great freedom in the positioning, grouping, insertion and deletion of stacks. Unfortunately this flexibility comes at a price. The implicit relationships between duplicate representations of functions is reliant solely on the visual appearance of those functions. The representations used must therefore concentrate on being *unique* and *distinctive*. It is relatively easy to fashion such properties in the case of a small visualisation (see example below) but it becomes very difficult when a large number of distinct functions are present.

The following example shows the construction of a CallStax visualisation using a simple "toy" program as the basis. Figure 1 shows a standard 2D call-graph of this program. The nodes on the graph have been shaded to show the main functions belonging to the program, whereas the plain (dashed line) nodes represent library functions called by the program. The CallStax visualisation is constructed by generating a number of stacks of function representations, each stack corresponding to a single path through the call-graph. Figure 2 shows a 2D representation of these stacks. The path represented by each stack begins at the lowest function (e.g. *main*) and proceeds upwards, the deeper the call nesting then the taller the stack.

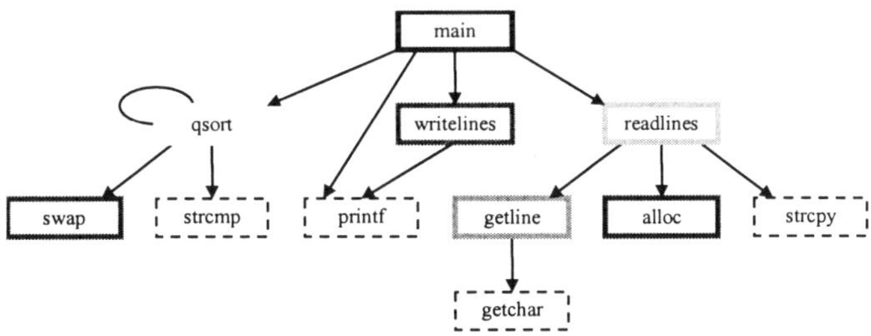

Figure 1. Standard 2D call-graph

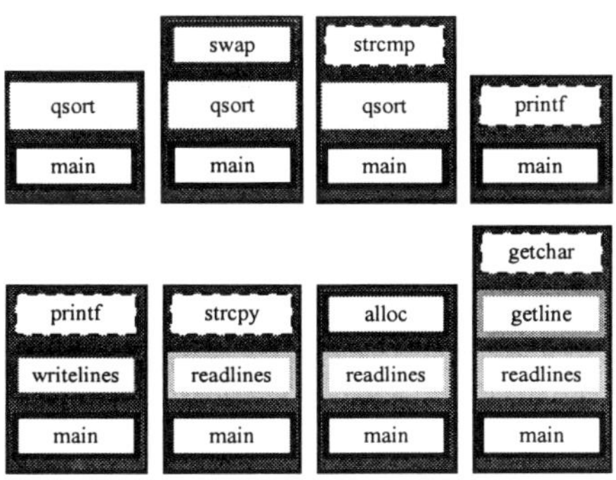

Figure 2. 2D callstax visualisation

Figure 3. 3D callstax visualisation with the function qsort selected

Figures 1 and 2 are intended for illustration only, figure 3 shows the actual CallStax visualisation which is displayed within a virtual reality system. Figure 3 shows the stacks in a position where the user has expressed an interest in the function *qsort*. The stacks have aligned themselves with all occurrences of *qsort* on the same horizontal plane. This 'selection plane' is indicated by a translucent mesh which gives a visual frame of reference for the user. All stacks which do not contain an occurrence of *qsort* have receded to the 'bottom' of the view. From looking at the currently selected stacks, it can be easily seen which functions call *qsort*, and which functions are called by *qsort*. Additionally the depth of *qsort* within the call hierarchy can be rapidly found by looking at the stack which extends the furthest down from the selection plane.

It is important to remember that the CallStax visualisation is not intended to be a single software visualisation in itself. CallStax was designed to provide a method for reproducing the dependency information shown by standard graphs, but in a form that allows for easier integration into a larger 3D visualisation. This property was the main driving influence behind the nature of the CallStax visualisation, it must provide maximum flexibility for integration into other visualisations.

4.2 FileVis

Another prototype constructed is the File Visualisation (FileVis) [5] which is aimed at providing a high level overview of a software system's structure (Figure 4). The goal of FileVis is to allow a maintainer to familiarise themselves with the software system and identify any important or interesting areas before they commence their maintenance work. It is often the case that the maintainer will have no previous experience with the software system they must work on. First contact with the system involves a high degree of learning during which the maintainer must understand as much as possible about the system as a whole before beginning work on a specific area. Visualisations such as FileVis attempt to support this learning process by providing a more intuitive and easily accessible method for browsing and investigating various aspects of a software system. The software system is no longer an abstract mass of files and information, it has become something tangible, you can *see* the software.

FileVis is an integrated WWW presentation consisting of three main frames. The primary frame contains the actual 3D visualisation itself, the remaining two frames are used to display any other information which is currently relevant in the 3D visualisation, such as detailed statistics or source code files.

Figure 4. Overview of a software system using FileVis

FileVis is based upon visualising the various components of a software system written using the programming language, C. FileVis is structured around the various C source files and their contents. The current version of the FileVis prototype has concentrated on just two components, the source code files and the functions defined within each file. Further work could be to expand the system to provide other information such as data structures, data usage and control flow.

Each source code file is represented within the virtual environment as a flat, coloured box or pedestal. To show the dependencies between the various source files a CallStax visualisation is constructed in the centre of the environment. From this it can be seen which files include other files or libraries, and also which files are shared through the system. Selecting any files or objects results in detailed information on that object to be displayed in one of the 2D browser frames, and the corresponding source code to be displayed in the other. This information includes hypertext links between each of the frames and the 3D world allowing the user to browse the software system using a variety of techniques.

In its current state FileVis shows only the function definitions within each of the files. Upon each file pedestal is a number of blocks which represent each of the functions defined within that file. These function representations have two levels of detail. As the user approaches closer to a particular file or function, they switch from a low detail to high detail representation which gives more information on the function definition. This has the effect of minimising screen clutter and information overload when viewing from a distance, but also emphasising the main characteristics of a function by reducing the number of others which are visible.

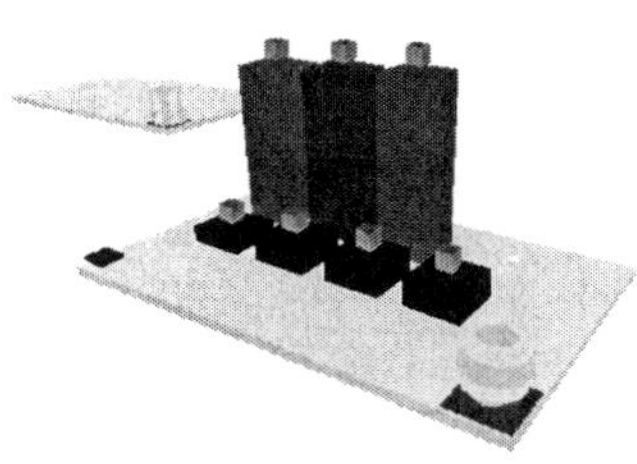

Figure 5. Low detail function representations

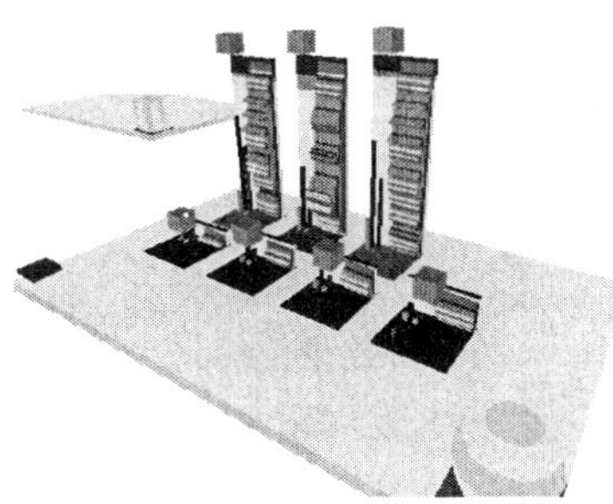

Figure 6. Moving in for a closer look

The low detail representation (Figure 5) emphasises only two characteristics of the function, its length (height) and relative complexity (colour). Using these simple attributes it is possible to quickly assess the distribution of functions within the software system. Long or highly complex functions or files can be identified quickly by simply surveying the virtual landscape. The high detail representation (Figure 6) consists of a number of different information items or attributes related to that function. This includes various information such as complexity metrics; a breakdown of the lines of code, comment and blank lines; and a simplified representation of the functions' control structure and textual structure.

An evaluation of how the various components of FileVis apply to each of the desirable properties, both as visualisations and representations, is described in [5].

5 Conclusions

The conclusions of this paper are that graphical representations are important for program comprehension. Software visualisation is complicated greatly by the size and complexity of typical software systems. All visualisations have both their own merits and shortcomings, the problem in hand is to find a suitable and effective compromise. New methods and techniques for visualising software systems are required. This paper presents initial guidelines for creating and developing new visualisations using 3D graphics and virtual reality.

The limitations of the 2D graph are highlighted when viewing the relationships within large software systems. The graphs will rapidly become very messy and unreadable [7], with little or no hope of finding an acceptable layout. 3D graphics and virtual reality have great potential for aiding program comprehension.

The two prototypes presented in this paper tackle very different problems within 3D software visualisation. The first, CallStax, is a conversion of an existing and much used 2D technique into a 3D equivalent. In doing so it harnesses the additional dimension afforded by the 3D environment and provides maximum flexibility for incorporation into other 3D visualisations. The second prototype, FileVis, provides a unique viewpoint on a complete software system. FileVis displays the files and functions within the system and highlights important metrics, characteristics and structural information.

References

[1] Young P. Three dimensional information visualisation, Technical report 12/96, Centre for Software Maintenance, University of Durham, 1996.

[2] Ingram RJ, Benford S. Legibility enhancement for information visualisation. In: Proceedings of visualisation '95, Atlanta, Georgia, 1995.

[3] Ingram RJ. Legibility enhancement for information visualisation. PhD thesis, University of Nottingham, 1995.

[4] Boyle J, Fothergill J, Gray P, Leishman S. Development of a visual query language. Aberdeen University, 1993.

[5] Young P, Munro M. Visualising software in virtual reality. In: Proceedings of IEEE 6th International workshop on program comprehension (IWPC'98), 1998.

[6] Young P, Munro M. A new view of call-graphs for visualising code structure. Technical report 03/97, Centre for Software Maintenance, University of Durham, 1997.

[7] Burd EL, Chan PS, Duncan IMM, Munro M, Young P. Improving visual representations of code. Technical report 10/96, Centre for Software Maintenance, University of Durham, 1996.

Visualisation of the OBJ Term Re-writing Process

Duncan S. Neary and Martin R. Woodward
Department of Computer Science, University of Liverpool,
Chadwick Building, Peach Street, Liverpool L69 7ZF, UK.
{dunc, mrw}@csc.liv.ac.uk

Abstract

Algebraic specifications have been promoted as an aid to the software development process. However, their usefulness has been restricted by a perceived unapproachability. This paper introduces an approach to the simplification of the algebraic specification language OBJ through visualisation and, more specifically, it focuses on the use of animation to represent the OBJ term re-writing process by which expressions are evaluated.

1 Introduction

It has long been argued that algebraic specifications can play a useful and critical role in the software development process. Their usefulness however has not been reflected in widespread use, except amongst the research community, perhaps indicating an underlying unapproachability issue for those only with experience in imperative programming languages. One method for tackling this unapproachability is to reduce perceived complexity through visualisation of specifications and the processes involved. The effectiveness of this approach has already been shown via the visualisation of specification notations such as Z [1] and VDM [2] and the logic language Prolog [3].

The OBJ [4] family of languages is one of the foremost algebraic specification notations. Visualisation has already been applied to the use of OBJ through its combination with nets [5] [6]. The approaches detailed in those papers however, require the user to input textual 'modules' to be included in the nets. By contrast the intention here is to develop a system that allows the user to create and execute OBJ specifications from within a completely visual environment, although the focus of this paper is visualisation of the OBJ term re-writing process. This process, which is an integral feature of OBJ, has proved difficult for users to understand, a fact underpinned by a pilot survey involving OBJ users conducted by the authors.

A number of visual notations for the representation of OBJ have been developed. When presented to prospective users all of the notations received a positive response. The most popular notation, the so-called Vertical Nested Box (VNB) notation, was then selected for initial experimentation with animated visualisation of the term re-writing process, although it is anticipated that any final system will allow use of any of the notations.

Section 2 gives a brief introduction to the OBJ language, before the VNB notation is introduced in Section 3. The use of the VNB notation in visualising term re-writing is detailed in Section 4 and the implementation of a proposed system to perform the process is introduced in Section 5. Section 6 summarises this paper and makes some concluding remarks.

2 OBJ

OBJ is a language for writing specifications in an algebraic or axiomatic style. As in mathematics, axioms describe fundamental properties, from which further results may be derived. This approach lends itself naturally to the definition of abstract data types, i.e. collections of objects and permissible operations on those objects.

A specification in OBJ consists of a number of modules, which may be either OBJECTs or IMAGEs. The IMAGE construct provides a simple copy-and-edit facility which will not be considered further here. An OBJECT may inherit information from other OBJECTs merely by naming the inherited modules in the OBJECT header. When writing an OBJ specification an OBJECT starts

```
                *** STACK SPECIFICATION ***
    OBJ Stack
    SORTS stack item
    OPS
       nilstack:                    -> stack
       push     : item      stack   -> stack
       pop      : stack             -> stack
       top      : stack             -> item
       isempty  : stack             -> BOOL
    VARS
       s : stack
       i : item
    EQNS
       ( pop ( push ( i, s ) )      = s )  *** equation 1 ***
       ( top ( push ( i, s ) )      = i )  *** equation 2 ***
       ( isempty ( nilstack )       = T )  *** equation 3 ***
       ( isempty ( push ( i, s ) ) = F )  *** equation 4 ***
    JBO .

                 *** TERM RE-WRITING ***
 top ( push ( b, push ( a, nilstack  ) ) )  *** expression 1 ***
 => b   *** becomes expression 2 after the use of equation 2 ***
```

Figure 1: OBJ specification of a stack and an example of term re-writing

with the keyword OBJ and finishes with the keyword JBO. It has four possible sections identified by the keywords SORTS, OPS, VARS and EQNS.

The SORTS section contains the definition of any abstract types used in an OBJECT. The OPS section defines the operations that may be performed on the types in terms of their domains and ranges. These operations may be performed on all argument values, so unless the user creates specific error-handling equations to force the re-write of erroneous expressions, such as *top(nilstack)*, to user-defined error values, such expressions fail to re-write any further and may be considered as not unlike a run-time error message. Operations by default have prefix syntax, although they may be defined with any syntax the user desires, i.e. postfix, infix and mixfix, through the use of placeholders which appear as underscore symbols. The VARS section contains the declarations of symbols (variables) to represent given types. The EQNS section contains equations relating expressions involving the operations and variables. An equation may also have an optional condition, indicating that it is valid only if the given condition is true. An example specification of the abstract data type 'stack' can be seen in Figure 1.

A feature of OBJ is its executability, achieved through evaluation of expressions, with equations being treated as re-write rules. Hence, given an expression to evaluate, a search can be made for a match of any sub-expression with the left-hand side (LHS) of any equation. If a match is found the sub-expression may be replaced by the right-hand side (RHS) of the corresponding equation. This process is known as term re-writing and continues until the expression cannot be re-written any further. An example of this process is given in Figure 1. In this example, expression 1 is evaluated using equation 2 from the *Stack* specification, giving the resulting expression 2, i.e. *b*.

3 The Vertical Nested Box (VNB) notation

Nassi-Shneiderman (NS) charts [7] form the basis for the VNB notation; however, a vertical aspect is introduced to the notation, allowing support for the differing syntax of operations. Further differences include the use of circles to denote variables (Figure 2(a)), rounded rectangles to denote operations (Figure 2(b)) and colour to represent type, although greyscale is used in the figures here. No differentiation is made between user-defined and built-in operations. For example the built-in boolean operations *and*, *or*, *not*, *T* and *F* are all represented by rounded rectangles, as is the user-defined operation *top*.

The VNB notation uses nesting to show to which entities an operation is applied. For example, in Figure 2(c), the variable *s* is nested inside a rectangle connected to the operation *pop*, indicating that *pop* is applied to *s*. The type of *s* is also denoted by the fact it is surrounded by the colour light grey, which represents the type *stack*.

The syntax of an operation is indicated through a visual version of placeholders, in that anything appearing to the left of the operation in textual form, now appears above in VNB, and anything to the right appears below.

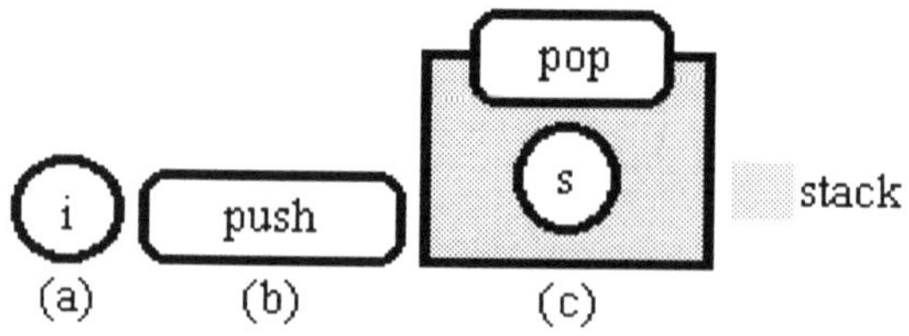

Figure 2: (a) a variable (b) an operation (c) operation application

4 Animating term re-writing

Visualisation of the term re-writing process takes place on-screen via animation. This requires visual indication of the matching that happens during the term re-writing process. The first step in this process involves substituting entities in the expression for the corresponding entities in the equation. The matching of the entities is indicated using 'matching lines', before the substitution is made via on-screen animation. For example, in Figure 3, *b*, from the expression, is matched with *i*, from the equation. This match is indicated using matching lines, before *b* is substituted for *i* using on-screen animation. The result is an instance of the equation with substitutions included, see Figure 4. This newly created equation has a LHS which is identical to the expression, allowing the next step in the term re-writing process to be taken.

The second step of the animated term re-writing involves substituting the RHS of the equation for the expression. This substitution is indicated by matching the LHS of the instance of the equation with the expression, again using matching lines, before animating the substitution of the RHS on-screen, completing the process.

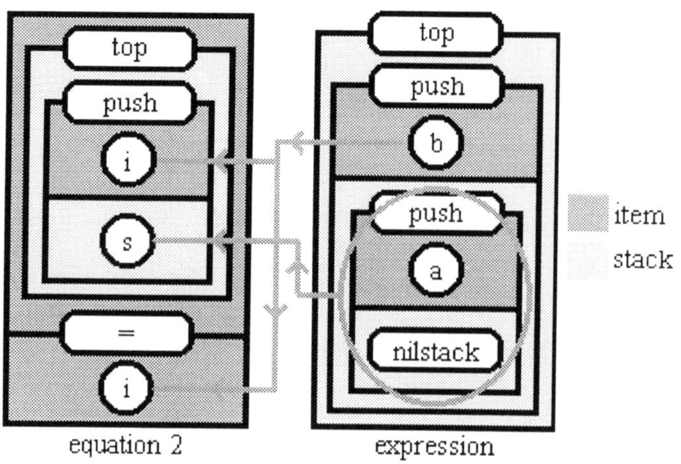

Figure 3: Expression matched with equation

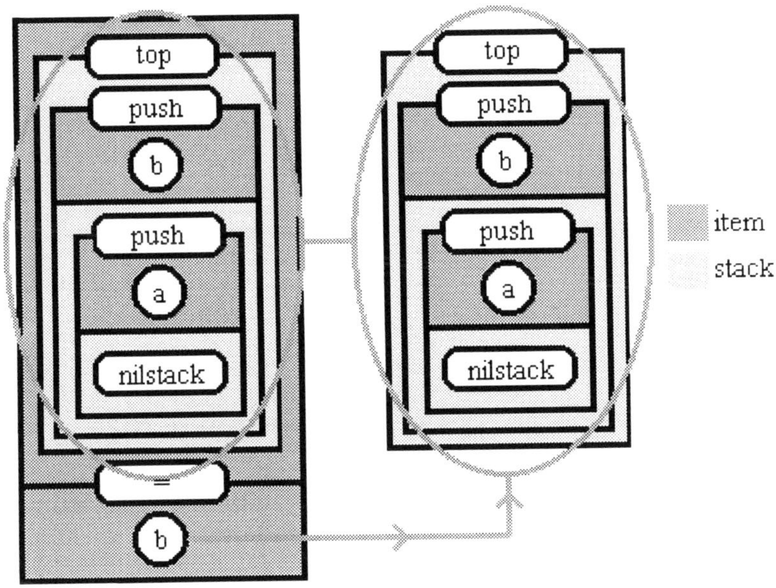

Figure 4: LHS of equation matched with expression

5 Implementation

Implementation at this stage is being concentrated on the development of a prototype system that will allow the input and visualisation of an OBJ specification. The system will operate by parsing the OBJ specification that is input and converting it into graphical form upon the screen. The system is being developed with the flexibility to support a variety of graphical notations and allow the inclusion of any number of further notations at a later date.

Progress so far includes the creation of an OBJ parser which will be executed using CGI, the results being passed to a Java applet which is used to display and animate the visual notation. Also some illustrative examples of animated term re-writing have been developed in Java for viewing with a web browser. Subsequent stages include incorporation of the ObjEx [8] implementation of an OBJ compiler and interpreter as the basic term re-writing engine and finally the development of a front end to allow direct input of a visual form of OBJ.

6 Concluding remarks

Although development at this time has concentrated on the term re-writing process, it is envisaged that this will be a small part of the visualisation of all aspects of the OBJ language. The final aim is a visual OBJ system offering all the functionality of the textual OBJ systems, but with greater usability. When fully implemented, the system will allow a number of different visual notations to be used, the layout rules for each notation being developed in

OBJ. It is hoped that the system will apply the positive factors associated with visualisation to the use of OBJ, and vice versa. Hence simplification and accessibility, the strengths of visual techniques, will be introduced to the use of OBJ, while quality and, above all, precision will be introduced to the creation of visual notations via the OBJ layout rules associated with the system.

References

[1] Yap, C.N. and Holcombe. M.: Using Graphical Icons to Build Z Specifications. Proc. of the 2nd BCS-FACS Northern Formal Methods Workshop. 1997

[2] Dick, J. and Loubersac, J.: A Visual Approach to VDM: Entity-Structure Diagrams. Technical Report DE/DRPA/91001, Bull, 68 Route de Versailles, 78430 Louveciennes, France. 1991

[3] Agustí, J., Robertson, D. and Puigsegur, J.: GRASP: A GRAphical SPecification Language for the Preliminary Specification of Logic Programs. Technical report IIIA 13. Institut d'Investigació en Intel-ligéncia Artificial, Bellaterra, Catalonia, Spain. 1995

[4] Goguen, J.A. and Tardo, J.J.: An Introduction to OBJ: A Language for Writing and Testing Formal Algebraic Program Specifications. Proc. Conf. on Specification of Reliable Software. IEEE Computer Society. 1979; 170-189

[5] Battiston, E., De Cindio, F. and Mauri, G.: Modular Algebraic Nets to Specify Concurrent Systems. IEEE Transactions on Software Engineering. Vol 22. No 10. 1996; 689-705

[6] Nakajima, S. and Futatsugi, K.: An Object-Oriented Modeling Method for Algebraic Specifications in CafeOBJ. Proc. 19th Int. Conf. on Software Engineering. ACM Press. 1997; 34-44

[7] Nassi, I. and Shneiderman, B.: Flowchart Techniques for Structured Programming. ACM Sigplan Notices. Vol.8 No.8 1973; 12-26.

[8] ObjEx User Reference Manual. Gerrard Software, 24 Duke Street, Macclesfield, Cheshire SK11 6UR, UK. 1987

Acknowledgements

Duncan Neary gratefully acknowledges receipt of a Research Studentship from the UK EPSRC (Ref No. 97306579). Both authors would like to acknowledge Gerrard Software for permission to embed the ObjEx system in a visual environment.

A Visual Representation of Mathematical Expressions

Chih Nam Yap, Mike Holcombe
Department of Computer Science
University of Sheffield
Regent Court, 211 Portobello Street
Sheffield S1 4DP UK
+ 44 114 2221870/2221812
{c.yap, m.holcombe}@dcs.shef.ac.uk

1. Introduction

Mathematical expressions are statements for describing the abstract world. Most kinds of mathematical expressions are of a textual form but they can also involve the use of graphical pictures as well, such as the use of Venn diagrams to describe the relationship between sets. This paper looks at a formal specification language used in software engineering called Z [1, 2] whose foundations are based on first-order predicate calculus and set theory. Z is often used for describing the properties of a system by structuring these properties into manageable constructs called *schema*. Each schema describes the system's properties using mathematical expressions that are formed by mathematical symbols with special meanings together with conventional alphabets. Two basic forms of expressions can often be found in any Z specification, unary and binary expressions. Their syntax are of the form:

Unary expression format:	Operator	Operand	
Binary expression format:	Operand	Operator	Operand

In its simplest form, an operand can be an attribute, a system state or even an input/output and it is represented by a user-defined name (e.g. `members`, `library`). Expressions can be more complex with the operand part of an expression replaced by another expression such as this one:

Operator (Operand Operator (Operand Operator Operand))

An operator is usually used to provide the required operations to link operands so that the required system properties could be presented. Operators are represented using special mathematical symbols such as $\cup$, $\cap$ and #.

To construct a Z specification in a computer system, the most earliest and common way is to write all the expressions in an ASCII text editor. However, because most of the keyboards do not support special keys for entering mathematical symbols directly, application-specific keyword systems had to be used to overcome this problem. we list, below two ways to create the expression "(A ∪ B) ⊆ C" in two different editors: $L^{A}T_{E}X$ [3] and CADiZ (Computer Aided Design in Z) [4].

$L^{A}T_{E}X$: $(A \cap B) \subseteq C$
CADiZ: (A sand B) sinc C

Using textual keywords to construct mathematical expressions often ends up with a very short statement. This is an advantage of using textual keywords. On the other hand, as different tools have their own keyword systems, users are forced to learn and remember the meaning of each keyword in order to use the tool efficiently. This increases the memory burden on the user. A user who already has the background domain knowledge may only need to spend some time learning these keywords. For those who do not learning keywords becomes a difficult task because they have to learn both the domain knowledge and the keyword system at the same time. Furthermore, because there is no correspond between a keyword and the conventional mathematical symbol the keyword is representing, there is a danger that the user (or the learner) may not recognise the actual mathematical symbol when they encounter it somewhere else. These are some of the reasons why these formal specification languages have not proven to be very popular in industry, despite having been taught in universities for over ten years.

Another most commonly known method to enter mathematical expressions into computer systems is the selection of symbols from pop-up windows. To select any of these symbols, the user either performs a mouse click or hits a combination of keys from the keyboard. Figure 1 shows a pop-up window used in a tool called Formaliser [5].

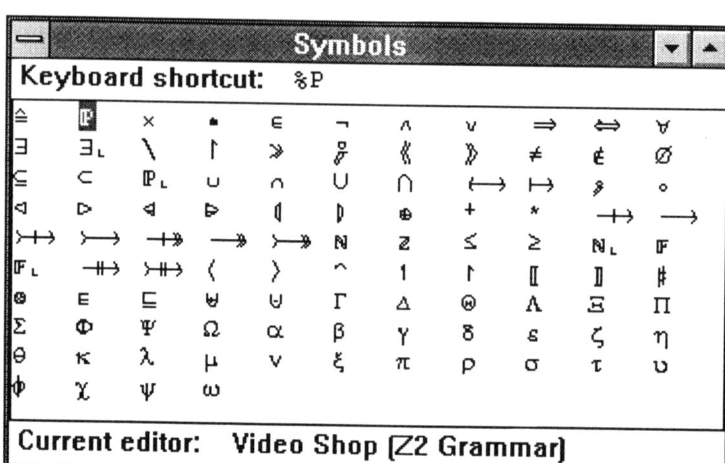

Figure 1: A pop-up window for the selection of symbols in Formaliser

The advantage of using a pop-up window for the selection of symbols over the keyword system is that the former does not required the user to learn any keywords. However, most of these pop-up windows arrange their symbols in an arbitrary form; symbols are therefore not categorised systematically. Apart from that, it is quite often the case that no help facility is provided to explain the meaning of each symbol inside the pop-up window. Like the keyword system, another drawback of using pop-up windows is they cannot prevent users from using the wrong operator symbols to construct mathematical expressions because any symbol (or keyword) can be used without restriction.

We are interested in developing a more satisfactory tool for novice formal methods users which helps them create Z specifications. In this paper we present an alternative, iconic way of constructing mathematical expressions. Our tool is called VisualiZer and it has now been designed, implemented and evaluated. We will illustrate how we have derived the system by showing a few designs that we have considered during the project. However, because we are also going to use our operand design to illustrate the tool, we begin by saying something about this approach to dealing with operators and operands.

The operand design idea of the VisualiZer tool is very simple. The window-like design is based on the metaphor of commonly used window interfaces. The advantage of using this kind of metaphor is that there is no need to provide extra training on how to use the operand constructions, the user can simply use the techniques he/she already knows about the windows interface and applies them to the element. For example, the user can move an operand by moving its title portion, or minimise the operand just like minimising a window. Our first design partitioned an operand into two portions: the title and the content. Figure 2 shows three different kinds of operand designs. We will illustrate the latest design when we come to section 4.

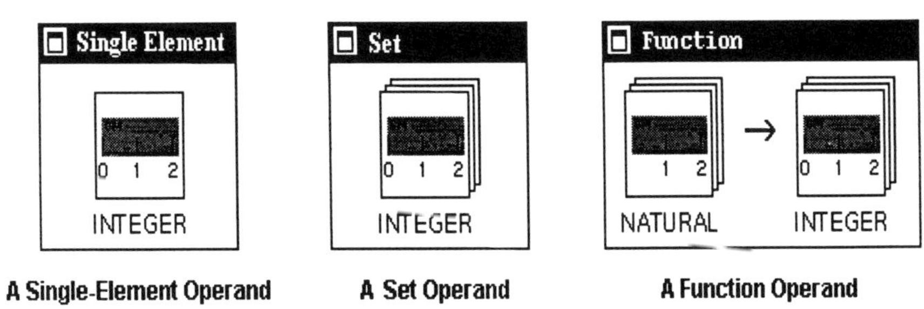

Figure 2: The single-element, set and function operand designs

2. The First Design

We do not want the user of our tool to use keywords to construct expressions. We arc more interested in the pop-up window way of representing symbols. However, we wish to categorise all the symbols into two groups: unary and binary. We could have done the categorising process within a pop-up window, but we didn't. The reason is simple. We discovered that users of the Formaliser tool invoked the pop-up window very frequently. This means that those mathematical symbols are in fact in use all the time. We think it is better to list these symbols on the user interface so that users can use them without having to keep invoking a pop-up window.

In our first design, we partitioned the unary and binary operators into two different user interface areas. There was also a working area. Figure 3 shows a portion of a screen shot of the first design.

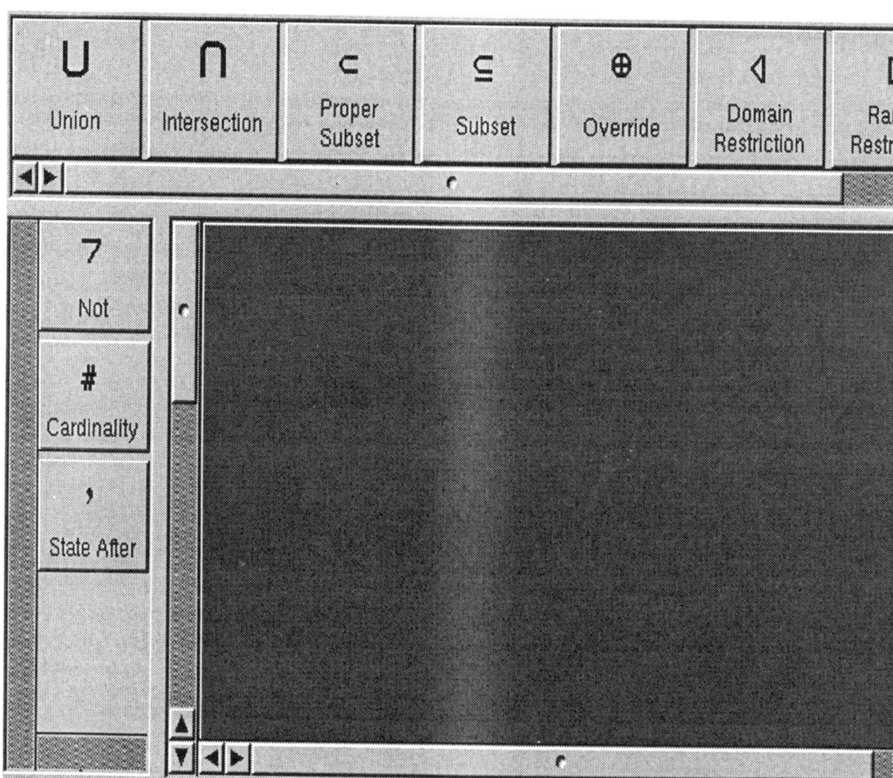

Figure 3: The user interface of the first design

We adopted a method called "The box method" [6], [7] for constructing expressions. The method is so called because boxes are used to represent operators. Every operator representation looks different but the procedure to form expressions was the same. To create an operator, the user simply needs to click on the button representing that operator. The tool will generate an operator in the working area. To form the actual expression, the user simply drags operands inside the operator and this is the end of the story. Figure 4 shows how the expression "SetA ∪ SetB" is created using our first design. Some of the operation required the user to drag operands to a specific location in order to achieve the required expression. The creation of the expression "SetA – SetB" is a good example. The user is required to move the operand represent "SetA" to the left of the "-" operator and the operand "SetB" to the right. Figure 5 shows how the expression "SetA – SetB" is created.

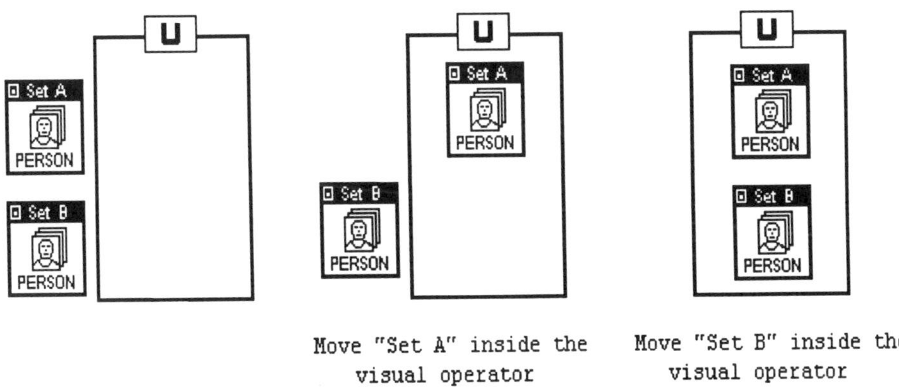

Figure 4: How the expression "A ∪ B" is created

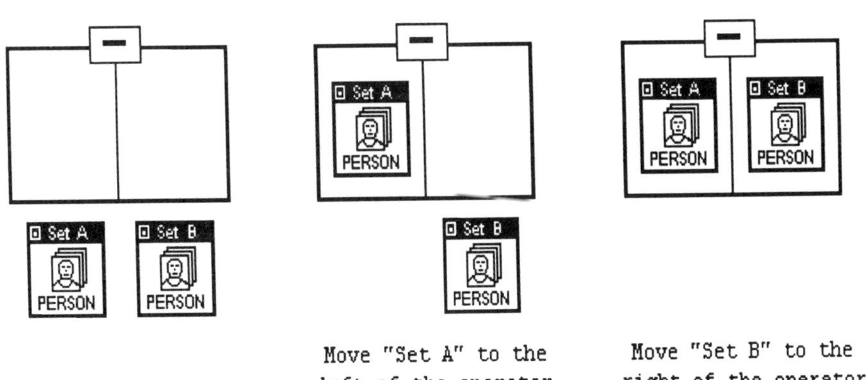

Figure 5: How the expression "A - B" is created

For unary operators, there are several possible ways of using a box style method of creating expression. Figure 6 shows how two different unary operations are carried out in our first design. The #(SetA) expression is created using the standard box method. The dom(FunctionC) expression is created in a different way. No button on the user interface needs to be clicked for this expression, the user simply clicks once on the left icon within the tool and the tool will automatically darken that icon to indicate that a domain operation has been taken place.

#(SetA) dom(FunctionC)

Figure 6: Two different ways to create unary expression

In the design, we also provided help facilities for the user to learn the meaning of each operator symbol by using the right mouse-button to click the corresponding button. A pop-up window with a small example to explain the selected symbol will be shown below.

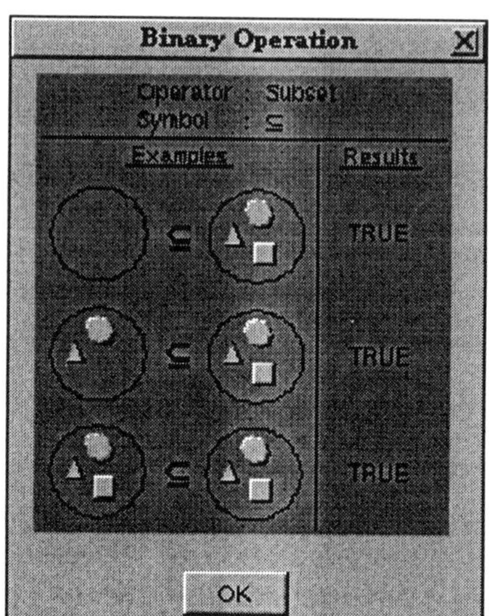

Figure 7: A help panel to explain the meaning of the subset operation

After conducting a few experiments, we discovered that there were many inconsistencies and deficiencies in our first design. First of all there were too many ways to create expressions in the design. Although users no longer needed to remember keywords and help facilities were available all the time, some users still had problems dragging operands to the correct slot in some of the operations. Furthermore, as there were more than 30 binary operators listed in the scroll bar, users had to scroll a lot in order to get the required operator they needed. The other problem was that we could still not prevent the user from using inappropriate operators.

3. The Second Design

In our second design, we made a dramatic change. After conducting a few experiments on our first design, we discovered that when first asked to create an expression, many users were reluctant to look for operators on the scroll bar. What most of them did was they moved one operand on top of the other and hoped to see something happen from there. This behaviour triggered us to think whether showing operators on the user interface was really a good idea or not. Based on this, we decided to use a "less is more" philosophy for our second design. This time we removed all the operators from the user interface. We wanted the tool to show these operators only when necessary.

The second design works this way. To form a new expression, the user only needs to move one operand on top of the other. A pop-up window with a list of operators will then be presented to the user. Only applicable operators for the current operation are listed in the pop-up window. Once an operator is selected, a visual expression will be presented to the user. Figure 8 shows an example of the new pop-up window and Figure 9 shows how a visual expression "SetA $\cup$ SetB" looks.

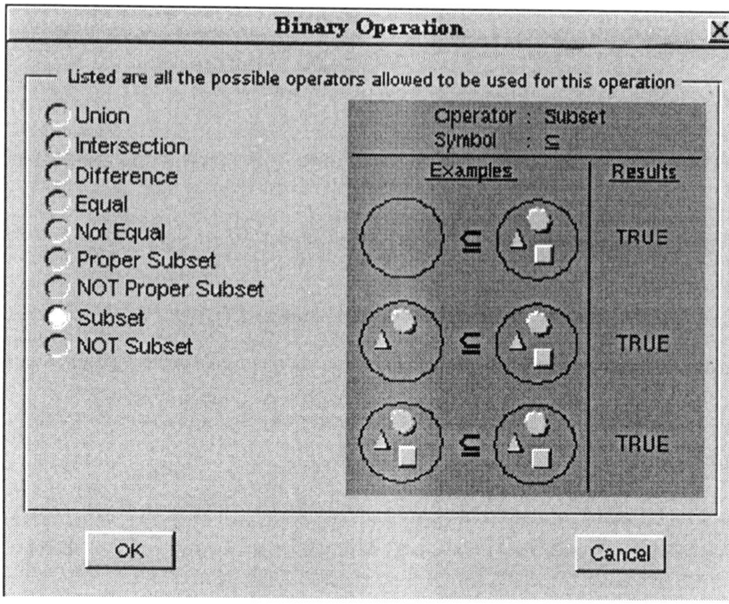

Figure 8: The new help panel

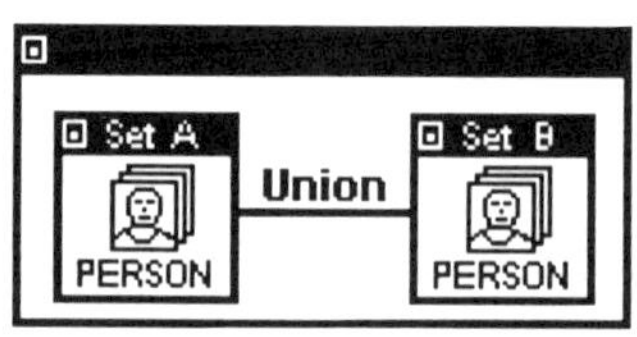

Figure 9: Visual expression "SetA ∪ SetB"

The advantages of the second design are that not only did it save a lot of precious user interface space, more importantly it also "partially" prevents the user from using the wrong operator. For example, when a user moves a set operand towards another set operand, the tool will only show a list of applicable set operators with the help facility for the user to choose from. Although the design might still not prevent the user from using the wrong set operator it at least prevents the user from using operators that cannot be applied on set operations at all. The other advantage is that all binary operations are now created in a consistent way, i.e., move one operand on top of the other and then select an operator from the pop-up window. The user no longer needs to remember so much. However the design has only partially solved all the problems.

4. The Third Design

The second design does not cover unary operations. As unary operation only involve one operand at a time, we felt that an unary operation should be self-contained within the operand so that the user can perform unary operations quicker. To make the unary operation self-contained we decided to add a bar between the title and the content of an operand.

Every unary operator is represented by a button and the button can be toggled between two states: *selected* or *non-selected*. Unary buttons always come as a set. At any one time, only one button in a set can be in the selected state, hence if another unary button within the same set is selected, the former will be toggled to a non-selected state automatically by the VisualiZer tool.

On the left of Figure 10 is shown the set of unary buttons1 used for a function operand and on the right of the figure shows how a "dom" unary operation is applied to that function operand.

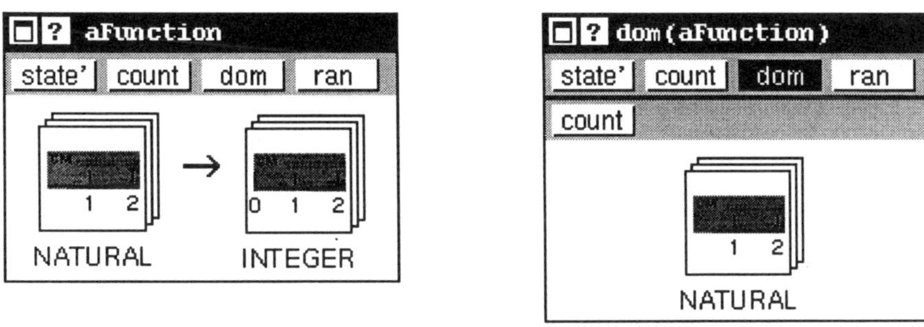

Nothing is selected The "dom" operator is selected

Figure 10: Applying a "dom" unary operator to a function attribute

Notice that when an unary operation is applied to an operand, both the title and the content portion of the operand will be updated as well. The updated title will show the new expression whereas the content will show the resultant type of the function operand after the operation. One could also go further by clicking the "count" on the second line so as to achieve the expression "#(dom(aFunction))". On the other hand, to remove all the unary operations applied to "aFunction", the user only

---

1 The "state" button represents the "state after" operator. The "count" button represents the cardinality "#" operator. The "dom" button represents the "domain" operator. The "ran" button represent the "range" operator. This terminology is part of the Z language

needs to re-select the "dom" button". This will toggle the "dom" button back to its non-selected state and the operand will look like the one on the left of Figure 10 again. New button "?" is also added. Once this button is clicked, a pop-up help panel will appear. This panel explains each unary operator on the bar in detail with examples.

5. Conclusion

We have performed usability tests on our second and third designs. The general results we have obtained have shown that novice formal methods users did learn something useful after using the tool. They made fewer errors when they constructed their own Z specifications than doing it on paper. The general comments given by students were that the tool is very easy to use and it provides very good help facilities for people to understand the use of the specific mathematical symbols of the language. They also commented that the way binary operations are created is very consistent and very easy to use.

References

1. Spivey M. The Z notation: A reference manual. 2nd Edition, Prentice Hall, 1992

2. Diller AZ. - An introduction to formal methods. 2nd Edition John-Wiley & Sons, 1994

3. Lamport L. LaTeX: A document preparation system; 2nd Edition, Addison-Wesley, 1994

4. Jordan D, McDermid L, Toyn I. CADiZ: Computer Aided Design in Z. In: Nicholls J (ed) Proc. of the 5th Annual Z User Meeting. Springer-Verlag 1991

5. Flynn M, Hoverd T, Brazier D. Formaliser: an interactive support tool for Z. In: Nicholls J (ed) Proc. of the 4th Annual Z User Meeting. Springer-Verlag, 1990

6. Yap CN, Holcombe M. Graphical Z specifications. In: Proc. PPIG '97, Psychology of Programming Interest Group, 9th Annual Workshop, Sheffield Hallam University, 1997.

7. Yap CN, Holcombe M. Using graphical icons to build Z specifications, In: Proceedings of the Northern Formal Methods Workshop, eWics (Electronic Workshops in Computer Science) series, Springer-Verlag, 1997.

Visualisation of an AI Solution

Brown, A.G.P.[1], Coenen, F.P.[2],and Knight, M.W. [1]

[1] School of Architecture and Building Engineering, The University of Liverpool, U.K.[2] Dept. of Computer Science, The University of Liverpool, U.K. www.liv.ac.uk/~mknight/VRI

Abstract

This paper describes the representation of output from an AI analysis of a Built Environment problem. A particular aspect arising out of the analysis is that we need to represent variables throughout a (tesserally defined) three dimensional space. This paper describes the two approaches that we have examined.

1 Introduction

We have developed an AI system, called SPARTA, which can undertake Spatial Reasoning using a technique to define spatial relationships known as Tesseral Addressing. Generally speaking Spatial Reasoning deals with the manipulation of the N-dimensional relationships that exist between objects in order to arrive at a solution that is application dependent. Traditionally the aim has been to determine the relationships that exist between two, or more specific objects in a space, given a set of known relationships between those objects and other objects in the space. In the case study presented later these objects are buildings, and the physical environment in which they are set. The noise generated by traffic in the geographical space around these buildings interacts with these physical phenomena.

This idea of Spatial Reasoning forms the basis of early work on temporal reasoning [1]. More recently there has been work on spatial reasoning such as that of Egenhofer [2] which uses point set topology [3] to represent a problem to which spatial reasoning can be applied. Once a system has been described in terms of sets of points and functions applied to those sets of points a method of solution can be applied. In SPARTA the solution technique used is that of Constraint Satisfaction [4]. In addition to using point set topology, SPARTA incorporates the notion of tessellation of space [5]. This tessellation involves sub-dividing a space into small *tiles* in 2d problems and small *cells* in 3d scenarios.

The paper is structured as follows. First the SPARTA technique is outlined, then the two potential approaches to visualisation of the data are described. We then give the details of a case study of a Built Environment problem to which

SPARTA has been applied. The techniques investigated to facilitate visualising the data for this case study, and in general, are then presented.

2 SPARTA

When applying reasoning techniques embodied in an AI system the representation of physical space using the Cartesian system tends to be computationally expensive. Our approach to tackling this problem is to use the concept of linear quad-tesseral addressing to describe the geometry of the space being represented. In this approach we replace the set of three Cartesian coordinates that define spatial locations with one single address [6]. The effect is to linearise the 3d space being investigated. The process involves taking two dimensional space and dividing it into sub-spaces called tiles (or cells in 3d). The tiles are each assigned an address that defines location and spatial relationship uniquely with reference to the remaining tiles in the space. An early application of the tesseral addressing technique is described by Morton [7] who used it in the investigation of atomic structures .

All of the different forms of tesseral addressing have, as their foundation, the subdivision of space into isohedral (same shape) sub-spaces. The ribbon illustrated in Figure 1 can effectively be unravelled leaving a one dimensional representation of the space. This property, in turn, leads to analyses which are computationally effective. In our system the method of addressing has evolved into a more direct left to right linearisation. The three main resulting advantages are that the linearisation is much more obvious than that associated with the Morton linearisation, especially if we also wish to consider negative space; conversion from Cartesian to tesseral addresses is more straight forward; and finally, translation through the space is achieved by simple integer addition and subtraction.

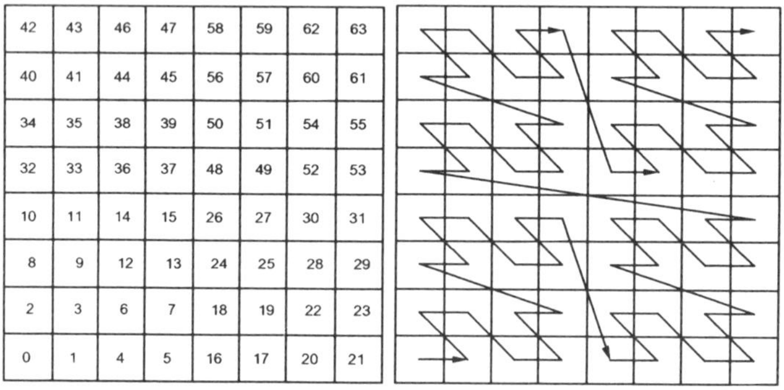

Figure 1: The numbering system (left) proposed by Morton and line (ribbon) following the numbering sequence (right).

Sign bit	Dimension 4 7 bits	Dimension 3 8 bits	Dimension 2 8 bits	Dimension 1 8 bits

Figure 2: Address bit pattern

In the work described in this paper the addresses have been limited in size to 32 bit signed integers (Figure 2). 64 bit integers can be used but the addresses then become unwieldy for the purposes of illustration. Eight bits are allocated to the first three dimensions and seven for the fourth. The sign bit provides the facility for translating addresses through the space in any direction. It is possible to calculate the tesseral address of a cell from:

$$address = r1 + r2(2^{8}) + r3(2^{16}) + r4(2^{24})$$

in which r1 to r4 represent the discrete coordinates in the four dimensions. r1, r2, r3 will normally represent the x,y,z co-ordinates of geographic space whilst r4 represents a fourth dimension (often temporal). All cell references are unique and conceptually simple to generate and the representation is applicable without modification to any number of dimensions. In addition the effective linearisation of N-dimensional space has significant benefits with respect to (a) data storage, (b) comparison of sets of addresses and (c) translation through the space [8].

3 Adding Constraint Satisfaction

We first define a volume that is of potential interest. This is referred to as the 'object space', and within it 'classes' are used to define the spatial objects. There are two particular types of objects that are most significant; 'fixed objects' (such as buildings in the example below) and 'shapeless objects' (for example sound in the case below). The existing or desired relationships between objects are prescribed by constraints.

The constraint satisfaction process starts with a single 'root node' from which a solution tree is dynamically created. If all the given constraints have only one solution the, tree will consist of a single (root) node. If, however, the scenario includes constraints that have more than one solution, the tree will consist of a number of levels, each level representing a point in the solution process where the satisfaction of a constraint generates more than one solution.

Whenever an additional level in the tree is created each branch is processed in turn until either all constraints have been satisfied, in which case the solution is stored; or an unsatisfiable constraint is discovered. On completion of processing a particular branch the current node is removed from the tree and the system backtracks to the previous node. If all branches emanating from this node have also been processed this node is also removed. The process continues until all branches in the tree have been investigated and all solutions generated. As a result of this approach the solution tree in its conceptual entirety never exists, only the current branch and those higher level nodes which merit further investigation

4 Visualisation of the Tesserally Represented Data

The nature of the quantitative representation, which is, in many respects, a raster encoding, is such that it is immediately compatible with all applications where spatial objects are represented using linear encodings. Examples include image encodings (such as GIF and PBM), some Geographic Information Systems (GIS) and the Admiralty Raster Chart System (ARCS). In addition a tesseral reference can be considered to be both a raster label and a vector quantity. Consequently the representation can also be interfaced to vector representations such as those prevalent in GIS and exchange standards such as the DX90 international drawing exchange standard used for maritime electronic charts.

A visualisation tool has been developed [9] which uses, as its input, tesserally defined, 3-dimensional objects. The output is in the form of a series of lines defined in terms of their start and end Cartesian co-ordinates referenced to the bottom-left corner origin of an appropriately dimensioned "drawing box". This then enables the output to be entirely compatible with graphical languages such as PIC where images are drawn in a procedural manner by specifying the motions that one would go through to draw the picture.

The visualisation assumes a view point from one of the "top" corners of the objects space under consideration; the possible options are "front corner", "right corner", "left corner" and "back corner". No account is taken of perspective; the view is fixed as an axonometric representation. We do not propose to go into detail here, but the nature of the resulting visualisation can be appreciated by consideration of the six different ways in which one cell can partly obscure another. (Figure 3).

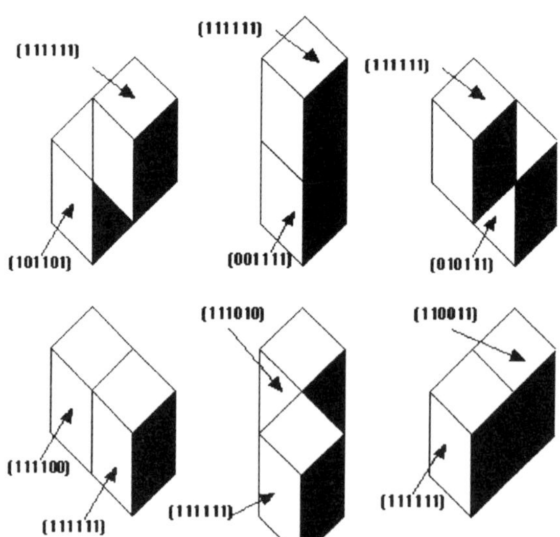

Figure 3 The six different categories of obscurity applied by the visualisation tool.

The second visualisation technique adopted uses modelling and rendering software (AutoCAD and Accurender) commonly used in architectural visualisation. Because the aim of this kind of software is to produce photorealistic representations of buildings they embody many useful features which allow the data be visualised in a variety of appropriate forms [10].

Unlike the previous technique the visualisation can be taken from any eye point and perspective can be used to show distance. In addition to that, the cells can be rendered in a range of ways, not simply as solid colours but with shadows for solid objects or degrees of translucency which allow us to see through cells in the foreground to cells of greater interest and importance in the distance. Yet a further advantage is that we can take cross sections through, or slices out of, the critical parts of the visualised space. Like Palamidese et.al. [11] who used the Renderman software in a different type of application, we aim to take advantage of the kind of facility offered by these relatively sophisticated visualisation packages.

The link between the visualisation software and the SPARTA system is made through a graphical data transfer standard, used frequently in architecture to convert drawings from one CAD system to another, called DXF (Drawing eXchange Format). A short routine had to be written to convert cell locations to the three Cartesian co-ordinates, and then output these co-ordinates, along with a value associated with each co-ordinate. In our case the value was the noise level at that location. The effectiveness of this technique is illustrated in the example given below.

5 An Illustrative Example

The system described has been applied to the study of a potential environmental noise problem resulting from traffic on a proposed new access structure to be added to a major exhibition Hall in London. The task was to examine the potential noise pollution as heavy goods vehicles passed close to existing dwellings as they used the proposed structure. Since our aim is to illustrate the visualisation technique we take the relatively straightforward case of a noise source (a lorry) at a particular location with the geographical space modelled by a fairly coarse grid of cells. We could, if we wish, add a temporal aspect to the problem or make to grid considerably finer. The tesseral representation of the physical objects is shown in Figure 4 in which the exhibition hall is the large object at the rightmost corner.

The vehicle was represented as a point [12] generating a sound power level of 108.5dB. The task was to find the worst case of noise pollution (in terms of the value and location) at the residential building close to the access structure. The geographic space around the exhibition hall was modelled over a volume 200x200x30m with a cell size of 2.5m. The problem was modelled as a four dimensional problem; three dimensions to represent geographical space and noise represented in the fourth dimension. A script was devised to represent the fixed objects in the geographic space (buildings etc.). This was then supplemented by a further script to represent a (shapeless) noise object in excess of 30dB. Levels below this were insignificant. A constraint was applied to fix the location of the sound source on the road.

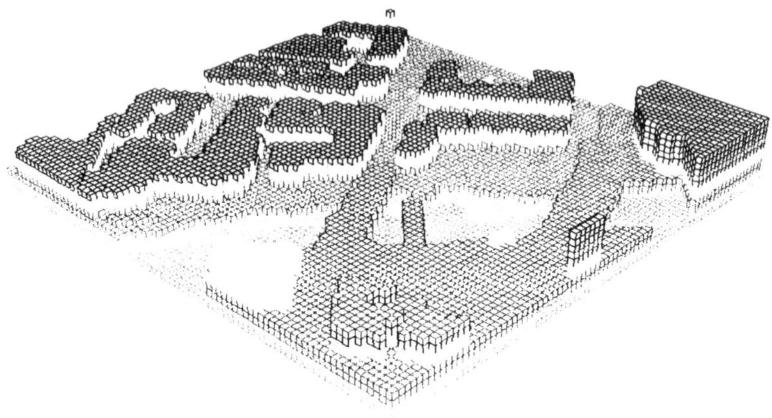

Figure 4: Tesseral representation of the site

Since each vehicle acts as a point source, then the sound pressure level at any location can be taken as:

$$L_p = L_W - 20\log_{10}R + 8$$

in which L_W is the sound power level of the source, L_p is the sound pressure level at a distance R from the source. Again, we used this simple relationship in the example, for the purposes of illustration, recognising that we could have readily incorporated more interesting and powerful techniques such as adopting a stochastic model to represent the generation of noise. Reflection can be modelled by treating sound as being analogous to light reflected from a smooth mirror. Obstruction can be allowed for by increasing the path length, R, by the appropriate amount.

The two images below illustrate the kind of representation that can be produced. In Figure 5 how, with the application of solid colour and shadow casting, the tessellated representation of the fixed objects can be made more clear. By applying a tinted colour to represent intensity of noise levels in the cells representing the space around the physical objects and modelling these cells as translucent glass cubes we can view the noise levels as they radiate out in three dimensions. Consequently the critical location in the accommodation block can be easily identified and, in Figure 6, we have taken a cross sectional slice across the space through the noise source and this critical location in the accommodation block.

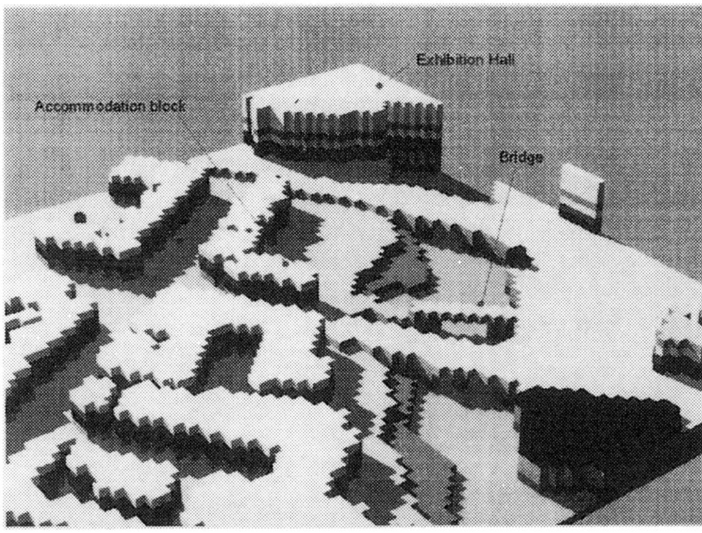

Figure 5 The tesseral representation of the site objects.

Figure 6: Orthogonal Cross Section through the site through the noise source and the critical part of the accommodation block (the hole on the right indicates a bridge over the railway). Shading in the cells defining space (top left) indicates noise intensity

5 Closing Observations

The advantages of the SPARTA AI system have been outlined. In short the main advantages are that it is computationally effective, conceptually simple and is effectively applicable in any number of dimensions.

Attention has been paid, here, to the visualisation of the solution data. It is important that for a complex multidimensional problem the solution can be viewed in a way that shows both particular detail and overall patterns. The two possible strategies that we considered to enable visualisation of the tesseral data have been described and we have shown how one of these techniques allows a very useful and informative visual representation to be achieved.

References

1. Allen, J.F. Maintaining Knowledge about Temporal Intervals, Communications of the ACM, Vol. 26, No. 11, pp. 832-843, 1983
2. Egenhofer, M.J. Deriving the Composition of Binary Topological Relationships, Journal of Visual Languages of Computing, 5, pp 133-149, 1994.
3. Spanier, E.H. Algebraic Topolgy, McGraw-Hill, New York, (1966).
4. van Hentenryck, P., Constraint Satisfaction in Logic Programming, MIT Press, Cambridge, Mass. U.S.A., (1989)
5. Coenen, F.P. Beattie, B., Bench-Capon, T.J.M., Diaz, B.M. and Shave, M.J.R. Spatial reasoning for Geographic information systems, Proc. 1st International Conference on Geocomputation,, School of Geography, University of Leeds, 121-131, 1996.
6. Diaz, B.M. and Bell, S.B.M. Spatial data processing using tesseral methods, publ. Natural Environment Research Council, Swindon, England, 1986
7. Morton, GM, A computer oriented geodetic database, and a new technique on file sequencing, IBM Canada Ltd. (1966).
8. Brown, A.G.P, Coenen, F.P., Shave, M.J. and Knight M.W. An AI approach to noise prediction Building Acoustics, Vol. 4 No. 2 1997.
9. Coenen, F.P. A visualisation tool for 3-Dimensional tesserally represented data, Dept. of Computer Science, Univ. of Liverpool, working paper.
10. Kirkpatrick, J.M. The AutoCAD book: drawing modelling and applications, Prentice Hall, 1998
11. Palamidese, P., Muccioli, G. and Lombardi, G. Enhancing Control on decoration and visualization of art worlds, in Visualization in Scientific Computing (Gobel, Muller and Urban eds.), Springer Verlag, 1995
12. D.O.T. Department of Transport (Welsh Office), Calculation of Road Traffic noise, H.M.S.O., (1988)

A Model for Multimodal Representation and Inference

Luis Pineda and Gabriela Garza
Department of Computer Science, IIMAS, UNAM,
Mexico City, Mexico
luis@leibniz.iimas.unam.mx

Abstract

In this paper some applications of a theory for representation and inference in multimodal scenarios is presented. The theory is focused on the relation between natural language and graphical expressions. First, a brief introduction to the representational structures of the multimodal system is presented. Then, a number of multimodal inferences supported by the system are illustrated. These examples show how the multimodal system of representation can support the definition and use of graphical languages, perceptual inferences for problem-solving and interpretation of multimodal messages. Finally, the intuitive notion of modality underlying this research is discussed.

1. Multimodal Representation

The system of multimodal representation that is summarized in this paper is illustrated in Figure 1. The notion of modality in which the system is based is a representational notion: information conveyed in one particular modality is expressed in a representational language associated with the modality. Each modality in the system is captured through a particular language, and relations between expressions of different modalities are captured in terms of translation functions from basic and composite expressions of the source modality into expressions of the object modality. This view of multimodal representation and reasoning has been developed in [13], [17], [9], [18] and [19], and it follows closely the spirit of Montague's general semiotic programme [5].

The theory is targeted to define natural language and graphical interactive computer systems and, as a consequence, the model is focused in these two modalities. However, the system is also used to express conceptual information in a logical fashion and, depending on the application, the circle labeled **L** might stand for first-order logic or any other symbolic language as long as the syntax is well-defined and the language is given a model-theoretical semantic interpretation.

The circles labeled **L** and **G** in Figure 1 stand for sets of expressions of the natural and graphical languages respectively, and the circle labeled **P** stands for the set of graphical symbols constituting the graphical modality proper (i.e., the actual symbols on a piece of paper or on the screen). Note that two sets of expressions are considered for the graphical modality: the expressions in **G** belong to a formal language in which the geometry of pictures is represented and reasoned about but which is expressive enough to express the translation of natural language expressions. It is an interlingua that permits to relate the natural language syntactic structures with the structure of graphics which is captured with a graphical grammar. **P** contains the overt graphical symbols which can be seen and drawn but cannot be manipulated directly and captures the underlying structure of graphical expressions.

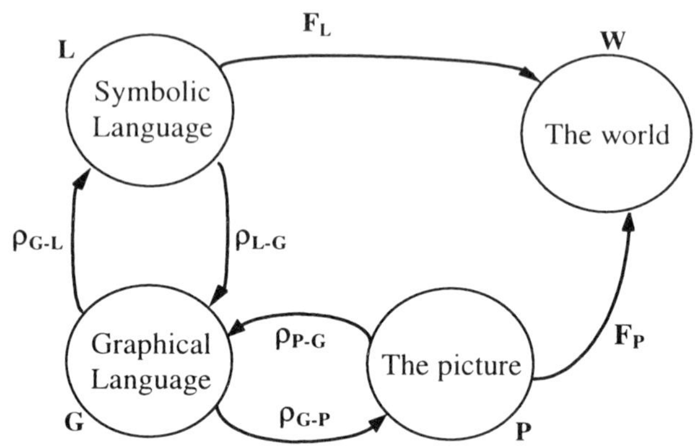

FIGURE 1. Multimodal System of Representation.

The functions $\rho_{L\text{-}G}$ and $\rho_{G\text{-}L}$ stand for the translation mappings between the languages **L** and **G**, and the functions $\rho_{P\text{-}G}$ and $\rho_{G\text{-}P}$ stand for the corresponding translation between **G** and **P**. The translation function $\rho_{P\text{-}G}$ maps well-defined objects of the graphical modality into expressions of **G** where the interpretation process is performed. The translation $\rho_{G\text{-}P}$, on the other hand, maps geometrical expressions of **G** into pictures. The circle labeled **W** stands for the world and together with the functions $\mathbf{F_L}$ and $\mathbf{F_P}$ constitutes a multimodal system of interpretation. The ordered pair $\langle \mathbf{W}, \mathbf{F_L} \rangle$ defines the model $\mathbf{M_L}$ for the natural language, and the ordered pair $\langle \mathbf{W}, \mathbf{F_P} \rangle$ defines the model $\mathbf{M_P}$ for the interpretation of drawings. The interpretation of expressions in **G** in relation to the world is defined either by the composition $\mathbf{F_L} \circ \rho_{G\text{-}L}$ or, alternatively, by $\mathbf{F_P} \circ \rho_{G\text{-}P}$. The denotation of a name in **L**, for instance, is the same as the denotation of the corresponding graphical object in **G**, as both refer to the same individual. The interpretation functions $\mathbf{F_L}$ and $\mathbf{F_P}$ relate basic expressions, either graphical or linguistic, with the objects or relations of the world that these expressions happen to represent, and the definition of a semantic algebra for computing the denotation of composite graphical and linguistic expressions is required. The functions $\rho_{G\text{-}P}$ and $\rho_{P\text{-}G}$ define homomorphisms between **G** and **P** as basic and composite terms of these two languages can be mapped into each other.

The purpose of this paper is to provide an overview of the functionality of the system and for that reason in the next section a number of examples involving multimodal inferences in different application domains are illustrated. The formalization of the multimodal representational system is presented elsewhere (e.g., [19]).

2. Multimodal Inference

In this section a number of problems involving multimodal representation and inference in different domains are illustrated. Once these examples are shown a summary of the kinds of multimodal inferences involved is presented.

2.1. Graphical Languages

Consider the picture in Figure 2.1 in which there are two triangles and two rectangles that have been assigned an interpretation through a graphical and natural language dialogue supported by pointing acts. The setting is such those triangles are interpreted as students and rectangles as subjects; additionally it is stated that if a student is in a subject he or she studies that subject, and if a student studies both subjects he or she is clever. According to this interpretation the picture in Figure 2 .1 is a graphical expression that expresses that both students are clever, but if the picture is manipulated as shown in Figure 2.b, a graphical expression is formed which expresses the fact that only John is clever.

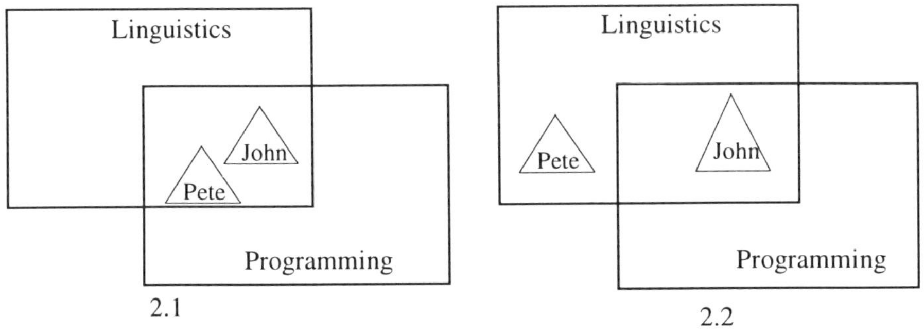

FIGURE 2. Graphical Expressions.

The question is how this knowledge is represented and, in particular, what is the relation between the expression of the abstraction (i.e., that a student is clever), and the geometrical fact that the symbol representing the student is contained within the rectangle representing a subject. For the interpretation of this particular situation the linguistic preposition *in* is interpreted as a geometrical algorithm that computes the relation in the graphical domain. To answer the question whether a student is clever or whether all students are clever, a deductive reasoning process is performed upon the representational structures in the language L; however, when the interpretation of the spatial preposition and its arguments is required to complete the inference, there is no knowledge available in L and the corresponding expression has to be translated into a expression in G in the graphical domain, which in turn can be evaluated by the geometrical interpreter with the help of a geometrical algorithm that tests the geometrical predicates involved. The result of this test is translated back into the language L to allow the reasoning process to succeed. As can be seen, in this kind of inference the picture functions as a recipient of knowledge that can be extracted on demand by the high-level reasoning process performed at the symbolic level. This kind of inference has been characterized as *predicate extraction* by Chandrasekaran in ([4]), and it is commonly used in graphical reasoning systems and the interpretation of expressions of visual languages, where large amounts of information are represented through graphics and geometrical computations improve considerably the efficiency of the reasoning process. For further discussion of this notion of graphical language see [12] and [13].

2.2. Perceptual Inference

One important feature of the multimodal interpretation and reasoning strategies used in the scenario of Section 2.1 is that the translation functions between expressions of **L** and **G** are defined in advance. The multimodal interpretation and reasoning cycle must move across modalities in a systematic fashion and this is achieved through the mappings defined in terms of the translation functions. However, there are situations in which the interpretation of a multimodal message or the solution of a problem involving information in different modalities requires to establish such an association in a dynamic fashion.

Consider, for instance, a problem typical of the Hyperproof system for teaching logic ([2]) in which information is partially expressed through a logical theory and partially expressed through a diagram, as shown in Figure 3.

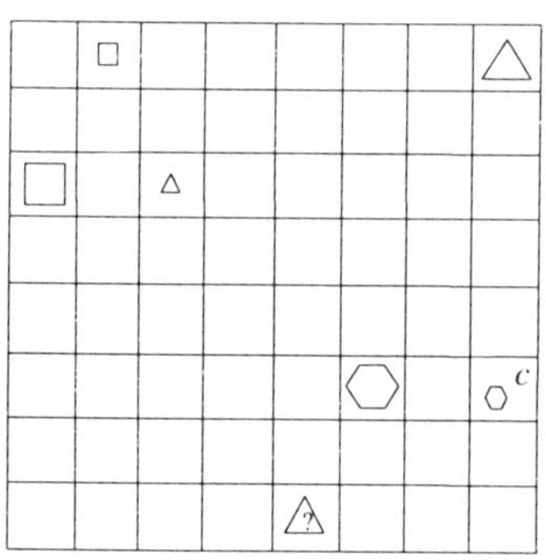

given:

$large(a) \vee small(a)$
$hex(b) \wedge below(a,b)$
$\forall x(triangle(x) \wedge large(x) \rightarrow left\_of(d,x))$
$\neg\exists x(small(x) \wedge below(x,c))$

prove:

$square(d) \vee small(d)$

FIGURE 3. Multimodal problem.

As can be seen the problem consists in finding out whether the object named *d* is either a square or small. This inference would be trivial if we could tell by direct inspection of the diagram what object is *d*, but that information is not available. Note, on the other hand, that under the constraints expressed through the logical language the identity of *d* could be found by a "valid" deductive inference. Note in addition that the information expressed in the diagram in Figure 3 is incomplete. In the Hyperproof setting, the question mark on the bottom triangle indicates that we know that the object is in fact a triangle but its size is unknown to us. However, the conceptual constraints expressed in the logical language do imply a particular size for the occluded object which can be made explicit through the process of multimodal problem-solving. This situation is analogous to the interpretation of images in which some objects are occluded by some others.

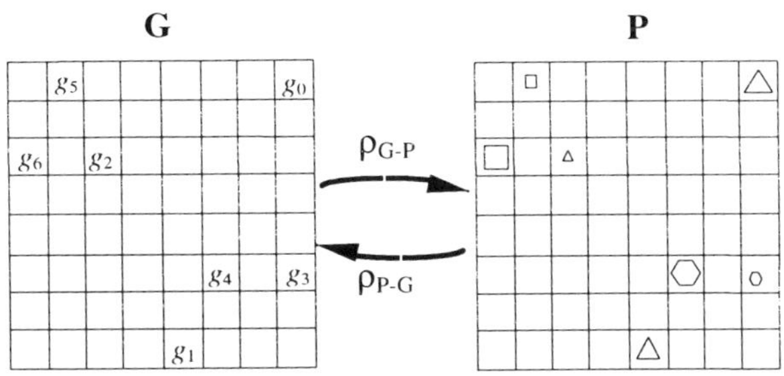

FIGURE 4. Relation between **G** and **P**.

In terms of our system of multimodal representation the task is not, like in the previous example, to make explicit information that was expressed only implicitly by predicate extraction but to find out what are the translations between basic constants of the logical language, the names, and the graphical objects of which they are names of.

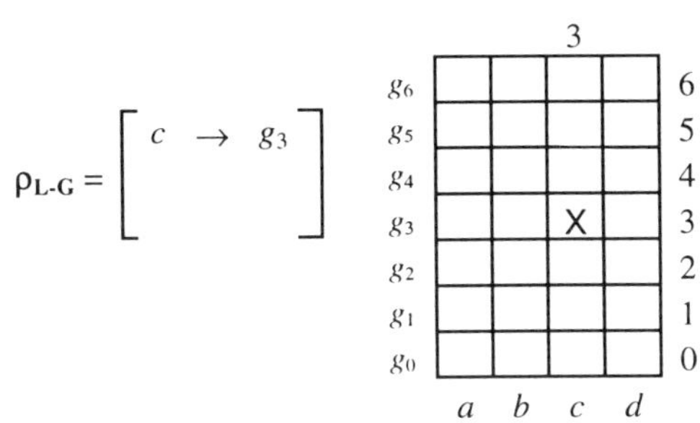

FIGURE 5. Initial interpretation function.

Another way to look at this is thinking of the graphical objects as the domain of interpretation for the logical theory. The multimodal inference consists in finding out all consistent models for the theory, and these can be found through a process of incremental constraint satisfaction. Consider Figure 4 in which a constant of **G** has been assigned to every graphical object (i.e., the objects of **P** properly). At the starting point of the interpretation process only the identity of the block *c* is known as can be seen in Figure 3. Accordingly, the interpretation of the linguistic theory is partially defined only. To see this consider Figure 5 in which a table relating the names of the theory in the horizontal axis with the names of the graphical objects in the vertical one is shown. This table can be interpreted as a partial function from individual constants of **L** to individual constants of **G** if no more than one square in each column is filled up. The interpretation task consists in completing this function by assigning a graphical object to each name in a manner that is consistent with the first-order logical theory expressed in **L**.

The strategy will be to find the set of consistent models incrementally in a cycle in which a formula of the theory is assumed to be true and all consistent models for such an assumption are found out through geometrical verification. Each cycle of assumption and verification is concluded with an abstraction phase in which all consistent models computed in the cycle are subsumed into a single complex object. To exemplify this cycle of model construction consider that the formula $hex(b) \wedge below(a,b)$ –in Figure 3– of the theory can be assumed to be true. With this assumption it is possible to extend the function in Figure 5 in two possible ways, which represent consistent models with the assumption and the given facts, as shown in Figure 6.

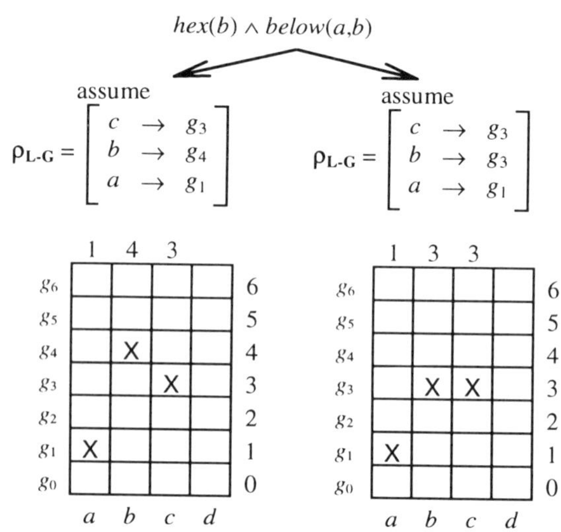

Figure 6. Two possible ways for extending the interpretation function $\rho_{L\text{-}G}$.

To end the incremental constraint satisfaction cycle it can be noticed that the two partial models in Figure 6 are similar in the denotations assigned to the objects *a* and *c*, and only differ in the denotation assigned to object *b*. Then, these two models can be subsumed into a structure by simple superposition as shown in Figure 7 in which the column for *b* that is filled with two marks is taken to represent either of both functions. This incremental constraint satisfaction cycle can be continued until the set of models for the theory is found and expressed as an abstraction, as was discussed above.

Another way to refer to this in the terminology of Chandrasekaran [4] is as *predicate projection* as the predicative information flows not from the picture to the logical theory, as the situation that was referred above as *predicate extraction*, but from the conceptual knowledge expressed through **L** into the graphical theory in **G**.

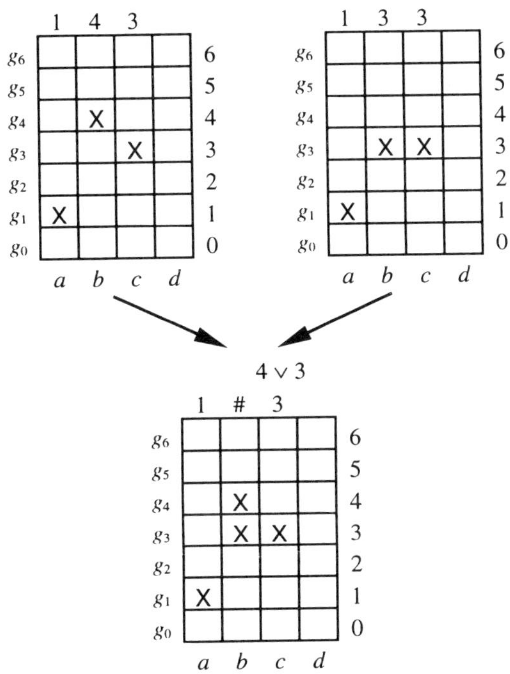

FIGURE 7. Abstraction

Consider that in the original stipulation of the problem the graphical information is incomplete, as the size of the bottom triangle is unknown. However, with the partial model obtained after the first inference cycle, in which such a block has been identified as *a*, the theory constraints the size of the block which can be found by an inferential cycle involving logical deduction in **L** and graphical verification in **G**. For this particular example, and in relation to the partial model in Figure 7, the proof that the size of such a block must in fact be large is given in Figure 8. This inference requires a cycle of assumption, deduction in **L** and verification in **G** which we refer as heterogeneous inference.

In summary, the incremental constraint satisfaction cycle involves the following steps:

1. Visual verification (geometrical interpretation).
2. Assumption and verification of theory (identification of consistent models).
3. Heterogeneous inference.
4. Abstraction

Prove (problem statement):	(0) $large(a) \vee small(a)$
Assume from theory:	(1) $\neg\exists x(small(x) \wedge below(x,c))$
Axiom:	(2) $\neg\exists x(P(x)) \leftrightarrow \forall x(\neg P(x))$
From (1) and (2):	(3) $\forall x(\neg(small(x) \wedge below(x,c)))$
Universal instantiation from (3):	(4) $\neg(small(a) \wedge below(a,c)))$
Morgan's law from (4):	(5) $\neg small(a) \vee \neg below(a,c)$
Direct inspection of the diagram:	(6) $below(a,c)$
From (5) and (6):	(7) $\neg small(a)$
From (0) and (7):	(8) $large(a)$.

FIGURE 8. Heterogeneous inference.

There is an additional way in which we can profit from the process. With the application of this cycle it is possible to find the set of consistent models for the problem stated in Figure 3, which is represented by the abstraction in Figure 9.1, and corresponds to the six graphical configurations shown in Figure 9.2.

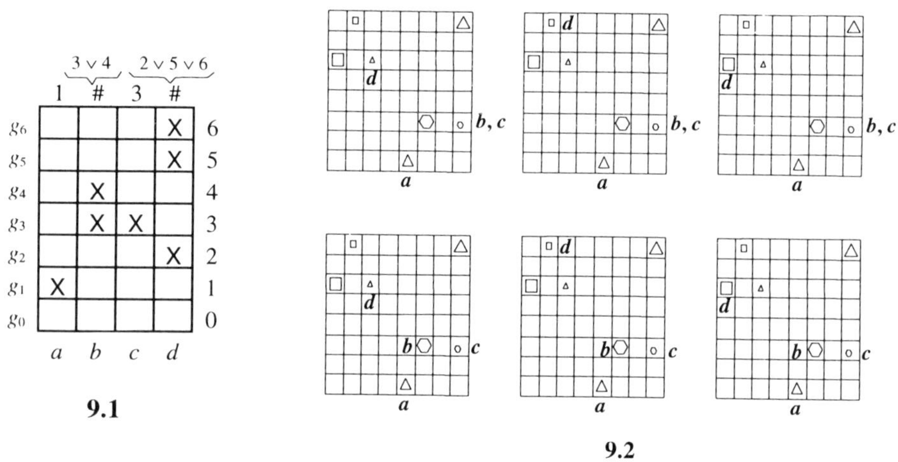

FIGURE 9. The set of consistent interpretations.

4.1. Multimodal Interpretation

The next kind of multimodal inference is related to one of the central problems of multimodal communication which we refer as the problem of multimodal reference resolution. Consider situation in Figure 10 in which a drawing is interpreted as a map thanks to the preceding text. The dots and lines of the drawing, and their properties, do not have an interpretation and the picture in itself is meaningless. However, given the context introduced by the text, and also considering the common sense knowledge that Paris is a city of France and Frankfurt a city of Germany, and that Germany lies to the east of France (to the right), it is possible to infer that the denotations of the dots to the left, middle and right of the picture are Paris, Saarbrücken and Frankfurt, respectively, and that the dashed lines denote borders of countries, and in particular, the lower segment denotes the border between France and Germany. In this example, graphical symbols can be thought of as "variables" of the graphical representation or "graphical pronouns" that can be resolved in terms of the textual antecedent.

"Saarbrücken lies at the intersection of the border between France and Germany and a line from Paris to Frankfurt."

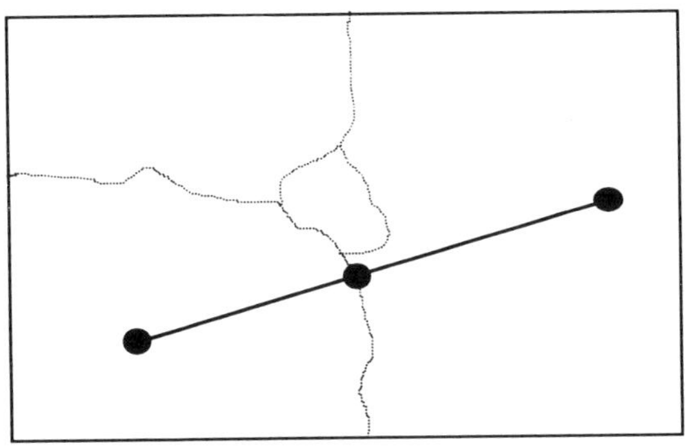

FIGURE 10. Instance of pictorial anaphor with linguistic antecedent.

The situation in Figure 10 has been characterized as an instance of a pictorial anaphor with linguistic antecedent and further related examples can be found in [1]. An alternative view on this kind of problems consists in looking at them in terms of the traditional linguistic notion of deixis [11]. To appreciate the deictic nature of the example consider that the inference required to identify the graphical symbols would be simplified greatly if at the time the words *Paris*, *Frankfurt*, *Saarbrücken*, *France* and *Germany* are mentioned overt pointing acts are performed by the speaker. In such a situation the overt ostension would be one factor of the interpretation context among many others. In this respect we can say that pointing is like describing. However, the opposite is also true: the names in the natural language text are like pointers to the graphical symbols and in order to identify the referents of the linguistic terms an inference process is required. For carrying on with such an identification process the context, including graphics and common sense knowledge about the geography of Europe, needs to be considered. For that reason, if we think of the names or other linguistic terms, like pronouns or descriptions, as pointers whose referent can be found out in terms of the context the situation is deictic. We call the inference process that has as a purpose to identify the referent of a graphical or a linguistic term in a multimodal context a *deictic inference*. This notion contrasts with the notion of anaphoric inference in which the referent of a term is found in terms of a context constructed out of expressions of the same modality of the term.

It should be clear that if all theoretical elements illustrated in Figure 1 are given, questions about multimodal scenarios can be answered through the interpretation process, as was shown for the interpretations of graphical expressions in Section 2.1. However, when one is instructed to interpret a multimodal message, like the one in Figure 10, not all information in the scheme of Figure 1 is available. In particular, the translation functions $\rho_{L\text{-}G}$ and $\rho_{G\text{-}L}$ for basic constants are not known, and the crucial inference of the interpretation process has as its goal to induce these functions. This is exactly the problem of finding the set of consistent models in the perceptual inferences carried out in the context of the Hyperproof system as illustrated in the previous section. According to our theory, the kind of so-called perceptual inferences performed by users of the hyperproof system can be characterized as deictic inferences.

5. Summary of Multimodal Inferences

From the examples in Sections 2.1 to 2.3 a number of inference strategies have been employed. Similar strategies can be found on examples about design (see [6], [15] and [16]). An analogous view of interpretation of pictures is developed in Reiter's Logic of Depiction (see [20]). Reasoning directly on expressions of a particular representational language, like **L** or **G**, corresponds to traditional symbolic reasoning. However, reasoning in **G** involves, in addition to symbolic manipulation, a process of geometrical interpretation as predicates in **G** have an associated geometrical algorithm. Another way to think about the geometrical representation is that it has a number of expressions representing explicit knowledge; however, it has a large body of implicit knowledge that can be accessed not from a valid symbolic inference, but from the geometry.

The multimodal system of representation supports an additional inference strategy that involves the induction of the translation of basic constants between the languages **L** and **G**, and this process is qualitatively different from a simple symbolic manipulation process operating on expressions of a single language. Examples of this kind of inference strategy are perceptual inferences and resolution of multimodal references which, as we have argued, can be characterized as deictic inferences.

In terms of the system, a multimodal inference can be deductive if it involves symbolic processing in both languages in such a way that information is extracted from one modality and used in the other by means of the translation functions. Multimodal inferences involving the induction of translation relations, or the computation of models, on the other hand, are related to deictic inferences. The use of these two main kinds of multimodal inference strategies is the characteristic of a multimodal inference process which has a deictic character.

6. A Notion of Modality

The multimodal system of representation and inference that has been illustrated in this paper has been developed on the basis of an intuitive notion of modality that can be characterized as *representational*. Representational in the sense that a modality is related in our system to a particular representational language, and information conveyed through a particular modality is represented as expressions of the language associated with the modality. The reason for taking this position is that one aim of this research is to be able to distinguish what information is expressed in what modality, and to clarify the notion of multimodal inference. If an inference is multimodal, it should be clear how modalities interact in the inference process.

This view contrasts with a more psychologically oriented notion in which modalities are associated with sensory devices. In this latter view one talks about visual or auditive modality; however, as information of the same modality can be expressed through different senses (like spoken and written natural language), and the same sense can be used to perceive information of different modalities (written text and pictures are interpreted through the visual channel) this psychological view offers little theoretical tools to clarify how modalities interact in an inference process, and the very notion of modality is unclear.

One consequence of our system is that modalities have to be thought of as related in a systematic fashion, and this relation is established in terms of a relation of translation between modality specific representational languages. One of the reasons to adopt Montague's semiotic programme is precisely to model the relation between modalities as translation between languages.

This view implies also that perceptual mechanisms are related to representational languages in specific ways: a message can only be interpreted in one modality if the information of the message can be mapped by the perceptual devices into a well-formed expression of the representational language associated with the modality. The algorithms mapping information in **P** to expressions of **G**, for instance, are designed relative to the syntactic structure of **G.** These algorithms might be different for different modalities, but once a multimodal system is set up these algorithms are wired, and are fired automatically if suitable input information is present to the input device. This let us to postulate two kinds of perceptual devices: physical, like the visual or auditive apparatus, and logical or conceptual, which relate information input by physical sensory devices with modality specific representational languages. Whether these views can be held is matter for further research.

References

1. Elisabeth André and Thomas Rist. 1994. Referring to World Objects with Text and Pictures, technical report, German Research Center for Artificial Intelligence (DFKI).

2. Jon Barwise and John Etchemendy. 1994. *Hyperproof.* CSLI.

3. A. Borning. 1981. The Programming Language Aspects of Thinglab, A Constraint-Oriented Simulation Laboratory. *ACM Transactions in Programming Languages and Systems*. 3, No. 4. pp. 353-387.

4. B. Chandrasekaran. 1997. Diagrammatic Representation and Reasoning: some Distinctions. *Working notes on the AAAI-97 Fall Symposium Reasoning with Diagrammatic Representations II.* MIT, November 1997. (Also in this volume).

5. David R. Dowty, Robert E. Wall and Stanley Peters. 1985. *Introduction to Montague Semantics.* D. Reidel Publishing Company, Dordrecht, Holland.

6. E. G. Garza and L. A. Pineda, 1998. "Synthesis of Solid Models of Polyhedra Views using Logical Representations, Expert Systems with Applications, Vol. 14, No. 1. Pergamon 1998.

7. Hans Kamp. 1981. A Theory of Truth and Semantic Representation. *Formal Methods in the Study of Language*, 136 pp. 277-322, Mathematical Centre Tracts.

8. Hans Kamp and Uwe Reyle. 1993. *From Discourse to Logic*. Kluwer Academic Publisher, Dordrecht, Holland.

9. Ewan Klein and Luis Pineda. 1990. Semantics and Graphical Information. *Human-Computer Interaction, Interact'90*. pp. 485-491. Diaper, Gilmore, Cockton, Shackel (eds). IFIP, North-Holland.

10. Wm Leler. 1987. *Constraint Programming Languages*. Addison-Wesley Publishing Company.

11. John Lyons. 1968. *Introduction to Theoretical Linguistics*, Cambridge University Press, Cambridge.

12. Luis Pineda, Ewan Klein and John Lee. 1988. Graflog: Understanding Graphics through Natural Language. *Computer Graphics Forum*, Vol. 7(2).

13. Luis Pineda. 1989. Graflog: a Theory of Semantics for Graphics with Applications to Human-Computer Interaction and CAD Systems. PhD thesis, University of Edinburgh, U.K.

14. Luis Pineda. 1992. Reference, Synthesis and Constraint Satisfaction. *Computer Graphics Forum*. Vol. 2, No. 3, pp. C-333 - C-334.

15. L. A. Pineda, "On Computational Models of Drafting and Design", Design Studies, Vol. 14 (2), pp. 124-156. April, 1993.

16. L. A. Pineda, Santana, J. S., Massé, A. "Satisfacción de Restricciones Geométricas: ¿Problema Numérico o Simbólico?", Memorias de XI Reunión Nacional de Inteligencia Artificial, Universidad de Guadalajara, SMIA, pp. 105 - 123, 1994.

17. Luis Pineda. 1996. Graphical and Linguistic Dialogue for Intelligent Multimodal Systems. In *G. P. Facinti and T. Rist editors, WP32 Proceedings, 12th European Conference on Artificial Intelligence ECAI-96*, Hungary, August. Budapest University of Economic Sciences.

18. J. Sergio Santana, Sunil Vadera, Luis Pineda. 1997. The Coordination of Linguistic and Graphical Explanation in th Context of Geometric Problem-solving Tasks, *technical report on the IIE/University of Salford in-house PhD Programme*.

19. Luis Pineda and Gabriela Garza. 1997. A Model for Multimodal Reference Resolution (submitted to *Computational Linguistics*).

20. Raymond Reiter and Alan K. Mackworth. 1987. The Logic of Depiction, *Research in Biological and Computational Vision*, University of Toronto.

Visualisation in Document Retrieval: An Example of the Integration of Software Ergonomics and an Aesthetic Quality in Design

Bernhard E. Bürdek
College of Design, Offenbach, Dept. of Industrial Design

Maximilian Eibl
Social Sciences Information Center, Bonn

Jürgen Krause
Institute of Computer Science, University of Coblence
and Social Sciences Information Center, Bonn

Abstract

Today, software ergonomics on the one hand, and media design on the other, are two separate schools that have few common goals in the area of designing user interfaces and, naturally, they come up with different solutions. Whereas ergonomics place the accent on the most effective operation, interface and media design put the artistic, creative aspect in the foreground, ignoring efficient methods of program handling. This article describes the practical attempt to combine both schools. As a working example we created a visualisation for a document retrieval system.

1 Introduction

In the mid-1980s, industrial designers in a number of countries started to examine the potential uses of computer technologies in the design process. The original objective was to use CAD/CAM systems in particular to optimise the design process itself. However, the available hardware and software systems were geared largely towards the needs of engineers in various disciplines. In particular, the cryptic user interfaces still normal at the time prevented the rapid spread of the CAD/CAM idea in design. Moreover, suppliers had no real interest in adapting to designers' needs because the potential target group was apparently too small.
On the threshold of the 1990s, however, the operation of products and equipment started to shift more and more to monitors or LCDs, and design itself changed - at

least in part - from three-dimensional modelling to the two-dimensional design of so-called user interfaces. This development can be described as the transition from a "linguistic turn" to a "visual turn". Today, Andy Grove (Intel) says that the "battle for the apple of the eye" has only just begun. We are now in the middle of the visual age, in which users need more structuring and orientation, i.e. form or design.

The terms "interface" and "interaction design" were therefore used to give a new name to a subject area located at the intersection of functionality and aesthetics. Engineering sciences, software human factors, and computer science are increasingly becoming reference disciplines for industrial design - in fact a new cognitive area for design itself has emerged. A new discipline - software design - can now be distilled from the long tradition of functionalism and from product-language knowledge about design itself.

The following article describes a project of this kind in the area of text retrieval. Text retrieval is, in general, a very interesting problem for visualisation, because Boolean algebra is difficult to use.

The visualisation presented in this article makes two basic assumptions about the use of Boolean search logic in document retrieval systems. Firstly, a user for whom working with such a system is only a means to an end (e.g. library information systems at universities) has great difficulty with the concept of Boolean algebra, and therefore produces too many invalid queries. The more specifically he wants to express his need for information, and the more complex his query becomes, the greater the probability of errors. There are several factors behind this, like for example the difference between the natural-language and the Boolean use of "OR", the difficulties in the Boolean "NOT", or the complexity of nesting with brackets. Here, a visualisation of the query can help free the user from the strictly logical ballast of the Boolean search, and allow him intuitive access.

The second assumption has to do with the search strategy of document retrieval systems. Normally, the user first formulates a broader query, and has the system show how many documents have been found. Their number decides whether the user displays the documents or reformulates the query, to narrow or widen the result. He therefore uses the number of documents found to determine the quality of his query.

2 Systems and Basic Questions

The attempt to make the query components of information retrieval systems user-friendly and efficient with the help of visualisation is by no means new. Michard

[1] already presents a system whose central interaction mode is a visualisation based on a Venn diagram. This approach very soon reaches its limits because of the problem of representation. It is just not possible to draw a Venn diagram for more than three descriptors. If the number of descriptors exceeds three, the user must take one or several intersections, call up a new representation, and fill one of the circles with the extracted set.

Spoerri [2] solves the problem of the closed nature of Michard's visualisation with the InfoCrystal system, which explodes the subsets of the diagram. The result is a representation in which the descriptors, reduced to icons, form the corners of a polygon, and the logical combinations of the descriptors within the polygon are also represented as icons, initialised with the number of documents found. Spoerri uses a large number of partly redundant codes: shape coding, rank coding, colour and texture coding, orientation coding, size or brightness and saturation coding. By these graphical means, the individual icons can be allocated clearly and unambiguously. However, the user must first learn the codes, and analyse them separately in the course of each query.

The VIBE system [3][4] exploits a principle similar to that of InfoCrystal. Here, too, the descriptors form a polygon. There are essential differences from InfoCrystal in that, firstly, users can alter the position of the descriptors in VIBE, and secondly, Boolean combinations of the descriptors no longer appear within the polygon; instead, the documents themselves are represented.

The LyberSphere, or sphere of relevance, in the LyberWorld system introduces the third dimension [5]. It consists of a sphere or planet, over the surface of which the descriptors are evenly distributed and hover like geostationary satellites. Within the sphere are the documents that match the descriptors. As in VIBE, the position of the documents results from their relationships to the descriptors. "The kernel of the metaphor turns out to be the physical notion of gravitation"[6]. This planetary gravitation metaphor must be treated with care though, because the central planet serves only as a pretext for the satellites and exerts no force of gravity itself. It therefore turns out to be not a planet, but just a bubble that merely separates the documents from the descriptors. Though LyberSphere may reduce ambiguities in the positioning of the documents compared to VIBE by using the third dimension, it can in no way eliminate them. Here, too, interaction is required if any ambiguities are to be resolved.

The galaxy model in the Vineta system [7] represents the logical extension of the planetary gravitation metaphor. In three-dimensional space, the descriptors appear as arrows that form an information space in which the documents float in the form of spheres. Here, too, the descriptors (suns) attract the documents (planets). The association of the documents is indicated by little pins stuck into the planets. The galaxy model dispenses with LyberSphere's central sphere, so there is no longer any definite spatial partition between documents and descriptors. The criticism of increased complexity of presentation must therefore be levelled at Vineta, in addition to the points already criticised in LyberSphere.

The comparison of the systems described here shows that three basic decisions must be made in the area of text retrieval: 1) Should the documents be presented singly or bundled? The individual representation of the documents can express the relevance of each document more distinctly. Bundled representation helps to avoid ambiguity more easily, and drastically reduces the complexity of the presentation. 2) Does it make sense to employ the gravitation metaphor, which, though seemingly appropriate at first, obviously raises serious problems on closer inspection? 3) Should a two- or three-dimensional representation be used? When representing the elements of an n-dimensional space, it seems appropriate to use the greatest number of dimensions that a human being can handle cognitively. On the other hand, if one has to "flatten" the n-dimensional space anyway to make it representable, would it not make more sense to go the whole hog and reduce it to a less complex, two-dimensional structure?

The visualisations presented here differ in these three points. In the search for a suitable form of representation, we cannot avoid answering these questions first.

We have decided to use set representation for the following reasons:

- The representation is greatly simplified. Whereas the single-document representations dealt with here are totally confusing even when the number of documents exceeds a mere dozen, the use of bundled sets of documents allows several hundred documents to be accommodated simultaneously, without making the representation too complex.
- When the documents are bundled in sets, their relationships are more clearly visible, and the user does not have to examine each document separately. This significantly reduces the time taken to process a query.
- The overall appearance of the visualisation of the single documents changes with each new or reformulated query. This forces the user to reorientate himself. When using sets of documents, as is the case in InfoCrystal, the user always has the same image before him, as long as the number of descriptors remains the same. The recognition value reduces the time taken here, too.
- The precision of the representation is not only negligible, it is actually obstructive. For a suitable search strategy, it makes more sense to use the

visualisation to limit the amount of text to be examined, and then to change the mode and display the text of the documents. Bearing in mind the example mentioned in the introduction, this change of mode comes too late in the single-document representation.

We consider the introduction of visual formalisms [8] and the rejection of the attraction metaphor as practical for the following reasons:

- The attraction metaphor does not work. It has serious flaws.
- The attraction metaphor is not capable of representing relevance in a way that is free of ambiguity.
- This problem is not solved but only retarded by introducing the third dimension. In addition, the extension of the metaphors into galaxy and planet metaphors arising from the addition of the third dimension also causes additional major crass flaws.
- As opposed to the attraction metaphor, visual formalism can show relevance unambiguously, and can solve the problem of dimension by introducing appropriate coding.

We have decided to use "only" two dimensions for the following reasons:

- The fact that, ambiguities crop up later in the three-dimensional representation, does not mean that no ambiguities crop up. It would, however, be desirable to create a visualisation that remains unambiguous in its representation, independent of dimensionality. As Roppel [9] demonstrates, the apparent advantage of the third dimension with regard to focus-context visualisation and space-saving is achieved at the expense of serious problems with interaction. The much heralded simplification of orientation is non-existent. The arguments of the 3D advocates are therefore untenable.
- The inclusion of the third dimension sharply increases complexity. Because the three dimensions are squeezed together to two again on the screen, the representation is in no way simplified. The aim of visualisation, however, should be to make complex situations as easy as possible to grasp.
- Human perception is by no means as three-dimensional as one might like to believe. "Given our lives on the surface of Earth, our experience is of a world with greater extent in the horizontal than the vertical; one might even call our every-day world '2.1-dimensional'" [10][11]. So, if one has to map the dimensionality of information space using methods other than space, it is recommended to limit the spatial dimensions to two.

3 Introduction of Media and Interface Design

Today, software ergonomics on the one hand, and interface and media design on the other, are two separate schools that have few common goals in the area of designing user interfaces and come up with different solutions. Whereas ergonomics place the accent on the most effective operation, interface and media design put the artistic, creative aspect in the foreground, at best ignoring efficient methods of program handling, sometimes even deliberately avoiding them.

Both schools have proved their justification over and over again, with regard to their goals and their way of implementing them. Modern computer programs have steadily increased in complexity over the last decades, and the opportunities they offer, above all the opportunities for user errors, have multiplied again and again. A knowledge of software ergonomics helps to gain mastery over this complexity, and make computer programs capable of effective use, instead of overtaxing the user with frustrating, error-fraught unwieldiness. Today, software ergonomics may in this way help to produce user-friendly user interfaces, but they have always avoided taking account of aesthetic aspects.

The aesthetic aspects, on the other hand, are taken care of by interface and media design, which present aesthetically pleasing interfaces which flaunt ergonomic aspects in favour of aesthetics. In fact, they actually break ergonomic rules in order to heighten the aesthetic effect and induce the user to come to closer terms with the interface; to explore it, so to speak, before starting to work with it. The two schools have not hitherto been united, so the design of a user interface presents the choice between the effective ugliness of ergonomics, and the involved, explorative grace of interface and media design.

In 1996, a co-operation agreement was made between the College of Design, Offenbach, the Institute of Computer Science, University of Coblence, and the Social Sciences Information Center. Their stated goal was to bring software ergonomics and interface and media design closer together in order to combine the cognitive but anaesthetic solutions of software ergonomics with the stylistically well-thought-out but less effective ones of interface and media design, and to find common solutions that do justice to both sides.

The visualisation presented here was conceived as part of this co-operation, to include aspects of interface and media design. The first rough idea was the result of a meeting between the authors, who discussed more than 40 draughts under the aspects of software ergonomics and of interface and media design. The purpose was to demonstrate that the two schools could, after all, be combined to advantage.

4 Implementation

Implementation began by reprogramming the basic concepts of InfoCrystal, as these seemed to come closest to fulfilling the requirements stated in 2. This remake was supplied with test data from the Social Sciences Information Center, Bonn. It was used for informal user testing by the researchers at the Information Center. In this phase, problems arose that indicated that the coding of InfoCrystal was too inconsistent and the representation too complex. In particular, the reorientation that is necessary when adding new descriptors led to persistent problems. The concept further led to the use of a wrong search strategy, in that mostly too many search arguments were entered, without evaluating the intermediate results. This contrasts with the search strategy discussed in the introduction.

Inconsistent coding not only caused problems for the users, but was unsatisfactory from the point of view of interface and media design because the use of very varied forms prevented the creation of a unified overall appearance.

Fig. 1 shows the newly created visualisation, and how it can be used to build up a query in stages. This visualisation does without metaphors, and is strictly formal from a visual aspect. In the area on the left, the search arguments are arranged vertically one below the other. Fig. 1a shows the initial representation. Here, the user can start by entering the search arguments. In the example shown, these are descriptors. In reality, the user can choose between titles, authors, etc. The entry of several search arguments in one field is also possible (OR-ing). As soon as the user has entered more than one argument, all possible combinations of the arguments appear on the right of the input fields. The combinations are arranged in columns according to their valence, i.e. whether they are 2-, 3- or 4-fold, etc.

The visualisation is designed as an open one; that is, in principle, an infinite number of search arguments can be entered without requiring a change to the basic appearance of the visualisation.

The coding of the set icons is now performed with colours. This does make identification more difficult, but it also leads the user away from the Boolean query towards a more intuitive search. Whereas InfoCrystal encourages the user to explore all the icons, he can concentrate here on the most important icons at the top of the combination columns. Should he feel the need to examine the exact relationships of the individual icons after all, he only has to drag the mouse over the set icons, and all the input fields that are not related to this set are dimmed.

A variety of further tools help the user to achieve an even more exact definition of the sets than would be possible with Boolean logic. For example, he can click on each separate set icon to display authors and titles, and a ranked list of all the descriptors of the documents in the set. He can thus ascertain the contents of the documents and the possibility of further queries.

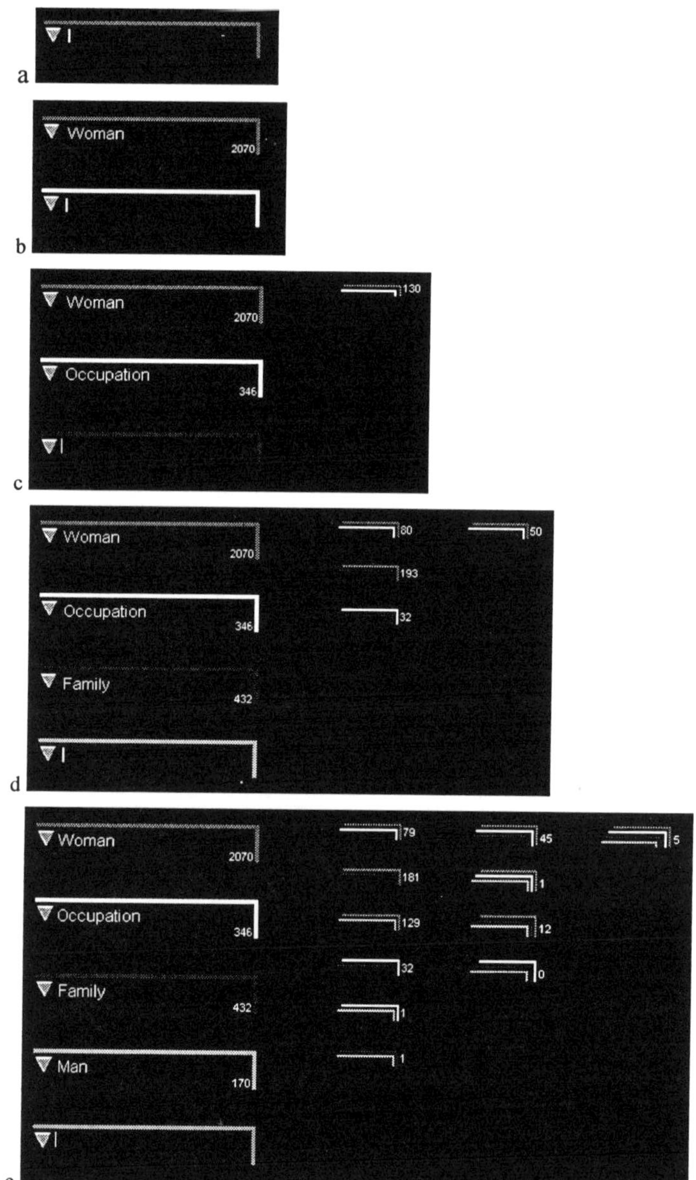

Fig. 1: Structure of a Query

Apart from considerations related to software ergonomics, interface and media design contributed to the style of the visualisation. The basic stylistic element is the bracket. Each input field is defined by a large bracket enclosing the search argument, a base-over-apex triangle that serves to open a drop-down list, and the number of documents found with the search argument.
The document sets are defined by a series of superimposed, small brackets which evoke associations with file cards. Here, the number of documents is deliberately placed beside the icons in order to make it clear that it applies to the total number of documents found. It is not the sequence number of the "uppermost" card. The choice of the angle as the basic stylistic device evidences on the one hand, the matter-of-fact, technical nature of the visualisation, and on the other hand it is reminiscent of the purpose of document retrieval because of the suggested association (It is not a metaphor!) of the file card. Through the choice and consistent use of this stylistic device, the visualisation receives a unified and appropriate appearance.

5 Conclusion and Outlook

The next step is to introduce probabilistic and vague retrieval. The position of the icons will be defined using the Binary Independence Retrieval Model. The position along the X-axis refers to the weights of the terms which are gained using the inverse document frequency. Since this is a wholly statistical approach the user might want to determine the weights himself. In order to free him from abstract weight measuring revision of the weights can be done by direct manipulation. He will have the possibility to drag the term icons along the X-axis by using the mouse. Concerning vague retrieval the user will have the opportunity to edit the size of the document icons. The system will fill up the sets with similar documents.
The visualisation presented here has not yet been submitted to formal user testing. However, informal user surveys have shown a positive response. On the whole, they have indicated a high degree of user acceptance, and have led to improvements in several details.
The approach of combining software ergonomics with interface and media design seems promising. In future, the GESINE information system, which offers this visualisation as an alternative query method, will be modified in a similar way, or its interface will be completely reworked. GESINE is a query system that integrates texts and facts, and was created for the heterogeneous GESIS database at the Social Sciences Information Center. It has already been partially optimised from a software ergonomics aspect and is therefore a good starting point. But a

development of the basic idea that can be implemented here on all levels of the interface calls for a complete - and exemplary - redesign of all controls and windows, because the standard elements of Windows programming can no longer be worked in without destroying the overall aesthetics.

6 References

1. Michard, A. Graphical Presentation of Boolean Expressions in a Database Query Language: Design notes and ergonomic evaluation. Behaviour and Information Technologies 1982;1,3:279-288
2. Spoerri, A. InfoCrystal: Integrating Exact and Partial Matching Approaches through Visualisation. RIAO'94 Conference Proceedings „Intelligent multimedia information retrieval systems and management", New York (NY), Oct.11-13, 1994:687-696
3. Korfhage , R. To see or Not to See - Is *That* the Query? Conference Proceedings SIGIR 1991: 134-141
4. Olsen, Kai A. Visualisation of a Document Collection: The Vibe System. Information Processing & Management, 1993;29,1:69-81
5. Hemmje, M. LyberWorld - Eine 3D-basierte Benutzerschnittstelle für die computerunterstützte Informationssuche in Dokumentmengen. GMD-Spiegel 1993; 1:56-63
6. Krause, J. Visualisierung und graphische Benutzungsoberflächen. IZ-Arbeitsbericht Nr.3, Bonn, 1996
7. Elzer, P., Krohn, U. Visualisierung zur Unterstützung der Suche in komplexen Datenbeständen. Proceedings of the HIM '97 - „Hypertext - Information Retrieval - Multimedia". Dortmund, 1997: 27-38
8. Nardi, B.A., Zarmer, C.L. Beyond Models and Metaphors: Visual Formalisms in User Interface Design. Journal of Visual Languages and Computing 1993; 4: 5-33
9. Roppel, S. Visualisierung und Adaption: Techniken zur Verbesserung der Interaktion mit hierarchisch strukturierter Information. PhD thesis, University of Regensburg, Germany, 1996
10. Chalmers, M. Visualisation of Complex Information. In: Bass, L., Gornostaev, J., Unger, C. (Eds.) Human-Computer Interaction. Third International Conference, EWHCI ′93. Moskau, August 1993. Berlin et al. [=Lecture Notes in Computer Science 753]1993: 152-162
11. Gibson, James J. The ecological approach to visual perception, Boston, 1986

Visualising Dynamic Browsing Patterns via Navigation Agents

David Reid and Chris Gittings
Connect: the Internet Centre for Merseyside Businesses
Department of Computer Science, The University of Liverpool
Liverpool, England
{david,gittings@csc.liv.ac.uk}

Abstract

This paper describes ongoing design and development of a system called MANTRA, for WWW site visitors and designers. We outline the MANTRA system, examining how Navigation Agents are modelled. We also describe current research into mechanisms for agent persistence.

1. Introduction

There are various systems which are designed to analyse and visualise the browsing behaviour of visitors to World Wide Web (WWW) sites. Some of these systems rely on analysis of static snapshots of browsing behaviour, captured in server log files; others attempt to adapt dynamically as a browse progresses.

Yan [1] proposes a system which analyses server log files and automatically suggests new links for categorised users. The Navigational View Builder (described in Mukherjea [2]) is a tool to develop effective overview diagrams of hypermedia systems. Chambers et al. [3] focuses on the representation of, and access to, Web-based information. A recommender tool tracks a user's browse and presents the URLs that appear to be most relevant to recently logged activity.

WebWatcher [4] is a software agent intended to give similar assistance to that provided by a human guide. It guides the user on an appropriate path through a set of WWW documents, based on its current knowledge of the user's interests.

Letizia [5] is a user interface agent that assists browsing. The agent tracks a browse and attempts to anticipate items of interest. Using heuristics derived from browsing behaviour, Letizia suggests potential links of interest. Alexa [6] is a plug-in addition to a WWW browser, which provides suggestions for related sites as a browse proceeds. Mapuccino [7] constructs visual maps of static WWW sites, without reference to browsing behaviour.

These systems described above are limited in their ability to react to the potential rapid changes in WWW site content, and the dynamic browsing behaviour of visitors to the WWW site. To address the dynamics of these rapidly changing environments, we are developing a prototype system called MANTRA (Multi-Agent Navigation TRAcking).

We take a novel approach by introducing concepts from genetics into our dynamic model representing the visitors to a site. MANTRA is intended to be utilised by both WWW site visitors and site developers. It can be used to visualise the dynamic behaviour of a collection of visitors. We can identify documents which attract many visitors, and may be able to identify improvements to the site layout, to make navigation through the site simpler.

In addition, by attempting to categorise a visitor based on their dynamic browsing behaviour, and then matching them with similar visitors, we can suggest potential links of interest, based on the behaviour of these matching visitors. We provide an overview of MANTRA in the next section.

2. Overview of MANTRA

2.1. Browse Signature

Conceptually, we regard a path through a set of documents visited during a user's browse, plus the length of time spent on each document, as defining a *signature* for the browse. The browse pattern is encoded in a *Navigation Agent*.

2.2. Navigation Agents

For each current user browsing the site, there is a corresponding Navigation Agent in MANTRA. As described later, agents can also exist in other circumstances.

2.2.1. Genetic Encoding

Rather than basing a match on static snapshots of a browse, we utilise a simple genetic algorithm which encapsulates the dynamic characteristics of differing browsing behaviour. In this context, the signature of a browse is regarded as a *gene*, encoded in the agent.

2.2.2. Agent Attributes

As a user moves around a WWW site from document to document in the site, this dynamically modifies the gene which is assigned that this user, encoded in the user's Navigation Agent. In addition to the encoded gene, an agent has other dynamic attributes. It has a location, which represents the document currently being visited. It also has an associated energy level, which reduces as the agent moves in the environment.

Each document in the site is represented by a node in the graph. An arc in this graph can correspond to a HTML hyperlink between the documents. Also, they can represent virtual links followed by a user as a result of suggestions from MANTRA; there might not be a corresponding hyperlink between the documents. Navigation Agents can move from node to node, along the physical or virtual arcs.

2.2.3. Genetic Matching and Agent Interaction

As well as the Navigation Agents associated with current visitors, other Navigation Agents can also exist. First, an agent continues to exist after its corresponding user leaves the WWW site, moving and interacting according to its encoded genetic information, until its energy level reaches zero.

Second, a new agent can be created as the genetic offspring of two current agents. If several agents exist at the same document contemporaneously, some of them may crossbreed. Two agents crossbreed if their genes are 'similar', based on a simple similarity metric. The offspring from these two agents inherits some of its genetic characteristics from each of them. These inherited characteristics determine how this new agent navigates independently through the MANTRA environment, interacting with existing agents.

If a specific document becomes too crowded, agents may become aggressive and fight other agents. This results in loss of energy to the fighting agents. An aggressive agent is represented visually in a darker colour. Non-tracking agents slow down as they lose energy.

New genetic material is added to the system as new users browse the site. As a result, the gene pool is continually evolving as new visitors browse the site, as the agents interact, and as the WWW site itself is modified.

2.3. User Interaction with MANTRA

There are two main methods for interacting with the proposed MANTRA system: via visualisation of the interacting agents, and following one of the suggested links from a matching signature.

2.3.1. Visualisation of Interacting Agents

For each user, a separate Java application window is used to visualise the current state of MANTRA. In this window, the MANTRA graph is displayed, together with the positions of existing Navigation Agents. The agents move in real-time; agents corresponding to a real user move as the user visits different documents. Non-tracking agents move according to their genetically-encoded behaviour.

The appendix shows screenshots of the agent visualisation tool. Figure 1 shows an environment containing a few agents; Figure 2 shows a more crowded environment, including some aggressive agents represented in the darker colour.

2.3.2. Displaying Suggested Links

When the Navigation Agent of the current user encounters a similar agent at the same document, MANTRA will suggested links to follow, based on the gene encoded in the similar agent. If the current user selects one of these links, their browser is taken to the new location. The agent making the suggestion will be rewarded with an energy boost. In this way, *fitter* genes survive in the environment longer. Other non-tracking agents which do not match with agents from current users, as well as matching agents whose suggestions are not followed, ultimately run out of energy sooner.

3. MANTRA Implementation

Navigation Agents perform two major roles: to gather browse data from visitors to a particular site, and to interact with similar agents. For the former role, the agent needs access to personal data from the browser, namely, its current location.

Each agent, programmed in Java, interacts with a user's browser, acquiring this information. Initially, a signed applet must be downloaded, to grant permission to access the browser location. On request from the corresponding Navigation Agent in the MANTRA environment, this applet transmits the documents visited, plus the time at each document, to the agent. This information is encoded in two arrays, representing the URL of each visited document in one array, and the time at each document in the other.

For the latter role, we compare individual alleles of a pair of agents. Two agents are considered similar if the alleles in each agent are in approximately the same location in the array of visited URLs. Consider two genes (arrays) of length m and n and where $z = max(m, n)$.

The arrays are compared pairwise; if a match is found, we define x_n as the difference in location in the respective arrays between the matching elements. The similarity metric (k) is defined as:

$$k = \frac{\sum_{n=1}^{z} \frac{(z - x_n)}{z}}{z}$$

A perfectly matching set of agent allele values has $k = 1$. This similarity metric is used to initiate breeding (if both parents have reached puberty - that is, have existed for a minimum time). Also, this metric is used when looking for URL suggestions to make, and to determine which agents fight when they turn aggressive.

4. Conclusions and Future Work

We have described ongoing work into a prototype system called MANTRA, to allow the visualisation of dynamic WWW browsing patterns. Using genetic ideas, we model WWW site visitors as Navigation Agents; multiple agents move and interact in this environment.

We are currently building a recording and playback facility, allowing dynamic agent activity to be saved for later replay. This will allow WWW site developers to determine the browsing patterns of visitors. They may be able to identify possible improvements to the design layout of the site. Also, the link suggestion interface is under development.

We are examining mechanisms for agent persistence. By storing the state of a Navigation Agent, we can reintroduce the agent to the same environment at a later epoch. Also, we can migrate the agent to a different environment and examine the effect of modifying the genetic pool of the new environment. We can already store agents on an iButton [8], a third-party storage device containing an embedded JVM. Another technology providing similar functionality is JavaCard [9].

We intend to extend the functionality of MANTRA to model a number of environments simultaneously. For example, Jini [10] allows multiple computers to be treated as a single entity. This will allow us to migrate agents between various environments modelled at different locations. Rather than being confined to a browse within a WWW site, an agent can track a browse across multiple sites.

References

1. Yan T, Jacobsen M, Garcia-Molina H, Dayal U. From User Access Patterns to Dynamic Hypertext Linking. Proceedings of the 5th International World Wide Web Conference, Paris, France, May 1996.
2. Mukherjea S. Visualizing the World Wide Web with the Navigational View Builder. Proceedings of the 3rd International World Wide Web Conference, Darmstadt, Germany, April 1995.
3. Chalmers M, Rodden K, Brodbeck D. The Order of Things: Activity-Centred Information Access. Proceedings of the 7th International World Wide Web Conference, Brisbane, Australia, April 1998.
4. Joachims T, Freitag T, Mitchell T. WebWatcher: a Tour Guide for the World Wide Web. Proceedings of the 1997 International Joint Conference on AI. Nagoya, Japan, August 1997.
5. Lieberman H. Letizia: An Agent That Assists Web Browsing. Proceedings of the 1995 International Joint Conference on AI. Montreal, August 1995.
6. Alexa. `http://www.alexa.com/`
7. Mapuccino. `http://www.ibm.com/Java/mapuccino/`
8. iButton, Dallas Semiconductor Corp. `http://www.ibutton.com/`
9. JavaCard. `http://java.sun.com/products/javacard/`
10. JINI. `http://java.sun.com/products/jini/`

Appendix - Screenshots from MANTRA

This appendix contains two screenshots from the prototype MANTRA system.

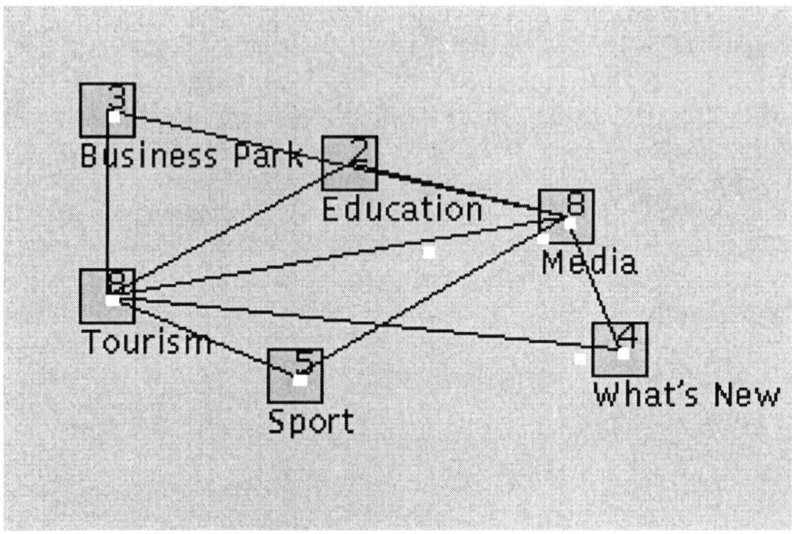

Figure 1: A small population of Navigation Agents

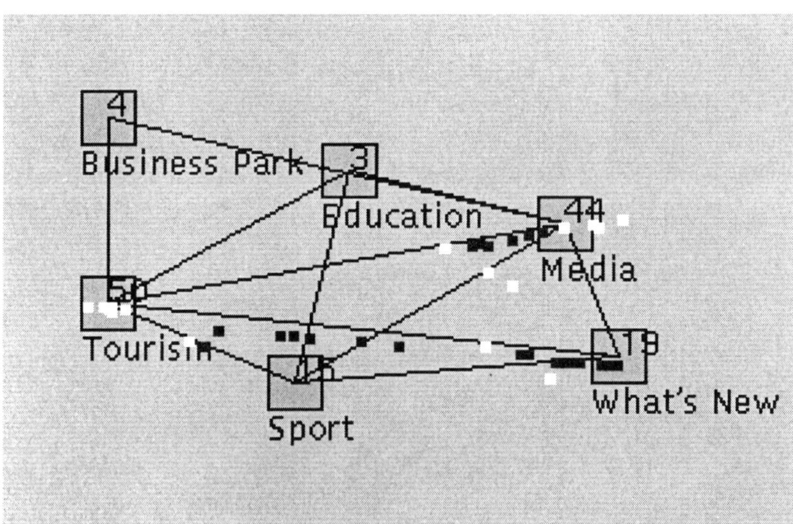

Figure 2: A larger population of agents, including aggressive agents

Author Index